INTERACTIVE LEARNING

INTERACTIVE LEARNING

*Vignettes from America's
Most Wired Campuses*

DAVID G. BROWN

Editor

*International Center for Computer-Enhanced Learning
Wake Forest University*

ANKER PUBLISHING COMPANY, INC.
Bolton, MA

Interactive Learning
Vignettes from America's Most Wired Campuses

ISBN 1-882982-29-0

Composition by Lyn Rodger, Deerfoot Studios
Cover design by Boynton Hue Studio

Anker Publishing Company, Inc.
176 Ballville Road
P. O. Box 249
Bolton, MA 01740-0249

www.ankerpub.com

ABOUT THE EDITOR

DAVID G. BROWN, as provost of Wake Forest University, chaired the committee that recommended ubiquitous computing for the university. He has founded both the Annual Conference of Ubiquitous Computing Colleges and Universities and the *Journal of Computer-Enhanced Learning*. He is chair of the Teaching and Learning Committee for the 1999 EDUCAUSE Annual Meeting. He has served as president of Transylvania University, chancellor of the University of North Carolina, Asheville, and has chaired several national groups including the American Association for Higher Education (AAHE), the Higher Education Colloquium, and both the NASULGC and ACE Councils of Chief Academic Officers. His service as provost spans 24 years at Wake Forest University, Miami University, and Drake University.

Among his books are *Leadership Vitality, The Mobile Professors, The Market for College Teachers,* and in 1999 *Always in Touch: A Practical Guide to Ubiquitous Computing,* and *Electronically Enhanced Education: A Case Study of Wake Forest University.* A frequent speaker at national meetings, Dr. Brown also regularly teaches courses in economics using technology. He has been recognized as an "inspirational teacher of undergraduates" by the University of North Carolina, Chapel Hill.

Currently, Dr. Brown serves as vice president of Wake Forest University and dean of the International Center for Computer-Enhanced Learning. For more information consult http://www.wfu.edu/~brown. Email: brown@wfu.edu.

TABLE OF CONTENTS

Social Sciences

Literature, Languages, Writing, and Humanities

Indexes

PREFACE

In this book, leading teachers of thought and experimentation tell about the computer-intensive courses they have designed and taught. Nominated by the provosts and deans from 36 of America's "100 most wired campuses" (1997 Yahoo rankings), each author

- Explains the educational beliefs behind the course redesign

- Highlights the computer tools and techniques used in the course

- Describes the course

- Cites measured impacts on learning

- Contemplates lessons learned that might be useful to others

These vignettes reflect state-of-the-art, best practices in computer-rich environments. The authors exude thoughtful concern for quality teaching, empathy with student learners, energetic commitment to self-learning, the courage of innovators, and the passion of disciples compelled to share their discoveries with colleagues.

WHO CAN BENEFIT FROM *INTERACTIVE LEARNING*?

Professors, teachers, trainers, and members of the new profession called instructional design will gain new insights from each vignette. Catalyzed by these stories, they may understand better their own educational convictions, discern new ways to use familiar computer tools, learn about new computer tools, reach new insights about the diversity of learners, gain confidence from measured results, and avoid blind alleys.

College presidents and deans, trustees and legislators, school superintendents and board members, directors of teaching-learning centers, and other leaders responsible for investment and policy decisions will find the specifics in these essays much more useful than the generalities in the speeches of advocates for, and detractors from, technology in education. Vendors and businesses serving education will get ideas about where best to focus their research, development, sales, and service.

ORGANIZATION OF *INTERACTIVE LEARNING*

Part I of *Interactive Learning* includes three important overview chapters. In Chapter 1, Educational Beliefs, the philosophies or educational notions behind course redesign are highlighted. What passion motivated course redesign, and what experiences in previous courses informed the adoption of computer-facilitated strategies? Which philosophies appear most frequently in the stories that follow? The chapter includes a typology of educational beliefs (interactive learning, communication, customization, materials and modes or presentation, and student initiative and responsibility) and lists vignettes that demonstrate each category within the typology.

Chapter 2, Technology Tools and Techniques, offers a typology of tools and computer techniques with examples of vignettes that illustrate them. How and how often are email, CD-ROMs, asynchronous discussion, PowerPoint presentations, self-paced exercises, and computerized course management being used?

Chapter 3, Assessment of Technology's Impact on Learning, describes the methods by which professors are judging the effectiveness of their learning innovations and the results of these studies. Provided here are early answers to the often asked question: "Are the new technologies worth the money and effort?" The chapter also includes a summary of lessons learned in the various situations.

Part II presents the 93 vignettes which are at the heart of this volume. The vignettes are organized by broad discipline categories: Physical Sciences and Engineering (Vignettes 1–17); Computer Science, Information Systems, and Mathematics (Vignettes 18–25); Biological Sciences and Medicine (Vignettes 26–36); Social Sciences (Vignettes 37–62); Fine Arts (Vignettes 63–72) and Literature, Languages, Writing, and Humanities (Vignettes 73–93).

Six separate indexes allow access to information by different routes: by author, college/university, computer tools and techniques, discipline, educational beliefs, and references. The variety of indexes should offer readers many useful ways into the vignettes.

As editor, I am indebted to many talents. Most of all, I thank the vignette contributors who have stepped outside their disciplines to share valuable experiences with a broader community. Our capable editor, Julie Edelson, gave coherence and, in some instances, increased clarity, to these diverse contributions. My administrative assistant, Janice Schuyler, coordinated communications with the many contributors and the movement of manuscript through many stages. Colleagues Craig Runde, Janet Bright, and Giz Womack—all from Wake Forest's International Center for Computer-Enhanced Learning—helped through Anker Publishing to bring the manuscript to public view.

Finally, in advance, I thank you, the reader, for extending our important conversation about computer-enhanced learning. Please share your thoughts by emailing me at brown@wfu.edu. This is to be the first of several volumes of vignettes. The typologies in Chapters 1-3 need to be refined and extended, and I am soliciting your suggestions. Extension of our list of lessons learned will also be helpful. Several readers may want to propose coediting a collection of vignettes relating to a particular discipline, geography, cluster of institutions, or users of a particular software program. For all of your ideas and proposals, I thank you.

REFERENCE

Yahoo Rankings. (1997). *America's 100 Most Wired Campuses.*

PART I
INTRODUCTION

CHAPTER 1

EDUCATIONAL BELIEFS: AN OVERVIEW

Scholars worldwide are creating a storm of experiments. With the computer have come many new tools of the mind that are being tested at a furious pace in a myriad of learning situations. The new tools have led to more conversations about teaching methods and more concern about assessment. When scholars assemble for annual meetings, corridor conversations, special panels, or vendor exhibits, they are seeking to engage in the issues and opportunities arising from computer-enhanced learning. The passion for testing the power of these new tools is unbounded by geography, discipline, or age.

At no time during my own 40 years in the profession have I seen so many professors undertaking fundamental remodeling of their teaching approaches. At no time has there been more thoughtful consideration of pedagogy. The appearance of user-friendly computer networks is the catalyst for this fervid focus on teaching and learning.

Most of us began integrating computers into our teaching because of a vague sense of guilt, thinking perhaps that "New learning tools are 'in the garage,' and I need to test their potential. Others say that their students are learning more. I must experiment. My students must not be left behind."

Immediately, the computer novice is confronted with a bafflement of choices. Our first impulse is to try out the new tools: email or a CD-ROM of images or self-help exercises with branches to additional reading when incorrect answers are detected. Soon, however, it becomes obvious that computer and computer-software are powerful, diverse, and expensive in terms of dollars and learning time. There are too many degrees of freedom. Choices among an overabundance of feasible alternatives must be made.

Some alternatives are inevitably ruled out because a local computer network is not sufficiently robust, the multimedia clips in a discipline are yet to be produced, or the learning curve on a particular program is simply too steep. Inevitably, however, even after many opportunities are eliminated, hard choices must be based on beliefs about effective teaching methods and the results from previous teaching experiences.

The contributors are motivated to expend an immense effort and risk in testing new methods. They seek to enhance learning by turning up the volume on practices that have been successful for them in the past. The most important step for each faculty member in translating the potential of computers into more effective teaching is the careful identification of past teaching successes. From these successes grow ideas, beliefs, and convictions about teaching and learning. From these beliefs, it is then possible to choose among the vast array of new tools and technologies.

When the authors of the vignettes that follow were asked to identify the educational notions and convictions that motivated them to pioneer the use of computers in instruction, the answer was nearly unanimous: They cited the benefits of "interactive learning," "collaborative learning," "learning by doing," "role-playing," and "integrating theory and practice."

This unanticipated response was so universal and so powerful that the title of this book was changed from *Computer-Enhanced Learning* to *Interactive Learning*. These innovative professors understand that computer tools can be used as a means to increase the quantity and quality of exchange both between themselves and their students and among students. Each of these professors had already left behind the "sage on the stage" stereotype to become the "guide by the side." They had also already been encouraging their students to collaborate on data collection and laboratory experiments and to work together in study clusters. Using computers, they realized, was another, very effective way to increase interactivity.

Computers provide an opportunity to activate some of the rich relationships between apprentice and master, to allow apprentices of differing intellectual maturity to teach each other, and to compensate for the loss of dialogue necessitated by increased student/faculty ratios. In the quotations that follow, the vignette authors further describe the benefits of computer-enhanced learning.

Interactive Learning

- *Enhances interactivity, and you have an engaged, committed, learning community of students*—Rebecca Gould, Hotel-Restaurant Management, Kansas State University, Vignette 62

- *Perhaps the most obvious advantage of the web-based forum is its capacity for interactivity.*—Jeffrey C. Barnett, Spanish, Washington and Lee University, Vignette 88

- *... we all learn best when we are active participants.*—Gail Sherman, English, Reed College, Vignette 79

- *The computer provides the instructional opportunity for learning to become much more interactive and, in turn, much more effective.*—John F. Wallin, Astronomy, George Mason University, Vignette 12

Collaborative Learning

- *Students appear to absorb the concepts presented in the modules more effectively if they work in pairs. Collaborative learning facilitates concept retention.*—Allen D. Bishop, Jr., Chemistry, Millsaps College, Vignette 2

- *Students learn from testing ideas with other students who are not in the same reinforcing in-group.*— Jean Goodwin, Communication, Northwestern University, Vignette 39

- *... collaborative learning enhances students' understanding.*—Carolee Larsen, Zoology, Connecticut College, Vignette 60

Learning by Doing

- *Students learn by doing science, not learning about it. Learn paleontology by doing what paleontologists do.*—John T. Omohundro et al., Anthropology, SUNY, Potsdam, Vignette 42

- *Students learn best by becoming teachers; they integrate what they themselves have learned by presenting it to others.*—Roger Brooks, Religion, Connecticut College, Vignette 93

- *Bringing students more directly into the research process is of prime importance.*—John Dobbins, Art History, University of Virginia, Vignette 73

- *They learned what can only be learned through experience, not through explanation: how to develop good intellectual judgment.*—Wilda Anderson, French, Johns Hopkins University, Vignette 82

- *Students should be asked to think deeply about a topic ... find supporting literature, critically analyze data and interpretations, and learn how to make their new understanding clear to their colleagues.*—Mark Sutherland, Biology, Hendrix College, Vignette 28

Role-Playing

- *Students react to literary passages by role-playing different genders.*—Donna Heiland et al., Psychology and English, Vassar College, Vignette 61

- *Students will not accept complex variability of judges' sentences until their class, through role-playing, issues variable sentences.*—Kent E. Portney et al., Politics, Tufts University, Vignette 57

Integrating Theory and Practice

- *Students profit from an early introduction to the real world, where engineers must put their theories to practice, and conclude with ambiguous outcomes.*—Michael Karweit, Engineering, Johns Hopkins University, Vignette 6

- *... true learning takes place when the student actively incorporates and utilizes concepts in contrast to receiving information passively.*—Jeffrey Barnett, Spanish, Washington and Lee University, Vignette 88

- *Learning modules are designed to help students gain information, practice what they learn, and construct new* their professors and fellow learners. These conversations can begin before the first class and extend for years beyond the final exam. Students can, while studying on their own or in small groups, get immediate help and/or feedback while working through multiple stages of complex simulations or preprogrammed homework exercises.

The computer enables students to work with continuous access to help on the challenges they encounter. Because the computer allows more people to be more active in more groups for more months and years, communication and learning can be increased substantially.

Prompt Feedback

- *The dominant new aspect is immediate online feedback. This is accomplished in three ways: 1) interaction between the students and the computer using materials and problems prepared by the instructor . . . 2) interaction between the instructor and the computer, providing the instructor with timely feedback on student difficulties so that such difficulties can be addressed . . . 3) asynchronous interactions between students and instructors via the network.*—Edwin Kashy et al., Physics, Michigan State University, Vignette 13

- *Communication, continuous and timely, is a key element in learning. . . . If possible, provide students instantaneous feedback that also allows them to monitor their own mastery of the material.*—Angela G. King et al., Chemistry, Wake Forest University, Vignette 4

ideas and create new knowledge.—James L. Stofan, Education, Johns Hopkins University, Vignette 29

Manifested in different ways, the authors I've quoted emphasize their desire to increase interactivity, facilitate exchange, and stimulate active learning. These categories are therefore grouped in Figure 1.1, Typology of Educational Beliefs. Most of the vignettes mention some form of interactive learning as a motivation for adopting computer methods.

COMMUNICATION

Frequent Dialogue

Equal to the emphasis on interactive learning, the quest for better communication with and among students was a major motivating factor in the adoption of technology. Students can be continuously in touch with

CUSTOMIZATION

Teaching toward modal learning styles and middle ability ranges can leave everyone frustrated. But learning research confirms that people learn in different ways and at different rates. Courses organized with many self-help exercises, optional hyperlinks to related materials, alternative methods of learning the material, and in some instances variable timetables accommodate much better those students at the tails of normal distributions. In turn, assignments that are individualized and personalized to special needs can better motivate learners at all points on the spectrum. Frustrated by their limited ability to provide experiences for different students in large enrollment classes, many of the vignette authors sought out the computer so that they could deliver "different strokes for different folks."

Different Strokes for Different Folks

- *... since levels of sophistication vary from student to student, I believe any course should ideally be structured so that it enables growth for all students.*—Gail B. Sherman, English, Reed College, Vignette 79

- *... because we believe that students learn in a variety of ways, we were committed to the use of multiple tools over the Internet.*—Elmer Poe, Industrial Technology, East Carolina University, Vignette 25

- *A multimedia web site, which addresses a range of learning styles... allows students to learn in the best way for them.*—Sally R. Hair, Chemistry, Dartmouth College, Vignette 1

- *Able learners are directed to higher-level tools and original research materials. Weaker students are sent to quizzes and tutorials online.*—Chris Impey, Astronomy, University of Arizona, Vignette 14

- *Virtual courses allow slower students more time to learn.*—Maurice Wright, Music, Temple University, Vignette 71

Repetition and Time on Task

- *You need to expose students to a concept at least three times before they will truly grasp it.*—Charles Grisham, Chemistry, University of Virginia, Vignette 35

- *Productive use of time outside class is a key to mastery.*—Angela G. King, Chemistry, Wake Forest University, Vignette 4

- *One of the reasons students are learning better is that they spend a significantly greater amount of time on their assignments.*—Edwin Kashy et al., Physics, Michigan State University, Vignette 13

NEW MATERIALS AND MODES OF PRESENTATION

Many authors knew the learning power of materials and techniques that, before computers, were inaccessible or prohibitively expensive. They wanted access to these materials, access that could be achieved realistically only through the computer, and they wanted all students to have equal access to the materials. Although the full range of creativity is best revealed by consulting all of the vignettes, a sampling of quotations reveals many ingenious ways to take advantage of new materials and methods.

Visualization

- *... although some students were able to grasp abstract concepts fairly easily through readings and lectures, many, if not most, needed to see the concepts in action.*—Charles M. Grisham, Chemistry, University of Virginia, Vignette 35

- *Most students learn how to integrate conceptual knowledge with practice by seeing and hearing real world cases: Visualization is the key.*—Harry R. Matthews, Pharmacology, University of California, Davis, Vignette 33

Comparative Analysis

- *Six representations of divinity, for example, can be juxtaposed side-by-side, at the same time, for comparative study.*—Eva R. Hoffman, Art, Tufts University, Vignette 66

- *It is through a comparison of things that we build meaning.*—Ed Epping, Art, Williams College, Vignette 67

Motivating Materials

- *... culture is no longer reduced to a series of facts about the other country but built on a dynamic process that involves interactions with multiple materials—raw or mediated—and multiple partners—learners, teachers, other students, and experts.*—Gilberte Furstenberg, French, MIT, Vignette 83

- *Students need first to provide their own answer, then learn the theories that might explain the variability of answers within a class.*—Kent E. Portney, Political Science, Tufts University, Vignette 57

Broad Spectrum of Materials

- *All transitions, from slides to face-to-face and vice versa, refocus attention.*—Andrew P. Barkley, Economics, Kansas State University, Vignette 46

- *... hypertext provides an ideal structure for organizing and making available literary research materials because it is similar to an archive.*—Wilda Anderson, French, Johns Hopkins University, Vignette 82

- *I strive in my courses for the flexibility to accommodate different learning styles and temperaments and thus view technology as part of a rich mix of experimentation, simulation, discussion, analysis, and reporting.—*Cindy Schwarz, Physics, Vassar College, Vignette 15

STUDENT INITIATIVE AND RESPONSIBILITY

Most authors seek ways for students themselves to take more responsibility for their learning. Without exertion and ownership, there is little growth. One instructor quips that his goal is for students to work harder than he does. By providing students access to rich databases, alternative lectures, cross-institutional discussions, self-paced exercises, and optional readings, the computer is a great enabler of guided independence.

- *...the more removed the professor is from discussion, the more actively the student takes responsibility for learning.—*Jeffrey C. Barnett, Spanish, Washington and Lee University, Vignette 88

- *Students' learning is more reliable if set in a "decentered" environment, where the instructor is a "guide by the side."—*Donna Heiland et al., Psychology and English, Vassar College, Vignette 61

- *It is my intent to put the students in charge of their learning experience...—*Joan Keck Campbell, German, Dartmouth College, Vignette 90

SUMMING UP

Early adopters in general share a passion for active learning. They aspire toward teaching environments—both face-to-face and virtual—where there is a lot of exchange, where interactive learning is facilitated. By offering many different routes to learning the essential material, they seek to individualize and to customize the experience of each student. For most of our authors, increased communication, both collaboration among students and dialogue between students and professors, is a key ingredient to increased learning.

By picking and choosing among the many philosophies in this chapter, I hope that others will be inspired to identify their own convictions about learning and to use the new technology to pursue those convictions.

CHAPTER 2

TECHNOLOGY TOOLS AND TECHNIQUES: AN OVERVIEW

The catalyst for rewriting lectures and redesigning courses is the arrival of new computer-based tools and techniques. For some scholars, the outcome of their course redesign may include new materials and new approaches that have nothing to do with computers. For all the teacher-scholars highlighted in this volume, computers were not only a stimulus toward course redesign, but also a major factor in the redesigned course.

MOST POPULAR TECHNIQUES

The spectrum of techniques pursued is captured in Figure 2.1, A Typology of Tools and Techniques Mentioned by Authors. Almost 100% of the authors posted materials on the web (almost always on a course web page), provided citations to digitized resources on the web, and communicated with their students via email. Asynchronous discussion groups were used in 80% of the courses. In Figure 2.1, these techniques are highlighted in bold type.

Roughly half of the vignettes describe computer-enhanced, self-paced exercises; PowerPoint presentations by either the professor or students; multimedia visualizations; comparative analyses; web searches by students; computer skills exercises; lecture notes online; simulation exercises; team projects; and some aspect of electronic course management. These, along with an array of strategies to enable class time to be used for discussion and not consumed by one-way information dissemination, are highlighted in italics.

OTHER TECHNIQUES

Although described in less than 25% of the vignettes, a number of other powerful computer-based techniques are being used in specific courses. These techniques are listed in plain type.

Students learn the web (sometimes HTML) by creating their own personal web pages. Quality student work is exhibited on publicly accessible web pages. Professors and students from several universities share databases, discussions, and self-paced exercises. Practitioners join in many of the asynchronous discussions.

Online office hours are an imperfect substitute when students enrolled in virtual courses cannot possibly meet with professors face-to-face. Chatrooms, where all participants must be online simultaneously, have for most proven disappointing, although a few authors report partial success with highly structured chat sessions.

Lecture notes and multimedia clips from lectures are being used often as effective review tools. Self-paced lectures and quizzes are used by fewer than 25% of our authors.

Professors who have prepared customized CD-ROMs, Image Archives, and Cybershows report spectacular results—but these time-intensive uses of the computer are still unusual. Only a few electronic textbooks have reached the market.

The most commonly used techniques—email, URL citations, and course web pages—promise great benefits in increased communication, while having a low cost in professorial learning and preparation time.

LINKING PHILOSOPHY AND TECHNIQUE

The tools and techniques chosen follow directly from the course designer's desired outcome. A few quotes related to each group of philosophies are cited here. To understand their context, however, the full vignettes must be read.

For Interactive Learning

- *Publishing papers on the web facilitates peer review and generally results in a higher quality paper.*—Robert M. Newton, Geology, Smith College, Vignette 11

- *Students work in teams of four to employ newly learned computer techniques in the presentation of a design problem. The presentation culminates in a fair with judges and prizes for the best.*—Richard Shiavi et al., Engineering, Vanderbilt University, Vignettes 8,10

- *Team teaching (scientist, pedagogist, technologist) is sustained by email, a common web site, a shared database…*—Angelo Collins, Education, Vanderbilt University, Vignette 51

For Increased Communication

- *The site contains all of the course information, including the syllabus, course calendar, list of covered concepts, daily goals, homework assignments, final project assignments, study questions, and animations.*—Stephen H. Loomis, Zoology, Connecticut College, Vignette 27

- *Last semester a student emailed a query to his hometown congressman and received not only a prompt electronic response but a package of previously inaccessible government documents.*—Linda S. Bergmann et al., English, University of Missouri, Rolla, Vignette 76

- *Class time is best devoted to work time for small groups to help each other understand the meaning and usefulness of the concepts. The concepts themselves, especially the vocabulary and the mechanics, are the component of the course that is most amenable to computer learning.*—William M. Clark, Engineering, Worcester Polytechnic Institute, Vignette 5

- *Students are encouraged to weave the computer discussions with ongoing discussions…in the classroom.*

Similarly, students weave online discussions with segments of text and image, whether native electronic texts or digitized print and images, into hypertextual papers, which also incorporate contributions from mail lists, web sites, and email with other students and professors (here and elsewhere), distance critics and theorists, and even, on occasion, authors of the texts under study.—Michael Joyce, English, Vassar College, Vignette 77

For Customization

- *Interactive tutorials on specific topics have been immensely popular with students.*—Angela G. King et al., Chemistry, Wake Forest University, Vignette 4

- *Virtual courses allow slower students more time to learn.*—Maurice Wright, Music, Temple University, Vignette 71

- *Self-paced quizzes help study strategy and feedback information to the instructor regarding where in class emphasis should be given.*—Gordon E. McCray, Business, Wake Forest University, Vignette 45

For New Materials and Modes of Presentation

- *Students search the web for the best URLs and state their criteria for ranking them.*—David G. Brown, Economics, Wake Forest University, Vignette 49

- *When photographs or slides are scanned, they can more easily be straightened, cropped, and adjusted. Properly stored and cared for, they can be more permanent than many types of color slides.*—Charles S. Rhyne, Art, Reed College, Vignette 65

- *All lectures and other course materials are available on the web. They are also available on CD-ROM so that students don't have to download from the web and so that the materials can be accessed even when the student is not linked to the web.*—Madison Daily et al., Engineering, University of Missouri, Rolla, Vignettes 7, 9

For Electronic Course Management

- *. . . exam-on-demand could be summoned from the computer at any time during a two-and-a-half-day period. Students are then expected to complete exams within the allotted time and time-stamp them in at the library.*—Fred Moore, Physics, Whitman College, Vignette 17

- *All exercises and sketches should be kept in a portfolio that stays with the student.*—Andrea Wollensak, Design, Connecticut College, Vignette 64

- *Twice each semester all students must state how things are going.*—Raymond A. Bucko, Anthropology, LeMoyne College, Vignettes 40, 41

SUMMING UP

The range and diversity of computer tools are almost baffling. By leading with the fundamental tools of communication—email, course web site, and URL citations—quick benefits can be realized without significant time delays or extraordinary effort. As computer-enhanced courses mature, more and more materials will become available on CD-ROMs and in shared databases. The richest of these materials, such as self-paced exercises, team simulations, and special routines for collaborative learning, are likely to involve interactive learning.

CHAPTER 3

ASSESSMENT OF TECHNOLOGY'S IMPACT ON LEARNING: AN OVERVIEW

The professors who taught these courses and wrote these vignettes were asked why, after observing the results of their change to computer-enhanced instruction, they continue to spend the extra time and effort that computer-enhanced teaching requires. From their answers, we have been able inductively to 1) craft a typology for the assessment of technology's impact on learning, and 2) collect a rich array of specific measured results.

TYPOLOGY

If the results of assessment studies are to shape decisions on the character of investment in computer infrastructure and the design of individual courses, the studies themselves need to be grouped into meaningful subcategories. This grouping is best achieved by answering three questions:

1) What unit will be served? (e.g., the whole college, all chemistry courses, or just Chemistry 101?)

2) What will be tested? (e.g., "do you as students [professors] like computer-enhanced courses over conventionally taught courses?" versus "are you [your students] learning more?")

3) How will we measure? (e.g., from formally gathered student perceptions, changed behavior, and/or conceptual outcomes?)

This chapter summarizes how learning gains are being tested at the micro, or individual course, level and presents a summary of the lessons that vignette authors learned in their use of particular instructional technologies.

The assessment studies associated with these vignettes are microlevel by specific course. A few authors cite metadata, especially those used to gain feedback during the conduct of their courses.

SIX VIGNETTES

Before presenting an overview of assessment methods and results from all 93 courses, let me highlight six of them.

Communications

Sally Jackson and her colleagues from the department of communication at the University of Arizona (Vignette 37) tested the effectiveness of their use of structured online dialogues. Ninety-six percent of their students agreed that "the lessons added an important component to the course," and 79% disagreed that "having to use the World Wide Web was an obstacle to learning." The four instructors authoring this essay concluded that "after three years of development and experimentation with structured online dialogues, we believe them to be the most important element of these critical courses and are continuing to phase them into this key course sequence."

Chemical Engineering

William Clark (Vignette 5) from the chemical engineering department at Worcester Polytechnic Institute (WPI) compared his two sections of the same course, one taught by the traditional lecture-homework format and the other by the multimedia group-project format. The number of "agree" and "strongly agree" responses to 14 statements about the instructor's delivery

A TYPOLOGY OF ASSESSMENT STUDIES

I. What Unit?
   A. Macro overview
      1. Whole college
      2. All courses in department
   B. Micro level
      1. By student type
         (e.g. level or learning style)
      2. By Instructor (e.g. discipline or age)
      3. By Specific Course

II. What Tests?
   A. Like
   B. Learn
      1. Technique
         a. Disciplinary
         b. Interpersonal
         c. Computer
      2. Substance
         a. Theory and concept
         b. Applications

III. How Measured?
   A. Perception
      1. Student
         a. Formal Evaluation
         b. Hearsay
         c. Feedback
      2. Faculty
         a. Formal evaluation
         b. Impression
   B. Behaviors
      1. Computer use metadata
      2. Self-reports re time on task, etc.
   C. Outcomes
      1. Externally measured
         a. Simultaneously matched pairs
         b. Matched pairs over time
         c. Other
      2. Internally measured
         a. Simultaneously matched pairs
         b. Matched pairs over time
         c. Other

of the course increased from 80% to 95%. When asked how they liked the multimedia format, over 70% of the students chose the top two categories for each of five components of the course (alternative to lecture, alternative to homework, group project in class, group project between classes, and working in groups instead of alone). In another survey, the percentage of students answering "agree" or "strongly agree" with the statement, "I learned a lot in this course" on the standard WPI course evaluations was 77% when traditionally taught and 97% when taught with the new approach. In his analysis of outcome data, specifically the average grades earned by students under the two methods, Clark concludes, "the multimedia group-project format did not hinder student learning and may have improved it."

Engineering
Edwin R. Carney and his colleagues at the University of Missouri, Rolla (Vignette 7) evaluated their effectiveness by student/instructor opinion polls, page counts revealing student behavior when using the material, and student performance on online homework problems. Pilot study results show that students using the optional online homework assignments are getting better grades and feeling that they are learning more.

Astronomy
Chris Impey from the University of Arizona reports in Vignette 14 that even with no particular incentive to participate, students average 30 web hits and ten emails with no negative effect on class or office hour attendance. Students who used both email and web tolls performed one letter grade higher than students who used neither, and, in entrance and exit polls, student responses to the electronic aspects of the course were overwhelmingly positive.

Information Sciences
In Vignette 13, Edwin Kashy and colleagues from Michigan State's College of Natural Science report results from teaching a class of 500. When compared with previous years, significantly fewer students dropped the course. Significantly more students earned A+'s, A's, and B's. Numerous student surveys confirmed their acceptance of and enthusiasm for the new course format.

French

Carl S. Blyth from the department of French and Italian at the University of Texas, Austin, working under an extensively evaluated FIPSE project, reports in Vignette 87 that there was a statistically significant difference in grades favoring the students enrolled in the computer-enhanced courses. Moreover, students enrolled in the computer-enhanced curriculum reported higher levels of satisfaction with the course and frequently wrote on their course evaluations that the computer lab was the most helpful and interesting part of the course. Blyth credits the new curriculum for the complete turnaround in previously declining enrollments in French.

RESEARCH METHODS AND RESULTS

Why are so many faculty willing to spend so much time redesigning courses and curricula in ways that are usually more time intensive? I just highlighted six courses, but equally interesting is an overview of the evidence cited by all of the authors.

Faculty Perception

Our scholars seeking more interactivity have been richly rewarded by results. Most of the vignettes include comments on assessment. Among the three strategies for assessment, by far the most frequently used is the perception of faculty and students. Seventy-six percent wrote about ways they observed more learning: the quality of class discussions, the frequency of "ah-ha's," student eyes lighting up with new insights, performance in more advanced courses, the capacity to customize assignments to student interest and ability levels, the popularity of computer-enhanced sections, the quality of term papers, the depth of conversations during office hours, the nature and frequency of questions asked over the Internet, etc. These qualitative judgments about the impact of computer enhancements seem to be the major reinforcers for continued computer use.

Let me cite a few quotes:

- *...the results...were unbelievably wonderful. The simplicity of the assignment let the students build something very complex and multilayered.*—Ed Epping, Art, Williams College, Vignette 67

- *Having the ability to conveniently review their materials is ... a great boon to their learning.*—John Kappelman, Anthropology, University of Texas, Austin, Vignette 43

- *My experience in a large classroom suggests that a combination of chalkboard and computer slides is superior to either format alone ... email not only has provided greater efficiency of teaching, but also has increased the number of students who seek help. ... The incorporation of technology ... allows instructors to review their course content, teaching style, and learning objectives and upgrade them.*—Andrew P. Barkley, Agricultural Economics, Kansas State University, Vignette 46

- *It is clear that word has spread that technology is a wonderful aid to learning. Students are now able to answer more complex problems with greater success, and more material can be covered in class. Their better understanding of biology is evident in their ability to synthesize various thought processes at an earlier point in the semester.*—Sarah Lea McGuire, Biology, Millsaps College, Vignette 30

- *The highest quiz average in my course was achieved on a section of materials that depends most heavily on the web site. The average scores for that particular quiz have doubled since I created the interactive tutorials. In addition, student response to the exercises has been extremely positive—they're asking for more.*—Charles M. Grisham, Chemistry, University of Virginia, Vignette 35

- *The incorporation of technology has made an incredible difference in this class. This difference can be measured not only in the amount and quality of writing produced, but in the enthusiasm students showed toward their assignment.*—Franziska Lys, German, Northwestern University, Vignette 84

- *I will continue and will encourage others to use Internet-based resources in teaching, in part because of some surprising results. More students completed their research in a timely way, with excellent content.*—Gail B. Sherman, English, Reed College, Vignette 79

Student Surveys

In many instances, these general observations by faculty are reinforced by end-of-course evaluations and perception surveys of students. Seventy-three percent of vignettes speaking to assessment mention student surveys. In virtually every instance, students felt that technology advanced their learning. Students reported that they prefer courses that include computer enhancements. They valued the increased communication, collaboration, and interactivity.

FIGURE 3.2

PERCENTAGE OF 83 VIGNETTE AUTHORS MENTIONING DIFFERENT ASSESSMENT STRATEGIES

Assessment Strategy	% Mentioning
Faculty Perception	76%
Formal Student Surveys	73%
Informal Student Feedback	63%
Matched Pair Outcome Studies	45%

Qualitative Feedback from Students

Elaborating the statistical results from formal student surveys were the qualitative comments by enrolled students and queries from students in other courses. Sixty-three percent of the essays covering assessment cite some of these comments.

Matched Pair Studies

Matched pair analyses, either before technology/after technology or with technology/without technology, were quoted by 45%. Although some of these analyses revealed no significant differences in students' grades as a consequence of using computer-enhanced techniques, a majority of the studies revealed statistically significant positive differences in favor of technology; and no study suggested a statistically significant advantage for the class taught traditionally.

Other Metadata

The results from the comparisons of outcomes and perceptions were reinforced by a wide variety of observed behaviors. Ten authors reported that their web-based resources were being used at other universities or by other professors within their own institutions. Web citations in research papers were more frequent than library citations. Successful completion of web-based problem exercises was related to success rates on final exams. One professor studied metadata on the number of times students tried and failed practice homework problems to determine where students were experiencing the greatest difficulty. Voluntary web site hits on evenings prior to exams were touted as evidence of the utility of web-based resources. Class percentages entering threaded conversations and item analyses of these conversations are being used to judge effectiveness. Clearly, the metadata generated by computer usage is becoming an important factor in evaluation, feedback, and improvement of teaching strategies.

SUMMING UP

Taken together, these assessments—perceptions, outcomes, and behaviors—are necessarily related to the objectives of the instruction. Although some professors are measuring whether students like a course and are having fun learning, most assessment is against objectives relating to understanding the theory, concept, and application of substantive disciplinary knowledge. However, a significant portion of our early adopters have expanded their course objectives and are also interested in nurturing and, therefore, measuring the capacity to work collaboratively in teams (mentioned by 20%) and in developing computer skills (mentioned by 26%).

Professor Stephen Loomis, who teaches human physiology at Connecticut College, sums it up well: "In overall learning, 68% of the students demonstrated an understanding of over 90% of the concepts. This compares with a ten-year average of 24% using the lecture format. In attitudinal surveys, 96% of the students rated this course as very good to excellent and would recommend it to a peer." It is no accident that virtually all professors who have added technological enhancements to their repertoire of teaching tools are persevering. Students win.

LESSONS LEARNED

Assessment Has Many Faces

In addition to measuring student learning, vignette authors cite their reactions to computer-enhanced-learning and their successes and disappointments. Themes repeated through many essays are presented here as the lessons learned.

The Time Demands Are Punishing

Learning the new media takes time. Redesigning courses takes time. Preparing failsafe plans if networks fail takes time. Capitalizing on the opportunities to treat students as individuals, not just groups, takes time. And the time these tasks takes seems always to be longer than estimated.

Extensive Support Is Essential

It is so easy to get stalled by the computer. Computer-savvy advice, through a help desk or consulting service, is essential. The network must operate predictably. Like subject matter specialists in our libraries, disciplinary faculty need coaching from disciplinary-savvy digital information specialists.

Plan for Glitches, Especially System Incompatibilities

Course shell software, email systems, security protocols, and even operating systems are still quite immature. Standards are only now, under the leadership of the National Learning Infrastructure Initiative, being adopted. And proprietary systems are still common. Although most incompatibilities can eventually be reconciled, delays are inevitable. Many student alibis are legitimate.

Mix Media: No One Approach Is Best for All

The real strength of the computer is as still another alternative learning tool. It is important to recognize that no single pedagogical method—not face-to-face and not virtual and not lecture and not laboratory and not self-learning—is best for all subjects and all purposes. The greatest strength is in diversity, in the opportunity to choose among many learning delivery systems.

Emphasize Interaction

Free face-to-face time for face-to-face interaction. Encourage interaction in between face-to-face times by creating assignments that require collaboration, with the assurance that new asynchronous strategies make such collaboration accessible to all.

Electronic Textbooks Are not yet beyond the Experimental Stage

If pedagogical software such as course shell are immature, electronic textbooks are still in their infancy. In this early stage, most digitized textbooks are translated versions of texts designed and written for hardprint presentation. This is changing, but it will be years before a critical mass of transaction mechanics and large databases designed for digitized teaching will be available.

Shift Course Management and Learning Responsibility toward Students

With computer management of courses comes a new degree of freedom, especially new opportunities to provide "different strokes for different folks." The challenge becomes, more than ever, time management. If the professor-in-charge is to pursue the advantages of customization, routine tasks must be performed by others. By performing some of the tasks, lead students can deepen their understanding of subject matter and enhance their self esteem. Thus, student involvement in course management is both educationally sound and pragmatically necessary.

Use Computers More Before and After Class, not so Much in Class

Most class time is best spent person-to-person, without the intervention of the computer. Between classes, however, the computer provides a means of continuing in the interactive mode. Discussions begun interactively before class can be completed in class. Projects begun interactively while in class can be completed, still in the interactive mode, after class. Although the computer can also increase interactive learning when face-to-face, the biggest gains are when face-to-face communication isn't feasible.

Encourage Students to Collaborate

It is usually important to structure the collaboration so that learners become interdependent. Among distance learners, the computer can be used to create some of the advantages previously reserved for face-to-face college communities.

Use Systems That Are Familiar to Your Students and Colleagues

Students need to capture economies of scale, wherein learning how to use the computer in one course is relevant to computer use in their next course. When familiar systems are chosen, all of us can more easily find a friend or colleague who can help us through the inevitable challenges.

Structure Online Discussions

Open chat sessions rarely work. Threaded discussions work only when student participation is rewarded and when the timelines for participation are short and explicit.

Keep Electronic Reading and Writing Assignments Short

The joy of reading a book online, of turning back pages and relating passages is still limited by awkward scrolling, limited screen space, and weary eyes.

Share Databases

The cataloging and indexing of electronic resources is still immature. Many professors still need to scan and digitize many of the materials they find useful. Departments from within colleges and professors with the same disciplinary subspecialities from different universities can avoid duplication of efforts by allocating responsibility for locating and cataloging different domains within the subject area. Without the constraints of geography and synchronous timing, the data may be pooled and therefore accessible to many students and faculty.

Enjoy the Teaching Profession More Than Ever!

The authors of the vignettes that follow exude a love of teaching and high delight in finding new ways to be even more successful with a broader spectrum of learners. Many suggest that, when struggling with new designs and tools, a little playfulness, a little self-congratulations for being among the leaders, and a little laughter over the absurdity of some of the glitches is essential if one is to stay with the hunt for better modes of teaching and learning.

PART II
THE VIGNETTES

PHYSICAL SCIENCES AND ENGINEERING

Vignette 1 An Interactive, Multimedia Web Site for the General Chemistry Laboratory

Sally R. Hair, Dartmouth College

This vignette describes ChemLab, a multimedia web site being developed for the general chemistry laboratory at Dartmouth (http://www.dartmouth.edu/~chemlab/). ChemLab provides still photos, audio, and interactive web-based applications for student use before and after their labs. It is my hope that the site will help students to understand and prepare for experiments more thoroughly than our current lab manual. This multimedia web site provides some novel ways to improve student learning before, during, and after a lab experiment.

BACKGROUND: PROBLEMS TO SOLVE

The general chemistry laboratory is often a student's first college-level laboratory course. Students sometimes struggle to make sense of Dartmouth's homegrown lab manual, no matter how clear and complete it seems to more experienced chemists. They conscientiously read it before coming to lab but still are not well prepared. They can be confused about terms, and even the pronunciation of unfamiliar words can be a problem. Things usually fall into place when a teaching assistant gives a demonstration or a short description of how to use a piece of glassware or equipment.

There tends to be a big gap between what students understand and take away from a laboratory experiment and what faculty have put into it. Students face a variety of challenges and tasks. They must complete the experiment correctly, measuring the right things in the right way; they must draw conclusions from their observations or calculate something from what they measure; they must write it all down in the proper form; they must put the experiment in the context of what they have learned in the lecture portion of the course. Typically, students focus on the procedure of an experiment at the exclusion of all higher-order thinking. They concentrate on learning the names of the equipment and how to use it properly. They learn techniques, but often leave the laboratory without an understanding of the chemistry of the experiment or how it relates to what they are learning in the rest of the course. They often fail to make connections to the molecular level, which is where the real understanding of chemistry lies.

The first goal of the ChemLab web site is to allow students to prepare better before coming to lab, so that they can understand more of the experiment while in the lab. If students learn about the procedure and equipment in detail, they will have more brain power available to think about the chemistry of the experiment. The second goal of the ChemLab web site is to foster higher-level thinking by enabling students to make connections between their experimental observations and the underlying chemistry. If we can build a link between the procedure or results and the underlying chemistry or theory of an experiment into the web site, we will pave the way for higher-level thinking and learning, before, during, and after the lab.

IMPLEMENTATION: MULTIMEDIA SOLUTIONS

The ChemLab web site addresses the problem of student learning in the lab in two ways. First, it presents still photos of all equipment, along with audio and text descriptions of how to use it. Photos are included of each procedure, so students will know what to expect. This supplements a more detailed procedure written in the lab manual and gives students a greater degree of familiarity with the equipment and techniques. It highlights key things to observe, like a color change or the formation of a solid. The site contains still photos of equipment with text descriptions of their proper use (http://www.dartmouth.edu/~chemlab/techniques/flasks .html, and following). One experimental procedure can be viewed at http://www.dartmouth.edu/~chemlab /chem3-5/week7/procedures .html.

The planned addition of audio to the photos will reinforce ideas and more explicitly connect each picture to the procedure or technique it illustrates. Audio will be concentrated on multistep procedures, so that students can look at the photos and listen to the description of the technique, rather than move their eyes between photo and text. An audio/photo slide show could be included as a review for students who have already read and listened to the step-by-step directions. Students learn in the best way for them and will go into the lab better prepared to do the experiment.

The second way of improving student learning in the lab is to include interactive applications that connect the experiment to higher-level thinking. These applications would be used as prelab exercises, to answer specific questions, or to analyze data after the lab. For example, a simulation of the experiment would enable students to practice the reasoning used in the lab. This type of application is especially useful for qualitative analysis experiments when an unknown substance is identified by its reaction chemistry. The analysis of this type of experiment turns into a logical puzzle with the laboratory observations as the clues. Giving students the opportunity to practice this analysis before lab will improve their ability to do it in the lab. A high quality, web-based application could include photos of the actual chemical reactions, which would also serve to prepare students to make accurate observations in the lab. Color photos showing the expected results of a qualitative analysis experiment can be seen at http://www.dartmouth.edu/~chemlab /chem3-5/week2/procedures.html.

A preliminary example of a Java applet is now on the ChemLab site and has been used by students (http://www.dartmouth.edu/~chemlab/chem3-5/java /hess/Hess.html). This application, written by Susan Schwarz and Brian Reid, allows students to choose reactants and test chemical reactions. It gives them information about a series of reactions and how to use them to reach the net reaction. This application allows students to go carefully through the analysis of the data before lab and again afterwards, if necessary.

In the future, the site will include an interactive prelab question form that will ensure that students actually use it. Students will be required to submit answers to questions via the site to their teaching assistants. These questions will be in addition to those turned in with the lab write-up and will address both the procedure and theory of experiments.

SCOPE AND APPLICABILITY

The general chemistry laboratory is associated with three lecture courses that teach the fundamentals of chemistry. These courses are taken by engineering majors, biology majors, and premedical students, as well as chemistry majors. In addition, many students use general chemistry to fulfill a distribution requirement and do not continue study in science. The backgrounds and abilities of students in these courses vary widely as do their interest and motivation. A multimedia web site that addresses a range of learning styles would be particularly helpful with this diverse group.

The ChemLab web site is used three terms per year by an approximate total of 660 Dartmouth students. This number represents about 15% of the undergraduate student body and 50%–60% of the students in a single class year. Clearly, this project has wide scope and broad applicability. In addition to use in General Chemistry, the descriptions of equipment, instruments, and techniques could be used in other chemistry courses.

FIGURE 1.1

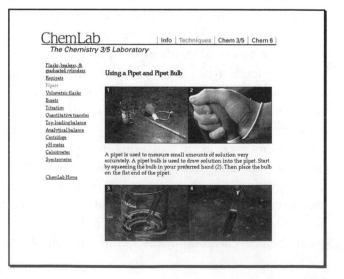

Figure 1.1 shows the navigation system of the ChemLab web site and the pictures of a procedure used in the lab. The four main sections of the site are selected in the banner across the top. The pages within each section are listed in the navigation column on the left. This is the pipets page in the techniques section. The page can be viewed on the web at http://www.dartmouth.edu/~chemlab/techniques/pipet.html.

Measured Results

Each term, students are asked to evaluate their TAs and experiments in the general chemistry laboratory. Questions will be added to the evaluation form including:

- Did you use the ChemLab web site?

- Was it helpful to you in preparing for lab?

- Was it helpful in understanding the concepts of the experiments?

- What could be added to make the web site more useful to you?

By examining responses, I hope to learn what aspects of the site are most helpful to students and how they regard its effectiveness.

LESSONS LEARNED

The ChemLab web site is an ongoing project, and some aspects are still under development. The primary lesson learned at this point is that major projects like this take much more time than anticipated. Aside from this, I have learned that students don't always take advantage of the resources available to them, even if they are colorful and high tech. Some students do not make use of the site in the same way that some students do not read the lab manual. I hope that including Java applets and an interactive prelab problem submission form will force students to the site. Once they are there, I hope they will be lured into learning something by the design and graphics. Lastly, my work with Sarah Horton, who designed the site, has demonstrated to me the importance of design details. The site is much more accessible and useful to students than some other chemistry sites on the web, because it is easily navigated, well designed, and easy on the eyes.

SUMMARY

The general chemistry web site, ChemLab, meets an important instructional need for a large number of Dartmouth students each year. By using still photos, audio, and interactive applications, students will be able to prepare more effectively before lab and better understand the chemistry underlying the experiments.

CONTACT INFORMATION

Sally R. Hair
Director of the General Chemistry Laboratories
Dartmouth College
6128 Burke Laboratory
Department of Chemistry
Hanover, NH 03755
Email: Sally.r.hair@dartmouth.edu
WWW: www.Dartmouth.edu/~chemlab
Phone: (603) 646-3532
Fax: (603) 646-3946

Impact of Technology on the Teaching of Chemistry

Allen D. Bishop, Jr., Millsaps College

When I entered college as a freshman, television and the electric typewriter were the cutting edge of technology. The availability of hands-on interactive processes, from arcade games to computer activities at home and at school, has dramatically changed information assimilation techniques for today's students from passive to hands-on. In order to help students understand the more abstract concepts in chemistry, I have been working for the past 18 years to develop and use various computer models, testing venues, and aids as adjuncts to my teaching style.

EDUCATIONAL THEORIES

Chemical bonding is one of the more difficult concepts for beginning chemistry students to understand. They nod their heads in agreement that something is holding the atoms together, although deep in their hearts they are not really sure, because they have never seen an atom. Just when they finally accept that a physical atom exists and these little tiny things called electrons form pairs and hold the atoms together, chemists slip in the idea that we can only talk about this in probabilistic terms. At this point, the concrete learner lapses into apoplexy.

The line between physical reality (those things you can touch) and visual reality is at best blurred for the technology generation. In order to direct students who are floundering in a sea of abstract information, we must tap into a process that stimulates senses honed by years of interacting with animated games and programs. The teaching of bonding concepts and molecular geometry has, out of necessity, become a hands-on and visual learning experience.

COURSE ACTIVITIES

I have developed a series of interactive tutorials in chemical bonding, ranging from a historical overview to the fundamentals of valence bond and molecular orbital theory. In addition, I have been able to parse the programs into segments that allow their use in a classroom. The students see some of the same visualizations in the classroom that they will encounter in the interactive tutorials.

- The concepts are introduced in the classroom in an exploratory format (e.g., if the charge clouds of two atoms overlap, what will happen?). This is augmented by parts of the tutorial showing various aspects of particular bond characteristics.

- The students are assigned the visualization tutorials before the topics are covered in class.

- The tutorials are delivered via the campus intranet along with an evaluation module.

- Computer-administered mastery tests on every major topic in the introductory general chemistry course are delivered via the campus PC network. The students receive a score at the end of each test and an opportunity to see what questions they have missed. They can take the tests as many times as they feel necessary to attain a mastery of the material. The student's PC network user name is parsed and stored with the test score and time and date of access. Only the highest of the first two scores will be used in assigning a grade on the material. Many students use the topics tests to evaluate their readiness to take a major in-class test.

- Weekly email messages suggest web sites containing additional or alternate presentations on the various bonding concepts.

One of the major problems with laboratory courses at all levels is assuring that students have read the experiment and the instrument instruction manual before coming to the lab. Traditionally, students have been asked to complete some form of prelaboratory and turn it in before running the experiment. This generally means scratching together a minimal description of the process the hour before the lab starts, which may work for lower-level labs but is not effective at the upper level. How can I assure that the students have read the requisite material in sufficient depth before the lab in order to efficiently use their time and mine?

A very efficient test design program, developed by Question Mark Computing, makes it possible to deliver tests over the campus network. The software allows the inclusion of graphic representations of the laboratory equipment and a variety of questions. The system stores the answers in a secure file along with a time and date stamp. This software has been used in all of my courses but perhaps most successfully as the prelaboratory component in physical chemistry.

The prelaboratory process must accomplish two major objectives. First, it must assure that the students have read the experiment in sufficient depth to understand the physical process of the experiment. That is, do they know what chemicals are needed and in what concentrations, and do they understand the fundamentals of the technique involved (chemical as well as instrumental)? Second, it must assure that the students have at least a minimal understanding of the basic concept that the experiment is trying to reinforce. With a considerable amount of time and effort on my part, the computerized test delivery allows the accomplishment of these objectives. It also solves the problem of assuring that students have completed the process prior to regular lab period with the inclusion of a time and data stamp on the results. The prelaboratory tests count as 15% of the laboratory grade, assuring student compliance. Once I found a set of experiments that I liked for the laboratory, then the same set of prelaboratory tests could be used year after year. The easiest part of the process is the grading. The software allows a variety of methods to evolve the results. Students grumble about the amount of time and effort it takes to complete the tests, but I have observed that, uniformly, the students are able to complete the experiment in the defined time period. Prior to using this type of prelaboratory experience, it was not unusual for a three-hour lab experiment to take five hours.

MEASURED RESULTS

One of the major problems in using multimedia components is obtaining useful and timely feedback on the effectiveness of the product. Various forms of evaluation documents have been handed out in class or made available on the campus network. The problem was that they generally were circulated following several multimedia experiences and, thus, information on specific modules was difficult to assess. I felt that the modules were effective teaching tools, but that was a biased opinion. How did the students feel about the modules? What was effective for them, and what was distracting?

I posed the problem to a student doing an honor's project with me, and she designed a series of module-specific evaluation questions (a maximum of ten).

When students finished a learning module, they were given the option to complete the evaluation. The results were mailed anonymously to my campus email address. In general, the students liked to have material presented in modular format where they could control the pace of information. Initially, the students were less complimentary about the attempts to present concepts via animated sequences. Further analysis of the responses showed that the dissatisfaction was not necessarily with animation concepts but rather with the speed of the process and the lack of student control. The students wanted to see and control every step of the sequence. I was showing the process too fast for them to comprehend all of the intermediate steps. Another interesting observation was that students did not seem to tolerate more than three colors on a presentation screen. The online evaluations are vital tools in finding both strengths and weaknesses in presentation media. Each year, I find new parts of the modules to modify based on the student responses.

How effective are the hands-on learning modules in understanding abstract concepts? I am not sure that I have a definite answer to that question. My colleagues seem to think they are effective, for one of the early assignments in organic chemistry is for the students to revisit the bonding tutorials.

LESSONS LEARNED

There is no single best way to present abstract ideas. Some students were excited by access to a hands-on learning experience; others were not.

- Students appear to absorb the concepts presented in the modules much more effectively if they work in pairs. Collaborative learning facilitates concept retention.

- Taking the students to a computer lab to run the modules as a part of class time was much less effective than allowing them to access the material outside of class. Because of the time constraints of the class hour, students felt rushed even with modular components. The time period—rather than their learning style or interest—was controlling how much material they could master.

- Computerized testing is an excellent teaching tool. Once students get over the fear of taking an online test, they find it more palatable than short, in-class tests. They like the ability to control the time of day and the length of time available for the process.

- Evaluate your multimedia presentations and computer-delivered test material every year. Student learning styles change, and the effectiveness of the medium is dependent, in part, on its ability to appeal to those learning styles.

CONTACT INFORMATION

Allen D. Bishop, Jr.
Professor of Chemistry
Director of Academic Computing
Millsaps College
1701 North State Street
Jackson, MS 39210
Email: bioshoad1@millsaps.edu or see
http://www.millsaps.edu/~bishoad1/
Phone: (601) 974-1406
Fax: (601) 974-1401

Vignette 3 Computer Modeling in First-Year General Chemistry

Arthur Glasfeld, Reed College

COURSE DESCRIPTION

The Reed general chemistry class is a relatively typical course by national standards. It is designed to introduce students to the structures, properties, and reactions of atoms and molecules, including examples drawn from inorganic, organic, and biochemistry. Specific topics include nuclear and atomic structure, types of chemical reactions and stoichiometry, gas laws, solution phenomena, chemical bonding, thermodynamics and chemical equilibria, kinetics, and electrochemistry. Laboratory work centers on quantitative analysis and is generally organized so as to illuminate lecture topics. To date, the use of computer graphics in our general chemistry course has largely drawn from the instructors' experiences with software packages used in advanced classes.

We are in the process of expanding the use of computer graphics in our first-year general chemistry course. Despite their utility in the relevant sections of our first-year course, the above packages do not provide visualization of more complex molecular phenomena. Why does the volume of a gas expand when it's heated? Why do reactions speed up when you increase the amount of reactant? Why do all processes tend toward equilibrium? Such questions depend on the behavior of large samples of a chemical species rather than individual molecules. Currently, we don't have high-quality software that can provide informative visual models that illustrate the processes that ultimately answer these questions. For example, Discover, which is packaged with Insight II, provides modeling tools. However, we have found that it is only really attractive in a demonstration context. The complexity of generating meaningful scenarios with this software doesn't lend itself to student experimentation. As a result, we would like to implement a simpler modeling package that accurately reflects chemical behavior without requiring a steep learning curve for its use.

COMPUTER MODELING

Two years ago, a Reed student, Grant Reaber, wrote a program that simulates the behavior of a gas in a closed container. Written in C++ with TCL, Gasbox is an interactive program that allows the user to define an initial set of conditions for a sealed, two-dimensional container of disks, which are meant to represent gas molecules. Students can change the number of disks, the temperature of the system, and the apparent mass of the disks. Students may then observe the effect of those conditions on the properties of the system. The multicolored disks, coded by their velocity, career around a black background, colliding with each other and the walls of the container. The container's pressure and the molecules' collisions, velocity, and energy are monitored. This software has been used as the basis of a general chemistry problem set over the last two years and has been well-received by students. Instead of interpreting an algebraic model of gas behavior (the ideal gas law) through calculations, students are given the opportunity to witness behavior, rationalize that behavior through the basic mechanics of visible objects, and then extend their understanding toward the creation of an algebraic model. In essence, students recreate the scientific process with a simple experimental tool.

The ideal gas law is a relatively simple algebraic model for a relatively simple system. We would like to extend the design of this software to capture more complicated phenomena like diffusion, chemical kinetics, and equilibrium. We're faced, however, with a difficult question: Do we continue in C++/TCL, or do we rewrite the program in Java, which is attractive because it is portable between platforms?

CONCLUSION

In general, computer modeling is a welcome activity for students. It bridges the passivity of textbook learning and the material and time-consuming aspects of the chemistry laboratory. While we can never replace the valuable experiences obtained by students working with the real materials of chemical research, we have found that computer models provide an excellent opportunity to conveniently capture the active process of learning that the laboratory environment fosters.

CONTACT INFORMATION

Arthur Glasfeld
Associate Professor of Chemistry
Reed College
3203 Southeast Woodstock Boulevard
Portland, OR 97202-8199
Email: Glasfeld@reed.edu
WWW: www.reed.edu/~glasfeld
Phone: (503) 771-1112 ext. 7679
Fax: (503) 788-6643

Using Technological Tools in General Chemistry

Angela G. King and Yue-Ling Wong, Wake Forest University

General chemistry (Chemistry 111/116) is taken by approximately 300 students each year at Wake Forest University. The courses are taught in multiple sections of 35-50 students each, with all professors agreeing on common coverage during the semester. The course sequence is filled predominately with first-year students, although there are some sophomores and even a few juniors and seniors signed up. Most in this course sequence are premedical students, and while they major in biology or chemistry, few are initially excited about general chemistry. The course has a reputation for being very demanding, with a great time commitment and low average grades.

Our initial question was how to best take advantage of the technology resources available at our university to improve communication within the class and to increase student motivation and level of performance. Most sections are taught in a classroom equipped with a state-of-the-art projection system to which the instructor's computer can be connected, and each student seat is equipped for Internet access.

COURSE DESIGN

Success in general chemistry is directly proportional to a student's thorough understanding of chemical concepts and ability to apply those concepts in solving mathematical problems. In reviewing past performance, three areas seemed to be universal candidates for improvement:

1) Communication between instructor and students

2) Motivation to increase students' willingness to work and study

3) Guidance for students outside of class as they independently applied what was learned in class

INCORPORATION OF TECHNOLOGY

Due to the implementation strategy of Wake Forest's Undergraduate Plan, students are issued computers upon arrival at campus. However, since the implementation began in 1995 with a pilot study, not all students in general chemistry currently have ThinkPads. While this situation will be alleviated next year, it did help us choose to present our teaching materials using web-based media in order to allow universal access. Since that decision was made, we have realized an added benefit of receiving recognition from chemical educators at different colleges and universities who have access to the materials at no cost. Keeping in mind our goals of improving communication, motivating students, and emphasizing conceptual understanding, we have incorporated the following activities into the general chemistry sequence:

1) Communication

- Establishment of a listserv

- Design and maintenance of a web page for the class

- Use of PowerPoint in lecture to allow students time for reflection

2) Motivation

- Development of self-paced interactive tutorials with instantaneous feedback on performance

- Development of online multiple-choice practice quizzes with instantaneous feedback on performance

3) Conceptual understanding

- Visual and 3-D conceptual problems to help students apply concepts on a molecular level

- In-class use of electronic concept tests

- Requirement of preclass exercises to improve preparation for class

COMMUNICATION

Communication has been dramatically improved through the use of these electronic avenues. Email has virtually replaced telephone calls from students. The listserv has allowed the instructor to send reminders, hints, and announcements to the class with ease. If an assignment is given out in class and a key piece of information was omitted from the assignment, the information can be sent electronically to all students immediately, without having to wait until the next class period.

An extensive web page for the class contains course materials such as a syllabus, schedule, and copies of all handouts. In addition, it contains scanned answer keys for all assigned problems, quizzes, and exams. Copies of exams from previous years are provided for students to practice. In addition, links to online tutorials, practice electronic quizzes, and other useful web sites are provided. While it does require time to maintain an extensive web page, that time is comparable to putting the equivalent material on reserve in the library and providing handouts to students. Students appreciate the constant access to solutions and often opt to print their own copies.

PowerPoint was incorporated into lectures in hopes of replacing time students spent writing with time they spent thinking. Handouts of the slide outlines, which contained some but not all information, were provided at the start of class. We hoped that students would stay engaged since they did not have all the notes beforehand, but that instead of copying definitions and theories, they could look at their print copies and reflect upon the implications. This approach yielded mixed results. Quiz scores for sections attending PowerPoint lectures were slightly higher than those of students attending traditional "chalk" lectures. However, student evaluations showed that the majority preferred the instructor to use chalk, thinking that they had to pay closer attention in class when taking their own notes.

MOTIVATION

Activities introduced to motivate students to work practice problems have been a success on all fronts. Online practice quizzes are created using a multiple-choice question database that allows for the incorporation of images. Questions are written by the instructor and entered into the database. Then quizzes are generated either to match the content of individual vignettes or to serve as exam reviews. Students access the resulting quizzes through links on the course web page. Students select the answer they feel is correct and submit it for grading. Within seconds, the computer responds to let them know if their answer was correct. At the end of each quiz, a score is provided for the students to monitor their own progress. They do not receive credit for taking the quizzes but do so anyway. Despite the fact that the instructor does not give multiple-choice exams, the quizzes are extremely popular with students.

The most extensive projects completed to date are interactive tutorials on specific topics. These tutorials guide students through example problems and then offer practice problems for the students to work independently. These exercises were designed for out-of-class use and provide the students with feedback and tips to avoid commonly encountered problems. Students can then practice independently while still receiving guidance as they would if in the professor's office. Development of the redox tutorial, for example, has drastically decreased the frequency of students asking the instructor for after-class assistance on this topic (Wong & King, 1999).

CONCEPTUAL UNDERSTANDING

Chemical education studies have shown that students may be able to master complex calculations without understanding their molecular basis. This was demonstrated in general chemistry at Wake Forest by presenting students with a calculation involving gas laws on an exam, followed by a problem in which they were asked to complete a sketch in which they showed the same laws applied to molecules. Many students could do the complex calculation but could not show the implications of the calculation on a molecular level. To combat this deficit of understanding, we developed a series of online problems that focus on visualizing molecules and the ways they interact. Most of these problems involve no calculations but simply the ability to recognize concepts on a molecular level. Most involve animations to simulate molecular motion, and some questions incorporate a 3-D approach to allow students to rotate a container and examine the contents from all viewpoints.

To help students focus on conceptual understanding rather than memorizing formulas, concept tests have been used in place of traditional lectures. Concept tests, designed to encourage active learning, present students with conceptual multiple-choice questions on discipline-specific subjects (Landis, 1998; Tobias, 1992). Students vote for the answer they select as correct, their votes are tallied, and the results presented to students for discussion in small groups. After their discussions, another vote is taken. The class vote should move toward consensus for the correct answer as students explain the concept to each other. One advantage of using concept tests in class is that instructors receive excellent feedback on how students are following the discussion (see http://www.chem.wisc.edu/~concept/). Initial use of concept tests in our class has revealed two problems: peer pressure and time constraint. Students who lack confidence coming into general chemistry are hesitant to raise their hands to vote for answers and, consequently, follow the lead of a few peers rather than struggling to master the concept. With the availability of student ThinkPads and in-class Internet access, we have alleviated this problem by developing an online voting program. Students vote anonymously using their ThinkPads, and the instructor can tally the votes electronically and project the results to the class.

The second problem with concept tests is the amount of time peer instruction takes. Much more material can be covered in a traditional 50-minute lecture than in a 50-minute class period of student discussions. To enable students to engage in active learning without sacrificing the content of courses due to time restraints, we have required more extensive preclass preparation. By reviewing students' answers and comments before class each morning, an instructor can briefly address the problems they are encountering before peer instruction begins. This approach allows students to cover the basic material on their own, and the instructor is freed to touch on more advanced topics and to assure the students' grasp of these concepts through their active participation in class.

MEASURED RESULTS

Student evaluations have supported continued use of technology in the general chemistry courses. Most valuable to students are the web page (for access to problems and answer keys), online practice quizzes,

and online tutorials. Most students have requested that tutorials be developed for most topics in general chemistry. While tutorials were developed for use outside of class, a study compared the quiz scores of students who were introduced to redox chemistry during class with either a traditional lecture and practice problems on paper or by in-class use of the tutorial. Quiz scores were higher on average for those students who first encountered redox chemistry through the online tutorial. This indicates that there may be advantages to using tutorials during class time. The effectiveness of Power-Point in lectures is not clear to either the instructor or students. A more extensive evaluation of the use of combined concept tests and preclass problem sets is being planned.

LESSONS LEARNED

While our experience introducing technology into the general chemistry classroom has been generally positive, we have developed strategies which should facilitate greater success in the future.

Demonstrate the Technology You Are Using

Instructors should demonstrate the technology they expect students to use at least once. Students who experience difficulties with any technology on their own may quickly become frustrated and not explore all of their options.

Develop Materials and Strategies Based on Your Priorities

Students are easily frustrated when they spend a lot of time mastering a technological application that is completely removed from the rest of the course. Our greatest successes have involved projects that mimic exam styles and emphasize important material.

Provide the Context for Online Material

Students are more motivated to work problems and explore options when they feel the exercises accurately reflect the instructor's priorities and expertise.

Provide Students with Instantaneous Feedback Whenever Possible

This allows students to monitor their own mastery of the material. For instance, our online quizzes are for practice only. While they do not contribute to a student's grade, we provide students with a score at the end, so they can determine if they need to continue studying.

Use Technology Appropriately

Use technology to increase student interest, but do not let bells and whistles distract students from the real goal of the material. If students are intrigued by animations, sounds, or images included in electronic materials, they are more likely to spend time using them. However, if the task at hand is for the students to learn content, that should be clear. Access to the content should not be hidden behind layers of visually stimulating but pedagogically useless displays.

CONCLUSION

Our experiences integrating technology into the general chemistry sequence show success can be achieved if thought and effort are put into both the planning and the delivery of materials. These materials do not replace other teaching tools, such as a quality textbook, but merely enhance the student's educational experience by making the material more engaging and providing direct feedback on student performance.

REFERENCES

Landis, C. R., et al. (1998). The new traditions consortium: Shifting from a faculty-centered paradigm to a student-centered paradigm. *Journal of Chemical Education, 75,* 741-744.

Tobias, S. (1992). *Revitalizing undergraduate science: Why some things work and most don't* (114-122). Tuscon, AZ: Research Corporation.

Wong, Y., & King, A. G. (1999). Application of interactive web tools in teaching redox chemistry. *Interactive Multimedia Electronic Journal, 1* (1). (http://imej.wfu.edu/articles/1999/1/05/index.asp).

Examples of applications that were discussed can be found at http://www.wfu.edu/~kingag/111/, http://www.wfu.edu/~kingag/116/, http://www.wfu.edu/~kingag/jittexercise/, and http://www.wfu.edu/~ylwong/.

CONTACT INFORMATION

Angela G. King
Assistant Professor of Chemistry
Wake Forest University
P. O. Box 7486, Reynolda Station
Winston-Salem, NC 27109
Email: kingag@wfu.edu
WWW: http://www.wfu.edu/~kingag
Phone: (336) 758-5511
Fax: (336) 758-4656

Yue-Ling Wong
Email: ylwong@wfu.edu

Learning Chemical Reaction Equilibria on CD-ROM

William M. Clark, Worcester Polytechnic Institute

A multimedia learning tool was combined with a co-operative group project to provide an alternative to the traditional lecture/homework format in a sophomore level, chemical engineering thermodynamics course. The CD-ROM learning tool included a motivational video of real processes; theoretical development including text, audio, video, and animation files; a virtual laboratory experiment; applications with worked examples; and self-tests for learners. Teams of four students were loaned two CDs and assigned the task of learning the material, while simultaneously completing a project requiring understanding of the fundamentals presented on the CD. The multimedia/group project format was evaluated against the traditional lecture/homework format with regard to student satisfaction, student learning, and faculty and staff time.

MOTIVATION

Having spent ten years teaching chemical engineering thermodynamics, I have come to realize that giving brilliant lectures doesn't always result in student learning. I was aware of extensive research indicating that active and cooperative learning has numerous advantages over the traditional lecture format (Felder & Silverman, 1988; Hagler, Marcy, & Wetzel, 1995), but I was reluctant to give up precious class time for students to actively engage the material. I had two main concerns: 1) There might not be enough time to cover the important material; and 2) misconceptions might be reinforced if students, helping each other, went down the wrong path unnoticed until too late. It occurred to me that a computer-aided learning tool might be used in conjunction with a cooperative learning approach to provide a more efficient learning experience. An interactive multimedia learning tool could present the fundamental information and techniques normally covered in lecture. A cooperative group project could serve both as motivation for learning and a concrete application of the fundamental material. A computer-equipped classroom would allow students to spend class time engaging the interactive learning tool, work-ing on the cooperative group project, and/or discussing the material with the instructor. This approach seemed like an ideal way for me to make the transition from "sage on the stage" to "guide on the side."

METHODOLOGY

The multimedia/group project approach was used for approximately one-third of a sophomore chemical engineering thermodynamics course. The first two-thirds of the course covered definitions and fundamentals underlying equilibrium calculations and phase equilibria using a traditional lecture/homework format. The final third of the course used a multimedia/group project format to teach reaction equilibria. The multimedia learning tool and the cooperative group project are both briefly described later in this vignette.

Student satisfaction was measured with standard WPI course evaluations and compared against those for the same course in previous years. Student satisfaction and attitudes were also gauged via pre- and post-course surveys covering attitudes about computers, cooperative learning, and chemical engineering. Student learning was evaluated by comparing scores on tests taken individually. Class averages on tests covering topics presented by the lecture/homework format were compared with the class average on a test covering the topic presented by the multimedia/group project format. Test scores were also compared to those from previous course offerings where the lecture/homework format was used for all topics. The time faculty and teaching assistants required to develop and to deliver the multimedia/group project format was compared to that required to deliver the lecture/homework format.

Computer-Aided Learning Tool

An interactive multimedia learning environment that provides a thorough nonlinear treatment of chemical reaction equilibria was created using the instructional media developer's software SIMPLE (Johnson, Johnson, & Smith, 1991). A main screen provided links to six sections, each leading to a series of interactive screens. Most screens provided text information and an opportunity for learners to input answers to questions or problems. Answers were checked and recorded in a log file, and feedback was provided depending on the answer. Some screens also delivered audio, video, or animation files that reinforced the concept presented on the screen. Each screen provided convenience buttons to advance, back up, return to the beginning of a section, or return to the main screen. Buttons were also provided to call a calculator, notepad, and Excel or Mathcad from the WPI Novell Network as needed. A fundamentals section provided interactive notes on reaction equilibria broken down into bite-sized subtopics. An illustrative examples section provided Excel spreadsheets to solve complex reaction equilibria problems. Students ran simulated reactions to see the effect of process variables and simplifying assumptions on calculated product compositions that were displayed on a pie chart. A laboratory experiments section contained a virtual titration reaction experiment, including a video showing a solution changing color as a function of pH. Students took virtual pH and spectrophotometric measurements and calculated the equilibrium constant for the reaction. An example problems section contained typical homework problems and their solutions. A test-yourself section provided sample questions for which learners provided answers. Feedback in that section indicated if the answer was correct, but detailed solutions were not provided. There was also a motivational film clip from a major oil company explaining the importance of the catalytic cracking process for producing gasoline. The multimedia learning tool was produced on CD-ROM.

Cooperative Group Project

Students were randomly assigned to four-member cooperative-learning teams and loaned two CDs per group. The teams' objectives were to learn the material on the CD, to prepare for a one-hour exam on the subject to be taken individually, and to prepare an oral and a written report on an assigned project. No homework was assigned, and no lectures were given. Students were free to investigate the CD learning tool or work on their projects during classes that were held in a computer-equipped classroom. The project placed the teams in the role of newly hired engineers asked to recommend improvements to a chemical reaction process. Two proposed improvements were to be ana-

lyzed, but the final recommendation was open ended. The project was related to the CD-ROM introductory film clip on catalytic cracking. All the background information required to complete the project was provided on the CD. Group members were required to sign a report cover page certifying that they contributed to and understood the contents of the report. All group members received the same project grade unless a group self-assessment instrument indicated that some members deserved a lower grade for failing to contribute their share. An individual exam, given the day after the final report was due, also included a group grade element. Groups in which all members earned passing grades (>70) received five bonus points as an incentive to work together and ensure the entire group learned the material.

MEASURED RESULTS

The multimedia/group project format was compared to the traditional homework/lecture format with regard to student satisfaction, student learning, and development and delivery time.

Student Satisfaction

The multimedia/group project format was well received. The standard WPI course evaluations solicited responses to 14 statements about the instructor's delivery of the course. These statements ranged from "established clear objectives for the course" to "assigned homework that aided my learning" to "was well above average," and all were phrased so that "agree" reflected satisfaction and "disagree" reflected dissatisfaction. The number of "agree" and "strongly agree" responses increased from 80%, when I taught the same course without the multimedia project, to 95% when the multimedia/group project format was introduced.

Pre- and post-course surveys taken for the multimedia/group project also indicated a high degree of student satisfaction. A five-level response option was given on most questions [i.e., strongly dislike (disagree), dislike (disagree), neutral, like (agree), and really like (strongly agree)]. Figure 5.1 shows the percentage of students responding at each level to several statements regarding learning formats. Clearly most students were pleased with the multimedia/group project format, and only a few disliked it. In keeping with these results, 75% of the students chose the multimedia/group project format when asked directly which format they liked better; 71% also felt that the multimedia/group project format helped them learn better than the lecture/homework format. These results indicate that neutral responders sided with the dislikes (and some of the likes) when forced to choose between the two formats. Thus, while few students disliked the new format, 25% to 30% still preferred the traditional lecture/homework format. A mixture of formats is probably the best approach for reaching all of the students.

The surveys also indicated improvements in student attitudes about thermodynamics as a subject and chemical engineering as a major, as well as their own abilities to solve problems and to use computers. Other indications that the multimedia/group project format was well received included numerous favorable oral comments from the students and my own impression that students were livelier and more engaged during computer/project classes than during lecture classes. Attendance was not recorded but appeared to be between 90% and 100%, with most students immediately going to work in their groups upon arrival before the beginning of formal class time, and many students continuing to work after class time was over.

Student Learning

Test scores for two course offerings are shown in Figure 5.2. In each offering there were three tests: one on definitions and fundamentals underlying equilibria, one on phase equilibria, and a third on reaction equilibria. The only test on material presented with the multimedia/group project format was the third test in year two. Averages presented are exclusive of any bonus points. Since the tests and students were different each year, no firm conclusions can be drawn from these data. However, it does appear that the multimedia/group project format did not hinder student learning and may have improved it (the improvement in test 1 compared to tests 1 and 2 was higher for year two). It should be noted that, while the technical content and material coverage remained the same, the year-two offering also included the important experiences of presenting an oral and a written report. Year-two students also expressed the perception that they learned as well or better than in previous offerings. The percentage of students answering "agree" or "strongly agree" with the statement "I learned a lot in this course" on the standard WPI course evaluations was 77% in year one and 97% in year two.

FIGURE 5.1

RESPONSES TO SELECTED POSTCOURSE SURVEY STATEMENTS

Strongly Dislike	Dislike	Neutral	Like	Really Like
Use of computer-aided learning tool in class as an alternative to lecture				
1%	10%	13%	60%	15%
Use of computer-aided learning tool outside of class as an alternative to homework				
0%	9%	10%	53%	28%
Use of cooperative group project in class as an alternative to lecture				
0%	13%	16%	50%	21%
Use of cooperative group project outside of class as an alternative to homework				
0%	6%	21%	46%	28%
Working in groups rather than alone				
1%	3%	16%	50%	29%

FIGURE 5.2

TEST AVERAGES FOR TWO COURSE OFFERINGS			
Year	Test 1	Test 2	Test 3
1	69.9	69.4	79.5
2	60.8	58.2	72.7

Faculty and Staff Time

The time required to prepare the multimedia learning tool and group project was much greater than that required to prepare lectures and homework. Much of the increased time can be attributed to the desire to give the multimedia presentation a more professional look than most overhead and blackboard notes. Even though SIMPLE is very easy to use, it takes time to type and format the screen information, especially when chemical and mathematical formulas are required. The fact that a learning tool for thermodynamics can be reused for several years helps justify the large initial time investment. Developing a group project that has both definite expected results and open-ended components and that requires application of fundamental principles also requires more time than selecting common homework problems.

There were some time savings that helped offset the large initial time investment. There was no need to prepare for and deliver lectures. Although I attended class, I did other work there unless questions arose. When questions did arise, I felt that students were actually learning from my responses as opposed to merely listening to me lecture. Although teaching assistants were employed to grade homework and tests for the class, their time was not required when the multimedia/group project format was used.

ACKNOWLEDGMENTS

This vignette was excerpted from Clark, W. M. (November, 1997). Using multimedia and cooperative learning in and out of class. Proceeding from Frontiers in Education Conference, Pittsburgh, PA.

Financial support for this project from the Davis Educational Foundation is gratefully acknowledged.

REFERENCES

Felder, R. M., & Silverman, L. K. (1988). Learning and teaching styles in engineering education. *Engineering Education, 78* (674).

Hagler, M., Marcy, W. H., & Wetzel, K. C. (1995, November). SIMPLE in Practice, Paper 3b31, Proceedings of the 25th Frontiers in Education Conference, Atlanta, GA.

Johnson, D. W., Johnson, R. T., & Smith, K. A. (1991). *Active learning: Cooperation in the college classroom.* Edina, MN: Interaction Book Company.

CONTACT INFORMATION

William M. Clark, Associate Professor
Chemical Engineering Department
Worcester Polytechnic Institute
100 Institute Road
Worcester, MA 01609
Email: wmclark@wpi.edu
Phone: (508) 831-5259
Fax: (508) 831-5853

What Is Engineering?: A Course That Incorporates a Virtual Laboratory

Michael Karweit, Johns Hopkins University

For the past several years, we have been developing an engineering laboratory course for freshmen: What Is Engineering? The course objective is to introduce students to engineering problem-solving early in their careers. Originally, the course consisted entirely of laboratory experiments, but when the interactive programming language JAVA became available, we began to explore the possibility of replacing or supplementing these experiments with web-based JAVA simulations. The result of this exploration is a virtual laboratory, which is now fully integrated into the course. We have a balance between virtual and real experiments, and students are learning more. With virtual experiments, they have more opportunity to experiment with what-if scenarios than they would in traditional laboratory experiments. Because some of the real experiments are now simulated, laboratory costs have been reduced. Further, scheduling problems have disappeared because the simulated experiments are available online at any time.

This vignette will focus primarily on the characteristics of this virtual lab and the impact it has had on student learning.

COURSE PHILOSOPHY

What Is Engineering?, in addition to providing a substantive introduction to a number of engineering fields, is designed to expose students to the whole process of engineering thought: theory, design (under constraints), construction, testing, and evaluation. It accomplishes this goal using four teaching elements:

1) Lectures: to provide the theoretical substance for the problems

2) Virtual experiments: to provide a click-of-the-button laboratory for experimentation and evaluation of ideas

3) Real experiments: to provide the hands-on validation of design ideas

4) Construction projects: to bring ideas to practical fruition

THE VIRTUAL LABORATORY

This laboratory is available to anyone on the Internet with a JAVA-enabled web browser. It includes ten simulated experiments with more to be added later. The experiments—ranging from the determination of the topology of hidden surfaces to the design of digital logic circuits—involve design, measurement, and estimation, and give students a taste of the type of problems found in engineering. Each of the simulations requires the student to set up the problem, perform the experiment, and extract information. In some cases, the information provides data for further calculations; in some cases, it provides a final result. Several of the experiments are intermediate steps in larger projects.

I describe here six of the experiments in the virtual laboratory.

1) Logic Circuits

Create circuits from AND, NOT, and NOR gates to effect logical outputs. Here, students assemble virtual components to produce logical properties. Circuits can be tested by assigning proper inputs and noting the results. Assignments vary from simple three-input AND gates to multidigit binary adders to robotic-control circuitry. Results from this experiment are further used in building a light-seeking robot.

2) Diffusion Processes

Visual simulation allows the process of diffusion to be explored and understood. Here, students can visually set up the elements of heat/diffusion problems in a nonmathematical way and then observe the process over time. Data may be taken from the display so that diffusion properties can be quantified. Problems include estimating heat loss from a poorly insulated window to calculating the largest chemical reactor that can accommodate a heat-producing chemical reaction.

3) Drilling for Oil

Suppose it were necessary to determine the curvature and orientation of a stratum of oil-bearing shale. The depth at which this stratum lies can be obtained only by drilling a hole until it is reached and then measuring the depth of the hole. Given a limited number of possible geometries, the problem is to determine the characteristics of this hidden surface at minimum cost. Cost factors include number of drill holes, terrain, and depth.

4) Robotic Arm Control

Consider a two-segment robotic arm whose tip is required to move through a sequence of specified trajectories. Control is affected by prescribing the rates of change of the angles between the links (i.e., by prescribing the angular positions of stepper motors). Assignments include: Prescribe a set of commands that will cause the arm to traverse its range along the x-axis at a fixed elevation y to within a specified tolerance; deduce the range of action of the arm; prescribe a set of commands that will take the arm through its trajectory at a constant speed.

5) Heat Transfer in a Duct

An experiment consisting of air blowing over a heated, ribbed surface is described. Motion holographic interferograms, taken during the running of the real experiment, are presented. The objective is to make measurements from these interferograms and deduce the Nusselt number—a measure of the heat transfer. The problem is to estimate temperature gradients based on visual data.

6) Bridge Designer

This is a design platform for developing simple truss bridges. By creating nodes, connecting them with members, and adding loads, students explore bridge designs and examine the compression or tensile stress experienced by every element of the structure. This module is used in conjunction with a project to design and build a load-bearing model bridge.

COURSE ASSESSMENT

What Is Engineering? has been well received. In post-course questionnaires, students said they like the diversity of teaching techniques used in the course: lectures, virtual labs, real labs, and projects. They commented in particular on the integration of these four components—unlike, for example, physics, in which they feel that lecture and lab are essentially unrelated. Since this course was taught before the inclusion of the virtual laboratory, we can evaluate its impact. It is substantial: Projects are more thought out, especially the bridge project. But there are some student grumblings: They say the course is very hard, because they have to think. For many of the assignments, there is no explicit or uniquely correct answer. This disturbs students who are accustomed to encircling an analytically derived result. Welcome to the real world . . .

LESSONS LEARNED

- When the virtual laboratory elements of this course were first being developed, the programming language JAVA was being touted as platform independent. Not true. The amount of effort that has gone into resolving inconsistencies among operating systems, web browsers, and web browser versions has been substantial. A perfectly operating JAVA simulation in one system may not work at all on another.

- Storing textual material—lecture notes, laboratory assignments, and project descriptions—probably wastes paper. Almost without exception, students print out material rather than read it on the screen. Then they discard rather than save their printout, because they can always retrieve it again.

CURRENT THOUGHTS

Multimedia courses are not new, but multimedia courses that offer interactive laboratory work are. The present effort is demonstrating not only that such courses are possible, but also that they can be effective. They appear to have the potential to extend the opportunity for science/engineering education well beyond the walls of the university campus.

ACKNOWLEDGMENTS

Development of this course is supported by the G. E. Fund.

CONTACT INFORMATION

Michael Karweit
Research Professor
Johns Hopkins University
Department of Chemical Engineering
3400 North Charles Street
Baltimore, MD 21218
Email: mjk@jhu.edu
WWW: http://www.jhu.edu/~virtlab/virtlab.html

 **Statics Online: Educational Software for the World Wide Web**

Edwin R. Carney, David B. Oglesby, Nathaniel Keen, Tuncay Akbas, Michael Garner, David Crites, University of Missouri, Rolla

Statics Online is being developed by the basic engineering department at the University of Missouri, Rolla. Its primary goal is to enhance the learning process through the use of computer technology and experiments in classroom pedagogy. To that end, Statics Online represents a model for a new environment where students can study and do their homework. This environment is accessible through the World Wide Web, but it is not necessarily intended for distance education. In fact, Statics Online is being developed primarily for use by on-campus instructors with their on-campus students. Over time, the components of Statics Online will free instructors to experiment with new ways to use their classroom time. Statics Online can be viewed as a new model for the academic textbook. Moreover, it is the first in a series of online pedagogical guides for teaching and learning.

EDUCATIONAL THEORIES

Statics Online consists of four main pedagogical components:

- Conceptual minilectures
- Conceptual self-tests
- Interactive example problems
- Homework problems

Conceptual Minilectures
Conceptual minilectures consist of a sequence of two- to three-minute audio lectures with synchronized graphics. They are similar to viewgraph presentations in that the graphics are automatically changed as students listen to the words. A minilecture usually introduces just one new concept. Often, they refer to more

fundamental material on which the current concept is based. When this occurs, students can click on a keyword that is linked to a minilecture covering the more fundamental material.

In many ways, minilectures are more efficient than classroom lectures. They are direct and to the point, they offer fewer distractions, can be repeated as often as one likes, and listened to when one is ready. On the other hand, we have found that the student's current perception of the minilectures is that they are not as important as the classroom lecture or the textbook.

Conceptual Self-Tests

Conceptual self-tests consist of true/false and multiple-choice questions that are used to test a student's understanding of a concept. They are simple questions that do not require long calculations. They attempt to trap and to correct any misconceptions that students have as soon as possible.

The interactive example problems are simulations. They include animation when appropriate. They are graphically rich and allow the user to change the input values to the governing equations and view the change in the graphics and the resultant values. They are used for classroom demonstration and also for discovery learning on the part of the students.

Online Homework

Online homework consists of randomized homework problems that are automatically graded when submitted and provide instant feedback on the results. The results are stored in a secure database. Students can view the results of their own work, and instructors can view the grades for their class. Students are given two chances to submit answers. A 2% tolerance is applied to all submitted answers, and 50% late credit is available for three days beyond the due date.

Some modification of the classroom experience may be possible using new technology. Introducing discussion groups, student board presentations, pairs problem solving sessions, group projects, and design problems could lead to a more active learning experience in the classroom. To some extent, Statics Online reduces the time spent in class collecting and passing back homework assignments. It also reduces the instructor's time grading papers outside the classroom.

Would it be possible for the students to rely on minilectures, the conceptual self-tests, and interactive example problems as a substitute for classroom lectures? To do this, their preconceptions would have to change, and some incentive would have to be provided. If this could be accomplished, the classroom experience might be adjusted to better accommodate all learning styles our students exhibit. Instructors would be better able to experiment with different ways of teaching through the cycle (Stice, 1997) and answering the why, what, how, and what-if questions posed in the minds of our students.

COMPUTER-ENHANCED TECHNIQUES

Statics Online is a work in progress for students, instructors, and experienced scientists and engineers. Eighteen homework problems are under development, with many more planned. During the fall 1998 semester, students at UMR were asked to complete 14 online homework problems. For each assigned homework problem, there are one or more conceptual minilectures, conceptual self-tests, and sample problems. The online problems are similar to the problems assigned from the textbook.

While homework problems are assigned for a grade, use of the other online material is completely discretionary. Students have classroom lecture notes, the textbook, and the online material to choose from when studying statics.

Portions of Statics Online are being used by instructors in the classroom with overhead projectors. Several of the interactive example problems, or simulations, provide a unique means by which to convey a new concept.

Some consideration is being given to modifying the Statics Online software in a way that offers incentives to students who visit material before it is presented in class. This can be achieved by having students log in when doing the conceptual self-tests or viewing the minilectures. Some credit may be given for attempting to answer the questions posed by the self-tests prior to the date specified by the course syllabus. This represents an attempt to better prepare students for class and would allow class time to be spent on more advanced topics.

Asynchronous communication among students is provided through a simple electronic bulletin board attached to each online homework problem. Students are encouraged to share approaches to solving the online problems. So far the competitive nature of the homework has precluded any significant use of this component. Virtual office hours are being considered for future experimentation. They would use online chat and white boards.

Concept maps are another pedagogical component not yet implemented. They promise to help tie together an otherwise disjointed curriculum in the minds of the students. They would be designed to map introductory or overview material in a way that would help the students better understand where the material they are asked to learn today will be used by them in the future.

MEASURED RESULTS

Three approaches are planned for evaluating the effectiveness of Statics Online as a learning/teaching aide: 1) student/instructor opinion polls; 2) page counts revealing student behavior when using the material; and 3) student compliance and performance with the assigned online homework problems. The results of the opinion poll combined with the measured patterns of behavior should provide insight into how the product can be improved. Over time, positive trends should be established.

Fragments of Statics Online were used by instructors and students during 1997. An early poll indicated that the students were generally favorable to the new material, although the actual traffic was light. During the fall 1998 semester, Statics Online was tested with five sections of BE50-Engineering Mechanics Statics at UMR. Approximately 120 students participated in this experiment. An opinion poll was available online, with credit given for student participation. The poll attempts to discover what aspects of the material the students find most valuable and how it can be improved. We also asked questions concerning how, when, and where the students use the material. These questions are intended to complement the measured patterns of behavior that are based on counter data.

Student behavior is measured by counters on the various pages in Statics Online. The following data consist of the number of hits on the Statics Online web site during the first seven weeks of the fall 1998 semester. During this period, seven of the 14 online homework problems were completed by the students.

120	Approximate number of students enrolled in the five participating sections of BE50
1827	Total visits to web site (welcome-page count)
3271	Total number of pedagogical component visits (excludes the welcome page)
5098	Total number of page counters tripped
131	Total number of pages with counters
7	Number of assigned homework problems completed
261	Number of visits per assigned homework problem
2.18	Number of visits per student per assigned problem
6.07	Number of pages with counters visited per student per assigned problem
1.71	Number of additional pedagogical components visited per student per assigned problem (minus the welcome page and the assigned problem for 2.18 visits)

From the data, we can see that, on average, each student visits the web site 2.18 times per homework problem. The welcome page and the homework problem page have counters. Counters are installed on all minilecture, example problem, self-test, and homework pages. The assignment pages and table of content pages do not have counters.

In visiting the web site to do homework, a student will accumulate a minimum of two hits (welcome page and homework page). The data indicate that, on average, each student views just less than two pedagogical components for each assigned homework problem.

The data analyses of web site hits are based on averages. In fact, the raw data would indicate that roughly 15% of the students account for the majority of hits. It is unknown whether the 15% are the same individuals each week. The results of the opinion poll should provide the information needed to better understand the student usage pattern throughout this first experiment.

Some additional data related to online homework performance are being accumulated. These will allow us to compare student compliance (percent of students doing their online problem compared to turning in problems in class) and performance (average score for online homework versus homework that is turned in). We will also look at the percent of problems solved correctly on the first and second attempts.

LESSONS LEARNED

Most authors of educational software report some difficulty in getting other members of the faculty to use the new material with their classes. Our introduction of online homework quickly overcame this problem. Half of the statics students and their instructors used the material during one semester, and we expect that number to grow.

CONCLUSION

Both students and instructors understand the conventional textbook and its relationship to a course. Statics Online is something new. Instructors and students alike will be adjusting to this new product for some time. While students may perceive it as more supplementary material, or more work, ultimately, as Statics Online matures, it will compete with, and eventually replace, the textbook. Statics Online represents a new model for the textbook, offering a new environment for study and homework. When students begin using Statics Online the night before an exam, we will know that we are there.

REFERENCE

Stice, J. E. (1997, February). Using Kolb's Learning Cycle to Improve Student Learning. *Engineering Education, 77* (5).

CONTACT INFORMATION

Edwin R. Carney, Lecturer
205 Basic Engineering
University of Missouri, Rolla
Rolla, MO 65409
Email: ecarney@umr.edu
WWW: www.Umr.edu/~oci
Phone: (573) 341-4639
Fax: (573) 341-6593

David B. Oglesby
Email: doglesby@umr.edu

Vignette 8 — Introduction to Computing in Engineering

Richard Shiavi, John Bourne, Arthur Brodersen, and
Edward White, Vanderbilt University

Almost all aspects of the engineering profession—including education—involve the use of computers. The introduction to computing in engineering course was designed with several general goals: to introduce students to certain computer applications that they will use in their educational and professional careers and to provide an asynchronous learning environment where the students have easy access to learning materials. The course is required for all engineering students in their first semester at Vanderbilt University's school of engineering; there are approximately 340 new students each year. The particular goals of the course are to introduce the computer as an engineering tool, develop a familiarity with Internet resources, develop communication skills, and develop an appreciation of working in teams. Two lecture sessions per week and one hour-and-a-half laboratory are scheduled. Nine instructors and nine teaching assistants staff the course in nine sections. All of the course materials are available on a web server. Instructors use the web pages to stimulate discussion in the time allocated for lecture, and students and teaching assistants use the pages to conduct the laboratories. Each laboratory page has complete instructions and methods, including demonstrations that the students can follow. Completion of the laboratory exercises usually requires more than the scheduled period, so the students complete the work on their own time. The software application Front Page is the development and management tool. The laboratories are integrated with the classroom material and require a written report. The reports are graded weekly.

Course Description

The material covered in the course is organized into topical areas in the brief outline that follows. The students are introduced to the computing environment at Vanderbilt University's school of engineering and the network environment at VU. Residence halls are connected to the VU network. Specifically, the students learn to set up accounts and get an overview of the hardware. They are introduced to Windows NT and Internet applications: electronic mail, web browser, and file transfer. They learn hypertext markup language (HTML), how to create their own home pages, virtual reality markup language (VRML), and visualization.

Communicating Tools

Communications is an important aspect of engineering The students learn to use a word processor, Microsoft (MS) Word, and slide presentation software, MS PowerPoint. All laboratory reports are written documents, and the students must make some presentations at the end of the semester.

Computing Tools

Computation and simulation are fundamental to engineering. For this capability, the students learn to use a spreadsheet application, MS Excel, and a professional computing environment, MATLAB. The learning and exercise of these environments are imbedded in useful topics: statistics, data plotting, solving simultaneous linear equations, and simulations of physical systems.

Team Project

One of the major aspects of the course is a team project. Teams of four students are formed after four weeks of the semester. Their goal is to select a design topic and develop a computer-based tool to implement their design. The project must use one or several of the computer environments learned. Past projects include campus tour guides in HTML, rocket and planetary simulations in VRML or MATLAB, and home pages for campus organizations. At the end of the semester, the students have two occasions to demonstrate their projects. First, each team makes an oral presentation during class. Second, at the project fair at the end of classes, each student group brings a computer, configures it and additional displays on a reserved table, and demonstrates its project. All students are invited and the Engineering Council presents awards for the five best projects.

SMALL GROUP DYNAMICS

To prepare for this group project, the students are given two classes in small group dynamics, which were developed by faculty in our department of human development and the counseling center. The activities are based on the Myers-Briggs Type Inventory (MBTI), which is administered to the students during freshman orientation. The activities include criticizing their MBTI versus what they think about themselves, solving an engineering problem in a team, and commenting on how each team member participated.

MEASURED RESULTS

At the beginning and end of the semester, questionnaires are administered to the students to determine their general background and their opinion of the course. To follow is a summary of their responses.

Student Responses

- 95% agree that the goals of the course were accomplished.

- Most liked learning about computers and having the course materials available to them online.

- 50% of the students remarked that they liked the modality of learning through the Internet the best.

- The percentage of students feeling comfortable with computers went from 37% at the beginning of the semester to 88% at the end.

- 95% of the students felt that the teamwork experience was very useful.

- 75% would recommend this course to someone in a nontechnical curriculum.

Faculty Responses

The faculty were questioned about the course material and their assessment of using web-based material. Their responses are summarized below.

Advantages to using web-based material.
- Students have continuous access.

- Materials can be updated continuously.

- Tests and questionnaires can be administered online.

- Students can take them when ready.

- Electronic access allows automated grading and tabulating.

- Authoring software makes courseware development straightforward.

Disadvantages to using web-based material.
- Some students still prefer using books and portable materials.

- A server must be allocated, and someone must monitor it.

- Extra time and energy is required to develop the materials.

CONCLUSION

This course has become a stable part of the curriculum. To maintain its quality and continually improve its content, several challenges are now apparent.

- Students are entering with more computer skills each year.

- Their background is very diverse, from the naive to the experienced.

- The residential network needs to be used more effectively.

- Students more and more tend to be bottom-up learners (integrators).

- The syllabus must be substantially updated biennially.

CONTACT INFORMATION

Richard Shiavi, Professor
Biomedical Engineering
Electrical Engineering
Vanderbilt University
P. O. Box 1554, STA. B.
Nashville, TN 37235
Email: Richard.shiavi@vanderbilt.edu
WWW: http://www.vuse.vanderbilt.edu/es130/
Phone: (615) 322-3598
Fax: (615) 343-7919

Vignette 9 — Developing an Effective Web-Based Engineering Course

Madison Daily and Susan L. Murray, University of Missouri, Rolla

Advanced Production Operations at the University of Missouri, Rolla (UMR) is a graduate-level survey course in the engineering management department. It provides students with a background in a variety of business and industrial engineering techniques. Topics covered include decision theory, forecasting, total quality management (TQM), statistical process control (SPC), acceptance sampling, product design, process selection, facilities layout, location planning, aggregate planning, material requirements planning, scheduling, and project management. With such a volume of material, it is easy for students to feel overwhelmed. A web-based course has been designed to reiterate this course material through a variety of teaching techniques.

Previously this course was taught in both traditional classroom settings and a distance-learning format, televised by National Technology University (NTU). Lectures used slides made in Freelance Graphics. Students were supplied course notes that contained copies of all of the slides, and a textbook supplemented the lectures. The current web-based course was a natural progression from the televised course. Students also get the benefits of chatrooms and email contact with classmates and the instructor.

Course Structure

Students in this course are required to purchase a textbook, supplementary casebook, and prepared class notes. The class notes contain all of the visual lecture material in addition to homework answers. An optional CD-ROM containing all lectures is available; it eliminates the need to download information from the web. On the first day of class, the professor meets with the students to discuss the course format and the Internet-based tools used in the class. There is no further face-to-face meeting until the final exam is administered. The course uses an Internet home page (http://www.umr.edu/~daily) that includes links to the class syllabus, assignment lists with instructions, grading policies, a bulletin board that is updated daily, class chatroom, class lectures, and quizzes. Students work

through the course material at their own pace and convenience. They are able to watch the lectures on the web or the CD-ROM which contain the same material. The lectures were developed using Lotus Screen-Cam software. The lecture modules contain Freelance presentation slides converted from the NTU television course. Text, figures, and other graphics appear on the screen, while the instructor's voice explains the various concepts. The audio and visual portions are synchronized. The students can stop, pause, repeat, speed up, or slow down the material.

Assignments, submitted electronically, are due throughout the semester. Students are encouraged to interact electronically with the instructor and other students by email and a chatroom. The instructor communicates both one-on-one and with the whole group via email messages and the class bulletin board as appropriate. Although office hours are also available for communication by phone or fax, students rarely use this option. Students are required to post an article relevant to the course in the chatroom and to comment on the discussion threads started by other students.

Measured Results

Data have been gathered for a traditional classroom lecture section and five sections of the Internet-based advanced production operations course. A pretest was given to determine the students' level of knowledge prior to the class. Surveys were given at the beginning, middle, and end of the course. The initial survey measured the students' expectations of a web-based course with respect to time required and effectiveness. The surveys during and at the completion of the course measured their actual experience in the Internet-based class. The final exam served as a post test to measure the course's effectiveness.

The expectation survey used a five-point Likert scale. Students responded that, compared to a traditional lecture course, they expected the Internet course would take the same amount of time (mean = 3.04, standard deviation = 1.01) and overall learning would be the same (mean = 2.98, standard deviation = 0.87).

They expected all of the learning techniques (email, chatrooms, textbook, casebook, prepared notes, and electronic lectures) to be effective. All of the students surveyed had an undergraduate engineering degree and reported a moderate to high degree of computer experience and knowledge. Their positive expectations about asynchronous computer learning should not be generalized to all educational situations.

The survey at the end of the course measured the experience of 87 students with the various teaching techniques. The students reported that on average the course took less time than a traditional lecture course (mean = 2.57, standard deviation = 0.87). This is likely because students can work at their own pace. Overall learning was rated as slightly more effective (mean = 3.17, standard deviation = 0.89). The students also rated the effectiveness of the teaching techniques. The electronic lectures and prepared notes were considered very effective (mean = 4.48, standard deviation = 0.75, mean = 4.56, standard deviation = 0.68). The textbook was rated as effective (mean = 4.05, standard deviation = 0.87) followed by the casebook (mean = 3.70, standard deviation = 0.92) and the email (mean = 3.60, standard deviation = 0.84). The chatroom's effectiveness was rated as neutral (mean = 3.15, standard deviation =0.83).

Five sections of the Internet-based course participated in this research. The control group consisted of 19 students who took the class in a traditional lecture format. The pretest average score was 51.14 % with a 8.11% standard deviation for the Internet-based students and 56.21% with a 6.49% standard deviation for the control group. Both groups experienced a significant improvement on the post-test final exam. The Internet-based group scored 89.09% with a standard deviation of 6.54%, while the control group's average was 90.58% with a standard deviation of 4.30%. The difference between the two groups was not found to be statistically significant. From these preliminary results, it can be inferred for this particular case that the web-based teaching techniques were as effective as traditional classroom lectures.

LESSONS LEARNED

The greatest benefit for students in an asynchronous course is flexibility. They enjoy the freedom to access course material any time of the day or night. They expect the course always to be available. The majority of students purchased the CD-ROM of the course material to avoid interruptions or delays with Internet service. They expect the same level of response from the course instructor via email, and this places a significant burden on the instructor to frequently monitor email messages throughout the day, seven days a week.

Just as many students are reluctant to speak in a traditional classroom setting, many Internet students are reluctant to speak in chatrooms. Requiring a specific number of contributions and comments to chatroom topics is an effective method of achieving the desired level of discussion among students.

Students seemed to particularly enjoy little extras that liven up the web-based material. Web-based lectures can become monotonous, just like traditional classroom lectures. Inserting a brief sound clip or humorous comment helps to liven up the course and keeps the students' attention. They help to make the instructor seem more approachable.

CONCLUSION

Asynchronous Internet courses provide many benefits to the student and the instructor. However, these courses require significant levels of instructor-time during both development and implementation. The instructor's efforts are not reduced; they are shifted from lecturing in the classroom to managing chatroom activities, monitoring individual student progress, and engaging in email discussions with students. With the necessary time and effort, asynchronous Internet courses can be effective and rewarding for both the students and the instructors.

CONTACT INFORMATION

Madison Daily
Email: daily@umr.edu or murray@umr.edu
WWW: http://www.umr.edu/~daily
Susan L. Murray, Assistant Professor
University of Missouri, Rolla
Engineering Management Department
Rolla, MO 65409
Email: murray@umr.edu
Phone: (573) 341-4038
Fax: (573) 341-6567

Richard Shiavi, Vanderbilt University

Signal processing is now being used in many engineering disciplines because of the omnipresence of desktop computers and sophisticated applications. Many concepts involved in signal processing are difficult to learn, because they are embedded in discrete mathematics and are not easy to visualize. This usually leads to erroneous implementation of techniques. A 1994 National Science Foundation Panel on Signal Processing and the National Information Infrastructure found that, although interactive teaching and learning modalities have developed very rapidly for simple textual data, there is a great need to develop interactive teaching modalities in signal processing. A second factor, adding a degree of difficulty to learning, is that the students lack a foundation for their learning. Time-series analysis is not anything one learns serendipitously, and the knowledge of real-world signals is complex at best. A third factor is that the students must also learn a computing environment in order to implement the techniques. A learning environment where students can visualize and interact with the results of mathematical operations is needed.

SOLUTION

To teach techniques, such as frequency analysis and signal modeling, a series of interactive notebooks has been developed. These notebooks are written in the integrated environment of Microsoft Word and Mathworks MATLAB. Each notebook presents a principle, reviews the relevant mathematics, and demonstrates its implementation via script in MATLAB. Students are then asked to exercise other aspects of the principle interactively by making simple changes in the MATLAB script. They receive immediate feedback on what is happening and can relate theoretical concepts to real effects on the signal. They are finally required to implement the learned procedure on a signal from a database of actual measurements. Students enjoy learning in this environment because it helps them visualize immediately the results of the mathematical manipulations.

Notebooks have been developed to treat the following topics: polynomial modeling, frequency analysis of deterministic, first- and second-order properties of random signals, signal modeling using autoregression, and spectral analysis of random signals using the periodogram and autoregressive models.

EXAMPLE

In each notebook, the history of the technique being studied is briefly summarized and is followed by a statement of the engineering application. In studying the calculation of the frequency content of deterministic signals, for example, the discrete Fourier transform (DFT) must be used. The theoretical result is given, and then the result of the DFT is presented. The notebook also shows the MATLAB script used to do the analysis. Figure 10.1 shows the script and the result of the application of the DFT to a truncated sinc function.

FIGURE 10.1

MATLAB

```
clear; close all; format compact; whitebg('w')
syms t
f0 = 0.5; %Hz
ft = 'sin(2*pi*0.5*t)/(2*pi*0.5*t)'; % SINC FUNCTION
% an indeterminate value exists at the peak of the waveform
figure (1)
subplot(1,2,1); ezplot(ft,[-5 5])
xlabel('TIME, seconds'); ylabel('AMPLITUDE');
title('SINC FUNCTION')
FT = zeros(201,1); FT(51:151) = ones(101,1);
fsp = 0.01; f = (-100:100)*fsp;
subplot(1,2,2); plot(f,FT);
xlabel('FREQUENCY,Hz'); ylabel('MAGNITUDE');
title('FOURIER TRANSFORM')
axis([-1.5 1.5 0 1.5]); grid
```

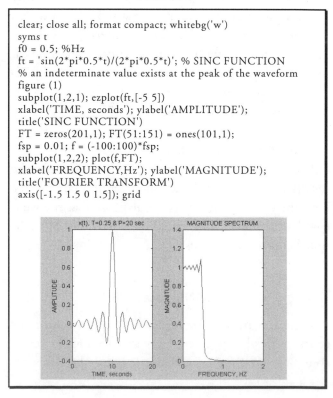

Figure 10.2

EXAMPLE

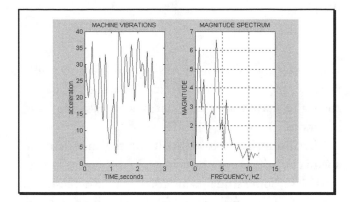

The student should both observe that the resultant calculation is not what is expected and see explicitly the error called "leakage error." Using the script available in Figure 10.1 the student is then asked to show the effects of signal length, zero padding, and sampling interval on the DFT and its leakage error. Thus, the student not only learns these effects, which are hard to learn directly from the mathematics, but also becomes more comfortable using MATLAB.

Next, students are introduced to the concept of windows and observe that windowing can improve the resultant DFT. They are then asked to apply other windows and see which one seems to produce the best magnitude spectrum. Finally, students are given a signal like the vibration signal shown in Figure 10.2 with its unimproved DFT. They are then asked to apply a procedure that will produce the best possible DFT.

MEASURED RESULTS

The students were given a questionnaire at the end of the semester that solicited their reactions to the notebooks. A summary of the responses follows.

- The notebooks were an excellent learning tool and easy to use on one's own time.

- The notebook approach took the drudgery out of learning MATLAB and facilitated experimentation.

- The use of actual signals embedded in real-world problems was an incentive to learn some of the dry mathematical details.

CONTACT INFORMATION

Richard Shiavi, Professor
Biomedical Engineering
Electrical Engineering
Vanderbilt University
P. O. Box 1554, STA. B
Nashville, TN 37235
Email: Richard.shiavi@vanderbilt.edu
Phone: (615) 322-3598
Fax: (615) 343-7919

Robert M. Newton, Smith College

Geomorphology is an intermediate-level geology course that involves the study of landscapes and the processes that form them. One of its principle goals is to teach students the skills needed to interpret the geologic history of an area from simple observations of landscape features.

The course has three hours of lecture and one three-hour laboratory scheduled each week. Approximately half the laboratories involve local field trips and one weekend field trip. Enrollment is ideally 14 students (the number that fit in a college van). All students live in wired dorms and either have their own computers or use computer resource centers that have both Macintosh and Windows-based machines connected to the network.

COURSE DESIGN

I believe students learn best in a cooperative learning environment where problem solving is emphasized. Therefore, as much as possible, I have students work in informal groups that stress positive interdependence and individual accountability. Assessment is done through both written assignments and hour-long exams. Students discuss questions, which are provided to them one week prior to the exams, both in small groups and in the class immediately preceding the exam.

Students develop the skills necessary to develop a geologic story from a view of the landscape in the laboratory portion of the course. The first labs are spent indoors, looking at maps and air photos, while later in the semester we apply these principles in the field. Each indoor lab is centered on a series of questions about features shown on a representative group of maps and air photos. Generally, students work together in small groups while I circulate the room answering their questions. I have found that it is important that students get immediate feedback. They need to know if they have correctly identified the features on a map before they move on to interpret their geologic significance. It

is not educationally sound for them to have to wait a week to get back their corrected lab assignments; by then, they have forgotten what was on each map and air photo.

Traditionally, it is difficult for the instructor to spend enough time with each group during the lab period. Also, some students are too shy to ask questions, especially if they feel that their question is too simple. Another problem is that students do not have easy access to the materials outside class. The only way they can study the maps, air photos, and photographs is to return to the lab at other times of the day or in the evening. Copies of the maps and photos passed out in class are generally of too poor quality to be of much use. The best solution I have found involves providing materials to students through the World Wide Web. This gives them access to high-quality images as well as a mechanism for immediate feedback, either through the use of web tutorials or email.

HOW COMPUTER TECHNOLOGIES ARE USED

The course web page is the principal vehicle for providing information, resources, and avenues of communication for students in this course. They are able to access the web page from anywhere on or off campus, using any computer connected to the web, regardless of the operating system. It provides them with general information, such as the course syllabus, assignments, and links to other sites, but, more importantly, it gives them full-color images of the maps and air photos used in lab. Some of these are provided as tutorials where students can get immediate feedback on their interpretation of landforms.

The tutorial helps students answer the type of question that they most ask me during labs. In the tutorial frame, clicking the mouse at some point on the map will cause an explanation of the feature at that location, displayed in a box below the map. This is fundamental in helping students build confidence in their landform identifications. It allows for a higher level of discussion in lab as we are not so concerned about getting the landform identifications but can now concentrate more on what these landforms mean in terms of the geologic history of the area.

The web page is also used to provide large data sets, in a variety of forms, for students to analyze. Hydrologic data, such as ten years of mean daily stream discharge, can be provided as a self-extracting archive so that students can download the data onto their computers in an application-specific form. This helps eliminate problems students have with data formatting. Image data is also provided from field trips. We now bring a digital camera along on all our field trips to take pictures of the landscape features. The images are posted on the web page and can be downloaded by the students to be incorporated in their written reports or incorporated directly into student papers published on the web page. Publishing papers on a web page facilitates peer review and generally results in a higher quality paper.

Perhaps the web page has had the greatest impact on the way I give examinations. Since students have a week to work on the answers, I can now ask questions that require more thought, and since they have access to high-quality images, I can ask questions from maps and air photos that they have not previously seen. The exam is no longer just a test of how well they can memorize what I have told them but now requires them to think. Students like it because it eliminates the stress of not knowing what will be on the exam.

I also use the computer presentation software, Persuasion, for most of my lecture, which easily allows me to provide copies of all the graphics used in lecture directly to the students. They do not need to spend time during lecture copying down complex diagrams but can struggle with the concepts being presented.

MEASURED RESULTS

It is difficult to measure the full impact of the implementation of this technology, as it is still very much a work in progress. Based on course evaluations, most students liked the system of web-based tutorials and would like to see more of them. Almost everyone liked the format of the exams even though grades tended to be lower. During the semester, there were approximately 1,200 hits to the web page, indicating a high level of use by the 15 students in the course.

LESSONS LEARNED

Course web pages have tremendous potential as learning resources, but it takes a lot of time to develop a good web page. No matter how interesting I may think other sites are, students will not browse through a series of links to other sites unless there is a direct reason to do so.

Scanning images like topographic maps and getting them up on the web page are time-consuming tasks that can be done by student assistants. The building of web-based tutorials is also time-consuming, at least initially. Once the general software design has been worked out, then the use of software tools like Webmap speed the actual production. Again, the use of student assistants could make this less time-consuming for faculty as well as educationally beneficial for the student assistant.

I worried that giving out exam questions prior to the exam would automatically result in everyone getting an A. This was definitely not the case. Exam grades were lower, especially on the first exam (C average). The more complex questions based on images of maps and landscapes revealed fundamental weaknesses in student thinking. This caused me to initiate a class discussion session prior to the exam to discuss exam questions. I did not give out answers during the discussion but instead let the students discuss the questions, while I steered the discussion toward the critical concepts.

I am not convinced that presentation software leads to better teaching. You can often cover more material in this type of structured presentation, but it is not clear that students learn more. Students may actually pay less attention during class if you provide them with presentation handouts, as they feel they can learn it later on their own.

The primary lesson I have learned from this venture is that computer-based technology has the ability to provide students with the resources to better learn the concepts I am trying to teach. The ability for a student to see, at any time, high-quality images of materials that previously were only available only in the lab greatly enhances their learning experience.

CONTACT INFORMATION

Robert M. Newton
Department of Geology
Smith College
Northampton, MA 01063
Email: Rnewton@science.smith.edu
WWW: http://www.science.smith.edu/geology
    /geomorph
Phone: (413) 585-3946

Vignette 12 | A General Science Class for Nonmajors

John F. Wallin, George Mason University

Astro 111/113 is a two-semester course in modern astronomy designed for first-year nonscience majors. In a typical semester, we have over 300 students enrolled in these courses and associated labs. The primary objectives for this class are to increase the students' scientific literacy and give them an appreciation of the physics and structure of the universe.

IDEAS BEHIND THE COURSE DESIGN

Large lecture classes are perhaps the worst learning environments on modern university campuses. Students enrolled in them typically spend most of their time frantically copying notes during each lecture, if they attend at all. They have virtually no direct contact with their instructor and little opportunity for feedback and interaction which would allow them to assess their understanding and remediate their misconceptions before formal testing occurs.

COMPUTER-ENHANCED TECHNOLOGIES

When I began teaching computer-enhanced courses, I began to improve the lecture sections by using a variety of electronic classroom and Internet-based technologies. First I developed a complete set of electronic notes to replace the chalkboard and overhead transparencies, and these notes are projected on the 25-foot projection screen in the lecture hall. I also use videotape, videodisk, and web-based resources to illustrate points throughout the lecture. All the lecture notes are also placed online immediately after the lecture, so students stopped mindlessly copying notes and began actively listening to the lecture.

Additional web enhancements developed during spring 1995 included a hyperlinked glossary, lecture summaries, online constellation maps, an email distribution system, and an online discussion system. Hyperlinks to external sites are also provided for each lecture to allow students to learn more about topics they are interested in.

Perhaps the most significant change in the class took place with the creation of a web-based electronic homework system. Before I began teaching this course, no homework assignments were given since there was virtually no grading support for the class except in the lab sections. I created an interactive electronic homework system on the web to allow students to complete weekly, extra-credit homework assignments. In this system, students are presented with a scrambled set of multiple-choice questions taken from a database. The order of the questions, the order of their answers, and even numerical data in the questions are randomly generated. After students have answered the questions, the computer automatically grades them and provides immediate feedback. Questions the student answered incorrectly are again scrambled and given to the student. To receive full credit for the assignment, the student must eventually answer all of the approximately 30 questions in these weekly assignments. If students complete all 14 of these assignments, they get a net increase in their grade of 8%.

In addition to providing students with feedback about their understanding, the system gave me a way to assess general misconceptions about the material. Statistical summaries of questions are provided to allow the teacher to learn which questions were particularly difficult. Since each homework assignment was only available for credit for a one-week period, students were also encouraged to keep up to date in their readings and lecture attendance.

Beginning in spring 1998, one section of the Astro 113 course was offered in a completely web-based format in collaboration with UOL Publishing, an Internet courseware provider. Lectures are replaced by interactive multimedia, and office hours are held online. Tests are still administered in class.

MEASURED RESULTS

During 1995, about 50,000 pages of online notes were accessed during each semester. However, there was no measurable impact on class performance. Although students were not busy copying notes during the lecture, their performance on in-class exams was not significantly better than in previous years. There was also no correlation between the use of the web notes and the final grade. Although students gave high marks for the class and for the online notes, there is no evidence that it affected learning outcomes.

During the spring 1996 semester, I introduced the online homework system. Over 85% of the students used the system at least once during the semester. Approximately 60% of the students used the system every week. Over 27,000 sets of questions were submitted for grading, and over 1,250 hours of online time were recorded by the quiz system. On average, students spent about five extra hours answering questions online, with additional time spent offline, studying printouts of these questions. Based on these statistics, there were no significant barriers to using the web as part of a large general education science class at George Mason University. The large amount of time-on-task as well as the number of homework sets graded also suggest that better feedback can be given through a computerized system than on a one-to-one basis.

Because of this online homework system, the average grades on in-class exams rose by more than 15% as compared to the previous year. Strong and weak students both did significantly better on these exams, and test performance was correlated with usage of the homework system. Despite the extra online material, attendance in lecture remained constant. The difficulty of the questions on the in-class exams remained approximately constant between the two years in this study, although the questions were changed to prevent memorization. By creating an incentive to keep up with the lectures and readings, students were better prepared to learn new material. The use of computer-mediated instruction has changed the way that students learn in this class. Although old exam questions were available for study in both years, the extra component of interactive feedback seems to have significantly altered the performance of students on objective in-class exams.

In the final year of the study, I was able to compare the students enrolled in my distance-learning section (web only) to those who attended my lectures. The students who were enrolled in the distance-learning class did slightly better on the in-class exams than the students who attended my lectures. There was a slight population bias in this study. The students enrolled in the distance-learning section were more likely to be juniors and seniors than in the lecture class. However, there is no evidence that my lectures actually helped students do better on exams.

LESSONS LEARNED

Technology can be effectively used to enhance the learning outcomes in large lecture classes.

- Students are able to use web sites. Over 99% of my introductory students had email addresses last year. All of them have used the web.

- Despite the hard work, good intentions, and great evaluations during the first year of this experiment, there is very little evidence that simply placing notes online has any effect in learning outcomes.

- Giving students feedback before formal evaluation, even if it is automatically generated, can make a significant difference in student learning.

- Even though I modestly feel my lectures are exciting, interesting, and well organized, there is little evidence they really help students learn. This may be because of the low attendance in the large lecture class. However, there seems to be little evidence that students really learn much better listening to a lecture than they do studying web pages and completing online homework.

CONTACT INFORMATION

John F. Wallin
Associate Professor of Space and
Computational Sciences
Institute for Computational Sciences and Informatics
George Mason University
Mail Stop 5C3
4400 University Dr.
Fairfax, VA 22030-4444
Email: Jwallin@gmu.edu
WWW: http://www.science.gmu.edu/~jwallin

Vignette 13 — Melding Network Technology with Traditional Teaching: Enhanced Achievement in a 500-Student Course

Edwin Kashy, Michael Thoennessen, Yihjia Tsai, Nancy E. Davis, and Guy Albertelli II, Michigan State University

INTRODUCTION

This vignette describes a three-year project to study and assess the impact of technology on learning and performance. We studied a 500-student introductory physics course for engineers. We have found significant improvements in student achievement with an approach that includes considerable use of Asynchronous Learning Network (ALN) technology within a relatively traditional lecture format.

Network technology has given instructors a wide array of new tools that make it now possible to efficiently implement in a large class an instructional environment normally restricted to a class with a small number of students. The dominant new aspect is immediate online feedback that immediately informs students if their understanding and solutions to problems are correct, and, consequently, lets their instructor know the areas where students are encountering difficulties so that these can be addressed in a more timely manner. Students learn by correcting their work without penalty for corrections. They can thus maximize their performance, and this is highly motivating.

Our initial goals were to take advantage of technology to address some of the factors that can contribute to students not performing well. These factors include 1) deficient preparation and a lack of awareness thereof; 2) misconceptions, especially in physics; 3) insufficient mathematical problem solving skills; 4) the tendency to fall behind; and 5) the students' perception of the quality of education. (For other factors, see Cheatham, 1994.)

COURSE ORGANIZATION AND DESCRIPTION

The 500-student physics course is a calculus-based introductory class for students in science and engineering. Traditionally, it included four lectures and one recitation session where a teaching assistant, quite often a member of the faculty, could interact with approximately 25 students, answering questions, giving quizzes, and helping with assignments. When there was no quiz, recitation attendance was generally quite poor. A fraction of the assigned homework was graded and typically not returned to students until the following week.

Our Asynchronous Learning Network (ALN) combined commercial conferencing software (First-Class and AltaVista Forum) with the use of CAPA (Computer-Assisted Personalized Approach) (see Kashy et al., 1993), a system developed at MSU to implement a computer-assisted personalized approach for assignments, quizzes, and examinations (Kashy & Morrissey, 1997). The course was reorganized without recitation sections, and the staff for the course was reduced to about two-thirds that of previous years. This staffing level was sufficient to maintain the network conferences and the Physics Learning Center (PLC). The network conferences were discussions of various topics or answers to questions, which were available to all students any time outside class hours. The Physics Learning Center provided a location where instructors and TAs interacted with students using the Socratic Method. The ALN and PLC became the major methods of providing student assistance. In addition to faculty and graduate students, several undergraduate students from the Honors College participated in the PLC helping their fellow students. These students were required to have the weekly assignment done correctly before the time they were scheduled in the PLC. A substantial fraction (~50%) of the time in lecture is devoted to students being actively involved in tasks related to understanding of basic principles and in discussing these ideas with neighboring students (see Sokoloff, 1995; Resnick, 1987). During the first year of the project, the emphasis was on establishing a higher standard for the course by having more challenging assignments and examinations. By the second year, most of the tools and materials were in place and were further refined for the third year (1997). With this reorganization, we strove to improve conceptual understanding. Demonstrations were designed to contradict misconceptions, and questions were constructed to stimulate discussions among students and with instructors, both on the ALN and in person.

A well-established difficulty encountered in introductory physics courses is the tendency of students to reach for a formula and then "plug and chug" to get an answer (Hestenes, 1986). To lead students away from this plug-in-the-formula approach, almost a third of every examination dealt with concepts and required no calculations. The importance of conceptual understanding is illustrated in Figure 13.1, which shows the relationship between student performance on conceptual and story-type numerical problems on the fall 1996 final examination. The correlation between scores on conceptual and numerical questions is easily seen. The correlation index r = .592 indicates the strong tendency for students who performed well on one type of question to also perform well on the other type of question. CAPA is especially well suited for conceptual questions because of tools and templates designed to facilitate coding of a variety of such problems (see Kashy et al., 1995). It is for this type of question that CAPA differs most significantly from other computerized assignment systems (see Mellema, Niederriter, & Thompson, 1993; Brown, 1997).

FIGURE 13.1

FREQUENCY DISTRIBUTIONS OF SCORES ON CONCEPTUAL QUESTIONS AND NUMERICAL PROBLEMS

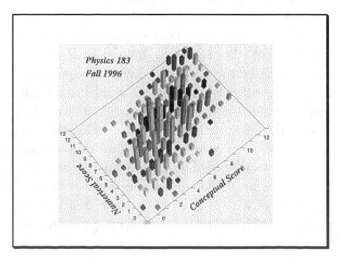

An example of a conceptual question used in assignments in fall 1997 is shown in Figure 13.2. The order of statements varies among students, and there can be several versions of each statement, keeping the concept involved within each statement the same for all students. Such questions generate considerable interaction and discussion among students.

Numerous problems and questions in assignments, quizzes, and in class lecture exercises emphasize concepts. In the exercise shown in Figure 13.3, only statements 1, 2, and 5 were initially selected by a majority of the students as possible actions even though all are possible. Following each poll, the action is discussed and demonstrated to clarify and cement the concept.

FIGURE 13.2

EXAMPLE OF A CONCEPTUAL QUESTION IN A HOMEWORK ASSIGNMENT

9. [2pt] A fisherman and his young niece are in a boat on a small pond. Both are wearing life jackets. The niece is holding a large floating helium filled balloon by a string. Consider each action below independently, and indicate whether the level of the water in the pond R-Rises, F-Falls, S-Stays the Same, C-Can't tell. (If in the first the level Rises, and in the second it Falls, and for the rest one Cannot tell, enter RFCCCC.)

A) The fisherman fills a glass with water from the pond and drinks it.

B) The fisherman lowers the anchor and it hangs vertically, one foot above the bottom of the pond.

C) The fisherman lowers himself in the water and floats on his back

D) The niece pops the balloon.

E) The niece gets in the water, loses her grip on the string, letting the balloon escape upwards.

F) The fisherman knocks the tackle box overboard and it sinks to the bottom.

Interactive Learning

MEASURED RESULTS

Assessment and evaluation of the data accumulated have shown that the project has resulted in significant measured enhancement of the success rate of students while maintaining high standards (Kashy et al., 1998). Students were clearly stimulated by the opportunity and the means to succeed. We also found that the fraction of those students doing extremely well increased significantly. Figure 13.4 shows the evolution of the grade distributions in the large introductory physics class for engineers.

From 1992–1994, results are for traditional classes. In 1995, we set higher standards for the class and introduced an ALN for the first time. Professor Norman O. Birge, who is not associated with the project, controlled the exam difficulty level from 1995 to 1997. The percentages in the middle column show the fraction of students achieving grades of 2.5 or better, while the third column shows the decrease in drop rate of students.

The change in distribution of grades and the improved student performance reflected in the data of Figure 13.4 are indeed gratifying. It is especially encouraging that the improved outcomes were observed in the context of a high level of student acceptance of

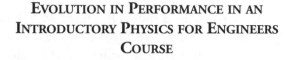

FIGURE 13.4

EVOLUTION IN PERFORMANCE IN AN INTRODUCTORY PHYSICS FOR ENGINEERS COURSE

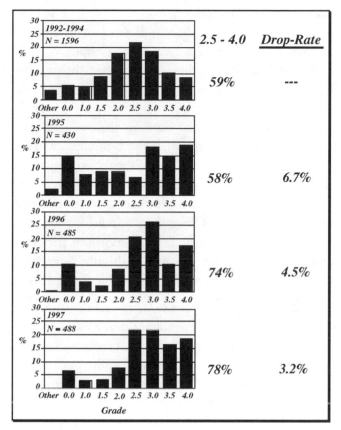

FIGURE 13.3

EXAMPLE OF A CONCEPTUAL EXERCISE DURING THE LECTURE.

A) Select all possible actions:
Frictional Forces can

1. Slow a body down

2. Increase the temperature of a body

3. Accelerate a body

4. Maintain a body's velocity constant

5. Keep a body stationary

6. Make a body move in circle

7. Lift a body

B) For each statement which you have selected, make a diagram (or describe) a practical situation for which a frictional force gives the indicated result.

FIGURE 13.5

TYPICAL RESPONSES OF STUDENTS IN SCIENCE AND ENGINEERING WHEN ASKED TO RATE CAPA AS A TOOL FOR LEARNING AND UNDERSTANDING

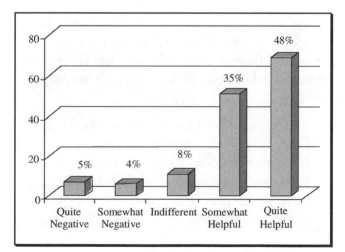

the technology, as measured by numerous student surveys (Thoennessen et al., 1998).

A typical response is shown in Figure 13.5. Since college students have been shown to be remarkably good judges of their scholastic achievement (Mabe & West, 1982), the high rating students give the system as helpful represents a credible indication of its positive impact. All such surveys have shown responses indicating that students consider the system helpful for learning and understanding. One of the reasons students are learning better is that they spend a significantly greater amount of time on their assignments (Thoennessen & Harrison, 1996). Student written comments in courses which used the technology show three dominant aspects which make the system popular: instant feedback, multiple chances to get a correct solution, and learning from their mistakes.

We can trace reasons for the improved performance to the implementation of a highly interactive learning environment with three main components:

- Interaction between the students and the computer using materials and problems prepared by the instructor. Students received instant feedback on their understanding of concepts and ability to carry out calculations properly and had access to specific help provided by an instructor.

- Interaction between the instructor and the computer provided the instructor with timely feedback on student difficulties so that such difficulties could be addressed.

- Asynchronous interactions between students and instructors via the network provided the opportunity for questions, answers, discussions, and elucidation of difficult concepts within the context of "anytime/anywhere."

The results shown in Figure 13.4 attest to the effectiveness which the ALN approach can have. These results were obtained with significant impact on productivity, including:

- The increased productivity reflected by the data in Figure 13.4. About 90 more students out of 500 (18% more students) achieved a grade of 2.5 or higher and could continue their engineering studies without repeating the class.

- A larger fraction of students excelled in the class, doubling the fraction of students achieving the highest grade (4.0).

- The cost reduction associated with having fewer teaching assistants in the course, due to replacing recitation sections with the Physics Learning Center and to grading of assignments by the computer.

CONCLUSION

We have demonstrated that networked tools can complement traditional teaching methods to enhance learning and improve efficiency while establishing and maintaining high performance standards. Motivated students have clearly benefited as they have taken advantage of the learning opportunities made possible by this technology.

On-campus ALNs can be useful for students in most disciplines and a growing number of students are benefiting as instructors adopt these methods. Finally, we believe that the many improvements which are reducing the additional work required will attract a greater number of instructors to employ network technology.

ACKNOWLEDGMENTS

This project was supported by the Alfred P. Sloan Foundation.

REFERENCES

Brown, D. J. (1997). Mallard: Asynchronous Learning on the Web. http://www.cen.uiuc.edu/Mallard/

Cheatham, M. (1994, December). *Study of undergraduate retention at Michigan State University*. Lansing, MI: Report of the Institute for Public Policy and Social Research, Michigan State University.

Hestenes, D. (1986). Toward a modeling theory of physics instruction. *American Journal of Physics, 55* (5), 440-454.

Kashy, E., & Morrissey, D. J. (1997). Individualized, computer-assisted, personalized assignment system. In S. Tobias & J. Raphael (Eds.), *The hidden curriculum: Faculty made tests in science.* New York, NY: Plenum Publishing.

Kashy, E., Gaff, S. J., Pawley, N. H., Stretch, W. L., Wolfe, S. L., Morrissey, D. J., & Tsai, Y. (1995). Conceptual question in computer-assisted assignments. *American Journal of Physics, 63* (11), 1000-1005.

Kashy, E., Sherrill, B. M., Tsai, Y., Thaler, D., Weinshank, D., Engelmann, M., & Morrissey, D. J. (1993). CAPA: An integrated Computer-Assisted Personalized Assignment system. *American Journal of Physics, 61*(12), 1124-1130. See also http://www.pa.msu.edu/educ/CAPA/

Kashy, E., Thoennessen, M., Tsai, Y., Davis, N. E., & Wolfe, S. L. (1998). Using networked tools to promote student success in large classes. *Journal of Engineering Education, 87* (4), 385-390.

Mabe, P. A., III, & West, S. G. (1982). Validity of self-evaluation of ability: A review and meta-analysis. *Journal of Applied Psychology, 67* (3), 280.

Mellema, S., Niederriter, C. F., & Thompson, H. B. (1993). A computer-based homework system with individual problem solving and instructor diagnostics. *Bulletin of American Physical Society, 38,* 1004.

Resnick, L. B. (1987). *Education and learning to think.* Washington, DC: National Academy of Sciences.

Sokoloff, D. R. (1995). Enhancing physics learning in lecture with interactive, microcomputer-based demonstrations, *Bulletin of the American Physical Society, 40* (2), 917.

Thoennessen, M., & Harrison, M. (1996). Computer-assisted assignments in a large physics class. *Computers and Education, 7* (2), 141-147.

Thoennessen, M., Kashy, E., Tsai, Y., & Davis, N. E., (1998). *Application of technology and asynchronous learning networks in large lecture classes.* Los Alamitos, CA: IEEE Computer Society Press.

CONTACT INFORMATION

Edwin Kashy
Professor
Michigan State University
Cyclotron Laboratory
East Lansing, MI 48824
Email: Kashy@nscl.msu.edu
Phone: (517) 333-6318
Fax: (517) 353 5967

Michael Thoennessen
Email: thoennessen@nscl.msu.edu

Interactive Teaching Tools for Astronomy: Web Tools in Support of an Introductory Science Course

Chris Impey, University of Arizona

INTRODUCTION

The educational promise of the Internet is enormous. In an editorial in the *Chronicle of Higher Education,* Neil Rudenstine, president of Harvard University, wrote, "The Internet has distinctive powers to complement, reinforce, and enhance some of our most effective traditional approaches to university teaching and learning" (1997, February 21). Around the country, universities are racing to install high bandwidth network connections and open-access computer labs. This surge in instructional technology is in part driven by student expectations, since many students arrive at college to find a poorer computing environment than they knew at home or at high school. Undergraduate ownership of computers is around 60% and rising. Nationwide, 77% of all faculty and 67% of all students have access to the Internet and the World Wide Web (Green, 1996).

Yet it is clear that providing hardware and connectivity is the easy part of this unfinished revolution. Set against these numbers are the facts that only 33% of all classes use email between students and the instructor, and only 11% of all classes use multimedia teaching aids. More ominously, only 8% of universities and colleges have mechanisms for rewarding faculty for the development of instructional computing (Green, 1996). The motivation to use networked teaching tools is extremely high, as evidenced by the continuing reports of the *Campus Computing Project.* When representatives from 600 colleges and universities were asked to rate the importance of 40 issues covering operating systems, hardware, networking, and user support, use of the Internet and the World Wide Web was ranked most important. The lag between interest in technology and its incorporation into the curriculum is easy to explain: The creation of effective instructional tools is an extremely time-consuming and labor-intensive enterprise.

After leading the early development, higher education will now benefit from the enormous economic momentum behind networked computing and web applications. The web has the potential to transform traditional models of teaching. Students can have more access to course information and research materials, can view their grades online, and can communicate by email with professors and other students. They can learn at any time and from any location—campus, dorm, or home. They can use a web browser to view multimedia subject matter, such as images, animations, virtual worlds, and links across the Internet. They can use interactive tools to access data, manipulate and plot it in different ways, control a simulation, or work through an interactive tutorial at their own pace. Distance learning is an obvious beneficiary of these new technologies. Multimedia learning on the web conveniently serves the faster growing segments of the student population: those with jobs and families and lifelong learners. Distributed learning also improves access to remote and underrepresented populations.

MOTIVATION

The primary vehicle for teaching basic science is the survey course for nonscience majors. For many university students nationwide, an introductory physics or astronomy course represents their last formal exposure to science. Ideally, science should not be taught as simply a body of information. If students are to understand the process of science, they must be empowered to make an observation or perform an experiment and formulate a hypothesis. They would then test the predictive power of the hypothesis by performing new experiments. In this way the hypothesis is either refuted or refined. Students must recognize the limitations and errors that attach to all observations, and they must understand how an interlocking set of observations can be used to support a theory. Science is a discovery process, and yet science is seldom taught that way.

The ubiquitous pedagogy in introductory science classes is the lecture presentation of factual material, typically to a large group of 100 to 300 students. Not surprisingly, this approach tends to produce a scientifically illiterate general population with an overall disinterest in the process of science. The project described here was motivated by a number of issues that highlight the shortcomings of traditional modes of instruction in science.

Dominance of Facts

A classroom lecture interspersed with a few demonstrations is a poor representation of science and its practice. If science is taught as a collection of facts about the physical world, students will respond by memorizing the facts of science and then regurgitating them at exam time.

Passivity

Because there is little direct contact between students and instructor, lecturing in front of a large class encourages student passivity. Few will typically come to office hours or otherwise seek help. Research shows that students often have preconceptions or naive beliefs about scientific concepts (Schneps & Sadler, 1988). In the standard mode of a lecture, that of transmission from expert to novice, these prior conceptual frameworks are rarely challenged (Novak, 1993; Lightman & Sadler, 1993).

Modes of Learning

Lectures are poorly suited to the range of ways that students learn. Cognitive research identifies four distinct learning styles (Witkin & Goodenough, 1981; Ausubel, 1978); traditional delivery-oriented education emphasizes procedures that best serve abstract and reflective learners while denying or limiting the active, hands-on, experimental approach that many students require.

Control of Information

Traditional classes invest the instructor as the primary information source. The instructor leads the students linearly through the curriculum and the textbook to reach a predetermined outcome. Student success or failure depends on their ability to master the body of information presented in lectures or textbook. Not surprisingly, then, most students perceive science as a dry, static body of facts.

Cooperative Learning

Large lecture classes limit the opportunities for cooperative learning. In an ideal world, students would break into smaller sections led by graduate students that would center on experimentation and student-driven inquiry. However, limited resources and rising enrollments mean that class sizes are never likely to get smaller. With the conventional mode of classroom lectures, there are few ways to encourage students to do research, work on projects and papers together, or communicate with each other.

Experimentation

There is a critical need to re-engage our introductory science students in a mode of experimentation and discovery that will lead to student-driven inquiry. With static lecture material, there is no practical mechanism for students to interact directly with the material via experimentation. The case for inquiry-based science education has been clearly made for the schools (National Research Council, 1996), but it applies equally well at the university level.

Many of the deficiencies of the lecture format can be alleviated by the addition of a hands-on lab experience. However, very few science departments have the resources, space, or personnel to provide lab experiences for all their nonscience majors. This project outlines a strategy to remedy some of these pervasive ills by the creative use of networked interactive experiments and instructional materials. This customized teaching environment can then be delivered to students on and off campus using the Internet and the World Wide Web. These tools are not designed to supplant the laboratory experience or to substitute for direct contact between the instructor and the student; they are designed to enhance both experiences.

TOOLS

A web site was created to serve about 1,000 students per semester in Natural Sciences 102 at the University of Arizona. This class satisfies a general education science requirement for nonscience majors, and it is typically composed of 70% freshmen. The site contains tools and materials intended to enhance the classroom experience—an electronic multimedia textbook, class information and notes, current news stories in astronomy, links to other sites with astronomy materials, online grades, a chatroom image and animation galleries, JAVA applets, and virtual reality markup language (VRML) worlds. Students log on with a secure password so that all use of the site is tracked. Readers of this document are encouraged to browse the materials at http://beast.as.arizona.edu,login=cimpey,password=c3impey. These elements of a virtual classroom try to actively engage the student in the course material. Current tools on the site include:

Image Galleries

We have digitized at high resolution a set of images covering the breadth of modern astronomy that are grouped into galleries according to common themes. Examples include the Hubble Space Telescope image archive, images from across the electromagnetic spectrum, telescopes and astronomers, and astronomically realistic space art. All images have captions at a level appropriate for an audience of nonscience majors.

Simulations

The site also contains a set of numerical simulations of astronomical phenomena. Many of these have been created at one of the five supercomputer centers. They include simulations of the formation of the solar system, the death of a star, the environment of a black hole, and the formation of large-scale structure in the universe. We have also created a JAVA front end for a modest N-body simulator that can display the future of the solar system, the orbits in star clusters, and the main features of stellar orbits within galaxies.

Animations

By permission of the Microsoft Corporation, we have created a set of educational cartoons using the 3D Moviemaker product. This is an application that can produce 3D rendered movies, incorporating various cartoon characters and geometric objects. Movies that will be placed online describe the life story of a gold atom, the prospects of life beyond earth, a cartoon version of the famous movie *Powers of Ten*, and animated tutorials on gravity and light.

Encyclopedia

An electronic version of the introductory astronomy textbook *The Cosmic Journey* (Hartmann & Impey, 1994) is available by arrangement with the publisher,

Wadsworth. The site has an HTML version of the text and all the line art and images. Images pop up with captions when their reference in the text is clicked. There is also an interactive glossary; clicking on any highlighted word will pop up the glossary explanation of the term. Another feature is a search engine that will take any term entered (e.g., big bang, quasar, Phobos, and supernova) and find all occurrences of that term throughout the book.

JAVA Applets

The JAVA language can make web pages come alive by expanding hypertext Internet browsing techniques to add arbitrary behavior that transforms static data into a dynamic application. An example would be a two-dimensional representation of a molecule, which the user can rotate around any axis by manipulating the mouse. The site has links to 14 physics experiments that can be run over the network in conjunction with a JAVA-aware browser (Netscape 3.01 or higher is recommended). Topics covered include kinetic energy, friction, forces, and inclined planes; momentum; ideal gas law; Maxwell's velocity distribution; thermodynamic equilibrium; inverse square law; galaxy photometry; galaxy sizes and the Hubble law; and combining stellar spectra.

Virtual Worlds

VRML is an extension of HTML that allows the creation of three-dimensional worlds on a web page. The VRML environment provides an excellent opportunity to convey the spatial relationships essential to astronomy that many students find difficult to grasp. This is a classic area of pedagogy, where conventional modes of teaching (diagrams in a book, drawings in class on a blackboard) are ineffective and where teaching is poorly coupled to student learning. In one VRML world, true images of the earth's and moon's surfaces were mapped onto spheres that are then positioned and animated with the correct relative motions and illuminated by a source that represents the sun. With the mouse, the student can observe the earth-sun-moon system from either the perspective of the earth or the sun or from a point above the plane of the orbit, viewing directly why the moon has phases and what causes the seasons and eclipses.

RESULTS

Initial results are very encouraging. Web site and email use run at 80–90% of the class, even with no particular incentive to participate. There is an average 30 web hits and ten emails per student per class with no negative effect on class or office hour attendance. In fact, the overall degree of contact with the instructor is increased, as many who would be reluctant to come to office hours use email or check grades on the web site. Male and female students use the electronic tools equally. Use of the tools is not a function of major or number of years at the university.

The web site automatically logs all student access, showing the level of activity as the semester progresses. We record the output from discussion groups set up in conjunction with the web site. One file anonymously logs student comments, complaints, criticisms, and suggestions. Another file reports student comments as they discuss among themselves the uses and limitations of the learning materials. Students complete two questionnaires. One, given on the first day of class, acts as a control for the prior level of computer and web use. The second is an exit poll that addresses issues of pedagogy and student access to, and satisfaction with, the materials. About 12 students each semester keep a detailed journal of their use and evaluation of the computer-based materials.

Direct feedback from students is overwhelmingly positive. On a four-point scale (1 = not at all useful, 2 = slightly useful, 3 = very useful, 4 = extremely useful), anonymous student questionnaires show averages of 3.5 to 3.8 when each of the tools is evaluated independently. There is some evidence that the features of the web site provide a good match to the different learning modalities of students in an introductory course. We have tracked multiple and intensive use of particular sections of the site as students explore materials at their convenience and their own pace. Able learners are directed to higher-level tools and original research materials. Weaker students are sent to quizzes and tutorials online. The interactive JAVA and VRML exercises allow students to explore physical concepts in a way that is impossible in the classroom. Each semester, a number of students use the web to create term projects which, when demonstrated in class, spur further use of the site by the rest of the class.

On standard questions that test common misconceptions—the cause of the seasons and the cause of the phases of the moon—students performed 20% better when they had access to VRML tools than in semesters before the tools were put in place. The only strong predictor of final course grade in the database is class attendance; better students come to class more often. After controlling for attendance, students who used both email and web tools performed one letter grade higher than students who used neither. Causation cannot be claimed at this point. A firmer conclusion awaits a full analysis of variance and the accumulation of another year of data.

LESSONS LEARNED

One encouraging lesson from this project is that large numbers of students can be served by hardware and software solutions that are cheap, flexible, and scalable. The current web server is an average desktop Pentium. Our software consists of three primary components: a web server, a database, and a collection of programs that we have created. All of these components, including the operating system, are freely available for download on the Internet and freely usable for noncommercial purposes. The operating system is Red Hat Linux 4.2 for Sparc systems, a powerful version of UNIX. The web server is Apache 1.2, the most popular server in use today. The database is mini-SQL, a speedy lightweight with all the features we need. Our programs are written mostly in the Perl and Java languages. These components are recognized by developers around the world for their ease of use, reliability, security, robustness, and rapid application development time. These components work very well together; even on an underpowered server like ours, the installation and integration took under one week. We have found good, fast technical support for all of these components through Internet resources such as mailing lists, newsgroups, and web pages.

The web site is secure, to allow students to view grades online and to permit full tracking. One program creates entries in the database for each user from the complete class list. Another set of programs lets students search the database for homework and test scores. We can link our class lists with other student information from the central administrative database at the University of Arizona. We can generate email lists from a class list for each section. Currently, we can create lists with 80–85% of the total class enrollment, and we are also working on methods to approach 100% (for comparison, attendance in these large introductory courses averages 65%). Other programs perform the tracking, enable us to see how each student uses the site, how often, from which access points, with what web browser, and so on. File sizes are kept small, and performance is optimal for T1 Internet connections or faster. For multimedia elements of the site, we consider that many users will have slow Internet connections via a phone line. Image galleries use thumbnails of 80 × 120 pixels, and only images of interest need be loaded at higher resolution. Video clips and animations use lossless compression by a factor of ten. The protocols for interactive materials are Java and VRML. Each of these uses readily available plug-ins for all the major web browsers.

While the hardware and software costs are modest, the personnel commitment needed to support 2,000 students a year is substantial. The site has been put together by one faculty member and four undergraduates, with an combined average of 60 hours per week committed to the project. However, continued support of these materials and training new faculty in their use is a major investment. Student contact increases, new materials must be created, and faculty workload goes up. Instructional computing has some visible innovators, but it is slow to percolate to most faculty. The reward structure still does not recognize the enormous time investment to create effective teaching tools. Put simply, the demographic timescale of faculty change is long, while each new set of freshmen is more web-savvy than the last. Our project involves 24 faculty members in a single department in a sociological experiment in the use of instructional technology. We will use our experience to come up with concrete recommendations on how to reward and motivate faculty to develop and use these tools.

REFERENCES

Astronomical Society of the Pacific. *A private universe* [film]. San Francisco, CA: Astronomical Society of the Pacific.

Ausubel, D. P., Novak, J. D., & Hanesian, H. (1978). *Educational psychology: A cognitive view*. New York, NY: Holt, Rinehart, and Winston.

Green, K. C. (1996). *Campus computing*. Encino, CA: Campus Computing.

Hartmann, W. K., & Impey, C. D. (1994). *The cosmic journey* (2nd ed.). Belmont, CA: Wadsworth.

Lightman, A., & Sadler, P. (1993, March). Teacher predictions versus actual student gains. *Physics Teacher*, 162.

National Research Council. (1996). *National science education standards*. Washington, DC: National Academy Press.

Novak, J., (Ed.). (1993). *Third international seminar on misconceptions in science and mathematics*. Ithaca, NY: Cornell University Press.

Rudenstine, N. (1997, February 21). The Internet and higher education: A close fit. *The Chronicle of Higher Education*.

Schneps, M., & Sadler, P. M. (1988). *A private universe*. Pyramid Films.

Witkin, H. A., & Goodenough, D. R. (1981). *Cognitive styles: Essence and origins*. New York, NY: International Universities Press.

CONTACT INFORMATION

Chris Impey
Professor of Astronomy
Steward Observatory
University of Arizona
Tucson, AZ 85721
Email: cimpey@as.arizona.edu
Phone (520) 621-6522
Fax: (520) 621-1532

Cindy Schwarz, Vassar College

Physics 113, Topics in Classical Physics, an introduction to basic concepts for students with both prior physics experience and a calculus background, emphasizes mechanics, wave motion, and thermodynamics. The course is meant to engage and to prepare potential physics and astronomy majors as well as other science majors, including students who express an interest in premedical studies. It combines a research interest in the pedagogies of science instruction and extensive experience as an author of interactive simulations and a workbook based on the Interactive Journey Through Physics CD-ROM with a practicing scientist's awareness of the importance of collaborative inquiry, discovery, and communication in the research process.

IDEAS BEHIND THE COURSE DESIGN

If I could use only one word to describe my current teaching philosophy, it would be interactive. Gone are the days of lecturing and looking out at a sea of faces staring back; gone are the days where I took full responsibility for my students' learning. I believe in shared responsibility for learning. Physics education research shows that the lecture format is not the most effective means of instruction, especially for introductory-level students. I have learned much from my colleagues, many of whom I have met over the Internet and many of whom I converse with by email. Often we share information about exercises that have worked well in our classes. In my courses, I strive for the flexibility to accommodate different learning styles and temperaments. I view technology as part of a rich mix of experimentation, simulation, discussion, analysis, and reporting.

COURSE ACTIVITIES

The course used technologies to stimulate discussion and to further experimentation and simulation. Class meetings on mechanics revolved around conceptual questions adapted from Eric Mazur's book on peer instruction (Mazur, 1996). One discussion involved an example of a man on a cart throwing a ball at a wall. Someone asked what would happen if the ball stuck to the wall rather than bouncing off of it. Students proposed at least five different scenarios, all supported by good physics reasoning. At the end of class, when no answer was clear, several students stayed on and simulated these ideas using interactive physics on the classroom computers.

The pattern of thinking prompted by the cart exercise recurred in quite a different class activity when I introduced computerized video analysis into the laboratory component. I asked students working in groups of three to plan what they were going to videotape and analyze. Although I half-expected everyone to throw a ball up in the air, students instead gave sophisticated analyses of swim team diving practice, particularly the motion of the diving board. This provided an unexpected discussion of whether oscillations were simply harmonic. This led to discussion about the physics of dancing, tennis, basketball, Frisbee throws, gymnastics, dolls parachuting off the biology building, and, of course, some bouncing balls.

Students also worked individually outside class with prepared simulations from Schwarz's *Interactive Physics Player Workbook*. Two of the four graded exercises were chosen at random by Schwarz, and students chose the other two to showcase their efforts and interests. In class, Schwarz used simulations to illustrate different thermodynamic processes for ideal gases. Following these sessions, students worked in small groups at the physics computer lab on early versions of thermodynamics simulation from the IJTP-CD for a few classes to consolidate their learning.

MEASURED RESULTS

I looked at Eric Mazur's study of an introductory physics class at Harvard, which supports the use of peer instruction and conceptual learning exercises in an introductory physics class at Harvard. Not willing to rely on Mazur's research completely, I collected students' written comments, which indicated that most viewed peer instruction coupled with simulations very favorably. I graded and noted improvement in my students' work when they used outside simulations. Student performance increased in limited testing on exam questions involving understanding motion graphs. Perhaps more importantly at a college like Vassar, which seeks faculty/student interaction and collaboration, I found that students often drop by my office to discuss interesting things that they discovered in the simulations. In course evaluations, many students said that the workbook and simulations were extremely helpful in illustrating difficult concepts; and several students, self-described as visual learners, said the workbook was excellent. In small group sessions, I could see that light bulbs were popping in heads all around the room.

LESSONS LEARNED

Because this is a foundation course for science majors, I feel it is important to balance testing of both conceptual and traditional knowledge in both formal exams and lab exercises. After offering this course for a number of terms, I am also convinced that collaborative work is most effective in small groups of not more than three students. I have learned that introducing computerized video analysis into the laboratory requires careful planning, capacious computers, and patience. However paradoxical it may seem to those who wonder about virtual inquiries in an actual, physical world, my experience convinces me that technology helps my students more readily and easily connect their knowledge of physics with their observations of the real world.

REFERENCE

Mazur, E. (1996). *Peer instruction: A user's manual.* Upper Saddle River, NJ: Prentice-Hall.

CONTACT INFORMATION

Cindy Schwarz
Associate Professor of Physics
Vassar College
Box 39
Poughkeepsie, NY 12604
Email: Schwarz@vassar.edu
WWW: http://noether.vassar.edu/~schwarz
Phone: (914) 437-7349
Fax: (914) 437-5995

Vignette 16 — Applying Technology to Introductory Physics

Robert E. Akins, Washington and Lee University

Our introductory physics laboratory has been modified to use a computer-based system for both data acquisition and analysis. All science majors take the course. The transition to a computer-based system was undertaken to make the laboratory more relevant and enjoyable and to better prepare the students for further experimental work in their respective disciplines.

A vendor for the entire package of instruments and associated software was selected from a relatively small sample. The system selected has proven versatile, the hardware robust, and the software easy to use. It includes a series of sensors, an interface box, and software compatible with the other components. The software is used both to collect and to analyze data.

The system and associated experiments were evaluated for an academic year in a single section of a laboratory. This section was taught by two faculty members in a genuinely collaborative environment with the students. We are now using the system for a second year with the entire enrollment of the introductory sequence (85 students).

Ideas Behind the Course Design

Our main goal was to allow a more complete observation and measurement of physical phenomena. In particular, we wanted to introduce the ability to measure quantities, such as velocity, acceleration, force, or temperature, as functions of time instead of values at a single instant. These measurements allow students to better relate physical principles to the theoretical concepts introduced in the lecture portion of the course. The addition of a computer-based system to the laboratory allows more variety in traditional experiments and students to apply analytical skills to new situations. The basic physical principles examined remained the same, but entirely new laboratory exercises were developed. Suggested experiments included with the system were appropriate for high school, but did not challenge our students nor make effective use of the equipment. Many new experiments started with traditional topics but then encouraged the students to ask relevant questions and to develop ways to use the system creatively.

An illustration of the velocity of a cart on an inclined plane as a function of time is an example of the typical results. The central portion of the trace indicates a linear relationship between velocity and time. This linear relationship indicates a constant acceleration, a conclusion that can be reached very quickly from the graphic representation of the data.

The analysis portion of the package allows the student to select a portion of the velocity versus time trace and to determine the slope of the curve, which is the acceleration, in this case. The student's ability to see a constant slope immediately and to determine the slope demonstrates the type of conclusions that can be readily obtained with a computer-based system.

Anticipated Outcomes

Only a small sample of students has used the system for an entire year. When tested, they seemed to have a good grasp of the system and were able to use it to make independent measurements.

In the large sections, the level of discussion of results and conclusions has increased substantially when compared to the lab settings which were based on more traditional measurements.

Lessons Learned

- The most difficult challenge in integrating technology into an introductory laboratory sequence is developing experiments that creatively use the technology to enhance the experience.

- The training of faculty and support personnel is a major challenge. One or two enthusiastic individuals cannot make a transition work effectively.

- The system selected must be reliable, versatile, and robust.

- Student interest is great and provides a major incentive for the faculty to adapt the equipment to the course material.

CONTACT INFORMATION

Robert E. Akins, Professor of Economics
Department of Physics and Engineering
Washington and Lee University
Howe 221
Lexington, VA 24450
Email: akinsr@wlu.edu
Phone: (540) 463-8883
Fax: (540) 463-8884

 **Web-Based Tools for the Effective Teaching of High Enrollment, Multisection Courses**

Fred Moore, Whitman College

The department of physics at Whitman College has implemented a new curriculum in its year-long introductory physics sequence. Historically, this sequence was taught as a lecture/demonstration course with enrollments of up to 100. The department and the college were committed to supporting the increased staffing needs and necessary building and laboratory modifications to permit small groups of students (24 maximum per class) to meet in both recitation sections and in the laboratory.

IDEAS BEHIND COURSE DESIGN

The physics education community has clearly documented that, in an introductory physics course, the traditional lecture modality does not result in maximum learning. This method of teaching has been shown most successful when used before highly motivated, well-prepared, and mathematically sophisticated students. Typically, these are the students most likely to complete a physics major, and even these students learn better in courses that use a discussion-based, discovery-oriented pedagogy. Our introductory course is primarily a service course, as only an average of 20% of its students complete a physics or physics-related major. Consequently, most of the students enrolling in this course are the least well served by a lecture style.

Realizing this, we have designed a strategy that moves away from the lecture and affords smaller class size and more discussion and discovery. The logistics of implementing this approach are onerous, since an important goal of this new sequence is to provide the students a congruent and consonant experience. This is a particularly challenging goal with students spread across five recitation sections and five separate laboratory sections. To provide logistical, organizational, and pedagogical support as we taught our new curriculum, we identified several areas where web tools are particularly important.

COMPUTER-ENHANCED TECHNIQUES

Prelab or Prerecitation Testing

"If you want the student to do it, put a value on it." This is a golden rule to which we adhere. We want students to arrive at laboratory or recitation having completed certain exercises and readings, and we need a testing mechanism. Doing this for more than 100 students meeting in small sections at various times and places is difficult. To address this problem, we implemented a web-based quiz facility that is accessed at students' convenience and that automatically evaluates and records their performance on multiple-choice or numerical answer questions. In addition to providing an incentive for the student to complete assigned readings and exercises, this strategy provides the instructor timely data on where the sticky spots are for the students, allowing these issues to be addressed quickly.

Exams-on-Demand

Exams should be common for all students enrolled in the course, regardless of their specific recitation or laboratory section. In addition, we wanted to allow students to take these exams at their convenience outside of regular class meetings. Our compromise makes use of web-based technology to distribute semi-unique exams to each student. During a specified period of time, students may take their exam. A web server responds to a student's request for an exam by packaging a pseudo-random set of postscript documents and logging the time at which they were requested. The documents are printed at a location that is convenient for the student, and the student is then expected to complete the exam within the allotted time and time-stamp it in at our library, which is open 24 hours.

Assignment Status and Grading Information

Since students face a variety of exercises (e.g., exams, quizzes, and lab work) given in a variety of settings (classroom, laboratory, their own rooms), we believe it is important to give them a single place to turn for a summary of their grade. This concern was also addressed with a web-based strategy that allows the different faculty responsible for different portions of a student's grade to enter information and allows students to review our record of their assignments, exams, and quizzes.

Facilitating Group-Based Learning

Our new curriculum makes use of a small-group learning strategy. Students are assigned to groups and are expected to perform tasks together. The groups are not static over the course of the year or even the semester. Educational research has shown that reconfiguring groups to address personality and performance issues is necessary if this pedagogy is to be successful. We have to provide the groups a means of interaction (e.g., bulletin boards, discussion lists, mailing lists, and individualized assignments). Students can be reassigned to groups using tools that automatically update mailing lists and access privileges to the proper bulletin boards.

MEASURED RESULTS

Fall 1998 was the inaugural offering of our reworked curriculum. The results we have so far are largely anecdotal (e.g., fewer students dropping the course after the first midterm and greater attendance at the common meeting times). Later this semester, we will be administering a standardized exam developed by a physics education group at the University of Maryland. We will then be able to compare the effectiveness of our new curriculum with the old as well as with the results from a number of departments across the country.

LESSONS LEARNED

With the students using various new web software for quizzes, exams, and the like, we found it absolutely imperative to have the authors of the software on call as the semester began. Despite several weeks of fairly careful testing, there were a number of small but important issues that needed to be resolved quickly. This response was primarily for the student's mental well being; all of them were new to this kind of instruction, and despite being quite computer-savvy overall, they tended to panic if small bugs in the software cropped up.

There is no substitute for having lots of faculty office hours available to the students as they become acquainted with the web-based tools. Despite being told by their computer that they've answered a question properly, students frequently want to double check their results with a professor.

CONTACT INFORMATION

Fred Moore, Associate Professor
Department of Physics
Whitman College
345 Boyer Avenue
Walla Walla, WA 99362
Email: Moore@whitman.edu
http://people.whitman.edu/~moore,
http://secphys.whitman.edu
Phone: (509) 527-5954
Fax: (509) 527-5904

COMPUTER SCIENCE, INFORMATION SYSTEMS, AND MATHEMATICS

Vignette 18 — Experiences Using a High-Quality MPEG Video Server to Aid Classroom Teaching

Mark Gaynor, Vijak Sethaput, and H. T. Kung, Harvard University

INTRODUCTION

Using a video-on-demand server as an aid to classroom teaching, we provided about 120 students with access to the complete lectures in Computer Networks taught by Professor H. T. Kung of Harvard University. Our video server system consisted of two server PCs (in the 200+ MHz range), a combined switched/shared ethernet network, and many client PCs for viewing the content. It was capable of simultaneously delivering 40 1.5Mbps MPEG (NTSC 352 X 240) streams of video. The video server software is Microsoft's NetShow Theater, previously available free from Microsoft's web site. We found that this solution worked well for our purposes, has a scalable architecture, and is affordable.

Video-on-demand servers are not new, but high-quality MPEG systems (like SGI's WebFORCE MediaBase or the Starlight system) use custom hardware that is more expensive than our class could justify. Our system, built with PCs running Microsoft NT 4.0 server, has storage for 22 90-minute lectures and costs about $10,000. Given our short time frame, limited budget, and current company support contacts, we felt that NetShow was a good option: We were able to set up a prototype system with our existing hardware quickly and determine that the product met our demands.

Judging by the feedback from our students, the video-on-demand project was successful. Students liked the web-based access and started using the service from the first week, before we were completely ready. The service became more popular as students began to appreciate the value that it added to the course. We found that the system was particularly useful in helping students review complex topics. We did not find an increase in absences because of the backup the video server provided. The students proved that this video service was more than "neat" technology by continuing to use it all semester.

VIDEO-ON-DEMAND SERVERS

A video-on-demand server provides a virtual VCR over a network. The user is able to view any title, no matter how popular, at any time of the day or night. Next, to allow notetaking or studying, the server supports pausing the video. Nice features are fast forward and rewind that help zero in on a point in the video. In addition to the normal VCR controls, a video server takes advantage of the random access abilities of the digital format to scan the video, quickly accessing any section.

Video quality is tied to resolution per frame and the number of frames transmitted per second. Our choice to use high-quality MPEG at 30 frames per second precluded our use of Real Audio/Video, a popular server for Internet and intranet video applications. We had adequate bandwidth on our network for the 1.5 Mbps required for NTSC MPEG video and felt we needed this quality to allow easy reading of the chalkboard.

A video server offers several advantages over videotape. Any client whose network connection possesses enough bandwidth can access the content, and it allows random access to the material. The tape requires the creation and distribution of physical objects, the logistics of which do not scale well. Also, it takes a long time to skip over 90 minutes of videotape. With a video server, once the network infrastructure is in place and the content added, the students can view at will from any client.

Multicast of video is a viable way to transmit live events; however, it does not meet the needs of busy students. Students used the service because of scheduling conflicts or for review, impossible with multicasting technology. A multicast service is not a good model for our course, intended only for on-campus students with diverse needs and nocturnal habits.

NetShow Theater

The distributed nature of this video server architecture allows building scalable solutions to reflect the actual demands on the system and to meet the budgetary and storage constraints. The minimal system, called an ice cube, uses a single PC. This scales easily to a two-system configuration, the minimum recommended by Microsoft. From there, additional content servers increase redundancy and capacity. By adding more disks per content server and increasing the number of content servers, the available bandwidth for streaming video increases. The ability to start with a single system as both content and title server and then migrate to a multi-content server configuration allows easy prototyping of a project, while maintaining the ability to build up the system as required for more video streams, better redundancy, and increased content.

The title server's function is to coordinate requests made by the clients into a distributed schedule of videos being served and to distribute this list to all content servers. To start a video, a client makes a request to the title server. When this new request can be satisfied given the existing schedule of videos being served, the title server then incorporates the new video into the existing schedule. This scheme guarantees that once a stream starts it can continue; however, it does not guarantee how long it will take for the video stream to start, which depends on the number of users currently receiving video streams. Once the content servers start the video stream, the title server maintains occasional contact with the client but is not involved with the transfer of data to the client.

The content servers receive a schedule from the title server and follow it, which is possible given the algorithm (Bolosky, Barrera, Draves, Fitzgerald, Gibson, Jones, Levi, Myhrvold, & Rashid, 1996; Bolosky, Fitzgerald, & Doucer, 1997) used by the title server in creating it. The design of the content server enables it to get as much data from the disks as the small computers systems interface (SCSI) bus allows. It then transmits this data on the high-speed switched network to waiting clients, shaping the traffic to provide a steady stream of packets on the network. Its configuration should include at least 96MB of RAM, a separate SCSI controller, and set of high-speed disks for content storage to achieve the high level of performance required. Connecting each content server with a switched 100Mbps link provides the capacity to serve over 50 MPEG streams per server.

The final component of the Microsoft Theater system is the administrator workstation that manages the entire system, completely independent of its operation. This design allows a lot of flexibility—any PC can be an administrator workstation, and any administrator server can administer many different video server clusters.

Why This Is a Scalable Solution

The design of this video server takes advantage of the inexpensive and increasing price performance ratio of PCs today. Many PC configurations have a single SCSI disk attached to a single controller, but the data transfer rate of the disk is typically much lower than the SCSI bus data transfer rate. To maximize the contribution of each content server, the SCSI controller connects to several disk drives, allowing a higher use of the SCSI bus (but limited by the bandwith of the 40 MBps ultra-wide SCSI controller, our system used three 7200 RPM Seagate drives). This proprietary stripping system also crosses PC boundaries by stripping data across up to 14 separate content servers under control of a single title server. This data stripping allows the title server to devise a conflict-free schedule, assuring that each disk in the system is free to provide the required amount of data within the specified time. By stripping data across several disks on a SCSI controller and then across several content servers, the number of video streams scales to the network capacity. An attractive feature of this video-on-demand server is the reasonable cost of a system with capacity to hold 22 90-minute lectures (over 25 gigabytes) and simultaneously serve 40 1.5Mbps video streams.

Our Network

The network used to transport the video traffic is critical to the performance of the entire video server. Real-time video of MPEG quality is a demanding service requiring about 1.5Mbps per client with low packet loss and small delays. Given the scalable nature of this video server, it is not unreasonable to build a system that supports hundreds of streams. These intensive data requirements demand switched high-speed networks (either ethernet or ATM) to have the performance needed to provide good quality service to the clients.

Our network, depicted in Figure 18.1, shows the local section in Pierce Lab connected with a 100Mbps link to a main distribution switch located in the science center. This switch acts as the campus-wide distribution point for the video traffic. Most backbone links in our campus network are switched 100Mbps links that will be upgraded to gigabit links in the near future. We have successfully streamed good quality video from our server in Pierce to a presentation given at the John F. Kennedy School of Government over a mile away. Our current network configuration provided a good baseline to study what we will need in the future to allow video streaming across campus.

As shown in Figure 18.1, our network is a combi-nation of switched ports required for the servers, along with shared links for the clients, used for student viewing. The sharing of client ports on a hub makes good sense given our network setup, but with the price of switched ports dropping, we would not build a hubbed system today. We found that sharing the client ports saved us valuable switched ports and still maintained good video quality.

CONTENT PRODUCTION

After solving the technical problems, we next worked on improving video quality by converting the analog video signal from the camcorder directly into the MPEG file in real time as the lecture was given, as shown in Figure 18.2 (path b). Originally, we put the content on a VCR tape (Figure 18.2, path a) and later replayed the tape into our real-time MPEG conversion board (made by Broadway), not the ideal situation because of the lousy qualities of VCR tape and the extra time required. We later installed a PC with the proper MPEG conversion hardware into the science center and fed the live video from the camera directly into the video jacks on the MPEG hardware, thus eliminating the transfer from the VCR, improving the clarity of the video.

FIGURE 18.1

OUR VIDEO NETWORK CAPABLE OF SUPPORTING 40 1.5 MBPS VIDEO STREAMS

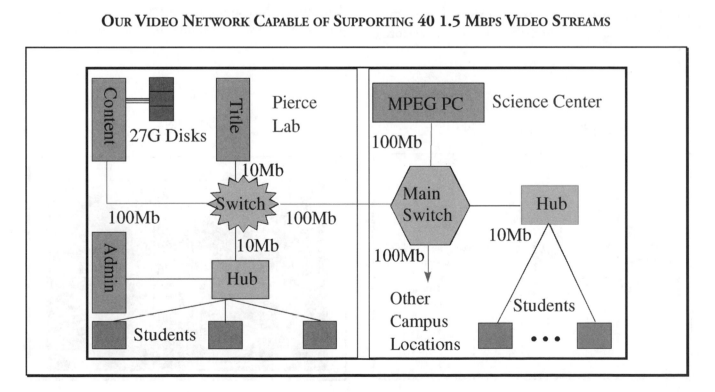

There are several options for backing up the content on the video server: VCR videotape, digital video (DV) tape, and online disk storage. We used DV tape for its quality and VCR tape for its ease of use. A better solution would be to set up NetShow to have redundancy in its data stripping and also to keep a copy of each MPEG file on a file server. While online disk storage is most effective, it was too expensive for us, so we used the dual tape backup scheme.

STUDENT USAGE

Our students used the video server for different reasons, as indicated by survey and discussion: reviewing a complex topic, doing problem sets, studying for tests, and watching a missed lecture. Students started to use the server within the first few weeks and, as word of its value spread, increased use throughout the semester. Some students became very consistent, always reviewing the previous lecture right before the next class started. As expected, the amount of use varied greatly from student to student, some relying on the video server for almost every lecture, while others used it only occasionally, if at all.

Whether or not we like to admit it, students miss classes for many reasons. Seniors were among the heaviest users, and one surprise was the number of students missing classes for job interviews. Many students interviewed with a different company every week, causing a major disruption in their course work. We found

that in a large class (over 100), we had students watching missed lectures for every single class. Although students did miss class, we did not notice a higher percentage of classes missed per student. In fact, students found the combination of first seeing the in-class lecture and then reviewing it with the video server provided the most benefit.

We like to assume that being in class will always be the preferred method of learning, but we found that for some students this was not true. With large classes, it may turn out that some students concentrate better with the video server, because the professor is so close. It is like sitting in the front row, something that we know improves the performance of most students. One student noted that he paid better attention to the server, saying that, with the instructor so close, he had to pay attention; the student lost track of the fact that it was only a video. By watching several lectures at one sitting, this student also found better continuity in the lectures and saved time.

Using a high-quality MPEG video server to review particularly complex sections of a lecture or for general review of the material proved invaluable to the students. The high quality offered by NTSC MPEG video allows for reading complex information from the blackboard, as seen in Figure 18.3. Understanding complex topics is even more difficult when the lecturer has an accent or speech impediment. We found that during the more difficult sections of the course, students would watch lectures in small groups, talking

FIGURE 18.2

OUR PRODUCTION PIPELINE

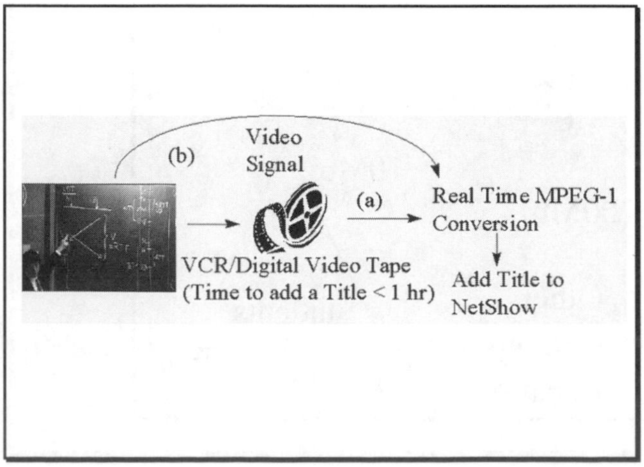

FIGURE 18.3

CONTENT

about the topics. After our midterm (average score 60%) we found that many students used the video server as an improvement tool, rewatching every lecture at least once. It is the random access abilities of the digital video media that are particularly helpful for this use, allowing students to quickly find a desired section or skip over an unwanted one.

Having lectures online allows students first to concentrate on the lecture and then to take careful notes while rewatching using the pause feature. We encouraged this by giving out computer-generated figures of all board work within a week of the lecture. We found students rewatching the lectures with these notes in hand, adding subtle points brought up in lecture, and increasing their understanding of the material.

The heaviest use of the video server was before the midterm and final or even before a problem set was due. Video-on-demand servers are a great tool for studying, allowing the students to review their points of confusion, very quickly hopping from topic to topic. We found that our client viewing stations were so busy before a test that students formed groups (to review the classes). Before a particularly difficult assignment was due, many students would rewatch selected portions of a lecture relating to the problem at hand. This proved a great backup to students who thought they had good understanding and adequate notes but then realized at the last minute while doing the problem set that this was not the case.

A bit of a surprise was that the teaching fellows (TFs) also made use of the video service to catch up on a missed lecture or to help answer a student's question. It is a great relief for a TF to be able to view a video to verify what happened in class. The TFs found the system easy to use, and, most importantly, it gave them an advantage. We could quickly compare what the professor said to what the students heard.

This project exposed our students to a cutting edge application—streaming video at high data rates—which demonstrated the theory of what we teach. It is great to talk about what packet loss means, but it is more effective to show students what the effect of losing packets is when watching a video. We invited students to stream video to their dorm rooms, something we knew would work only occasionally. This allowed them to compare viewing from the lab on a fast switched network to viewing from their dorms on a slower, shared network. We found that most students

enjoyed seeing how network concepts like quality of service (QOS) work in real life.

Overall, most students liked the video service with its easy-to-use web-based access. They were happy with the quality and valued the random access abilities of the digital video. Usage patterns showed that students continued to use the system all semester, something that would not happen if it were not an effective tool. We had only a few complaints. From our point of view, the students were able to get the educational content, and we feel the quality was reasonable in that the glitches, when they occurred, were short and infrequent.

Lessons Learned

While very happy with our results, we did have our share of problems. These included software glitches, not being able to hear questions from the audience, network capacity problems, and insufficient planning. The problem-reporting feature of our beta software was particularly poor. Occasionally, the system would fail to add a new title and only provided a cryptic diagnostic message that gave no information about the cause of the problem. The common fix seemed to be reinstalling all the software, including the NT operating system—not the most practical way to solve a problem. Overall, the software worked well for us.

Ultimately, the production of the MPEG is very important and time-consuming. We had a dedicated camera operator plus a graduate student who maintained the video server. If lighting, sound levels, camerawork, and creation of the MPEG file are low quality, then so is the video. It was frustrating that once we ironed out the technical glitches, and looked at the content, it was sometimes hard to see the instructor's face because of bad lighting. Next time, we will be very critical of the factors that account for quality video.

Real-time transport of video traffic is new at Harvard, and part of the motivation for this project was to assess its impact on the network. We asked students to try streaming video to their dorm rooms to see what the network would do when overloaded. The parts of the network that had switched bandwidth worked well; it was only when we ventured to the slower, shared parts of the network that we started having QOS problems. It did surprise us when the occasional student would successfully watch a lecture from their room.

We will do this again since we feel it had a positive impact on the course but realize that improvements to the system will increase the benefit to our students. Some improvements, such as production techniques, are under our control, while others (network upgrades and sophisticated video indexing) are beyond our control.

Students want access to video services from their dorm rooms, but two problems made this difficult: The network is not up to the task, and many students do not have systems with the CPU power to play the MPEG videos. The short-term plan is to distribute video servers and PC clients to each student house, allowing real-time video viewing from all on-campus dorms. Our experience shows that video streaming can enhance the educational experience, and Harvard is building the network infrastructure to allow video streaming campus-wide.

Indexing the video content like a book would greatly enhance its educational value. Video indexing is a current topic of research at Harvard and elsewhere. It will be a fundamental improvement, moving digital video into a new era as a tool for education.

Conclusion

The video service worked well, and everybody was happy with the results. The students found the web access easy to use and the MPEG video of high quality. Our fear that students would not attend class was unfounded, as most students used the video server for reviewing lectures rather than for making up missed classes. At the end of the semester, both students and staff felt the video server added value to our network course.

Acknowledgments

The authors wish to thank Intel for hardware, Microsoft for beta NetShow software, and our support staff at Harvard.

References

Bolosky, W., Barrera, III, J., Draves, R., Fitzgerald, R., Gibson, G., Jones, M., Levi, S. N., Myhrvold, N., Rashid, R. (1996, April). The Tiger Video Fileserver. Proceedings of the Sixth International Workshop on Network and Operating System Support for Digital Audio and Video, IEEE Computer Society, Zushi, Japan.

Bolosky, W., Fitzgerald, R., & Douceur, J. (1997). Distributed Schedule Management in the Tiger Video Fileserver. OSDI France.

Contact Information

Mark Gaynor
Research Assistant
Harvard University
29 Oxford Street
Cambridge, MA 02138
Email: gaynor@eecs.harvard.edu
WWW: www.eecs.harvard.edu/~gaynor
Phone: (617) 496-4513

Vijak Sethaput
Email: vijak@eecs.harvard.edu

H. T. Kung
Email: htk@eecs.harvard.edu

Mark Urban-Lurain and Donald Weinshank, Michigan State University

Designing instruction to provide computer literacy for students who are not majoring in computer science is a challenge faced by computer science departments in many colleges and universities. Based on interviews with the chairs of 67 departments on our campus, we created a fixed course structure with continuously evolving content. The structure provides feedback for assessing students and revising the course content to meet the changing demands of client departments, student experience, and hardware and software environments.

IDEAS BEHIND COURSE DESIGN

We expect students to learn underlying computing concepts and principles so that they can use computers to solve problems in a variety of disciplines. Instruction and assessment must focus on genuine problem solving tasks rather than static measures of component facts, such as those measured by multiple-choice exams.

In addition, concern for student motivation is important when designing instruction from which we expect a high degree of retention and transfer. A collaborative learning model specifically addresses student engagement and motivation. Exercises are designed to help students help each other succeed and to engender feelings of competence rather than to stratify and categorize them in a competitive manner. Finally, the assessments are designed as authentic tasks that require the students to solve problems similar to those they will encounter in courses in their majors and in the workplace.

CPS 101 uses a modified mastery assessment model. At regularly scheduled intervals, students take a bridge task (BT) that requires them to synthesize the concepts and competencies acquired to that point in the course. Bridge tasks are individualized by defining a number of dimensions that encompass the concepts and competencies for that task. The specific text for each student's bridge task is selected from among a number of possibilities in each dimension.

Bridge tasks are criterion-referenced assessments (Pearson, DeStefanno, & Garcia, 1995), evaluated on a mastery-level, pass/fail basis. If students demonstrate sufficient mastery on the first BT, they will receive a grade of 1.0 in the course. If a they fail a BT, they continue in the class. However, students must repeat until they have successfully passed it before being allowed to take subsequent BTs. On the average, students pass each BT in two attempts. For each subsequent BT passed, students' course grades are increased by 0.5 until they pass the 3.0 BT. Once students pass the 3.0 bridge, they may choose to complete an integrative semester project that may increase their course grades to 3.5 or 4.0. Course grades are determined by the highest BT passed by the end of the course plus any contribution from a semester project.

COMPUTER-ENHANCED TECHNIQUES

- All classes are held in computer labs.

- All course materials other than the textbook are on our web site.

- Class outlines and PowerPoint slides are used by TAs and students to progress through each lesson.

- All students have their own networked file space that may be accessed from all public computer labs, student residence halls, and off-campus residences.

- Most communication among students, TAs, and instructors outside of class is by email and electronic news discussion groups.

- Individualized BTs are delivered directly to student work stations.

- Students receive the results of their BTs from a similar system that displays their original BT together with the grading criteria and their individual results.

MEASURED RESULTS

Approximately 3,500 students take CPS 101 each year: fall 1997 (N=1,680) and spring 1998 (N=1,770).

Figure 19.1 shows the distribution of final grades for both fall 1997 and spring 1998. The overall GPAs were 2.98 (FS97) and 3.00 (SS98). The nearly linear relationship among the grades determined by the BTs (0.0 through 3.0) is expected for a mastery-model course where student effort is the key factor in determining grades (Bloom, Madaus, & Hastings, 1981).

FIGURE 19.1

FINAL GRADES

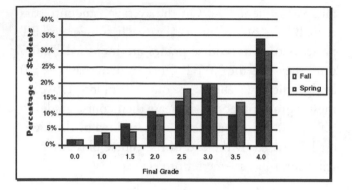

We obtained feedback from the students on the university's Student Instructional Rating System (SIRS). On the eight questions about the course, the student ratings improved very significantly by two-tailed T-tests from fall to spring. We attribute these improvements to extensive revisions to the course content and BTs we made in that period.

LESSONS LEARNED

Now that the course has been offered for a year, we perceive three changes:

1) We have a firmer grasp of methods for explaining this model to students. For instance, at midsemester, we discuss with the students the previous semesters' performance at midsemester versus final grades the students received. This helps current students understand how their midterm standing is likely to translate into a final grade. In turn, students are motivated to prepare thoroughly for their remaining BTs to maximize their chances of success.

2) Faculty and student advisors across campus now understand the model and explain it when advising students.

3) In the student culture, the word on the street prepares the incoming students for the instructional and assessment model.

Students have mixed reactions to the course. For some, this new assessment protocol is puzzling because they are thoroughly imbued with the model of getting points, irrespective of what these points measure. For others, the fact that BTs can be repeated without penalty leads to a subtle trap: They fail to take into account the fact that the course is of fixed duration. Therefore, toward the end of the semester, they have to take BTs at a fairly rapid pace to raise their grades to levels they consider acceptable.

On the positive side, most students become independent learners, turning naturally to the help system, their textbooks, and their peers when confronted with a problem rather than simply raising their hands for help. By the end of the course, more than half of the students can do very competent semester projects on topics appropriate to their majors, suggesting strongly that they will carry forward what they have learned in this course to future courses and careers.

REFERENCES

Bloom, B. S., Madaus, G. F., & Hastings, J. T. (1981). *Evaluation to improve learning.* NY, NY: McGraw-Hill.

Pearson, P. D., DeStefanno, L., & Garcia, G. E. (1995). *Dilemmas in performance assessment: Beginning a conversation.* Urbana-Champaign: University of Illinois, Urbana-Champaign.

CONTACT INFORMATION

Mark Urban-Lurain
Instructor
Department of Computer Science & Engineering
Michigan State University
3115 Engineering Building
East Lansing, MI 48824
Email: Urban@cse.msu.edu, cps101@cse.msu.edu
WWW: www.cse.msu.edu/~urban,
    www.cse.msu.edu/~cps101
Phone: (517) 353-0682
Fax: (517) 432-1061

Richard Vigilante, New York University

I teach the introductory systems analysis course in New York University's online Virtual College program. Through the Virtual College, students receive instruction, ask questions, conduct analyses, resolve problems, and complete projects—all largely at their own convenience and from practically anywhere. The program was designed to address the access problems facing part-time, working, adult students and provide them the same level of dynamic, hands-on instruction that characterizes the best on-campus course available to full-time students.

IDEAS BEHIND THE COURSE DESIGN

Systems analysis is characterized by two broad categories of knowledge: declarative and procedural. Declarative knowledge represents the concepts of the field and is readily learned from faculty lectures and presentations. Procedural knowledge represents the processes inherent in the field and is best acquired by doing, through faculty/student discussions and collaborations.

When teaching this course on-campus, I tried, to little avail, to get students to meet after class and team up on group projects. Time and again, I observed students' frustrating attempts to meet, only to have them spend more time in agreeing on a time than they actually spent meeting. The result was a course that instructionally reduced the key procedural concepts to declarative how-to lists.

By offering the course online, my students were able to collaborate continuously at times that were convenient for them. I divided the typical class of 20 students into four groups to work on various phases of information systems projects. Functioning as members of their virtual project teams, the students established discussion guidelines, critiqued and edited each other's work, and managed online workplace responsibilities. This level of interaction was maintained even when many students were traveling on national and international business trips.

COURSE ACTIVITIES

My six-week course is divided into six variable-length online sessions. Unlike on-campus courses whose two-hour class sessions always meet on the same night each week, online classes are always in session and run for as many days as are necessary to cover their topics. The online sessions meet as follows:

Session 1: Course Overview (5 days)

This session familiarizes students with the conferencing and electronic mail features of the Lotus Notes groupware package and introduces them to the systems development life cycle, the case-study systems project and client, and each other.

Session 2: Preliminary Analysis (10 days)

Within their five-member project workgroups, students identify, survey, and analyze data on aspects of the case-study database and communications system.

Session 3: Alternatives Analysis (8 days)

This session requires the four project workgroups to propose and analyze alternatives to the current case study system. Students identify the scope and objectives of their proposed alternatives and analyze their costs and benefits.

Session 4: Output Design (6 days)

This session designs the initial set of information outputs for the new case-study information system. Two of the work groups are chosen to identify the data elements and output formats for the new case study system.

Session 5: Input Design (6 days)

This session covers the principles of data input and data file design.

The other two project workgroups are chosen to determine the client's input requirements and translate them into final Lotus Notes input forms for the new system.

Session 6: System Implementation (7 days)

This session completes the development of the prototype case study system. All four groups work on completing the system's final Lotus Notes output views, online help, and user documentation.

To get a clearer understanding of what actually goes on in this online course, let's look in more detail at the course session called Preliminary Analysis. During this ten-day session, students work online to collect the fairly detailed procedural and cost data necessary to prepare the preliminary analysis of a case study system. In the interests of time, the students are divided into four equally sized groups, with each group responsible for one aspect of preliminary data collection and analysis. Each group conducts its work within its own Lotus Notes discussion database.

During the first two days of the session, the students and I discuss the overall requirements of a preliminary analysis, and we review the organizational and operational environment of the case study project. I provide each group with their particular preliminary analysis responsibility. Students use their own group database to discuss approaches, divide responsibilities, and formulate questions for the case study client or me. Both the client and I actively monitor each group database to ensure that work progresses satisfactorily and that we answer all questions promptly. While each group's deliberations are private, there are often questions or findings that have to be shared with the class as a whole, and these I post in the course discussion database.

Each group's survey form or questionnaire has to be completed by 11:00 a.m. on day six and transmitted to the client. The client then collects as much data as possible and returns the completed survey forms to the work groups by the evening of day eight. The student groups analyze the returned data and prepare a short summary for me by 9:00 p.m. on day ten. I incorporate the four group summaries into the completed preliminary analysis report.

During the course, students and I typically generate 1,100 course and group database documents related specifically to the curriculum. This is an average of 50 discussions, analyses, questions, and assignments per student, a level of participation that would be rare in most on-campus courses over a similar time period.

MEASURED RESULTS

At the completion of the course, students were asked to complete an online course evaluation form consisting of 23 multiple-choice, Likert-scale questions and an optional written evaluation. The questionnaires were completely anonymous, and all completed evaluations were sent to a public display area of the course. The questions on course content and instructor performance were similar to those asked of NYU on-campus students. The students' evaluation of these factors was quite positive, with the content and performance items averaging an 80% "very good" or "excellent" response.

I have conducted ongoing comparative evaluations of student performance in on-campus and online sections of the course. Student performance was measured by a combination of written assignments, group participation, and project reports. In terms of their educational and experiential input characteristics, both groups were essentially identical. The mean cumulative final grade (on a 0 to 100 scale) earned by the on-campus students was 84, while that earned by the online students was 92.

While not based on a formal evaluation design, I believe that most of the eight-point difference between the online and on-campus students was due to the increased knowledge acquisition of the online students, made possible by the greater degree of student/faculty interactions in the collaborative environment.

LESSONS LEARNED

I discovered that while faculty-led computer conferencing could effectively instruct students in the process inherent in a subject area, it could sometimes be unnecessarily labor-intensive in conveying the subject's content. I have been experimenting with online multimedia presentations to cover in minutes what asynchronous discussions might take an hour or more to complete.

As up to 20% of systems analysis topics are generally familiar to graduate students through previous education or experience, I plan to use computerized pretests to allow students to test-out of redundant course material and to study more individualized topic sequences appropriate to their backgrounds.

Responding to student requests for more flexibility in course scheduling and delivery, the course will soon be offered in an education-on-demand format. Students will be able to register for the course anytime and have from 4 to 12 weeks to complete it. A new computerized delivery system will continuously track, prompt, and record student progress through the course. The new system will help me to create and to sustain student collaborations and will provide students continuous electronic access to me for questions, assignments, examinations, and advising.

CONCLUSION

The physical infrastructure of the global economy is rapidly changing from concrete and steel to computers and communications. My online course will likewise change to give students those collaborative and technical skills necessary for working within as well as on net-worked workplaces. It is part of a virtual college preparing professionals for tomorrow's virtual organizations.

CONTACT INFORMATION

Richard Vigilante, Senior Director
The Virtual College
New York University
48 Cooper Square
New York, NY 10003-7154
Email: Richard.vigilante@nyu.edu
WWW: www.scps.nyu.edu/virtual
Phone: (212) 998-7199
Fax: (212) 995-3550

Vignette 21 Computer-Enhanced Calculus

David Pravica, Michael J. Spurr, and James Wirth, East Carolina University

The teaching of calculus has undergone intensive redesign on a national level during the last decade. Much of this redesign has centered on harnessing technology to allow a more active learning mode for students interested in mathematics and computation. We at East Carolina University have been involved in this effort, seeking to integrate computer-based activities and learning into the calculus curriculum. We have designed many activities and labs that fit into any calculus course, and we have also offered sections of Project Calc, a calculus-reform project pioneered by David Smith and Lang Moore at Duke University.

IDEAS BEHIND THE COURSE DESIGN

We approached the process of integrating technology by attending several conferences on the use of mathematics-related technology, learning the available software, and visiting various programs, in particular, Duke's, to observe their practices. After this initial exploration, we began incorporating the best features we found, infusing our ideas and approaches, evaluating which projects worked, and editing and revising any projects needing improvement.

Our main goals were the following:

- Make mathematics more concrete and meaningful by directly connecting it with physical and visual phenomena that students can experience

- Make the process of learning mathematics more active and interactive

- Have the students make a mathematical discovery for themselves, when possible

The technology and activities chosen were means to these ends. Their use made it possible to have the students engage in a variety of activities:

- Harness computational power to illustrate and model physical and mathematical phenomena

- Gain experience with numerical and computational software

- Work in a collaborative setting

- Participate in physical demonstrations

- Perform more independent investigation

- Interpret results in written reports using mathematical word processing and spread sheet features

COURSE ACTIVITIES

Incorporating technology into the course allows for a wide array of activities that add to the depth of a student's understanding, intuition, visualization, and general enthusiasm. The following are some of the types of technological applications we've employed.

Computer-Based Calculus Demonstrations

Not only can students visualize traditional images of functions and surfaces via the very powerful graphics capabilities, but they can also relate them to familiar physical experiences. For instance, a motion detector can graph the position and velocity of a student moving across the room, and thermal sensors can measure the heat of a cup of coffee as it cools. Patterns and relations can be inferred, observed, and related to the concrete situation.

As an example, if a student walks across the room in a straight line, reaches a farthest point, and backs up,

what happens to her velocity when she is farthest from a motion detector? The motion detector provides graphic analysis of the student's position and velocity at a given time. This analysis quickly reveals that when she is farthest away her velocity is zero, when she is moving forward her velocity is positive, and when she is moving backward her velocity is negative.

Students will make these observations themselves, not only because the motion detector instantly pictures the graphs for them, but also because the students know such facts from experience. Yet these very facts form a cornerstone for the study of functions in calculus: Finding an optimal point (farthest distance, in this case) on a smooth curve is related to finding those points with vanishing derivative (zero velocity, in this case).

Physical Demonstrations

As explained, these physical demonstrations often overlap with demonstrations as chronicled above, but we often have hands-on demonstrations of physical phenomena without involving a computer. For instance, working with torque, levers, balance beams, and balance points of plates gives the students direct experience with fundamental ideas that have mathematical analogs.

Numerical Computation of Approximate Solutions

The computational power now available in a desktop computer allows for rapid and accurate approximation of a wide range of mathematical and physical phenomena. One type of approximation includes estimating the area of a circle of radius one, where we use

FIGURE 21.1

APPROXIMATING π WITH RECTANGLES

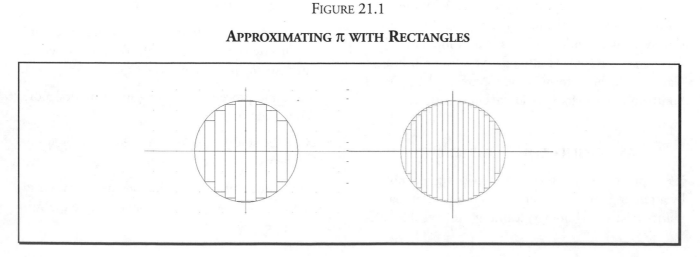

thin rectangles inside the circle to estimate the area, π. A succession of approximations using thinner and thinner rectangles leads to increasingly accurate approximations of π, which can be directly computed and witnessed by the students on their computers.

Another very pragmatic approximation technique connects line segments together to approximate a curve, as illustrated in the picture below (in an application of the so-called Euler's method). Such approximate curves are relatively easy to compute (being constructed from lines), and they are quite useful in studying rates of change when the exact curve is difficult or impossible to compute.

FIGURE 21.2

APPROXIMATING A CURVE WITH EULER'S LINE SEGMENTS

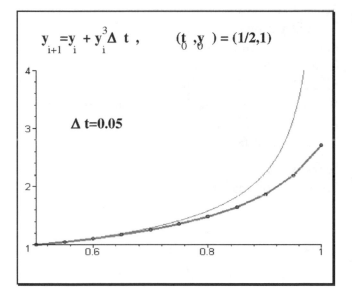

These apparently different examples—approximation of area and linear approximation of curves—can be linked through one of the central theorems in calculus. Even though this link is quite subtle, we have had students with no prior calculus background make this link themselves.

Laboratory-Based Activities

We obtained funding for a computer lab through a National Science Foundation grant and local matching and maintenance funds. Our lab activities have allowed rich, in-depth student experience with technology in their mathematics courses. Most of our labs involve each student working with a partner, performing independent team investigation, and writing reports on their methods, results, and ideas. Use of the computer in conjunction with some of the approximation techniques I've mentioned has allowed students to investigate more sophisticated problems than they would normally tackle at their level without technology.

Collaborative Work

Group work occurs not only in lab projects, but in class projects, with three to four students working together. Students enjoy hashing out an idea, debating it, explaining it to each other, and generating questions. This intellectual yet social process can be quite valuable.

Experience with Technology

Students gain a great deal of exposure to the type of technology they will use later in various professions. In our case, this technology includes symbolic manipulation, numerical computation, graphical representation, word processing, and spreadsheets. While experience with these types of packages is to their advantage, we also work to ensure that each student retains the ability to perform traditional calculus computations.

Mathematical Modeling

A very pragmatic feature of technology is that it allows for rapid analysis of actual data. The students attempt to fit various curves to the data by varying parameters or comparing competing curves that claim to model the data. Such data analysis and modeling are a valuable feature of the course. For instance, population growth provides a natural setting for discussing rates of growth and for fitting various population models to actual data.

MEASURED RESULTS

We performed a four-year analysis of students who completed our technologically based yearlong Project Calc course and who then enrolled in our standard Calc III course. It showed that 73% earned A's or B's (equally distributed), and 96% earned at least a C. These results are tempered by the fact that many of these were honors students. Survey of student opinion in all of the technologically based calculus courses has revealed a great deal of enthusiasm. There were generally one or two students in each section who would have preferred a more traditional course, but overall, we've experienced strong support from the students.

LESSONS LEARNED

Teaching a technology-based calculus course is a labor-intensive endeavor, rewarding for both the instructor and the students. The students must be willing to put more time into the course because, in addition to the usual time spent learning concepts, there are also lab and class activities, written reports, and teamwork and scheduling issues. The instructors must be willing to learn new technologies, maintain them, and deal with equipment and compatibility issues. There is more written work to interpret, and grading is subtler than that in a more traditional math course. The instructor also must find a reasonable balance between group and individual student work.

Technology is woven throughout the course and is not limited to computer lab settings. We rely on portable units equipped with computers, sensors, and overhead displays which allow for maximum usage and flexibility in offering these courses. When faculty design labs for their courses, these labs are made available to any other faculty wishing to try them. Another strategy we have tried is to have a team of faculty take turns teaching certain technology-based courses, comparing notes and exchanging practical information on their experiences.

CONCLUSION

The rewards of teaching a technologically based course are quite high. The students react very favorably. It is a gratifying experience to hear the students gasp over a particularly beautiful computer graph or to witness them reach a discovery or realization of their own. For their part, the students complete their technology-based calculus course with the awareness that mathematics is a very pragmatic and powerful discipline that directly impacts and is motivated by their real world.

CONTACT INFORMATION

David Pravica
Email: pravica@math.ecu.edu
WWW: http://www.math.ecu/~pravica/tea_pra.html

Michael J. Spurr
Associate Professor
Math Department
East Carolina University
Greenville, NC 27858-4353
Email: Mjs@math.ecu.edu
WWW: http://www.math.ecu.edu/~mjs/mjs.html
Phone: (252) 328-4110
Fax: (252) 328-6414

James Wirth
Email: wirthj@mail.ecu.edu

Vignette 22 Student-Centered Learning of Statistics Using Multimedia

John D. Emerson, Middlebury College

The introductory applied statistics course has long had a perhaps deserved reputation as being dry, dull, and difficult. Students may enroll in it because their programs require it, or because they see statistical training as good medicine and a valuable credential for the job market.

At Middlebury College, my colleague Bill Peterson and I have been offering a course that emphasizes the logic of statistical science—its relevance to issues in the world our students experience and how computers can aid the careful exploration of data, using simulations to reveal sampling distributions, and implementing formal inferential procedures. Ma 106, Introduction to Statistical Science, has successfully used Data Desk by Data Description, Inc. for weekly hands-on laboratory projects that keep students in close contact with data through its graphical and dynamic interface.

In my sections of the course, I felt that a different learning paradigm was needed that would involve students even more actively in all phases of learning statistics. A course development grant to Middlebury College from the Davis Educational Foundation provided me the time and resources needed to reinvent our introductory course.

EDUCATIONAL THEORIES

Two educational assumptions are the cornerstones of the course's development:

- Successful learning takes place when students connect new concepts to their existing understanding and knowledge. A relevant and secure intellectual foundation best supports the acquisition of new conceptual structures and related information.

- Successful learning takes place when students have active responsibility for their own learning; The active engagement of new concepts is a key to student success, whereas passive involvement in the learning process at best gives lowered efficiency in learning.

I enjoy relating new and sometimes difficult concepts to what is familiar to my students. But the second educational assumption poses a challenge. It implies a shift in focus from my strategies for presenting new material to a focus on how student learning really occurs. Although I have always given statistics students daily problem sets and weekly lab assignments, I sensed that I needed help in moving students to take a more active role in their first encounters with new statistical concepts. Could computer multimedia technology help?

INTEGRATING MULTIMEDIA INTO THE STATISTICS COURSE

In spring 1998, I adopted a multimedia package called ActivStats as an integral part of the course. ActivStats was developed by Professor Paul Velleman of Cornell University and marketed by Addison-Wesley Interactive. Velleman also developed the interactive statistics package, Data Desk, that I liked so much and was already using for the course lab. In fact, the ActivStats CD integrates a student version of Data Desk in a seamless fashion into the multimedia environment. It also provides links through the user's web browser to the World Wide Web and to web pages that relate to the topic or application area at hand.

ActivStats comes on a single CD, which was purchased by all of my students. It runs equally well in a Windows or Macintosh environment. It uses the statistics textbook as a paradigm: The electronic course has 24 chapters, and students use mouse clicks to turn pages, use the index and glossary, and access homework problems and projects. The differences between ActivStats and a textbook are sharp. ActivStats always uses sound and full color, and it incorporates video clips, statistical tools that dynamically illustrate and teach new concepts, as well as interactive quizzes that assist students in checking their level of mastery. The program encourages students to review earlier concepts to ensure a firm foundation for new statistical material. Velleman as narrator is an ally of the students. He is always patient and reassuring, and students can ask him to repeat himself as many times as needed, simply by clicking a mouse.

From a student perspective, the greatest strength of ActivStats may lie in its video presentation of examples that are both fascinating and real. For example, in discussing Bernoulli trials and binomial experiments, ActivStats asks whether NBA basketball players have hot shooting streaks. The surprising conclusion is that they do not. The CD shows a video from an NBA game, which then provides the background for a statistician's discussion of the substantive statistical issues. ActivStats offers students a link to the current NBA web page, where lots of data are available. Students also see adjacent sequences of actual hits and misses by the NBA player and simulated sequences that are generated by assuming that hits and misses arise independently. The strong message is that we can't tell the two situations apart.

Given the sound scientific content and strong motivation provided in ActivStats, the central question for me was about how to integrate it into the course and how to change my own teaching strategies to use ActivStats to good advantage. I decided to ask students to use ActivStats as their first introduction to new material. I also used the integrated activities and homework problems to engage them in the new concepts. Students were invited to bring questions to class. Besides responding to these, I used class time to go over the deeper homework problems that I assigned from our textbook, *Introduction to the Practice of Statistics* by David Moore and George McCabe. I also tackled examples that were more complex, some of which became the basis for subsequent work in the weekly lab. I tried to make much of our class work relate to the problems and projects that students were actively engaging in the other parts of the course.

The revised version of *Introduction to Statistical Science* also used computer technology in two other ways. I referred students to some web pages on certain topics (e.g., correlation and simple regression) from web-based statistics courses; the purpose here was to make an alternate presentation available to students who wanted reinforcement. In one of my labs, I used a clever web-based applet to teach students more about the meaning of null and alternative hypotheses, the p-value, and Type-I and Type-II errors. This applet, called Drawing Conclusions About Proportions, was developed at Dartmouth College by Dr. Tor Tosteson and his colleagues as part of the Dartmouth Math Across the Curriculum project.

ASSESSMENT OF OUTCOMES

Because I viewed the course as substantially new and experimental, I invited student input and advice at three points during the course. Their responses to the two-page questionnaires were voluntary and anonymous. With the first two surveys, I promised students to report back on what their responses told me and whether and how I planned to make adjustments to the course.

The first midcourse feedback came on the last day of the second week. Students felt strongly that they enjoyed learning in the ActivStats environment more than they would enjoy learning from a text, and they tended slightly to report that ActivStats introduces and explains statistical concepts as well as or better than would be done if a teacher lectured on the concepts in class. (Half the students were neutral on the second point.) They indicated that they enjoyed both the ActivStats and Data Desk environments more than they would have liked a traditional course format (e.g., using the text as the locus of most assigned written work).

Several students urged me to use part of class time to explore and review the major key concepts of the course. Others urged me to do a few more of the assigned problems in class. One student concern stood out: About half the students reported spending between ten and 12 hours each week on the course outside class and lab time, and the rest reported spending more than 12 hours. At that point, many students characterized the time demands of the course as "excessive," and several even checked off "absolutely ridiculous." I resolved to make careful adjustments to address their concerns; I had not intended that my use of ActivStats would be just an add-on or a significant burden for my students.

The second midcourse feedback, administered at the half-way point, used a questionnaire that was nearly identical to the first. Students continued to be positive about ActivStats. They were even more likely to appreciate the self-paced aspect of the environment but were slightly less positive about the homework problems assigned from ActivStats. Now, students reported a median workload outside of class of eight to ten hours weekly, and they characterized this as "heavy but manageable" or "excessive" but not as "absolutely ridiculous." I view the workload students were now reporting as consistent with my goals for them.

A substantial majority of the students mentioned that the course had improved as a result of my responses to their earlier input. I was somewhat surprised and gratified by this outcome. When asked what further changes they would recommend, one suggestion emerged clearly: Students wanted me to give less advice and guidance for weekly Data Desk labs and let them forge ahead more independently, while relying on the detailed written instructions I was providing. I agreed to try this; the change worked well, and I used it throughout the remainder of the course.

The last course feedback was provided by students on the last day of class. Again, I used essentially the same format, with a few different questions where appropriate for the end-of-course feedback. The student responses were slightly less positive about ActivStats, and noticeably more positive about Data Desk, the labs, and my work with students in class. Near the end of the course, we were doing significant applications, such as chi-squared tests for association, two-way analysis of variance, and multiple regression. My course develops the related inferential tools and concepts more fully than the ActivStats software, so the shifts in student sentiments may have been predictable. However, student ratings clearly reflected that they appreciated adjustments I had made along the way in response to their advice.

There was near unanimity that students liked the labs and the way I structured them in the last half of the course; instead of sharing general perspective and offering guidance to everyone, I kept quiet, circulating around the room, and responded to lots of individual questions. Workload was no longer an issue for students; they reported spending either six to eight or eight to ten hours on their work outside of class and lab. There were strong indications in students' replies to open-ended questions that they felt the last half of the course was better than the first.

Middlebury College has long had its own general student ratings of all courses by all students. These are almost always done in class on the last day of the 12-week term. Students are invited to rate the course, the instructor, and their own work in the course. There are several open-ended questions and two additional questions with responses on a five-point Likert scale. Of 14 completed student ratings, one student rated both the course and the instructor as "fair" (this student gave no other feedback). All others rated both the course and the instruction as "good" or "very good"; when the ratings differed, the instructor always got the higher rating. I was surprised that so few students commented

explicitly on the role of ActivStats in the course; several students did comment positively on their use of Data Desk and the substantial lab projects that they completed. Students probably felt no need to comment again on a point they had already addressed in their responses to my own questionnaire.

My previous student ratings for Ma 106 were from spring 1996, just before Middlebury added the quantitative sections to the ratings forms. Thus, I cannot compare my recent course with its predecessor on the numerical student ratings; the qualitative student responses were more positive for the recent edition of the course that used the multimedia package. In particular, student responses to the lab part of the course were considerably stronger in spring 1998. Some of that change may be attributed to adjustments I made in response to the previous year's feedback, but some of the improvement is likely attributable to the very smooth and friendly tutoring that ActivStats provides in the use of Data Desk.

LESSONS LEARNED

I have learned a number of things from this teaching experience:

- Students can give useful advice for improving a course while it is underway.

- Students respond positively when faculty members apprise them of changes they are making in response to student feedback.

- A multimedia learning environment, though enthusiastically received by students, can make substantial demands on their time and energy; a teacher needs to consider this realistically when developing the course.

- A highly interactive and engaging multimedia environment offers the advantages of flexibility that allow students to review a tough concept as much as needed and unlimited patience.

- The integral use of multimedia forces us to refocus our teaching emphasis from the content of class presentations to students' learning and their active involvement in the learning process.

Did students learn introductory applied statistics better with the new course format? I have no objective empirical data to support my answer, but I am convinced that they did learn more in three respects. First, I think that they better internalized the underlying and most fundamental concepts of statistical reasoning. Second, I think they developed a fuller appreciation for the broad range of fascinating applications of statistical reasoning. Finally, I think that they learned to stay in close contact with the data using a computer. I will use the ActivStats multimedia package again, and my teaching will benefit from this first experience in using this new teaching environment.

ACKNOWLEDGMENTS

I am grateful for Middlebury College's support of this project, and for the generous support of the Davis Educational Foundation. This vignette benefited from the suggestions of several colleagues who read it, including Susan Campbell, Bob Churchill, Marcia Collaer, Amy Jo Emerson, Fred Motseller, Sheldon Sax, Cleo Youtz, and Clara Yu.

CONTACT INFORMATION

John D. Emerson, Professor of Mathematics and Computer Science
Middlebury College
Warner Hall
Middlebury, VT 05753
Email: jemerson@middlebury.edu
Phone: (802) 443-5589
Fax: (802) 443-2080

Vignette 23 Inserting the Web into Precalculus

David Slavit and Joshua Yeidel, Washington State University

This vignette addresses the use of web-based activities in a precalculus course at a large university. The purpose of this paper is to discuss how instructors who did and did not receive instructional mentoring made use of web-based activities in their classrooms. It is important to note that the activities were incorporated into an existing course and were not the primary instructional medium. Hence, the course structure suggests that the presence and impact of the educational technology were transpositional in nature, as the web-based activities were inserted into an existing format.

COMPUTER-ENHANCED TECHNIQUES USED

The students encountered five web-based activities throughout the semester, all of which were worked in a computer laboratory. The five activities used simulations to facilitate exploratory learning behaviors, such as the creation of data and conjectures about contextualized problems based on the data. In general, the students were asked to make decisions about parameters and variables that controlled a given functional situation (e.g., the price of a plant), followed by questions that asked them to interpret the situation based on their model. Two key assumptions were made in regard to the construction of the activities:

- Students should be required to conjecture, explore, report, and justify. The web affords an interactive potential that can support these learning behaviors.

- Web-based activities should be visually appealing, technologically transparent, interactive, contextually based, enjoyable, connected to course content, and conceptual.

The students were able to submit their completed activities via email, although this was not used as a frequent means of student-instructor communication.

Early on, some of the students became frustrated by occasional computer crashes and lost work, but these occurred less frequently as the semester progressed. Because of the instructors' and students' facility using the WWW, the classroom implementation of the activities required no technical instruction or introduction of any kind. Further, no instruction of specific software commands was required, a situation very different from most laboratories that use software like Mathematica or Maple and even graphing calculators.

RESULTS

Instructional observations and interviews were conducted on and with two mathematics doctoral students, Greg and Luci (pseudonyms). We worked closely with Luci, a young Eastern European woman, in incorporating the web-based activities into her course and instructional approach. The mentoring focused on four basic ideas:

- Using the activities to introduce and extend course topics

- Generating student discussion in the classroom

- Focusing on functional properties as a theme in the course

- Connecting skills to concepts

We chose to work with Luci in order to support an instructor whose style and general mathematical framework were different from that of the activities. The bulk of Luci's mentoring occurred prior to the semester and during the first four weeks, with meetings approximately once every two weeks thereafter. In contrast, Greg, a middle-aged American man and former middle school social studies teacher, received no instructional support at any time. Observational data indicated that Greg was primarily interested in developing problem solving ability and exhibited teaching behaviors often referred to as student-centered. His instructional approach contained aspects of problem solving, exploration, and student justification, which were in line with the goals and characteristics of the activities.

Although Luci received instructional mentoring, her instructional presentations and assessments made very little use of the mathematical ideas and situations in the activities. The mismatch between her instructional objectives and framework and that inherent in the activities was too much to overcome in a single semester. On the other hand, Greg's instructional approach meshed very well with that of the activities. Although Greg received no mentoring, classroom observations indicated that he more frequently used the activities during in-class discussion than did Luci. More importantly, Greg made frequent references to the functional growth behaviors and properties that were highlighted in the activities to support his own classroom instruction, something Luci rarely did. Observations and student interviews indicated that this resulted in class discussion that was not generally perceived to be useful by Luci's students. This result supports the conclusions of Lloyd and Wilson (1998) who found that algebra instructors are enhanced by the use of curriculum materials consistent with their function, concept image, and instructional style.

To provide an illustration of the differences in instructional approach and presentation in the two classrooms, we will discuss the classroom conversations surrounding Lab 1, which occurred during the second week of the semester. Lab 1 used a plant-growing context to illustrate linear growth, requiring the students to supply two different plants with water, sunlight, and nitrogen. Once the students made decisions on these parameters and input them into the computer, a graph based on their inputs was immediately generated. The activity was designed so that each graph would be approximately linear regardless of treatment, but the rate of increase was dependent on the input amounts. The amount of water was the most important parameter in determining plant growth. The students could then monitor the growth rate of the plants for each element they supplied by analyzing the corresponding graphs. Questions about the context as well as the linear functions that defined the models were then given.

Classroom observations immediately after Lab 1 illustrated that Greg discussed specific problem solving strategies for changing parameters and interpreting data. The following discussion then ensued:

Greg: *What was the optimal condition for plant growth?*
Jim: *Sixteen ounces of water.*
Greg: *Yes, and nitrogen doesn't matter.*

Greg then made several comments that related the mathematical ideas they were discussing in class to other aspects of the activity. These included slope, functional notation, and the calculation of specific function outputs. Greg reemphasized the importance of the activities by stating, "We're not going to do the second lab for about two weeks, so don't forget this." It was clear that Greg was already placing great importance on the activities as an avenue for student learning.

Luci made little use of the activities in her classroom, and this affected their potential impact on her students. During a student interview after Lab 1, Ken, a student in one of Luci's sections, indicated that his group missed the mathematics embedded in the activity, stating:

> We didn't see the point in doing the lab. It really didn't connect up to any equations or anything. I mean, it was like playing, like being in third grade where we plug in numbers for sunlight and things and watch the plants grow. I really didn't see how it connects to the math.

Results of a questionnaire after Lab 5 found that Greg's students consistently rated the activities as more relevant to the course and helpful in their understandings. In addition, Greg found that more of his students were focusing on the what's happening kinds of things than on the procedural kinds of things. He illustrated this with a story of a student who asked a question extending the discussion of a trigonometric property that was introduced in the activities into a subsequent course topic:

Student: *I've never seen that before. I've never seen that before. I've never seen that before!*

Greg: *Usually they'll come to me and say I can't do these steps, but she was saying I'm thinking about this and I can't see how to think about this next idea.*

Greg's comments suggest that the activities provided an avenue for both students and instructor to explore mathematical ideas in ways not previously afforded by the textbook alone. The activities combined with classroom discussion provided the students an opportunity to develop understandings of important aspects of mathematical functions and to conjecture about the consequences and implications of these understandings. In contrast, Luci's lack of inclination to use the activities in the core of her instructional approach and assessment led the students, in part, to feelings that the activities did not help them develop such understandings.

Data show that these differences did have an effect on student learning outcomes. Although very few differences were noted early in the semester, the students in Greg's sections were able to more accurately analyze the functional situation of later activities. For example, Lab 4 required the students to input amounts of various pesticides and determine which was most effective in eliminating a harmful plant bacteria. Analysis of student responses revealed that 96% of Greg's students investigated, analyzed, and determined which pesticide most quickly eliminated the bacteria, while 64% of Luci's students failed to do so. These differences were mainly due to the manner in which both groups attended to the specific mathematical features of the situation. In essence, the students in Greg's sections were more attuned to the goal of the activity and were better able to discuss the functional situation by using more appropriate understandings. These differences were typical in student responses that occurred late in the semester. Hence, the emphasis on the web-based activities Greg placed in his own instructional practice had real implications on student learning, most of which surfaced after a period of time.

CONCLUSIONS

Based on this evidence, we can conclude that brief but intense periods of mentoring may not be enough to overcome incompatibilities between instructor's goals and those inherent in technologically driven activities inserted into an existing course format. Mentoring may be insufficient to change an instructor's philosophy and practice in a manner that allows for effective use of technology. However, instructors whose goals and practice are in line with such web-based activities are able to use them effectively. This study also shows explicit connections between how instructors make use of web-based activities and student learning outcomes. Instructional behaviors that supported the goals of web-based activities led to differences in student gains in relation to these goals.

Adding technology to classrooms will not necessarily improve educational outcomes. The relevance of technology to teachers and students depends on attitudes that are not easy to change. It is not enough to couch large-scale educational uses of technology in an environment that is conducive to the stated goals of the associated instructional setting. The technological environment must be designed and supported in a way that connects these goals to those of the participating instructors and students. However, in the case of Luci, mentoring was not sufficient to support the formation of these connections.

ACKNOWLEDGMENTS

Portions of this manuscript were made possible through a grant from the Center for Teaching and Learning, Washington State University. We are solely responsible for the contents of the manuscript and wish to thank Phil Scuderi for his assistance during numerous phases of this project.

REFERENCE

Lloyd, G. M., & Wilson, M. (1998). The impact of a teacher's conceptions of functions on his implementation of a reform curriculum. *Journal for Research in Mathematics Education, 29* (3), 248-74.

CONTACT INFORMATION

David Slavit. Assistant Professor
Mathematics Education
Washington State University, Vancouver
11420 NE Salmon Creek Road
Vancouver, WA 98686-9600
Email: Dslavit@wsu.edu
Phone: (360) 546-9653
Fax: (360) 546-9040

Joshua Yeidel
Email: yeidel@wsu.edu

Vignette 24 What You Expect Is Not Always What You Get: Ruminations and Recommendations from Teaching and Taking an Online Course

Frank W. Connolly and Teresa Fernandez, American University

INTRODUCTION

Offering and taking a course totally online seemed like a great idea—innovative, future-oriented, and a real challenge. It turns out it was innovative, future-oriented, and a real challenge, but not what either of the authors expected. Beginning in fall 1996, the instructor investigated, proposed, coordinated, planned, justified, explained, and defended offering a special topics graduate course in information systems titled Legal, Ethical, and Social Implications of Information Technology. Students who were interested in the material as well as the opportunity to experiment with new technologies eagerly registered. This course was unique in offering convenience, leading-edge technologies, and content that appealed to students from a wide range of disciplines.

EDUCATIONAL THEORIES

The course was driven more by pedagogy than technology, since in the field of information systems, the world is a better lab than the classroom. By design, class members would never meet face-to-face; rather, everything from course registration to class meetings would occur via computer.

COMPUTER-ENHANCED TECHNIQUES

Although the delivery and interaction media were different, the course was to closely resemble a typical class arrangement. The initial course design called for a combination of videoconferencing (CUSeeMe from WhitePine Software) and groupware (Lotus Notes), to conduct regular class meetings and discussions, with telecommuting enabling the students to carry out group projects and meet in project teams. Technical difficulties required on-the-fly modifications to this design. By the fourth week, attempts to use videoconferencing were abandoned, the course shifted entirely to Lotus Notes, and the format for activities solidified.

Prior to each class, students were expected to complete readings detailed in the syllabus. For class, the instructor would post additional content for review and pose several questions for discussion. The additional materials prepared for each class included the following.

- Administrivia regarding class: reminders about assignments, concerns, or problems, etc.

- Lecture pieces: the equivalent of material the professor would present as a brief lecture in a regular class

- Current articles from online periodicals and electronic newspapers

- Online sites or resources for student investigation and analysis

Participation was disappointing. It would be 45 minutes or an hour before the first response arrived and then others trickled in or an unsatisfying "I agree" was added. It was taking the instructor many hours to prepare material for each class: Writing brief lecture pieces was much more time-consuming and demanding than sitting in class and talking; locating and vetting online materials, even at familiar sites, took time; preparing challenging, open-ended written questions was more time-consuming than asking similar questions as part of a typical class. The instructor shared his concern with the class, and the response from students was immediate and unanimous. The students felt they, too, needed a great deal of time to review the current material and then to form and to write their responses. It wasn't a casual in-class discussion, but a reflective piece they were preparing. Just as the instructor needed significantly more time to prepare for each class, they needed significantly more time to think about and to respond to questions.

The result of this interaction was a refinement of the model and, gradually, a relaxation of the tight time constraints. Refining the model meant preparing material and making it available to the class earlier. Online resources for their review were identified at least one class ahead; current readings from electronic journals and newspapers were kept to short articles with longer selections offered for personal consideration outside the class discussion. Lecture pieces and questions for consideration and response were posted no later than noon of class day. Relaxing the time constraints meant that although many postings and responses still occurred during the scheduled meeting times, significant numbers also were posted outside of those hours. From the instructors' perspective, this meant that class meetings were significantly extended.

MEASURED RESULTS

At the end of the semester, class members were invited to dinner at a local restaurant. The instructor's objective was to engage the students in a discussion about the experience to gain insight about the course from their perspective.

Student feedback indicated the following reactions:

- The course was demanding in terms of the depth of cognitive processing, the research needed to support answers, and the greater care and precision demanded over writing face-to-face communication.

- Not having to fight traffic to reach campus was a major advantage.

- Taking classes from home required unexpected family cooperation to provide time and quiet.

- They missed the normal social interaction associated with class.

- The experience was educational, fun, and worthwhile.

LESSONS LEARNED

The students and teacher all learned numerous lessons, some surprising, many that could have been anticipated.

- Don't develop and teach an online course unless you have technical support such as

  - Hardware and software for the faculty teaching the class and for full student participation

  - Institutional expertise to install and maintain the software and hardware on a high-priority basis throughout the course. This includes the institutional software and hardware resources needed to create a virtual classroom and individual systems for faculty teaching the course and students taking the class.

  - Help desk support to allow faculty and staff to resolve minor problems over the telephone or via email. Help Desk staff must know the applications being used and be aware that they are critical to the course. Delayed responses or corrections have a direct and immediate impact on the course.

- Developing and teaching an online course is both wonderful and exhausting. It is wonderful to have students access today's *Washington Post* or *San Francisco Chronicle* to discuss a news item related to the class. No excuses—everyone can get and read it. The same is true of material from the Library of Congress, and innumerable public and private organizations and associations. A discussion of free speech can include reviewing material not only from the far right, but the far left and center as well. Students and the teacher can support opinions and arguments by having everyone go directly to the source material. While it might take an hour to update and prepare a lecture on a concept (e.g., the four-factor test for fair use under copyright law), writing the same material at a reasonable level of quality and detail for electronic distribution takes many hours, and then it represents only a small portion of a class.

In *EDUCOM Review,* Judith Boettcher, the executive director of CREN and former head of Penn State University's Multimedia Teaching Center, estimates that an online course takes 18 hours of faculty preparation time for every hour of class time, and that assumes the instructor is knowledgeable in the subject matter (Boettcher, 1997).

Students also felt that they invested significantly more time in this class than in others. Offering all responses in written form takes more thought and time than face-to-face interactions, and retrieving and reading current articles and materials were not requirements in other courses.

- Don't offer a course using technology that is brand new or that technical staff are unfamiliar with.

- You have to go with the flow. The instructor becomes just as frustrated with the technology as the students.

- The frequency of interactions among and between the instructor and students was significantly lower than in regular classes, but the depth of analysis and discussion was deeper. The literature on education indicates this is to be expected as all interaction was via the written word. It takes greater thought to structure a response in clear written form. Student feedback indicates that they felt they learned at least as much as in other courses but in greater depth. They had better mastery but over fewer topics.

- Online courses are not for everyone—faculty or student. A dyslexic student was at a distinct disadvantage when the course shifted away from interactive video to become solely text-based.

Not all students are suited to take courses online. In addition to obvious technical skills and learning preferences, there are physical requirements of ADA to be considered and personal characteristics, such as the self-discipline to participate when there are no apparent external forces to encourage it.

- Social interaction is important. In a regular classroom, even if students do not enthusiastically participate in discussions, the instructor gains a great deal of feedback from facial expressions and body language. Students, too, use visual clues to better understand an instructor and each other. None of that is available online. The instructor was surprised at how much he wanted to see students' faces and chat face-to-face with them. Especially when there were technical problems, he set up telephone conference calls to review progress and chat as much for his own benefit as for the students'.

- Students will be students whether the classroom is virtual or real. One of the requirements for the course was to complete a team project. Student dyads had to select a topic for research, with each team required to conduct an online class and prepare a joint paper based on their research. While no personality conflicts were reported, one student did not fully participate and was later charged with plagiarism.

- Students and faculty who decide to follow an online path must be taught about the expectations and the feelings of isolation and frustration that go with such technology-based courses. In addition, there must be clearly defined procedures when technical problems arise.

- Only when discussing course registration with potential enrollees did an unintended bias come to light. While we intentionally excluded undergraduates, the computer hardware requirements for participating in the course limited the pool to individuals with sufficient wealth to own a fairly sophisticated personal computer.

- When it became obvious that students would defer to the instructor's postings no matter what, he wrote responses directly to individuals or held his comments until all student reactions were heard. Initially, the instructor wanted to be just one of the participants, hoping that the students and teacher would learn together from this new experience. But, just as in face-to-face classes, the instructor's remarks stifled further discussion as the students assumed he had the answers.

- A major benefit to teaching a course online is telecommuting. Once all of us were comfortable with the technology, it was no longer necessary to come to campus for class. In fact, the instructor conducted a number of classes from his home and, when attending professional conferences, from hotel rooms in Minnesota and Florida.

- As students became more comfortable with the medium, class sessions were extended. Students felt compelled to check the course database regularly to add to discussions or view peer opinions.

REFERENCE

Boettcher, J. (1997, July/August). How much does it cost to develop a distance learning course? It all depends... *EDUCOM Review, 32* (4).

CONTACT INFORMATION

Frank W. Connolly, Professor
Computer Science and Information Systems
American University
Washington, DC 20016
Email: frank@american.edu
Phone: (202) 885-3164
Fax: (202) 885-1479

Theresa Fernandez
Email: Tfernan@American.edu

Elmer Poe, East Carolina University

EDUCATIONAL THEORIES

Our program is an MS industrial technology course offered entirely over the Internet. Our average student is 30 years old and employed full time in a technical field. As we planned how to offer our program, we were faced with four constraints. First, because we believe that students learn in a variety of ways, we were committed to the use of multiple tools over the Internet. Collaborative activities and student-student interactions were important elements in our design. Second, we were constrained by the fact that the degree program includes three different technical concentrations—digital communications, safety, and manufacturing—which had included lab activities when offered in a face-to-face setting. Third, the bandwidth of most of our student connections to the Internet prohibited real-time video. Finally, while many students thought they had network experience, most only had some experience with email and a web browser. We decided to set up our own servers to allow maximum flexibility in the selection and use of tools.

COMPUTER-ENHANCED TECHNIQUES

We initially tried teaching the use of network tools along with the content of the courses in the program but found that to be unsatisfactory. Our solution was to initiate the Internet research tools course. It is the first required course in the program, and when students complete it, they have mastery of all of the tools required. They also have a clear idea of the amount of time required in an online course.

Email

Email is an essential but time intensive tool for interaction between faculty and students and among students. We learned that other tools can foster a broader discussion with the bonus of greater time efficiency.

Listserv

Listserv is used in two formats. We use one-way lists to distribute announcements, lessons, course FAQs (frequently asked questions), etc. This is not only efficient, but as students change ISPs, they maintain their current email address on the listserv. We also use discussion lists for class discussions. By operating our own server and our own listserv, we can have multiple lists per course and create them quickly without red tape.

Newsgroups

Newsgroups are used as discussion forums. Since we operate our own server, it is possible to have multiple groups per course. In the tools course, for example, we have five groups. Multiple groups allow the instructor to direct pointed and limited discussions over time. We have found that for many activities these groups are much more efficient than email lists and naturally promote more participation in the discussion. Sometimes we will reserve one or more newsgroups for small group project discussions. One group is an open discussion group on which assignments are never required but on which students can discuss topics of their choice.

Keyboard Chat

Keyboard chat is used in a variety of formats. We operate a chat server so that students can set up their own groups for use in collaborative projects. We have whole class meetings where lecture material is discussed. Instructors use availability on chat at preset times as office hours. We have learned the hard way that chat sessions must be managed carefully, just as one would manage a face-to-face meeting with a class, and have developed written rules of protocol for participation in a class chat. One or more students is designated to capture the sessions and distribute the transcripts. The live interaction has created a real sense of community among our students, who never see each other. It is important to schedule into a chat-based meeting some social time for that student interaction that normally takes place around the soft drink machines.

Whiteboard and Workgroup Tools

We were faced with the teaching of statistical process control in a manner that would allow student participation. The instructor used a whiteboard application, dividing the class into problem solving teams that reported the solution of an assigned problem via the whiteboard. Other teams could then interact with the solution. The teams developed a competitive spirit, and the course was very effective. Workgroup tools supported collaboration on projects in a variety of settings. Finding a functional yet cheap whiteboard was difficult.

Web Pages

Web pages were used to distribute course materials and lecture notes, including photos and demos. Instructors have direct FTP access to the web server so the pages can be modified as each course proceeds. We have included small video files (in the ten- to 20-second range) to illustrate machine operation.

Audio and Video

We have successfully used audio at modem connect rates for whole group discussions and made limited use of streaming audio and video. As overall bandwidth improves, these will see more use, but overall their effectiveness is no greater than that of the other tools. Talking heads are interested in real-time or slo-mo.

LESSONS LEARNED

We discovered that talking head audio/video was not as important as we assumed and that students preferred to be active learners. The result is a successful low bandwidth program using a variety of other tools.

Because students had narrow experience with network tools, we realized that we must teach their use. We initially tried teaching the use of tools with the content of the courses in the program but found that to be unsatisfactory. The courses were already demanding. Students often lost the content while learning the tools. Our solution was to initiate the Internet research tools course. It is the required first course in the program, and when students complete it, they have mastery of all of the tools required. They also have a clear idea of the amount of time required in an online course.

We found that by centering problems in our students' workplaces, we were able to overcome the lack of traditional lab experience. Since there are many students in the program, there is no lack of appropriate and good problems. Also, teaming students from different employers produced a synergy that has paid dividends in both their educational and work experiences. The use of teams allowed the students to build a sense of community and a surprising amount of out-of-class online sharing occurred.

The use of continual feedback and collaborative activities provided an ongoing evaluation of student work. As one of our colleagues says, "You know when a student falls asleep at the switch" when active participation is a requirement for successful course completion.

Finally, we learned that a variety of tools really is essential. We learned that one must always have an alternative plan for synchronous activities. We have used a "If We Don't Connect by 15 Minutes After the Hour, Go Here" approach that allows students who can make the connection to work through the materials and activities without the instructor present. The role of the instructor has changed from knowledge-giver to knowledge-facilitator. Some of our faculty members have adapted to this new role easily, while others have struggled.

CONTACT INFORMATION

Elmer Poe, Professor and Director of Graduate Studies
School of Industry & Technology
Department of Industry and Technology
East Carolina University
105 Flanagan
Greenville, NC 27858-4353
Email: Poee@mail.ecu.edu
WWW: http://www.sit.ecu.edu
Phone: (252) 328-6705
Fax: (252) 328-1618

BIOLOGICAL SCIENCES AND MEDICINE

Vignette 26 — Science Education for Hostile Nonscience Majors

Richard H. Falk, University of California, Davis

For many years, I have taught a large enrollment biology class designed for nonscience majors. At the beginning of the term, when I poll my class about why they might be taking this course, no one ever volunteers that biology is interesting or relevant. To an individual, they take this course because it is seen as the easiest way to satisfy a requirement that some university committee has inflicted on them. They are quite hostile to any study of science.

The nature of general education courses has always bothered me. We have science courses for nonscience majors and humanities courses for science majors, where we encapsulate science or the humanities as unrelated to one another. Our doing this has rewarded us with students who regularly tell us that science has no relevance to their lives or that any study of the humanities is fluff.

Where does the average individual encounter science? In general, it is when he or she is faced with a contentious issue at the intersection of sociology and science. Most individuals bump into science when they hear about Chernobyl or Dolly or Viagra. If they wish to engage in any meaningful discussion of these topics, they must have some understanding of science and how it is done. Without this understanding, they are reduced to making simple, emotive responses to complex issues. What we tend to do in our teaching of science is to present classical, unequivocal "truths" in a totally uncontentious manner. We detach science from sociology and make it value-free.

As computers and the Internet became more available to students, I began to consider ways I might use this technology to facilitate my students' learning and perhaps even change their attitudes about biology in general. I had also been reading extensively about the purported benefits of cooperative or collaborative learning and thought I might explore its use in my biology class.

COURSE DESIGN

A major disappointment with my biology course had always been the discussion sections. Topics were meant to unleash vigorous discussion in small groups under the supervision of graduate teaching assistants. In practice, however, it was always painfully difficult to elicit discussion from most of the students. Many simply failed to attend these meetings.

My solution was to choose contentious, contemporary topics from newspapers and news magazines for discussion. I replaced the in-person discussion sections with virtual discussion sections. For each of eight weeks, I posed a topic and had students discuss it among themselves through the use of an email list processor. Participation in these virtual discussion sessions became a significant part of their overall grade in the course.

Writing is an important component of education. I foster it by requiring that my students respond to a series of virtual essay questions over a period of eight weeks. They prepare their responses on their favorite word processor and submit them as an email attachment to their graduate teaching assistant. Their responses are graded for content and grammar.

I design the questions so that most of the material necessary to address them can be found with web search engines. A few questions, however, require a physical trip to the library. I believe that we must teach our students how to use both Internet resources and primary reference materials.

Finally, my students are required to write an 8- to 12-page term paper on a biological topic of their choosing that is graded for content and grammar. Their chosen topic needs my approval to ensure that it is neither too broad nor too narrow and that it is appropriate. The papers are prepared on their favorite word processor and submitted as an email attachment to their graduate teaching assistant.

The last thing that I modified was my lecture material. While my in-person lectures allowed me to expound brilliantly on various topics in biology, I sometimes spoke too rapidly or projected particularly complex diagrams or photographs for too brief a time. My solution was to prepare my lecture materials as web pages.

I quickly realized that simply moving lecture notes to web format was not sufficient. Such material is rather dry. Why not just assign readings in a text? I was simply not exploiting the medium.

One can add a great deal of interactivity to a web page that is not possible in a lecture, such as the following which I added:

- Molecules that could be rotated for more complete study

- Drop-down questions to query a student's retention or understanding of information in a preceding paragraph

- Small multiple-choice quizzes at the end of each module that act as self-test instruments

- Carefully chosen hyperlinks to sites that treat topics in a different context

MEASURED RESULTS

When I compared student performance between conventionally taught classes and my newer method, I saw no real difference, which is not surprising. One can teach well using a variety of methods. But what was surprising and totally unexpected were unsolicited student comments to the effect that my new manner of teaching had changed their perceptions about the relevance of biology and science to their everyday lives. A few examples:

- *I thought this WWW class was a mistake when I could have taken the traditional form of this class. Instead, I have found that taking the class has been interesting, demanding, and has kept my focus on biology and its concept.*

- *By the way, while I'm writing to you, I just wanted to say that I am pretty impressed with this whole email course thing.*

- *...this course has been balanced by the interesting though somewhat intimidating issues presented for discussion and by the writing assignments. I really don't like science. I have learned a lot from this course though, and because I found it stimulating, it is information that I won't immediately forget.*

- *...I would like to start by saying how much I enjoyed this discussion part of the class.*

- *It was not until this class (which I took reluctantly) that I realized that science is important and relevant to our daily lives and that a basic understanding is necessary to be decently educated.*

- *At the beginning, I was thinking, "Oh great, here goes another boring standard general education course.'" But I have been quite surprised to find that our discussion and essay topics have been real issues. It has been a joy and has opened my eyes to new aspects of biology.*

LESSONS LEARNED

Many students like being taught by the means of a well-designed, web-based biology course; however perhaps 40 of 200 students did continue to attend traditional lectures. At the same time, these 40 admitted that the web materials were quite useful—they just liked an in-person lecture.

Student computer configuration for dial-up network communication was initially a problem for a small number of students. This was addressed largely by careful instruction where necessary.

Students particularly liked the virtual discussion and virtual essay aspects of the course. Many remarked that they appreciated the freedom associated with attending discussion at their convenience. Others remarked that it was a new experience to be able to think a bit about what they wished to say and correct their statements before they pushed the send button. Still others liked the pseudo-anonymity that this kind of discussion offered. In the case of the virtual essays, many students praised being pushed to use the Internet and its search engines.

While my teaching assistants and I were always available for in-person office meetings, we found collectively that our students were more likely to send us email questions. Many remarked that we were more available in this manner than their instructors in other classes.

In some respects, what I have constructed is an issue-based collaborative learning course done via distance education. It appears to be a powerful educational tool.

CONTACT INFORMATION

Richard H. Falk, Professor
Section of Plant Biology
University of California at Davis
One Shields Avenue
Davis, CA 95616-8635
Email: Rhfalk@ucdavis.edu
WWW: http://bio2000.ucdavis.edu/
Phone: (503) 752-0623

 **Human Physiology**

Stephen H. Loomis, Connecticut College

Human physiology was completely redesigned as a studio course, which allowed the faculty to focus on different learning styles and to use daily assessments of student learning. Instead of lectures, the classes included various activities designed to build on conceptual understanding gained by the students in homework assignments. As homework, students were required to complete sections of Adam Interactive Physiology, CD-ROMs that present virtual lectures using rich animations and interactive activities. The students were able to repeat sections of the lectures pertaining to concepts that they did not understand and to test their understanding using interactive quizzes. Therefore, they entered class with a base of understanding similar to, or better than, what they would have left class with using the lecture format. In the classroom, the faculty facilitated further learning through a variety of activities designed to take advantage of different learning styles. Activities included bioplays in which students acted out a biological concept, drawing activities in which students were asked to draw a representation of a concept, physical model building, intellectual model building and testing, case studies, discussions, and virtual and real experiments. All work was performed in groups of two or four, and students spent a great deal of time teaching each other.

COURSE DESCRIPTION

This course examines human physiological processes with an emphasis on interactions among the physiological systems. We (myself and a lab instructor) approach this study using systems of thinking and require students to build more sophisticated intellectual models as they progress through the course. The final project requires the students to build a model of the normal control of blood carbohydrate concentration and then test their model using a diabetes case study.

They present their model in both verbal and written formats. The course used a rich variety of instructional technology.

Electronic Textbook

Students were given out-of-class assignments in the Adam Interactive Physiology CD-ROMs. This set of five CD-ROMs acted as an electronic textbook; however, they did not include some of the topics covered in the course. We surmounted this problem by giving supplementary reading assignments, developing our own CD-ROM on the digestive system, and developing a set of interactive tutorials that play on the web. Students used the CD-ROMS a great deal, with 100% of them responding that they used them several to many times (the top two categories out of five). They also found them extremely useful in learning physiology (100% responding in the extremely to very useful categories).

Short, Web-Based Animations

We have developed a number of short animations on individual concepts ranging from tutorials to interactive modules, which request that the student make predictions and test them. We have used these animations to initiate discussions and to review concepts. Most of the students (69%) found these animations extremely to very useful in learning physiology.

Computer Data Acquisition

For much of the experimental work, students collected, analyzed, manipulated, and graphed data using computers. Downloading the raw data into spreadsheets allowed students to make more sophisticated analysis and presentation. We did not ask the students to rate their perceptions of the use of computers in this way, although 67% responded that the laboratory was a useful learning experience.

Computer Simulations

For a series of experiments on the nervous system, the students used a computer simulation program of the squid giant axon called Loligo Electronicus. This program allowed students to design and to carry out their own experiments in a virtual laboratory that contains all of the components of the real laboratory (microscope with nerve chamber, stimulator, and oscilloscope). Students make all adjustments as if they were adjusting the actual equipment, and results resemble the actual oscilloscope tracings. The experience allowed students to do rather sophisticated experiments without the expertise to do intracellular recording.

Web Site

We have developed a web site for this course (http://camel2.conncoll.edu/Academics/zoology/courses/zoo202), which is designed mostly as a means of increasing communication among students and between students and faculty. The site contains all of the course information, including the syllabus, course calendar, list of covered concepts, daily goals, homework assignments, final project assignments, study questions, and animations. In addition, the site contains a chat room, which the faculty use for virtual office hours in the evening and on weekends, when the students are most likely to be working on the course, and a suggestion box for continual feedback from students about the course. Students are allowed to log on to the chat room and to leave suggestions anonymously. This policy was designed to promote honest communication and increase quality feedback.

The World Wide Web

The students used several web sites to initiate discussion of specific concepts. In addition, students performed informational searches in developing their case study reports.

Presentations

The faculty used computer projection for demonstrations, and the students used PowerPoint and computer projection for some of their oral presentations.

MEASURED RESULTS

Student learning was informally assessed on a daily basis through oral presentations to the rest of the class or examination of the results of the activity. Formal assessment instruments included essays in which students were required to apply their understanding of concepts to novel situations; laboratory reports; case study reports; and project reports. These instruments were designed to test student understanding of 59 concepts covered in the course. Students were usually given more than one chance to demonstrate understanding of each concept. In addition to assessment of student understanding, an attitudinal survey was given at the end of the course. In overall learning, 68% of the students demonstrated an understanding of over 90% of the concepts. This compares with a ten-year average of 24% using the lecture format. In attitudinal surveys, 96% of the students rated this course as very good to excellent and would recommend it to a peer.

LESSONS LEARNED

I was generally pleased with the results from this experiment and plan to revise it. The assessments show that students learn better when actively involved in their learning and have a better attitude about their learning. Not everything worked as well as I would have liked, however, and elements will require some changes in the future.

Chat Room
Students did not take advantage of the chat room as much as I would have liked. None of them stated that they used the chat room many times, and only a few used it several times. Most disappointing was the fact that 59% of the students did not use it at all. Of those students that did use it, all found it useful in learning physiology.

Web Site
Since this was the first time that I taught human physiology using this format, there were constant changes in the schedule. It was difficult for me to keep the web site updated. When I was late in updating the site, it created a good deal of confusion. Hopefully, I have corrected this problem by developing a one-page assignment calendar that can be corrected quickly and easily.

Short Animations
Most of the short animations were developed for Power Macs and were not available for students with DOS machines. This meant that these programs were not available outside the classroom for a number of students. We have recently shocked all of our animations and included them in the web site so that they will now operate on both platforms.

CONCLUSIONS

The great advantage of using technology in this course has been enhanced learning both in and out of class. Students have understood concepts at a deeper level and been more engaged in their learning. Communication with students has been facilitated in a way that promotes honesty and allows the faculty to make adjustments on the fly rather than waiting until the next time the course is taught. Based on the first experience teaching this course in this way, we have already planned adjustments. Continual assessment and reflection should allow the faculty to create a rich environment that promotes positive attitudes toward learning and develops conceptual understanding.

CONTACT INFORMATION

Stephen H. Loomis
Professor of Zoology
Connecticut College
Box 5496
New London, CT 06320
Email: shloo@conncoll.edu
WWW: http://www.conncoll.edu. http://camel
.conncoll.edu/ccacad/zoology/faculty
/loomis.htm,

http://camel2.conncoll.cdu/Acadcmics/zoology
/courscs/zoo202
Phone: (860) 439-2135
Fax: (860) 439-2519

Mark Sutherland, Hendrix College

COURSE DESCRIPTION

I have been teaching advanced cell biology for eight years. This is a senior-level course in which I try to maintain more of a graduate-school tone than in most other courses. I make it very clear to the students that I am more concerned with the academic level of the course (scientific rigor, critical analysis, and data interpretation) than with the specific topics we deal with.

Many biology courses in graduate schools involve heavy student participation, both in discussion and presenting new material to their peers. Students are expected to read the current research literature, prepare seminar-like presentations, and then present them in a formal class setting. Biological literature primarily describes experiments and so is very data-intensive, with most papers having a variety of charts, tables, graphs, photographs, and microphotographs. In addition to talking about the results of the experiments, the presenter must also show the original research data and explain how it is interpreted. Conversation often becomes heated as the audience interprets the data differently.

To prepare my advanced cell biology students for this graduate school experience, I require them to present similar seminars to their classmates. In the past, I had students photocopy the original data onto overhead transparencies for classroom display. Our debates on the research tend to be less volatile due to the undergraduates' unfamiliarity with the concepts being presented and the natural classroom reticence that fades in graduate school. However, the students doing the presentations benefit tremendously, as they are required to think more deeply about a topic than they have before, find supporting literature, critically analyze data and interpretations, and learn how to make their new understanding clear to their colleagues. Students in the audience also benefit as they are exposed to several different types of research data and a variety of presentation styles.

THE PROBLEMS

There have been a host of problems associated with these seminars.

- Since I feel that these presentations are so important, I include the material they cover when writing tests. Students have complained that this is unfair because they find the presentations hard to understand and almost impossible to take notes from. In an initial effort to remedy this situation, I had the presenters make photocopies of the data to pass out to the audience. This lessened the criticism but only to a small extent.

- I do not assign scores to individual presentations. I find that most of our seniors are sufficiently motivated and do not need the threat of a grade to take this assignment very seriously. However, a few will try to slip by with a shoddy performance, leading to more complaints. Most complaints are not about some students getting away with less effort. The class does not want to be tested on material presented in a poor seminar.

- The quality of the photocopied overheads and handouts was poor. Many research publications in cell biology now feature high-quality, full-color photomicrographs and other color graphics. Subtle changes in color or shading can be critically important to correct interpretation of the data. These nuances are diminished or totally lost in a photocopy. Thus, the quality of the presentation is reduced by illegible data, and studying the material for a test is a frustrating process.

- Although most students told me on course evaluations that they found preparing the seminars a valuable experience, it was also a joyless process; furthermore, they found listening to other seminars marginally worthwhile.

THE SOLUTIONS

Most of the problems described above have been successfully addressed by having the students prepare their seminars using scanners and PowerPoint. The seminars are presented in a classroom with a video projector connected to a computer, and the files stored on the network server where they can be accessed while preparing for exams. Although we have had this equipment in place for only one year, the difference in student appreciation for the seminars has been so striking that I am confident that many of the problems have been solved. A list of improvements follows.

Quality of Student Preparation

Since making these changes, the quality of presentations has increased dramatically. Students clearly enjoy working with the program and making elegant presentations. On their own, they have figured out neat tricks with PowerPoint. For example, one student found a paper describing intracellular transport of membrane-bound materials. The authors included a web site where they had stored actual videotapes of material being transported inside the cell, the same tapes from which they had collected data to write their paper. The student was able to download these videos and show them from within PowerPoint, giving the class an unsurpassed understanding of a process that is normally very difficult to describe or sketch.

Quality of Presented Materials

The use of color scanners and a video projector allows the presented material to be almost the same quality as the original data. The quality of our scanner still presents some limitations, and putting the images into PowerPoint may also distort some detail, but the improvement over photocopied material is tremendous. The presentations are more enjoyable to watch, and the science is quite superior.

Storage and Retrieval of Presentations

Because the materials are all in the computer, I can save them to a network server. From the server, any student can retrieve them at any time for further study. Hendrix College has a large computer laboratory, and all the computers have PowerPoint on them. In addition, over 30% of students have computers in their dorm rooms that are hooked to the campus network. However, the presentations are not stored on the web server, so they are not accessible off campus without considerable hacking skills. In addition, I remove the files as soon as the test covering that material has been given. These steps are taken to ensure that we have no problems with copyright compliance.

ASSESSMENT OF RESULTS

Because of these improvements, student complaints have greatly diminished. I got mostly favorable comments from students about the presentations. To help assess their impact, I asked the students to address them specifically in the comments section of their anonymous course evaluations. In past years, the evaluations of the presentations were generally neutral to negative. To follow are some relevant comments from my students.

- *Presentations were a crucial part of the course. The experience of doing a presentation was very helpful.*

- *The presentations were informative, and I enjoyed them and learned from them.*

- *The presentations were a good way to learn extra info, and they made the class involved in teaching and learning. [They] also kept cutting-edge info flowing into the class.*

- *I think the presentations are very helpful because they get you ready for senior seminar. The class had a good deal of discussion, which was fun and interesting.*

- *I loved learning up-to-date research in the subjects we were studying in class. I learned a lot from mine and enjoyed all the others.*

- *It was good for me to do mine. I got a lot out of reading the paper and getting a clear understanding of it (also PowerPoint). But I never got much out of listening to the (other) presentations.*

- *Keep the presentations!*

- *The class format is good because it stimulates discussion more than any previous class I have had.*

I also asked the students to state whether they wanted me to start assigning scores to the presentations. Of the eight who had something to say on this issue, five wanted some points or at least a few bonus points, while three were adamant in stressing how much more enjoyable their experience was without that added pressure.

CONCLUSION

In conclusion, I believe this added technology has significantly improved an important aspect of my cell biology course. I plan to make more use of PowerPoint myself in all my classes, especially when covering data-rich material and storing the presentations on the server for student access.

CONTACT INFORMATION

Mark Sutherland
Associate Professor
Biology Department
Hendrix College
1600 Washington Avenue
Conway, AR 72032
Email: Sutherlandmv@hendrix.edu
http://www.hendrix.edu/homes/fac/sutherlandm/
Phone: (501) 450-1217

 **Empowerment for Electronic Education: Building Student Confidence in a New Way of Learning**

James L. Stofan and Linda H. Bruce, Johns Hopkins University

When the Internet-based Graduate Certificate Program in Public Health began at Johns Hopkins University in 1997, we knew that the online courses it contained would pose some serious challenges to our target audience: global health-care professionals who, as adults long-since out of school, would likely have minimal computer experience. In order for these returning students to perform well in the program and to find it a satisfying experience, they would have to gain a host of technical competencies as well as to adopt new learner attitudes and strategies.

To address these challenges, the distance education division created a special web-based, noncredit course called Internet Skills (http://www.jhsph.edu/~distance/gcp/iskills/). Delivered in a six-week format, the course guides students through progressively more complex skills, such as understanding basic computer functions, navigating the web, downloading and installing plug-ins, and using advanced communication tools. Completing the course requires roughly seven hours per week, and participation is mandatory for all students enrolled in the graduate certificate program.

EDUCATIONAL THEORIES AND LEARNING IDEAS

When we set out to design Internet Skills for online delivery, there was no doubt that it would need to be a truly exciting and engaging course. Not only would it serve as the students' introduction to an entire graduate program at Johns Hopkins, but it would also mark almost every student's entry into the world of distance education. It was paramount that we demonstrate up front that distance learning worked well and that the graduate program would be an educational experience of quality and value.

We created the course primarily by following our instincts as former distance learners, adhering to the principle that learning should be active and enjoyable. "The learner and your materials must bond," advises Eric Parks, president and CEO of ASK International, so that the learner will be willing "to let the learning in." We integrated multiple and varied opportunities for students to engage with the material, to explore it, to interact with it, to ponder and to share it, and, ultimately, to make it their own.

A major factor that influenced the shape and delivery of the course was our conviction that while taking it, students should be freed to the greatest extent possible from other academic focuses and undue time pressures. In truth, it may have been daunting for students to think about completing a rigorous, 18-month program of study, let alone to have to learn and depend on a whole new set of technology skills. Acknowledging that the tasks ahead might be formidable, we designed Internet Skills to run before any other courses in the program. A generous amount of time was built in for guidance and support as students experienced the material in depth. Ultimately, we hoped that those taking the course would become so comfortable with the distance-learning process that the technologies would become transparent, and the online experience would be nearly as seamless as traditional classroom learning.

COMPUTER-ENHANCED TECHNIQUES

The main organizational unit of the course is the module, or major topic area, in which students are given opportunities to 1) gain information, 2) practice what they learn, and 3) construct new ideas and create new knowledge.

In each of 14 modules, consistent text and graphics-based elements included are:

- A written introduction, often supported with a pithy or provocative quote from an authority in that topic area

- A list of competencies for each skill area

- A skill-building session, usually a multimedia lecture, an interactive tutorial, or a detailed set of instructions

- An exercise or practice session, varying significantly in design from module to module to keep student

interest at a high level (for example, an automatically scored quiz, a round-robin discussion, a critical analysis, web site exploration, preparation of a PowerPoint presentation)

- Frequently asked questions

- Links to multiple related web sites for supplemental learning

- An interesting statistical Tech Tidbit relating to the module topic (e.g., "More people use the Internet for email communication than for any other purpose"), with sources cited

In addition to the text and graphic elements, the course also contains interactive mechanisms to facilitate its delivery and to help bridge time and distance barriers between students and instructors. These are:

- Email for asynchronous, person-to-person interaction and file sharing

- A bulletin board (by Allaire Forums) for asynchronous, public discussion and file sharing

- NetMeeting (by Microsoft) for synchronous chat-style interaction and collaboration on documents

- LiveTalk (a tool custom-designed by the Distance Education Division's systems developer) for synchronous, radio talk show style communications (web broadcasts)

Working in tandem, the communication tools and the text and graphic elements in the modules are the foundations of the course and serve as the principal discovery zones for learning.

MEASURED RESULTS

During summer 1998, when Internet Skills debuted at Johns Hopkins, students provided the instructors and technical staff with a steady flow of informal feedback. In addition, they completed a formal evaluation, which assessed the overall course, the core elements and individual modules, content and organization, instructional effectiveness, and learning support. Seventy-eight percent of the class completed the evaluation.

Students were overwhelmingly pleased with the course. Ninety-six percent indicated that they agreed or strongly agreed that it was a valuable learning experience, relevant to their career goals, managed effectively, held their interest, and they would be willing to take another course from the instructors. Encapsulating these responses, one student commented, "I'm very, very grateful that we had the Internet Skills course before Quantitative Methods. It helped me focus on what distance education is all about, gave me exposure and access to the new tools I'll be using, reinforced the knowledge that I did have from eight months on the Internet, and taught me how to be disciplined and get assignments done and turned in on time." Another student wrote, "You made it a very positive learning experience, one that I was rather apprehensive about initially. To your credit, the learning was fun and prepared me to handle the technical portion of this program with much more confidence."

While most comments were positive, concerns were also expressed, sometimes strongly, about elements of the course that did not meet expectations. Almost invariably, these concerns were technical. For example, the bulletin board system sometimes ran slowly, NetMeeting stymied students at nearly every turn, LiveTalk at first proved inaccessible to a number of would-be participants, and personal hardware and software problems beset a few students with regularity. Addressing these issues, one participant wrote an optimistic but telling comment: "Keep up with improvements in technology. The somewhat difficult parts of LiveTalk and NetMeeting are sure to [get better] as the software and hardware improves."

LESSONS LEARNED

Creating and conducting the Internet Skills course was a great opportunity to learn about delivering online courses. Above all, it showed us how important interaction is for students and teachers. It was clear in monitoring the volume and tone of email and bulletin board communications that we all found genuine value and enjoyment in interacting. Of course, it helped that in most exercises students were required to interact. For example, the module on using NetMeeting asked them to work in small groups to develop joint responses to a specific issue and then to share the response with the class as a whole. Activities like these set the stage for many levels of collaborative learning and helped to provide instructors with ongoing feedback.

Because interaction is so important to students, the tools for communication become valued, too. We also learned that when the tools don't work properly or effectively, students can become frustrated and even disillusioned with the distance-learning process. Our best solution whenever this kind of situation arose was to immediately communicate our intention to resolve it. Though quick resolutions were not always possible, students realized that there was an active commitment to helping them succeed and that they were not alone in cyberworld. Eventually, their frustrations were assuaged by a solid sense of trust that was built with the instructors and the distance education division as a whole.

The most salient lesson at this point, as we prepare to offer the course a second time, is that reworking it requires almost as much effort as initially developing it. When Internet Skills was being delivered, students sent many suggestions for changes, such as "More practice time should be built in between modules," and "Slow down the pace to accommodate novice users." The instructors and developers also made their own set of discoveries about what needed to be revised. Incorporating all these ideas into a new iteration of the course will be a time-consuming endeavor, albeit necessary and no doubt satisfying.

CONCLUSION

Fundamentally, the Internet Skills course can be seen as a structured collection of information, exercises, and experiences designed to help students gain critical technical skills needed for succeeding in the graduate certificate program. But gaining technical skills is only part of what we hope students achieve during the course. The other, equally important part is that students expand the boundaries of what they think is possible in online education and in using the Internet for thinking, learning, and communicating. When combined, these outcomes can empower students to begin and to persist through their technology-based program with a sense of accomplishment, a reduced fear of technology, and a belief that they can wield new tools in exploring the world.

CONTACT INFORMATION

James L. Stofan
Director, Distance Education Division
Johns Hopkins School of Public Health
111 Market Place, Suite 850
Baltimore, MD 21202
Email: Jstofan@jhsph.edu
WWW: http://distance.jhsph.edu
Phone: (410) 223-1830
Fax: (410) 223-1832

Linda H. Bruce
Email: lbruce@jhsph.edu
WWW: http://www.jhsph.edu/~distance/gcp/iskills/

 **Genetics and Multimedia Technology: A Meiosis Made in Heaven**

Sarah Lea McGuire, Millsaps College

As I finished teaching my first semester of genetics in the same manner that I had been taught, I faced a sobering realization. My students were memorizing problem solving techniques that allowed them to answer problems successfully, but they were not gaining an in-depth understanding of the material. Yes, they performed well, even on standardized exams; however, when asked questions that required complex thought processes and synthesis, they were not as advanced as I had hoped. In the midst of my frustration, I was presented with an idea: Why not use multimedia technology to enhance students' learning? My first question was, "What is multimedia technology?" and my second, "What is a CD-ROM?"

EDUCATIONAL THEORIES

The educational theories on which I based the integration of multimedia technology into my genetics course were four-fold:

1) Problem solving and problem-based learning are essential for students to gain an understanding of the concepts.

2) Learning must be active and inquiry-based.

3) In order to understand principles of genetics, learning must be quantitative.

4) Collaborative learning enhances students' understanding.

These are addressed in most traditional genetics courses, but I felt they could be significantly enhanced by incorporating multimedia technology.

COMPUTER-ENHANCED TECHNIQUES

Students are quite adept at learning problem solving techniques that allow them success at answering typical Mendelian genetics problems, but when asked how or why they arrived at their answers, most are unable to provide a satisfactory response. To remedy this, I designed an interactive, animated program that takes students through the basic processes in meiosis, while simultaneously showing them what various genes and alleles do during the process. Students understand the individual events when taught in sequence but have difficulty making the connection between meiotic events and gene/allele movements; this connection is essential for understanding genetics. The program includes both aspects throughout as well as several problems. Incorrect answers are discussed, and then students are routed back to the original problem.

The inquiry-based and quantitative experience the students had in the traditional course was laboratory-based and fraught with technical problems from the beginning. Using biological organisms lends itself to numerous problems, all of which prevent students from obtaining reliable, interpretable data. Because there is an inherent value in allowing students to learn by doing, we have continued the laboratory investigation component of the course albeit with a more amenable organism. However, it has been significantly enhanced by using of a number of interactive World Wide Web-based laboratory modules. The use of these modules allows students to explore numerous genetic traits as they design and execute experiments and analyze data. For example, the Virtual FlyLab (http://cdl-flylab.sonoma.edu/) allows students to analyze many different types of traits in an investigative manner, and they must plan their experiments appropriately to obtain usable data. Quantitative analysis is both required and aided by the program. Students have the opportunity to learn by making mistakes. If, upon analysis, students realize they have useless data, they must examine their procedures and experimental outline, adjust them accordingly, and perform another set of virtual experiments. This understanding of the investigative process would not be possible in a traditional setting.

We have also used commercially available interactive CD-ROM programs, which contain laboratory experimental modules or three-dimensional animated depictions of various cellular processes. Students work on these in groups, varying parameters according to the group's desires. These programs have allowed the students to more quickly grasp complex cellular processes, allowing the class to cover a wider variety of topics and experimental protocols.

In addition to the use of interactive, group-based or CD-ROM modules, I maintain a personal web page that students use as a reference. The page contains current course syllabi, allows for updating and posting exams, and it also contains a list of helpful genetics sites for students who wish either to expand their knowledge or to practice their skills.

MEASURED RESULTS

The impact of these tools on my genetics class has been amazing. Students often stop me outside class to say how much my multimedia lessons have helped them to understand the material. Students who are not in my classes will often approach me wanting to gain access to these tools. It is clear that word has spread that technology is a wonderful aid to learning. Students are now able to answer more complex problems with greater success, and more material may be covered in class. Their better understanding of the biology is evidenced in their abilities to synthesize various thought processes at an earlier point in the semester. Finally, student written responses on course evaluations frequently indicate that one of the most beneficial aspects of the course is the use of multimedia technology.

LESSONS LEARNED

I have learned much from incorporating multimedia technology in my classes.

- Using interactive programs not only helps students learn the materials, but, from the questions they ask while using the programs, I learn their weaknesses.

- The collaborative way we use the computers (students work in groups of two or three) not only helps less computer-literate students learn quickly, it also helps the groups to interact with each other. Students with varying computer skills and genetics backgrounds help each other learn, and more is accomplished.

- Students can become tired with technology just as they become tired with chalkboards and overhead projectors. A successful course uses a balance of traditional and technology-based learning.

- Students who use many of the interactive investigative laboratory modules are better laboratory scientists because they are able to think on their feet in analyzing data and problems.

CONTACT INFORMATION

Sarah Lea McGuire
Assistant Professor
Millsaps College
Box 150305
Jackson, MS 39210
Email: Mcguiresl@millsaps.edu
WWW: www.millsaps.edu/~mcguisl/
Phone: (601) 974-1414
Fax: (601) 974-1401

 **Computer-Enhanced Teaching of Cell and Molecular Biology**

Robin S. Treichel, Oberlin College

Biologists agree that laboratory instruction is essential if students are to learn biology as "a body of knowledge applied to a process of organized investigation" (Miller & Cheetham, 1990). After all, scientific knowledge is derived from experimentation, and laboratories provide students with opportunities to think about, discuss, and solve problems. However, designing an effective laboratory experience that illustrates important concepts and develops the ability to perform standard techniques and to use essential equipment is challenging, especially given budgetary restraints and the time constraints of a typical three-hour laboratory period.

Cell and Molecular Biology Lecture and Laboratory is the third and final course in our biology core curriculum. The course is required also of biochemistry majors and is an upper-level elective for neuroscience majors; prerequisites include two semesters of introductory chemistry and one semester of biology. The lecture portion of the course is designed to introduce and to integrate the essentials of molecular biology, biochemistry, and cell biology so that students are prepared for the advanced courses in our curriculum.

The formal goal of the laboratory is to teach routine procedures used in modern cell biology and molecular biology research labs. We also want our students to become skilled and comfortable using the sophisticated equipment that is standard in these disciplines. Over the course of the semester, we want each student to develop the habit of working safely, efficiently, and with active awareness. We want students to use their imaginations to envision what is happening at a cellular or molecular level during lab procedures. This requires that they understand the purpose of each step in a long procedure. It also requires that they draw on what they have learned previously in their chemistry, physics, and biology courses. We want them to appreciate that learning and problem solving should not be compartmentalized by discipline or by course. Students should develop good skills for finding needed information. Finally, we want students to think analytically and to appreciate the importance of quantitative skills in biology.

To accomplish these goals, we have developed for each lab exercise a problem set that guides students to think deeply about the procedure they have just performed. "What is the effect of heating the solution? Does heating at this temperature affect primarily the protein, or does it affect the DNA? How?" Answers to such questions can be deduced using information presented earlier in lecture or obtained from library or Internet sources.

The responsibilities for lecture and lab are equally divided between two instructors, one with training in molecular biology, the other with training in cell biology. The lecture typically enrolls 105-125 students and meets three times per week. The lab is optional but enrolls 95-100 students. Five lab sections, each with a maximum of 20 students, meet once per week for three hours. The classroom and the lab are equipped for Internet access, and the department houses a computer laboratory with 15 Pentium machines.

EDUCATIONAL THEORIES

Teaching multiple lab sections that require timely preparation of living cells combined with the workload of grading weekly homework sets for 100 students makes the lab course burdensome for instructors who are also teaching the lecture course. I thought that computer tools should be able to relieve some aspects of this burden, while providing more effective means for students to learn.

I approached the use of computer resources with the idea that all education involves communication between faculty and students. Computer tools clearly provide opportunities for enhanced communication, but they supplement rather than replace traditional teaching modes (lectures, textbooks, laboratory mentoring, or one-on-one advising). Computer tools also offer unique opportunities in biological sciences. For example, computer graphics and graphic simulations allow dynamic processes to be represented visually in a way that cannot be achieved with pencil or chalk. Com-

puter tools also allow students to access tutorials and practice remedial skills in private, without the embarrassment of asking a peer or faculty member for help.

I believe that students learn best by applying and practicing what they have learned. In biology, one way to accomplish this is to have students answer word problems that force them to apply theory to familiar situations. I have found that providing data from real experiments and having students draw conclusions is an excellent exercise. Similarly, describing experiments that were set up incorrectly (replicating common lab errors) and asking students to identify what went wrong can enhance their understanding of major techniques and foster the critical skills a practicing scientist needs. We do not have graduate students to serve as TAs or graders. Thus, the challenge is to provide adequate feedback to students so that they can learn from these exercises.

COURSE ACTIVITIES

Email

Email has revolutionized my accessibility. I find that students are very willing to ask questions about the lecture or lab via email; this makes their study time more effective, because they are not hung up on a key aspect of some mechanism or confused about some important detail. Email also facilitates scheduling face-to-face meetings and is a useful way to make general class announcements.

Online Lab Tutorial

Pipetmen are among the most important pieces of equipment that we want students to learn to use in the laboratory course. They are used in modern research laboratories to dispense very small volumes of liquid with accuracy. Students must master the use of pipetmen if they are to succeed in upper-level laboratory courses and if they wish to pursue a research career. Students are instructed in the proper use of the instruments during the first two weeks of lab. Invariably, however, 20%–30% of the class requests refresher explanations at various times throughout the semester. To supplement the in-class instruction, I created online instructions and a tutorial. The first pages at this site include text and photos that identify the key parts of the pipetman and explain those aspects of its function that are important from a user's perspective. In the past, we have found that many students have difficulty dialing in the correct setting so that it delivers the desired volume. The web site provides photos of actual dials on a pipetman, which are set to a variety of volumes. Further, the web site tests the student's ability to read the dials accurately. The volumes selected are those that have given students difficulty and/or illustrate key differences among the pipetmen in the set. A subsequent tutorial gives students practice in this critical step. The final pages include step-by-step instructions for using the pipetman as well as a few "tips for the pros" for getting the greatest accuracy and precision.

Virtual Lab

I have developed an online exercise designed to help students understand and appreciate one of the most important experiments in the field of molecular biology, namely, the experiment that revealed how the information for making millions of different types of antibodies is stored within our genetic material. The exercise is designed as a tutorial. Interspersed within the text are questions that test the student's understanding; an incorrect answer elicits further clarification that directs the students toward the proper answer before proceeding. The tutorial concludes with additional problems that apply and build on the concepts presented. Again incorrect answers elicit responses that guide the student to a correct understanding.

Online Lecture Outlines

Outlines for the lecture course are available at the course web site. These may be printed out before class and used to direct notetaking during lecture. My motivation was to provide a general outline for those students who want one, without having to make paper copies for the many students who might not find an outline useful.

Online Study Problems

I have three sets of study problems that focus on particular methodologies and concepts presented in lecture (more are in development). The questions are designed to reveal common misunderstandings by students. Rather than grading each student's work, I post the answers, with extensive explanation, to the course web site. The answers are posted several days after the problems are assigned. I find the ability to use color and graphics allows me to explain the answers more clearly than I could if the assignments were hand-graded or if a paper answer key were posted. Using HtX, an extensible web development system, makes it easy to turn the answers on or off simply by changing one line in the source file.

Relevant Web Sites

The course web pages include a list of hot links to other web sites. Many of these have kinetic graphic images that illustrate key concepts from lecture. Others are good for reviewing foundational information, such as basic chemistry. Still others are selected to illustrate the tremendous wealth of good information available on the web.

Internet Search. In the lab, we include several exercises that help students to practice web-searching skills. We direct them to the home page for the Howard Hughes Medical Foundation, where they are asked to search for the safety and disposal information pertaining to methanol, a chemical that they use in the laboratory. Knowing where to find such safety information will be an ongoing need for someone who wants to pursue a research or teaching career in cell/molecular biology.

LESSONS LEARNED

I have found that construction of related web pages has been simplified by using a HtX, a web development program that was created by a member of the Oberlin faculty and is available free to educational institutions. The program converts text in a source file into a set of related HTML pages. The advantage of HtX over other web page builders is that all of the linked pages have a similar look; this look can be formatted according to any of several existing styles, which, in turn, can be personalized. The application automatically manages the various pages making up a web site. I chose this program because it can be used to produce interactive documents, hyper-programmed texts, slide-show lectures that can subsequently be converted to lecture notes, and it can manage cross-linked, multiply-sorted information, such as college activity calendars—all with less effort than using HTML directly. Additional information about HtX can be viewed at the HtX home page: http://www.cs.oberlin.edu/htx/.

Although I have identified dozens of hot link web sites that are relevant to my course, I have discovered that most students do not have the time to utilize these resources. Therefore, I point out in lecture the handful that I think every student should view, because they significantly enhance a lecture or lab topic.

Students love having the study problems and answer keys posted online so that they are accessible whenever or wherever the student is studying. I have noticed that there is a significant improvement in how well students understand the concepts that have been fleshed out through these exercises. In previous years, as many as 40% of students might incorrectly answer exam questions testing a homework concept. Since introduction of the online answer keys, that percentage has dropped to around 5%.

Student evaluations this past semester included specific questions pertaining to the course web site. Of the 93 responses, 58 (62%) students consulted the web site during the semester. Of these 58 students, 48 (or about half the total class) reported that the electronic posting of the "Answers to the Practice Problems" was useful. The syllabus and course policies were also popular among web users (40 students). Fewer students (21) used the "hotlinks to relevant sites," but of these, several spontaneously praised their favorite site. Thirteen students reported that they found the online "Pipetman Tutorial" useful; although small, this number does indicate that the site was moderately successful in reaching the estimated 20%-30% of students whom we predicted might desire supplemental training. The Virtual Lab has not yet been made available to students and so it has not been possible to get feedback regarding its educational benefit.

REFERENCE

Miller, J. E., & Cheetham, R. D. (1990). Teaching freshmen to think: Active learning in introductory biology. *BioScience, 40* (5), 388-391.

CONTACT INFORMATION

Robin Treichel
Associate Professor of Biology
Oberlin College
Department of Biology
Oberlin, OH 44074-1082
Email: Robin.Treichel@Oberlin.edu
WWW:
www.oberlin.edu/~rtreiche/Homepage/robin.html,
http://www.oberlin.edu/~rtreiche/b213/b213.html,
http://www.oberlin.edu/~rtreiche/pipette/pipets.html,
http://www.oberlin.edu/~rtreiche/iggenes/iggenes.html,
http://www.cs.oberlin.edu/htx/, home page:
http://www.oberlin.edu/~rtreiche/Homepage/robin
    html
Phone: (440) 775-8015
Fax: (440) 775-8960

David A. Damassa, Walid El-Bermani, Myra Rufo, and
Robert F. Willson, Tufts University

Anatomy is simply defined as the study of the shape and structure of organisms and their parts. Under this subterfuge of simplicity lies a monumental endeavor for both students and faculty in the health professions. It is estimated that the language of medicine comprises at least 10,000 terms, and a majority of these are encountered in anatomy courses (Educational Affairs Committee, American Association of Clinical Anatomists, 1996). Thorough knowledge of anatomical terminology is required for localizing disease processes and for clear and precise communication among health practitioners. In addition, practitioners are expected to comprehend the three-dimensional structure of the living human organism and to use this understanding to properly diagnose and successfully treat their patients.

Gross anatomy is the study of structures that are visible without magnification and constitutes a significant part of the first-year curriculum for both medical and dental students at Tufts University. Our gross anatomy courses are team-taught, and both include dissection laboratories. Although the emphasis for the dental students is focused on head and neck anatomy, both courses cover all major systems of the human body.

EDUCATIONAL THEORIES

Traditional courses in gross anatomy consist of lectures and laboratory dissection sessions. Both of these teaching modalities immerse students in the anatomical language and strive to provide an understanding of other facets of human anatomy, including three-dimensional anatomy, functional anatomy, and anatomical variation. During the last 20 years, the importance of diagnostic imaging in medical practice has increased dramatically. Modern imaging techniques, such as computerized tomography (CT) or magnetic resonance imaging (MRI), yield serial, two-dimensional sections (cross sections) of the body that must be related back to the three-dimensional patient. Laboratory dissections are essential for understanding anatomical relationships and variations but do not adequately address all aspects of the mastery of cross-sectional anatomy. Combining web technology with computer imaging provides a clear, easily accessible, and diagnostically relevant means of teaching cross-sectional anatomy. The exercise of visualizing and interpreting cross sections also helps to validate one's understanding of a structure's relationships and its topography in three dimensions.

COMPUTER-ENHANCED TECHNIQUES

By downloading and labeling individual images from the National Library of Medicine's Visible Human project, we prepared a series of study units for different areas of the body: extremities, thorax, abdomen/pelvis, and head/neck. Images were selected by the course faculty, and relevant structures were identified, outlined, and given identifying letters. The images were placed in appropriate radiological orientation, cropped, and enhanced for better viewing on the course web page. Images were provided at two different levels of resolution to facilitate viewing from home via modems. In addition, serial cross sections were reconstructed into a 3-D data set, and movie clips were generated showing object rotation or fly-through. These movie files were also mounted on the web site.

The images were introduced to the students during scheduled laboratory sessions in our Multimedia Resource Center (MRC), a 45-station computer laboratory. Four two-hour sessions were held during the semester. In faculty-led sessions, the students were asked to deduce the identities of labeled structures and to justify their answers. Groups of approximately ten students worked as a team, with two teams assigned to each of the cross sections. At the end of the laboratory period, one member from each of the teams shared their findings with the class. During the student presentations, faculty would introduce radiological images or cases to help students transfer their understanding of the anatomical cross sections to a clinically relevant setting. Following the scheduled sessions, the answers were posted on the web, so students could continue to work with these sections in the library or from home. Students were formally tested on the concepts learned in cross-sectional anatomy as part of their regular anatomy exams.

MEASURED RESULTS

Questions regarding the usefulness of computerized cross-sectional images have been included on medical school course evaluations for the past two years. Response rates to these questions were very high, with more than 90% of the students in each of these two classes responding. The evaluations revealed that the cross-sectional images were used by most of the students. For the first year, only 11% of the respondents indicated that they did not access the images, and for the second year, the percentage of nonusers was 10%. When asked to rate the usefulness of the cross-sectional images on a scale of 1 (not at all) to 5 (definitely), mean ratings for both years were very high (4.2 and 4.4). However, responses to a question on whether the computer laboratory is an effective way of learning indicated a somewhat lower level of enthusiasm. The mean scores on a 5-point scale were 3.7 for the first year and 3.5 for the second.

LESSONS LEARNED

It was not surprising to learn that many students considered web-based delivery systems to be highly effective for the study of cross-sectional images. Virtually all of our students had used web browsers prior to entering medical or dental school. This was also a boon to the faculty, since no computer interface training was required, and discussions could focus immediately on the subject. Comments from the students also reflected the importance of being able to access the images from home and the usefulness of the images in understanding structural relationships.

Scheduling issues surrounding the computer laboratories were found to be an important consideration. The MRC only accommodates half the class, and no extra class hours were provided for the study of cross sections. Therefore, computer laboratories were scheduled during dissection labs, with half of the class assigned to each. Several students expressed concern that we were sacrificing precious dissection time for computer-based instruction. This may have influenced their views on the usefulness of the computer laboratory sessions. In addition, the faculty found that the computer laboratories were more effective if scheduled after the students had completed the dissection of a given region rather than running concurrently with the regional dissection. It was much easier to use the cross sections to refine perceptions of structural relationships than to teach anatomical concepts and terminology. Overall, our experience was positive, and we expect to increase our use of computer-based teaching methods as improvements are made in software and hardware for web-based visualization and interaction with anatomical structures.

REFERENCE

Educational Affairs Committee, American Association of Clinical Anatomists. (1996). A clinical anatomy curriculum for the medical student of the 21st century: Gross anatomy. *Clinical Anatomy, 9*, 71-99.

CONTACT INFORMATION

David A. Damassa, Professor Anatomy and Cellular Biology
Director of Medical Information Technology
Tufts University School of Medicine
136 Harrison Avenue
Boston, MA 02111
Email: Ddamassa@infonet.tufts.edu
WWW:
    http://iris3.med.tufts.edu/medgross/gross.html
Dental Gross Anatomy:
    http://iris3.med.tufts.edu/dentgross/gross.html
Phone: (617) 636-6603
Fax: (617) 636-0375

Harry R. Matthews, University of California, Davis

University teachers can be divided into those who espouse the lecture approach and those who prefer group discussion, of which problem-based learning is a subset. The strengths of lectures include an organized approach to the subject matter and a comprehensive coverage of topics deemed appropriate by the instructor. The strengths of discussions include better context and more active student involvement. I have developed the concept of virtual lectures, now evolving into a virtual course, which aims to combine the advantages of both approaches to improve university-level teaching.

The prototype course, a class of 95 to 102 students, has been given once and is now in progress for the second time. The course is part of a series on molecular and cell biology. The students are at the beginning of their first year in medical school and come with a wide range of backgrounds. They are intelligent and motivated to learn medicine but not necessarily molecular biology. The new approach was evaluated by comparing examination results with historical performance and by a detailed, anonymous student questionnaire. The results show that factual and conceptual learning was at least as effective as with the traditional methods and that student acceptance was very high. Students believed their intellectual skills improved, but this has not been evaluated objectively or historically.

IDEAS BEHIND THE COURSE DESIGN

Our students do well on our examinations and on those set by the National Board of Medical Examiners. Nevertheless, when they have completed their two years of basic science and move to the clinical environment, they often feel that their basic science knowledge is irrelevant, and clinical instructors complain that the students lack basic science knowledge. More likely, the students lack the ability to take a general principle and apply it to a specific situation.

Many of our students learn very well visually and aurally. In my own lecturing, I found that illustrations,

particularly scientific cartoons and animations that illustrated concepts visually, helped students to understand quickly and completely. Encouraged by student feedback, my lectures incorporated more and more animated graphics. It seemed a small step from showing the graphics with live narration to showing both graphics and narration on the computer. Students could choose their own pace through the material as well as their own time and place for studying. Second, once the transformation to the computer was complete, my time was freed to focus on the development of the intellectual skills that I feel our students need badly. This time was used for small group, case-based discussions. Unlike traditional problem-based learning, these groups have no responsibility for content because content is provided by the virtual lectures on the com-

FIGURE 33.1

VALUE FOR STUDYING: VIRTUAL LECTURES OR TEXTBOOK

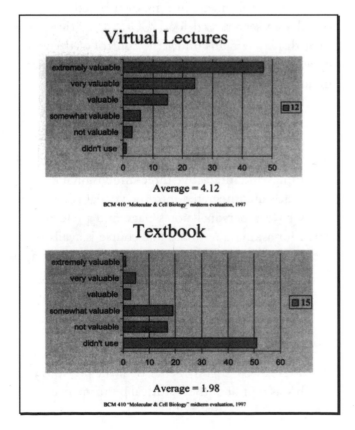

puter. Thus, they can be truly student-based, without focus on specific learning issues or concepts, so long as the students are practicing their critical thinking, deduction, and out-of-context recall skills.

COMPUTER TECHNIQUES

The complete course content is now provided exclusively through a web browser running on a computer. I have in-person office hours, but students rarely use them. Students attend the small-group discussions, but these are oriented toward specific clinical cases that may or may not be germane to the topics in the virtual lectures.

The course is a prototype for a MoBy Virtual Course that uses a database that resides on a web server. The database integrates all aspects of a course including content, assignments, and examinations. The structure allows instructors to select the parts they want to use and ignore the rest, which is then hidden from both instructor and student until the instructor wants to extend the application. The course content is both structured and flexible. Many different types of multimedia can be accommodated, and the prototype includes animation, video, sound, hypertext, and interactive three-dimensional molecular models. In the prototype, the multimedia files are distributed over additional web servers and local CD-ROM drives while their display remains under the control of the central database. This architecture provides good performance under heavy load and over standard phone lines.

The virtual lectures include animated graphics, sound, and text. The text is hyperlinked to a glossary, and the lectures are linked to a bank of self-test questions. Additional tutorials and advanced topics as well as readings and interactive three-dimensional molecular models are integrated into the virtual course. Students have a personal notes page and preformatted email for asking questions. The course is available on the Internet at http://trc.ucdavis.edu/coursepages/bcm410a/.

MEASURED RESULTS

Examination results from the first virtual offering of BCM410A were slightly better than the previous year, which was typical of the historical performance in this course. The format and difficulty of the examination did not change, so I conclude that the students learned at least as well from the virtual lectures as from the real lectures. In addition, the average time each student spent per lecture was about two hours (students' own estimate), which compares favorably with the three hours my institution assigns for each normal lecture (one hour in lecture and two hours outside). Learning, therefore, was also time-efficient. Anonymous student evaluations showed strong acceptance of the virtual lectures. Figure 33.1 compares the virtual lectures with the available textbooks in their value for learning. The students expressed an overwhelming preference for the virtual lectures.

Students cited main strengths and weaknesses when asked for a narrative evaluation of the virtual lectures. Strengths clearly outweighed weaknesses, and the three most important features were:

1) Ability to choose one's own pace

2) Visuals

3) Ability to back up and repeat sections

The students believed that the small group discussions helped them develop their thinking skills. In narrative evaluations of the small groups, the three main points revealed by textual analysis were

1) Liked working with other students

2) Liked the application of biochemistry to medicine

3) Liked interacting with a clinician

Figure 33.1

THE GROUPS WERE VERY STUDENT CENTERED

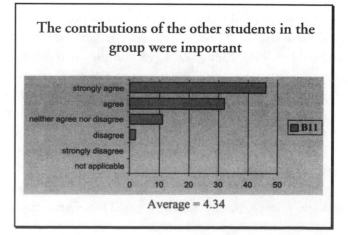

The contributions of the other students in the group were important

Average = 4.34

Interactive Learning

Figure 33.2 shows that the discussions were highly student-centered.

The full evaluation results are available on the web at http://trc.ucdavis.edu/coursepages/bcm410a/evaluations/.

LESSONS LEARNED

Students like a properly developed multimedia, web-based course better than a textbook or written course syllabus. Students prefer to ask questions by email rather than to come to office hours, but students like interacting with the professor in small group, student-centered discussions.

The biggest problem we noted was getting students' home computers set up to run the virtual lectures. We approached this by changing the structure of the computer materials and switching from a largely client-based approach to a largely server-based approach. The server-based approach has been very successful so far, and by using a distributed system for delivering the multimedia files, we have avoided performance problems. Students can now choose either a Macintosh or a Windows client. We still have difficulties, but now these are due to students' computers needing repair and/or upgrade, rather than to installing the application.

The system in use now keeps track of each individual student's use of each part of the course materials. We will begin analyzing this data and expect to learn more about how the students are using the material and how that correlates with their examination results.

CONTACT INFORMATION

Harry R. Matthews
Professor
University of California, Davis
MED: BIOL.CHEM.
Davis, CA 95616-8635
Email: hrmatthews@ucdavis.edu
WWW: http://moby.ucdavis.edu/HRM/,
http://trc.undavis.edu/coursepages/bcm410a/,
http://trc.ucdavis.edu/coursepages/bcm410a
    /evaluations/
Phone: (530) 752-3570
Fax: (530) 752-3516

 Patient Assessment: Physical Examination Skills

James A. Karboski, University of Texas, Austin

The role of the pharmacist is rapidly changing from the traditional focus on drug distribution to direct patient care. This new role involves hands-on assessment of patients at a level similar to that of a nurse practitioner or physician's assistant. Much of patient assessment is evaluating what can be seen, heard, and felt. The frustration of trying to explain to students what something looks like, feels like, or sounds like led to the development of a multimedia approach to classroom instruction in a patient assessment course.

EDUCATIONAL PHILOSOPHY

In most traditional assessment courses, students attend lectures that focus on gross anatomy, physical examination terms, and description of techniques. This is generally followed by a laboratory section, where students practice assessment techniques on each other.

I was struck by the number of illustrations and photographs in my preparatory materials. I had two options: 1) Take the material to our Learning Resources Center and have color slides made, or 2) scan the material and import it into my Microsoft PowerPoint presentations. Slides were going to cost me about $100–$200 for the course, and use of the scanner was free. I also wanted to distribute copies of the graphics to students for use in the laboratory and as study aids. These two concerns led me to begin the process of developing media for in-class presentation.

While it would have been easier to offer the more traditional lecture, I felt that the gains in student interest and learning would be worth the effort invested in bringing multimedia elements into the classroom. This led to the incorporation of digital video, digital audio, animation, and virtual reality elements into my classroom presentations.

COMPUTER-ENHANCED TECHNIQUES

CD-Quality Sound

Many of the skills involved in patient assessment require the identification and differentiation of sounds. In my lectures, I use digitized heart and lung sounds to demonstrate the differences between rales and wheezes, midsystolic clicks and third heart sounds, as well as many others. These sounds are digitized from either CD or cassette sources, converted to QuickTime movie files, and imported to PowerPoint for classroom use. I can play these sounds side-by-side to help students hear the subtle differences between normal and abnormal heart and lung sounds. These collections are then made available to students via the course web page. I encourage students to turn the speaker volume down and use their stethoscopes to listen to the sounds as they will hear them when listening to patients.

High-Resolution Digital Video

Since most students in this course are young and in relatively good health, there are very few abnormal findings for students to experience. To broaden the range of responses to the examination techniques they are learning, I have started bringing digital video clips that highlight abnormal findings into the classroom and the laboratory. I record patients whom I care for at a local hospital with a digital video camera. This can be imported to a video editing package, such as Adobe Premiere, and saved as high-resolution, QuickTime movies. Because of recent advances in digital video compression, these movies are very portable and will soon be streamed via the Internet for students to review outside of class.

Interactive Drills

To maximize the effective use of time in the laboratory sections, interactive drills and quizzes were implemented. Using Macromedia authorware, I have developed simple drills to reinforce the skills described in class. One drill asks the student to drag a marker to the correct location of various anatomical landmarks. If the student drags the marker to the correct location, confirmation is heard. If the student drags the marker to an incorrect location, the marker returns to its original position, and the student is prompted to try again.

Animations

Animating graphics to demonstrate a dynamic process is one of the strengths of computer-generated multimedia. I use animations to show how blood travels through the blood vessels of the heart, how turbulent movement of blood through a damaged heart valve results in an audible murmur, and the sequence of palpating the chest wall for palpable murmurs. Out-of-the-box animation programs, such as Macromedia Director, simplify and speed the process of developing animations for the classroom or web distribution.

Graphics

Since patient assessment is such a visual topic, I use graphics extensively in the course. I can save a lot of time describing something that can easily be shown. Graphs, charts, pictures, and photographs are all used to help fix an image in the student's mind that is both correct and long-lasting. I use a flatbed scanner connected to my computer for capturing images, and Adobe Photoshop to edit scanned images. These images are used in classroom presentations and included in materials distributed to the students.

QuickTime VR Movies

A particularly useful tool for teaching/reviewing gross anatomy is Apple QuickTime VR (virtual reality). A series of pictures can easily be stitched together to create a three-dimensional object that can be manipulated on-screen. For this course, I created a 3-D heart that I use in class to review the heart chambers and coronary artery anatomy. This movie can be linked to another movie or graphic.

MEASURED RESULTS

No formal evaluation of the impact of multimedia elements has been performed, but student comments have been universally favorable. While at first students are interested in the bells and whistles that multimedia brings to the classroom, their comments on the course evaluation describe how valuable this approach was to their ability to learn the material. I've gotten into trouble with a few of my colleagues who also teach in the course when students ask during lecture to play an example of the sound they are talking about, or show a picture of how something would appear in a patient.

Skeptical faculty will often ask if I can prove to them that the students in my portion of this course are actually learning more of the content. I usually respond that the data don't matter to me. When I'm lecturing about heart sounds and I play examples of the sounds that I've been trying to explain to them, the looks of acknowledgment, the nods of understanding, and the smiles of interest validate the time and effort spent in development. Even if it only results in more interested and excited students, that's good enough for me.

LESSONS LEARNED

- Don't force content into the computer purely for the sake of having it there. Some information is better presented on a chalkboard or overhead projector.

- Wait for good software tools to simplify the development process. I remember Apple Computer's first attempt at VR software: It required command, line-style scripting. The newest VR tool is a very simple drag and click tool that any computer user can easily master.

- Make the content available for students to review outside class. Some students need more time than others to master material.

- Identify multimedia experts in your area to consult before and during the construction of your multimedia projects. This can save a lot of time otherwise spent with your nose buried in the software manual.

CONTACT INFORMATION

James A. Karboski
Lecturer
College of Pharmacy
University of Texas at Austin
Austin, TX 78712-1026
Email: karboski@mail.utexas.edu

Vignette 35 — Interactive Biochemistry

Charles M. Grisham, University of Virginia

Two-dimensional drawings and traditional ball-and-stick models of molecules are severely limited teaching aids for students in biological and organic chemistry. The processes of molecular interaction are the important notions to grasp, and static depictions of structures do precious little to advance students' capacity to visualize and understand these dynamic changes.

The Interactive Biochemistry course web site includes a comprehensive library of three-dimensional renderings of molecules. Students can rotate and manipulate images to see and understand their chemical composition and their interaction with other agents. The site also includes interactive programs that simulate chemical interaction and lead students through complex problem solving exercises. In these tutorials, students use mouse clicks to simulate how one molecule reacts with another. A correct match generates an animated sequence of the real life reaction.

IDEAS BEHIND THE COURSE DESIGN

This undergraduate biochemistry course is a year-long sequence that is critical for all students intending to pursue careers in medicine and biomedical research. Some 125 students typically enroll in the course, which is generally agreed to be among the most challenging offered to undergraduates at the university.

To assure that the students had ready access to essential educational materials, I co-wrote a biochemistry textbook that was published in 1994. I was frustrated not only by the limited number of drawings and photographs in the textbook, but also by their inability to tell a chemical story. In creating the Interactive Biochemistry materials, I set about filling the gaps with the following specific pedagogical aims:

- To deepen students' understanding of the subject matter, I recognized that although some students were able to grasp abstract concepts fairly easily through readings and lectures, many, if not most, needed to see the concepts in action. The digitized materials render the abstract visible in ways that two-dimensional texts cannot.

- To engage students through interactive exercises, the interactive tutorials and drawings give students the opportunity to gain a more practical, even tactile, appreciation for complex chemical processes. The web site talks back to students and coaches them along to correct interpretations.

- To allow students to focus out-of-class time in more productive ways in working through the exercises on the web site, students are able to tailor study sessions to meet their needs. They may linger on particular sections with which they are having difficulty, manipulating molecules and using the tutorials time and again until the concepts are clear to them. The focus, the time, and the direction are theirs.

COURSE ACTIVITIES

The Interactive Biochemistry web site is used in conjunction with my traditional textbook and in-class lectures. The slides from my PowerPoint lectures are available to students. An adjunct to traditional teaching, the Interactive Biochemistry materials are used exclusively as out-of-class supplements. The renderings and tutorials are extensive and complement a substantial portion of the concepts covered throughout the year. As the class works through topics that have digital corollaries, I alert them to the web site components.

Certain exercises on the site are designed to help students understand and make decisions about various chemical sequences. Others are created with the primary purpose of helping students visualize molecular structures. All components are intended to encourage students to reason through the images and problems and then to reevaluate their thinking.

MEASURED RESULTS

The highest quiz average in my course was achieved on a section of material that depends most heavily on the web site. The average scores for that particular quiz have doubled since I created the interactive tutorials. In addition, student response to the exercises has been extremely positive—they're asking for more.

LESSONS LEARNED

Creating digitized instructional materials is an enormous, time-consuming process. We struggle to stay ahead of the student programmers who work for us. My reliance on a large team of students compounds the problem and amplifies the amount of time I have to spend writing scripts for them. One potential difficulty in using student programmers is the unpredictability of their schedules: Exam periods, vacations, and the like can cause serious delays in development of the educational materials.

Still, the ready supply of student programmers from the computer science department is the key factor in my success. The students are eager, technically savvy, and very inexpensive by traditional market standards. They are delighted at the chance to help create a substantial, sophisticated product, and those who have graduated have parlayed the experience into interesting and lucrative job offers.

CONCLUSION

The creation of digital complements to in-class lectures can require an enormous investment of time; even if they are not writing the programs, faculty must assure that their design concepts are correctly interpreted and executed by their employees. Because I have found interactive materials useful, I have undertaken an expansion of the web site and creation of a compact disk with funding from the National Science Foundation.

CONTACT INFORMATION

Charles M. Grisham
Professor of Chemistry
Department of Chemistry
University of Virginia
Charlottesville, VA 22903
Email: cmg@virginia.edu
WWW: http://cti.itc.Virginia.EDU/~cmg/
Phone: (804) 924-7012
Fax: (804) 924-3710

Vignette 36   The Virtual Fetal Pig Dissection

Earl W. Fleck, Whitman College

With few exceptions, biologists are persuaded that the only way to learn the structure of an organism is to dissect it, accompanied by a well-written laboratory guide and a patient, observant instructor. However, owing to the resistance of some students to animal dissections and the need of others to have review material, I became convinced that I must provide my students with substitute or supplementary material for these dissections. Thus, as an initial effort to test this conviction, I created an animated program that presents a Virtual Fetal Pig Dissection. We call it VPD (http://www.whitman.edu/offices_departments/biology/vpd/).

I started this project with a senior biology major, who is highly skilled in computer use, and a local retired physician. Later, another senior biology major and a multimedia specialist from our computer center joined the team. The talents brought to bear on the project have allowed a far more sophisticated and appropriate approach than what I might have done on my own. The physician has a depth of anatomical knowledge far superior to mine, while the multimedia specialist brings sophisticated and dedicated computer animation talent. Moreover, the two seniors who performed the dissection in lab only a few years ago bring a student's perspective to bear as well as fine computer and photography skills. The Howard Hughes Medical Institute funded this effort.

IDEAS BEHIND THE COURSE DESIGN

My introductory biological principles course covers material typical of any introductory college-level biology course. Students receive a rigorous introduction to the molecular, cellular, and physiological processes of life. I use a three-week series of labs on the fetal pig as a supplement to the lecture discussions of whole animal physiology. On my class evaluations, students cite this section of the lab as the most interesting and exciting exercise. However, each year I have several students who refuse to participate owing to ethical or moral qualms; they have a strong aversion to performing any dissection on an animal, especially one that looks so much like a human. Various antivivisection agencies provide educational material as substitutes for a dissection. For example, videos of a fetal pig dissection and molded plastic models of pigs are available at modest costs. Unfortunately, my students and I find these substitutes inadequate; the videos are of poor quality and lack interactivity, and the molded models lack detail. Hence, those students who refuse to do the dissection miss a valuable learning experience. Further, the students who perform the dissection in lab complain that they lack a way of reviewing the material once they complete their dissection and prepare for the lab practical exam. Clearly, here are opportunities to enhance the education of my students using electronic multimedia tools and provide a measure of interactivity.

COMPUTER-ENHANCED TECHNIQUES

When I initially started the Virtual Pig Dissection (VPD) project about three years ago, I intended to use HTML format for the project—a rather crude technical conception. However, when Macromedia Shockwave became available a few years ago, I decided to use Macromedia Director as the basis for the interactive animations. Director provides the software tools to create animations, while the Shockwave plug-in allows a browser to play Director animations over the web. Using Director and Shockwave allows much more sophisticated and dynamic interaction between simulation and user. The drawback is that Director, especially higher level use, demands quite high technical expertise.

Initially, my team spent much of a summer preparing high-quality 35 mm photos of a fetal pig dissection. The following fall and spring, we organized the photos, scanned appropriate images, formatted the images using Adobe Photoshop, and completed a few more dissections to fill in gaps in the coverage. More recently, we have switched from a 35 mm camera to a digital camera. This allowed us to upload images directly to our computer. Unfortunately, the image quality of our Kodak DC120 Zoom Digital Camera is less than that of the images taken with our 35 mm SLR camera. I am unsure whether this represents the poorer quality of a digital camera or our inexperience in its use.

After we took most of the photos, we embarked on the next and most important step: creation of a storyboard for the first module. A storyboard is a simple method of mocking up the animation and making organizational decisions using static frames. We prepared rough drawings of the dissection photos we wished to use. To these images we appended labels, text, and descriptions of the transitions from one panel to the next. We worked on this storyboard until we were satisfied that it represented the content we thought essential in the order that was appropriate for the students.

Once we finalized the storyboard, we began integrating the images into the animations for our first module. This required gaining command of the Director programming language, Lingo. After we created an animation that roughly represented the storyboard, we played through the animation and operated the interactive elements. Often, we markedly changed text, enhanced labels and highlights, and changed the order of presentation after viewing our efforts. One beneficial aspect of Lingo script in Macromedia Director is the ease of moving elements of the animation once you construct them.

I decided to reduce our task into modules that roughly correspond to the main physiological systems (e.g., the digestive, respiratory, and excretory systems). At this time, we have four modules of about ten completed with three more in the final stages of completion. Each of these modules has high quality images of the dissection coupled with appropriate text and links to further information or additional dissection views.

Mated with each module is a student self-assessment activity. Most of the questions are objective, but all make use of graphics from our pig dissection image file. For example, in one exercise on anatomical reference terms, students view an image of a pig and apply correct orientation labels. In another exercise on the digestive system, students match a series of definitions with the appropriate structures. Although this sounds like a simple matching quiz, there is immediate feedback. In a third exercise that focuses on the circulatory system, students place the names of structures in an appropriate loop on a schematic diagram representing the pattern of circulatory flow.

MEASURED OUTCOMES

Although the project remains incomplete, we uploaded each module when finished and provided access to our students. We now have four semesters of experience using these modules in my introductory biology principles lab. On a supplemental student evaluation form that contains specific queries on the course, I ask students to indicate which of the half dozen computer-enhanced learning opportunities they consider most beneficial. Although exact percentages vary from semester to semester, students rank this enhancement as the best computer learning aid available. These survey results are supported by an analysis of the hits to the VPD web page, information that is available from our computer center. Our VPD site sustains a large number of hits from college sites outside my teaching lab.

Although I envisioned student use only for those withdrawing from the dissection exercise and for review just prior to the lab final, I find that students make extensive use of the animation during the lab period to preview the dissection on the computer before they actually perform the incisions. They tell me that they find the interplay between the actual dissection and the computer dissection very helpful as they embark on their first serious dissection.

LESSONS LEARNED

First, the students who opt out of the dissection are grateful for the chance to view quality images with matching labels and text. Although the animation is markedly inferior to performing dissection, they feel they learn something. Further, these students now feel more part of the class, since they have not completely withdrawn from the exercise. Second, most students report that they use the animation as a review for the exam. Third, use of the animation during the dissection exercise was a pleasant unintended consequence. Clearly, in my view, this has been a successful addition to my course.

Finally, I learned that having this animation on the web has led to use by students and faculty outside the college. Analyses of the hits to the site show that a significant fraction is from educational sites around the country and the world. This is gratifying, as it shows the power of the web to span large distances.

There are some serious drawbacks in developing such exercises. The animation is still incomplete in spite of spending two years on the project. The demands on my time—to supervise the preparation of high-quality images, to manipulate the digital images, and to write Lingo scripts for Macromedia Director animations—is tremendous. Without the help of a dedicated computer center multimedia specialist, I know that the product would be of much lower quality.

ACKNOWLEDGMENTS

I wish to thank Dr. Robert Schaeffer, Miso Mitkovski, Ben Houston, and Mike Horn for their help on the VPD project.

CONTACT INFORMATION

Earl W. Fleck
Provost and Dean of the College
Centenary College of Louisiana
P. O. Box 41188
Shreveport, LA 71134-1185
Email: efleck@centenary.edu
WWW:
http://www.whitman.edu/offices_departments
    /biology/vpd/
Phone: (318) 869-5104

SOCIAL SCIENCES

Vignette 37 | Disciplining Commonsense Explanations of Communication with Structured Online Dialogues

Sally Jackson, Stacy Wolski, Joseph Bonito, and Leah Polcar, University of Arizona

One challenge faced in teaching communication as a social science is to get students to reflect on their naive theories in light of contradicting perspectives and to close the gap between these naive theories and social scientific principles. Pretheoretical understandings are common in other fields as well. In science education, researchers have shown how these pretheoretical understandings can interfere with learning, by motivating rejection of contradictory material or reinterpretation of the material to make it consistent with prior beliefs (Chan, Burtis, & Bereiter, 1997). This is especially likely to happen when instruction allows the student's exposure to new material to be largely passive and unintegrated with commonsense thought. It is less likely to happen when instruction is designed to call attention explicitly to the contradiction between commonsense beliefs and expert beliefs.

Communication 280 (Laboratory Methods) and 281 (Field Methods) have the difficult curricular task of convincing students that theoretical explanations of communication processes grounded in careful observation and analysis are in some sense better than the commonsense explanations that follow from their naive theories. The general expectation is that by the end of this sequence of required courses, communication majors will be able to reason as social scientists, employing the skills needed to recognize the difference between commonsense and expert explanations. Students are required to practice the evaluation of both types of reasoning against some disciplined standard, such as coherence or consistency with observational evidence. Most students beginning communication study have no expectation of having to learn these skills, and their surprise at being required to do so is an additional challenge for the teacher.

CONFRONTING COMMONSENSE: A RATIONALE FOR STRUCTURED DIALOGUES

Overcoming pretheoretical beliefs about a subject requires, at a minimum 1) getting students to articulate their initial understandings, 2) presenting a challenge to that understanding, 3) guiding students toward more sophisticated understandings, and 4) inducing them to reflect on the difference between the original understanding and the achieved understanding.

Various dialogue protocols will serve this purpose. One well-known protocol used particularly in physics instruction is the Peer Learning Sequence developed by Eric Mazur (1997). In this protocol, students are presented with a physics problem, asked to commit to an answer and to try to persuade another student of the correctness of this answer, given the opportunity to revise their initial answer, and then shown the correct solution. There is no chance here to miss the contradiction between a correct solution and an incorrect conjecture and the reasoning leading to it.

In Communication 280 and 281, each of which enrolls over 200 students, we have used in-class dialogue protocols of this kind, but our greatest gains come from the incorporation of protocols into online lessons.

STRUCTURED ONLINE DIALOGUES

To support routine use of structured online dialogues, it was necessary to create lesson templates that could be reused with varied content. CGI scripts written in Perl were developed to support five distinct dialogue types: 1) an online version of the popular one-minute essay;

2) an online recitation (question/answer/correction/response); 3) an online debate; 4) a virtual peer sequence, modeled after the Mazur protocol; and 5) a standard text/quiz tutorial. The recitation, debate, and virtual peer protocols are most relevant to the specific intellectual tasks at the heart of these two courses, but all five protocols create interactive lessons that take student responses and continue adaptively (Jackson & Madison, 1997).

Supplying different content to the templates allows for creation of a rich and varied set of lessons. We implemented these within a web course construction kit that allows instructors to build new lessons as often as desired using forms that publish to the web instantaneously. Within Communication 280 and 281, we have developed a large library of online lessons, allowing us to assign two or three each week.

In a typical online lesson, a student is presented with a problem or controversy and asked for some form of explanation. This format allows for the student to provide either a commonsense or an expert explanation. Throughout the lesson, the student is given opportunities to develop more sophisticated explanations based on provided scientific evidence. For example, in one lesson, students are asked whether they think rap music might have the effect, as many people claim, of encouraging hostility or violence against women. Whatever position the student takes, the lesson continues with several stages of counterconsiderations involving data and disciplined reasoning. Students denying that rap music breeds misogyny are shown the results of an experiment in which men exposed to rap music for an hour behaved more aggressively toward a female partner than men exposed to neutral music, and students are asked to explain the results.

In another set of lessons, students are asked to judge whether a speech by President Clinton is or is not liberal. In the first lesson, they are supplied with the speech text and asked to rate each paragraph. In the next, they are given a statistical summary of the class's ratings and required to generate a final judgment of the speech as a whole. Students who judge the speech to be liberal are reminded that most of the paragraphs were rated conservative or neutral by a majority of raters, while those who judged the speech as not liberal are reminded that more paragraphs were rated as liberal than as any other category.

Additional counterconsiderations are presented to try to show students that the classification of the speech as liberal or conservative is not a simple matter of measuring opinions of the individual paragraphs and aggregating these into a final judgment.

In the best of these lessons, the culminating step is not simply the revelation of a correct answer but some form of reflection on the gap between a commonsense response and a disciplined response. In the rap music lesson, this culminating step reflects on how political and aesthetic preferences shape our beliefs about factual issues. In the speech-rating lesson, the culminating step reflects on the role of aggregated opinion data in justification of expert judgments.

This is a point we make even more explicitly in other lessons, where self-interest is purposely engaged as a bias. We draw attention to the possibility of using disciplined reasoning strategies to control the biases all of us bring to everyday decisions and judgments. In a series of lessons on the moral and practical consequences of workplace surveillance, for example, students are first asked to debate whether employers should monitor their employees, using the debate protocol. Students are then asked to examine the debate for subordinate issues that could be settled by reference to data (recitation protocol). Finally, students are given the opportunity to reflect more abstractly on how disciplined argument plays a role in questions that first appear as mere matters of opinion (essay protocol). In addition to reflecting the gap between commonsense and scientific reasoning, a focus on the limited but important role of empirical evidence in value conflicts is central to this lesson series.

OUTCOMES

In the first year, we gathered survey data on student opinions of online lessons and found overwhelming agreement that the lessons were valuable. Of those students surveyed, 96% agreed that "the lessons added an important component to the course"; on a scale from 1 (strong disagreement) to 5 (strong agreement), the average rating was 4.4. Students generally disagreed that the online lessons created difficulties: 68% disagreed that "the online lessons presented too many technical problems to be worth the effort," and 79% disagreed that "having to use the World Wide Web was an obstacle to learning." The average ratings on these two items were 2.3 and 2.1.

Since then, we have been gathering data from standard instructional evaluations which unfortunately contain no quantitative scales assessing the online lessons. However, the online lessons are important enough to the students that over 40% of free response comments in both courses focus on this topic. The frequency of comments attests to the importance of the lessons, and the evaluative content attests to their effectiveness. In the most recent evaluations available for Communication 280, over 90% of the comments were positive; in Communication 281, 70% were positive.

After three years of development and experimentation with structured online dialogues, we believe them to be the most important element of these critical courses and are continuing to phase them into this key course sequence.

Lessons Learned

Protocols of the kinds we have used have also been evaluated in standard face-to-face interaction in a wide range of other subjects (e.g., Kuhn, Shaw, & Felton, 1997). We have reason to believe that the incorporation of structured online dialogues would be beneficial in any subject where the aim is to develop knowledge that can support explanation—at least throughout the sciences and social sciences.

A year after introducing structured online dialogues into our own classes, we made the lesson templates available as a campus-wide instructional computing resource, within a web kit known as POLIS (http://www.u.arizona.edu/ic/polis). POLIS has now supported several hundred different courses at the University of Arizona and an unknown number at other schools and universities. In fall 1998, about 80 courses were registered with the system.

Structured dialogue can be worked into instruction with or without online technology. However, certain features of online environments offer special advantages for the kinds of protocols we felt necessary to our purposes. To begin with, structured online dialogues can be designed to assure confrontation; in-class alternatives must leave this largely to chance. Structured online dialogues offer unrestricted opportunities to respond; there is no time limit, as there must be in class. Finally, online dialogues eliminate one inhibitor of disagreement and argumentation in face-to-face settings: the standing concern students have for identity and status. Overall, these advantages make it well worthwhile to develop structured dialogues online.

References

Chan, C., Burtis, J., & Bereiter, C. (1997). Knowledge building as a mediator of conflict in conceptual change. *Cognition and Instruction, 15,* 1-40.

Jackson, S., & Madison, C. (1997). Protocols for online learning: A problem of discourse design. Northern Arizona University/Arizona Board of Regents: *http.//star.ucc.nau.edu/~nauweb97/papers/Jackson.html*

Kuhn, D., Shaw, V., & Felton, M. (1997). Effects of dyadic interaction on argumentative reasoning. *Cognition and Instruction, 15,* 287 315.

Mazur, E. (1997). *Peer instruction: A user's manual.* Upper Saddle River, NJ: Prentice Hall.

Contact Information

Sally Jackson
Professor of Communication
University of Arizona
209 Communication Building
Tucson, AZ 85721-0001
Email: sjackson@u.arizona.edu
WWW: www.comm.arizona.edu/sjackson.html
Phone: (520) 621-1366
Fax: (520) 621-5504

It's the Process That Counts! Communication Tools and Techniques for Teaching in the Virtual Classroom

Concetta M. Stewart and Stella F. Shields, Temple University

The first courses we taught online at Temple University were Global Telecommunications, and then Organizational Communication Systems. While these courses may sound quite different, the core of both courses is learning how people communicate in a mediated environment—be it around the world or within a given organization. Consequently, it seemed quite natural to us to take advantage of the opportunity to teach these courses in cyberspace—the emerging community environment. We had already been incorporating Internet tools, such as email, MOOs, and listservs, into our courses for a number of years. Our goal in using these tools is not only for the students to develop a comfort level with them, but also to develop an intimate understanding of these mediated environments along with the issues involved in traversing them.

For sake of simplicity, we will talk primarily about Global Telecommunications, although we use similar tools and techniques in the two courses. The course is offered to both upper-division undergraduates and graduate students; it is conducted almost exclusively on the Internet, using email, conferencing and chat systems, and the listserv. There is an optional face-to-face meeting held monthly to ease the transition from the traditional classroom and to give students a chance to see each other. The course also has a web site, which includes the syllabus and assignment pages.

EDUCATIONAL PHILOSOPHY

Teaching with technology forces one to confront very basic questions about teaching, such as: What do we want students to know when they leave this course? What processes and techniques can help us to achieve those goals? What do the students come into the course knowing? What do the students come into the course expecting? How do our teaching styles fit in these new environments? What about the topic or material lends itself well to this environment? What doesn't? How important are the things that are lost? Can they be

compensated for in other ways? What matters is that we are thinking self-consciously about what it means to teach and to learn.

We determined that knowing how to use information and communication technologies, the impact of these technologies on human interaction, and how to access and evaluate key information sources is important. However, equally important (yet far more complex) is how to develop an understanding of international and intercultural communication as components of human interaction. We needed to look more closely at how we could actually teach these people-related issues in what is typically thought of as an impersonal environment.

COMPUTER-ENHANCED TECHNIQUES

Given our focus on communication processes, the selection and application of communication tools was vital. We realized that we needed to select tools that serve the needs of both individuals and groups, for private as well as public communication (i.e., communication broadcast to the entire class), and for sharing short messages and long documents. Consequently, we analyzed each of the processes we were seeking to support and looked for a best fit with the technologies available:

- Electronic mail is the first and most obvious communication tool for many of these tasks. Since some students still have not used this technology, we ask them to begin sending us messages as soon as they register for the course—that is, before the semester begins.

- Next, we ask them to visit the web site to get the syllabus and list of assignments, because, again, a number of the students were not familiar with surfing the net. From that process, we get a chance to discuss the course goals and processes with the students individually and address any questions and concerns they raise. We also use these first steps as a way to begin building a relationship with the students, which is key to the formation of a sense of community and sharing. It is through these initial processes that we are able to learn about students' interests and backgrounds, which we are then able to integrate into the course.

- At the outset of the term, we ask students to subscribe to the listserv. Through this process, they learn what the listserv is used for, along with some of its features, such as the archive. Right away, we begin using that tool to make class announcements, such as general issues related to the readings or to post the exercises and related URLs. In this forum, the students are able to get questions answered not only by the professors but by other students as well. Since we do encourage group work on the exercises, extended discussions will often ensue once an exercise is posted.

A week or so into the semester, we introduce more elaborate technology systems and processes. For instance, students are required to submit their completed exercises to us via email. While this sounds simple, it is not. The exercises are usually four to six pages in length and are not conveniently read as regular email messages. Consequently, we have asked students to send them as attachments, so that they can be read by our respective word-processing packages.

We have also adopted a threaded conferencing system that supports live chats. We establish conference threads for the weekly discussions so that each group can work on its project. Each student is expected to check the conferencing system several times each week and participate in the discussion threads by reading and posting comments. Obviously, we are able to tell who participates by the postings. However, we can also tell who visits the system just to read, since the system provides a variety of usage statistics. Then we can ask them if they are having problems with either the system or the discussions themselves. This is much like what instructors would do in the face-to-face classroom if they saw a student who obviously had something to contribute but needed to be drawn into the discussion. Students are advised that we will be doing this but that it is more of a shepherding than policing activity. To create a more playful atmosphere on occasion, we'll run contests for the most visits or postings to the conferencing system.

ASSESSED OUTCOMES

The Online Learning Program administers evaluation questionnaires to the students at the end of each semester. While the response has been somewhat low, the responses have been quite positive. Given the fact that the students are already being surveyed and that the response rate is low, we also seek feedback ourselves. We do this in several ways. We monitor both the listserv and conferencing systems regularly to see what issues the students are raising. In this way, we can address concerns and questions immediately as they arise. Also, occasionally we will post questions to the listserv, directly asking students how things are going with the systems and processes. While we have found that many students will post their responses publicly to the listserv, there are some who prefer to email us privately. We have found that students often think that they are the only ones who don't get it, so they feel more comfortable with private communication.

We also use the monthly face-to-face meetings to hold focused discussions on issues related to the course materials, exercises, class processes and procedures—and, of course, the technology. Frequently, these discussions start out slowly, with everyone saying that things are okay. But then either we or one of the students raises a concern or brings up a critical incident, and then the floodgates open. It is this free association and sharing that help us get an understanding of the issues facing us in the virtual classroom. We have found that this semi-structured format works best to address issues for which we do not always have a common language. The students start off by addressing their comments to us, but then they do a lot more sharing with each other—at various times offering praise and critiques. It is through this process that the students are also building their own sense of community.

LESSONS LEARNED

Perhaps the most important thing we have learned is that this new environment is not obvious. Since we have been negotiating cyberspace for some time, we tend to forget what it is like to be a "stranger in a strange land." We are constantly finding ourselves taking a step back and putting ourselves in the students' shoes. One of the course goals is "learning to see the world from behind someone else's eyes," and that goal applies to us as well. The gap between the haves and have-nots is widening. We teach in a public, urban institution. While our students come in eager to learn and work hard, some of them are not learning computer skills in their high schools. We've come to realize that technology support is vital to the success of these courses, even at the most basic level.

Tasks are not as simple as they appear on the surface. So we've learned to be prepared to render lots of help for basic things like subscribing to listservs and attaching document files to email. The Online Learning Program has been most helpful here. In fact, there is now a web site that offers our online students a basic tutorial in many of these processes and procedures.

We have also found that chats are not particularly useful as a teaching or collaboration tool. They can be fun for the students and even help to break the ice, but they are not effective for thoughtful, managed discussion. To this end, we have redoubled our efforts to use the threaded conferences more and more for the various group and class-based processes.

Student cooperation and collaboration is key. We, as faculty, must be effective facilitators, though. We must help to set the ground rules for process and behavior and help students based on their individual needs. In some ways, the virtual classroom is best for this. It is much more practical, for instance, to send a private message to a student you're not hearing from on the listserv or in the conference discussions than it is to stop the class and make the same point.

Constant communication is key. We have learned that it is essential that both we and the students are prepared to check our email and log into the conferencing system daily. We note in the syllabus requirements that regular participation is vital and part of the grade. Most of all, it is through communication that we are able to foster learning, excitement, and confidence among the students, so our emphasis is on using these communication processes for encouragement and support.

CONTACT INFORMATION

Concetta M. Stewart
Faculty Fellow
Temple University
Annenberg Hall 011-00
Philadelphia, PA 19122
Email: cstewart@astro.temple.edu
Phone: (215) 204-5181
Fax: (215) 204-5402

Stella F. Shields
Email: sshiel00@astro.temple.edu

Vignette 39 Teaching with an Online Public Forum

Jean Goodwin, Northwestern University

Contemporary Problems of Freedom of Speech is an upper-division course enrolling about 80 students annually. The course acts as an informal capstone, joining the diverse disciplines within Northwestern's School of Speech. Its goal is to get students to develop their views on the functions of speech in our common life. The class proceeds by the case method: examining different sorts of problematic speech—violent speech before abortion clinics, harassing speech on campus, sexual speech online—and considering what, if anything, should be done about it. The primary readings are the arguments made by the Supreme Court in deciding similar cases. And the primary method is to induce students to start making arguments for themselves.

EDUCATIONAL THEORIES

Students at Northwestern are articulate. Among their friends, in conference with teachers, in small discussion sections, they readily assert and argue for their opinions. All these interactions, however, typically take place under conditions of intimacy. The people involved know each other well, already comprehend and often share each other's views, and can rely on a basic level of mutual trust and understanding. What Northwestern students, like most traditional college students, have rarely encountered are situations of publicity. These are situations where they must interact with their fellow citizens—people they don't know but with whom they share a common life. One task of college teaching must be to initiate the student into the skills needed for civic life—the skills of publicity. These include the ability to present oneself in a way that demands respect, the ability to defend one's position against a broad range of criticism, and the ability to respond to views very different from one's own.

My goal for the last three years has been to use a technology with minimal constraints to enable students to address a public: each other. The online public forum aims to establish conditions as close as possible to those that prevail in public life generally. The

individual has to address and respond to people unaccountably different from her, facing a real risk of misunderstanding and being misunderstood.

COMPUTER-ENHANCED TECHNIQUE: THE ONLINE PUBLIC FORUM

The syllabus directs students to the local USENET newsgroup that will serve as the public forum for the class. It advises students that they should post to the forum forcefully (i.e., taking a position on any free speech issue and arguing it) and responsively (i.e., commenting on other students' posts). It also points them to some resources from which they might draw ideas (e.g., the Controversies Bank on the course web site at http://faculty-web.at.nwu.edu/commstud /freespeech/.

I try to keep the boundary between the newsgroup and class time permeable. To get students started, I suggest in class they try posting online their initial and rough philosophy of free speech. After some momentum builds, I raise questions about managing the newsgroup such as strategies for how to sort through the hundred or so postings made each week. I bring relevant newsgroup threads into class discussion. Within a few weeks, students begin to break the class/newsgroup boundary the other way, posting online commentary on issues raised in class.

Like any public forum, the newsgroup is self-regulating. I impose no rules beyond a requirement that everyone must sign their posts. When someone sees something problematic occurring, we talk about it. With almost clockwork predictability, for example, the first serious "flame war" or online shouting match occurs about four weeks into the quarter—just about the same time as we're discussing "fighting words" in class! The students themselves intervene, and then we deliberate on whether we should impose rules on the forum. Other typical recurrent issues include whether non-class members should be allowed to participate and whether requiring online participation "chills" it.

At the beginning, one can already find expressed an attitude that students rarely allow into their official work: what I think of as the "they're stupid" stance of garden-variety closed-mindedness. It is, oddly enough, a sort of victory when students say things they ordinarily never would to the teacher's face:

> My biggest pet peeve is stupidity—and unfortunately there seems to be epidemic proportions of it in this world. A lot of the subject material in our newsgroup centers around stupidity.

Within a few weeks, some early starters are engaging in a sort of active open-mindedness, finding issues with two defensible sides and debating them soberly, all the while setting an outstanding example for the rest of the class. I try to continue to loosen things up by declaring "inversion week" once a month or so, encouraging everyone to argue the opposite of their actual opinions.

RESULTS

A snapshot of the newsgroup in the seventh week of the quarter shows almost 200 messages on 68 different topics; about 20 of these were continued from previous weeks, a dozen were news clippings posted by me, and another half dozen were announcements. Popular new threads—all student-initiated—included beer advertising on the scoreboard at the football stadium, speech codes at BYU, Snoop Doggy Dogg, and local news coverage of gruesome auto wrecks—each generating six to ten messages that week. Some students posted multiple short messages; most posted one longish one (two- to three-page equivalents).

The online public forum, however, is not a means but an end; its primary product should be the enjoyable and frustrating experience of arguing with this group of gathered strangers. Whether such public debate is worthwhile is, of course, a legitimate subject for public debate, one always opened by the students themselves at some point in the quarter.

In the final course evaluations, more than half of the students agreed that "I enjoyed developing an online 'personality,'" and "I feel I got to know several people on the newsgroup, although I never met them face-to-face." About the same proportion spontaneously discussed themselves and/or their fellow students in the unstructured part of the evaluation. For

example: "You'll learn about your own views and the views of others." "We didn't just learn from the instructor; we learned from each other." "I learned about how annoying NU dorks are."

Interestingly, slightly more than half the students strongly agreed that "there was more B.S. on the newsgroup than in a regular discussion section." Personally, I don't think there was more breath (or electrons) wasted in the newsgroup than in other teaching situations; instead, it would seem to be a matter of salience. B.S. in discussion fades and is forgotten. B.S. in the online public forum gets its due reward: It sits there and stinks.

LESSONS LEARNED

- The problem of propaganda. While online discussion sounds like regular discussion, only less fun, online papers sound like regular papers, only less work.

- The problem of access. At Northwestern, students have good network access—almost three quarters, for example, strongly agree that "I have easy access to the Internet where I sleep at night." Obviously, if routine participation were a greater burden, an online forum might be unworkable.

- The problem of usability. The technology itself created more problems for the instructor than the students. While 90% of students found the newsgroup easy to use by the end of the quarter, probably half encountered problems and contacted the instructor to help resolve them. One solution might be to dedicate a TA to technical problems. Another is to shift to a web format, which allows the same sort of asynchronous communication in a more familiar interface.

- The problem of grading. As often, less turns out to be more. In the first few tries, I attempted to impose quality control through grading, penalizing students for not using the course readings or not responding to their fellow students. As well as being a pain for the TAs, this created a climate of censorship for the students: They felt that someone was watching them while they wrote. I've found that a more or less pass/fail system (three points every week the student posts at least once, up to 24 points in the ten-week quarter) elicits the same quality work without the intrusion.

- The key remaining difficulty. The curve for the class is bimodal, with peaks at relatively high and relatively low grades. In the cacophony of the on-line public forum, nonparticipation or just going through the motions is hard to catch; I fear I'm losing a chunk of students here to complete passivity or anti-newsgroup bitterness. In the final course evaluations, about 15% advised, "lose the news-group." To capture these students, I offer an alternative to online participation: a real-world discussion group organized by the students themselves. This is not an opportunity the unattached have been willing to seize. I'm going to try next year placing students in small, permanent work groups, in the hope that fewer will be able to opt out of the

course this way. Whether the intimacy of the work groups can be combined with the publicity of the public forum, however, remains to be seen.

CONTACT INFORMATION

Jean Goodwin
Assistant Professor
Northwestern University
1815 Chicago Avenue
Evanston, IL 60208
Email: jeangoodwin@nwu.edu
http://pubweb.nwu.edu/~jgo259/
Phone: (847) 491-5854
Fax: (847) 467-1036

Vignette 40 Native American History and Culture

Raymond A. Bucko, Le Moyne College

COURSE GOALS AND STRATEGIES

Native American History and Culture focuses on issues of importance to contemporary Native Americans by carefully examining their cultural and historical backgrounds. We also contextualize these issues within a global community and with relation to other indigenous peoples. This course uses Internet and computer facilities extensively both to enhance the classroom experience and to expand the community of discussants.

The course emphasizes communications across cultural boundaries with regard to both the material we cover and the students we teach. Three Native Americans from around the United States act as consultants for the class via the Internet. They visit various discussion groups on the enclosed workspace and make comments. They also answer students' questions. The course is taught collaboratively, with a shared work-

space containing course resources and asynchronous discussion areas. A professor of Indigenous Law at the University of Deusto leads a class of European students in Bilbao, the Basque country of Spain, and a professor of anthropology leads the class in Syracuse, New York, at Le Moyne College. The students represent a wide variety of cultural and ethnic backgrounds, including Native American.

Class discussions are highly structured and based on readings as well as informed opinions. Students have specific deadlines for making comments in the discussion areas. Faculty and outside consultants also engage the students in discussion in these areas. Because of the time differences and the vagaries of the Internet, we do not engage in real-time conversations. Both professors conduct class in their own schools. One semester, the course was taught as a distance course with no professor present. The results were largely unsatisfactory.

The enclosed workspace (Basic Support Cooperative Work) acts as an archive and knowledge base for the class. Students and professors can easily make links to relevant Internet sites both for anthropology and contemporary issues. The professors also post a rich variety of scanned images, sound files (primarily indigenous music), and relevant documents to the workspace.

COURSE ACTIVITIES

Email

The course uses email extensively to communicate with students who are located around the world. Students are expected to be comfortable with electronic communications or at least be willing to climb the learning curve quickly.

Adding to the Information Base

Students are expected to actively enhance the workspace by adding relevant links from the Internet as well as documents and images. The professors generally add scanned materials. The workspace is highly effective for adding links and alerting students to their presence.

Sharing Papers

Students are asked to write three papers. All of them are posted in the workspace, and students are encouraged to read each other's works. The papers are listed in a more or less better-to-worse order to highlight the better papers. All papers are posted anonymously.

Active Discussions

Discussions, which are the core of the course, are begun on the workspace and continued in the classroom.

Periodic Evaluation

The course schedule links a course evaluation form that students are required to fill out twice a semester. The form is anonymous and geared to specific aspects of the course.

Student Self-Evaluation

Because this factor is so essential to the success of the class, the students are made aware early what constitutes active participation, and they receive 20% of their grade for it.

Electronic Grade Book

Both professors share an electronic grade book. Grades are emailed to students using a program called Vargrade. Discussion groups, in particular, are graded to encourage students to participate. Students are encouraged to discuss the grades if they are not satisfied. Professors clearly link quality of work and quantity—a willingness to contribute to discussions and the information base beyond what is required.

Electronic Syllabus

The course material is outlined on an electronic syllabus. There are numerous links to this syllabus throughout the workspace.

Electronic Schedule

Because Deusto and Le Moyne start and finish classes at slightly different times, it is necessary to coordinate class schedules. This is done through an electronic schedule with links to the required evaluation forms.

ICQ

The professors used ICQ or "I Seek You," a real-time chat program to discuss class issues (for the freeware, see www.icq.com). This saved an incredible amount of money in terms of international calls and allowed the class to flow more freely. Electronic meetings were also scheduled between the professors when necessary.

MEASURED RESULTS

According to both the electronic and traditional evaluations, the students tend to be satisfied with the course and the way it is conducted. Keep in mind that because this course is so computer intensive, the group self-selects; students not interested in computer-enhanced learning drop it. Most students recognize the unique opportunities in the way this course is conducted and are confident that the skills learned, both moral and practical, will serve them well in life. There is some deserved dissatisfaction with the speed and accessibility of computers as well as the amount of work required in the class.

TECHNICAL LESSONS LEARNED

Because this course is so computer intensive one

quickly learns the problems and limitations of Internet communications. Slow servers, slow connections, and server breakdown all contribute to irritations in the class. Both professors are careful to emphasize to the students that using computers does not mean instantaneous communication and that problems will arise (normally at the most crucial period in the class). Also, the course relies on support from local information systems personnel at each college, and we must squeeze in with their 100 other computer priorities. Le Moyne has its own server for the Basic Support for Cooperative Work (BSCW) program, and Deusto plans to mirror all the course materials to help with student access. Le Moyne is also upgrading the server to a faster processor. A course like this requires changes in infrastructure and must be coordinated with many different departments.

LESSONS LEARNED

- Be flexible. Students must learn how to use the workspace. At times, servers don't work, the net is slow, or procedures misfire. Keep to a schedule, but allow for exceptions. Students must make the professors aware of the problems ahead of time.

- Keep communication flowing both ways. Electronic gradebooks allow weekly grade feedback to students. Email facilitates intercommunications. Electronic evaluation forms keep you abreast of the "barometric pressure" of the class. All this allows students to have some control of the class and see changes based on their suggestions.

- Monitor student progress. The BSCW gives precise details of who has done what on the workspace. Students are reminded that this accounting is meant to allow faculty to reward outstanding work rather than to act as "big brother."

- Be physically available. Although there is a plethora of help files available on the workspace, it is vital that students have contact with professors. This is particularly true for students unfamiliar with the Internet and computers in general.

- If you use technology, teach technology. While this course requires computer literacy, few students are

familiar with workspaces and specific tasks required for this particular class. Each professor takes a week to teach students how to use the computers specifically for this class. The beginnings of classes early in the semester are also used for questions and answers about the technology. Later in the class, problems are moved to office hours unless there is a large number of students with the same difficulty.

- Don't rely on computers always working. Students have an illusion of the instantaneous and trouble-free computer. Teachers must make expectations realistic.

- Set realistic work levels. Having taught this course internationally twice, both professors realized that there is a dual workload—normal course material and Internet delivery. Until students become very familiar with computer techniques, and this may not happen in a single course, there is a dual learning curve.

- Find out what students know. We use a form in the course for basic biographical data. We are also careful to find out from students how computer-literate they are so we can adjust our early seminars to accommodate their needs.

COURSE RESOURCES

- Course syllabus: http://vc.lemoyne.edu/ant212/ant212_eng_syl.html.

- Course schedules: http://vc.lemoyne.edu/ant212/ant212_lemo_sch.html and http://vc.lemoyne.edu/ant212/ant212_deus_sch.html

- Course evaluation form: http://vc.lemoyne.edu/ant212/ant212_eng_form_course.html

- Self-evaluation form: http://vc.lemoyne.edu/ant212/ant212_eng_form_self.html

- Student biographical information form: http://vc.lemoyne.edu/ant212/ant212_eng_form_bio.html

- Basic support for cooperative work home page: http://bscw.gmd.de/

- Customized help files for the enclosed workspace: http://vc.lemoyne.edu/help/help_index.html

Conclusion

This is the most exciting course that I teach, and it really allows for a classroom situation that would be impossible in any other circumstance. However, the more technology, the more possibilities of breakdown. Because the course is interesting and students are invested in this form of communication, we have been able to endure despite computer breakdowns. Most importantly, indigenous voices are heard, students from vastly different backgrounds interchange ideas, and a new generation becomes aware of the intricacies of the modern world both in the medium and the message.

Contact Information

Raymond A. Bucko, S.J.
Le Moyne College
Syracuse, NY 13214
Email: bucko@maple.lemoyne.edu
WWW: http://web.lemoyne.edu/~bucko/index.html

Aitor Esteban, Co-Professor
email: ustas01@sarenet.es
WWW: http://www.deusto.es.esteban/index.html

Vignette 41 Museums and Social Science

Raymond A. Bucko, Le Moyne College

Course Goals and Strategies

This course is designed to teach social theory by looking at the history of museums and how they express assumptions about culture and the world. Students are expected to work in groups to prepare seminar presentations based on course readings. The project for the semester is to create a virtual museum. The topic of the museum can be anything, and students work to help each other refine their topics. Students are held to the ethical standards of actual museums as well as copyright and publishing laws. One day a week is devoted to teaching web page authoring so that the students have the technical skills necessary to produce credible museums.

Course Activities

- Students visit three actual museums and reflect in groups on what constitutes these collections as museums.

- Students use a workspace program, Basic Support for Cooperative Work (BSCW), and conduct asynchronous pre-seminar discussions based on readings. Students from two schools, Le Moyne in Syracuse and Fairfield University in Fairfield, Connecticut, engaged in the course last semester.

- Students took turns writing summaries of live discussions and posting them to the workspace so that members from each group could review the other group's live discussion.

- Students created links in the workspace pointing to virtual museums that they felt were particularly effective. They also articulated why they rated these museums highly.

- Students wrote three papers on aspects of museums and posted them to the workspace so that other students could read them.

- Students were encouraged to assist each other in climbing the Internet HTML publishing curve.

- Students used email to discuss problems with the class or with the computing facilities.

- An electronic gradebook kept students informed of their progress with weekly updates. Workspace discussions were graded each week based on quality and quantity of the interaction.

- Students viewed a wide variety of museum floor plans and images of museum displays on the enclosed workspace. This material allowed them to begin formulating effective means of displaying and organizing their own virtual materials.

- Weekly reviews of progress on museum sites and a museum of the week created by a student were used to set high watermarks for accomplishment.

MEASURED RESULTS

Students were largely satisfied with this course. It used both Internet web-based forms geared to periodic evaluation of the course as well as the official end-of-semester evaluations distributed by the college. While students were content with the quality of the instruction, there was some concern about availability of computers and scanners for web work. At one of the colleges, we experienced a semester with almost continual hardware failure. This generated a lot of discontent. Students did recognize the importance of the computer skills acquired in the class and appreciated the innovative quality of the presentations. One student was hired for an entry-level museum position based, in part, on her Internet work. She created a second virtual museum for Onondaga County in collaboration with high school students. Another student's web site was selected as a Microsoft Site of the Week.

TECHNICAL LESSONS LEARNED

Students work consistently on acquiring HTML skills. The first year, there were two students who did not complete the class as they waited until the last week to try to complete an entire museum. They simply did not have enough skills to construct a basic web page, and while students were generous in helping each other, no one in the class would do it for them.

Creating a virtual museum is quite effective in bringing home the lessons of theory, ethics, and history in the study of museums. Students are faced with constraints of time and space, budget, legal and ethical issues, issues of attribution and ownership, and control of cultural property and representation itself. They also learn a valuable lesson in focusing and limiting research topics and museum presentations on a very practical level.

One semester, I taught the class at two different schools, Le Moyne College and Fairfield University. I was at Fairfield and conducted the seminars. Students at Le Moyne held discussions on their own based on RealAudio prelectures I had constructed and had an adjunct come in to teach them web authoring. I had hoped to create teams of two students, one in each school, to work on joint museums. The students opposed this due to the amount of work involved in learning HTML techniques. Students did not want to be teamed with someone who did not work up to speed. I suspect that a class in which learning how to publish on the web was not an issue would be more amenable to this type of structure. Unfortunately, few students in small undergraduate schools are up to this level. Clearly, the more computer technology is incorporated into a variety of classes, the more faculties can use rather than teach techniques. For now, technology instruction is vital in almost all classes, if students are to progress.

LESSONS LEARNED

- Show the relevance of the computer aspects of the class. I begin by taking the students on tours of virtual museums so that they can see how effective and, at times, problematic they can be. Writing web pages is a useful skill, but using the web in a scholarly manner is far more germane to what we do as educators.

- Keep students working consistently. The best model I have found is progressive graded assignments.

- Integrate computer knowledge with classroom learning. Show that computers are relevant to the subject at hand. I stress that this is a museum course and that virtual museums are a vital outgrowth of traditional museums.

- Encourage conversation in the discussion areas of the workspace. Students often need to be encouraged to talk and to examine ideas. The professor should not dominate a conversation but also should not simply watch from afar. A good balance is vital.

- Teach raw HTML code. While there is a controversy over the usefulness of teaching raw code versus teaching web authoring with a WYSIWYG editor, it is clear that for a class in which the final paper is an intensely graphical web page, control of the medium is essential. This is harder to achieve with editors. Also, one of the best ways for students to learn effective layout and presentation is from other people's pages. If they are unable to read and understand the HTML code, they cannot transfer what they see on another's page to their own work.

- Keep students ethical and courteous. Part of creating virtual museums involves copyright, attribution of information, and accuracy of citation. I insist that students contact publishers before using material. I also ask them to reference works used in preparing their museums. If students find graphics or specific attractive site layouts on the web, I ask that they request permission to use them and send thank-you notes.

- Review work with students often. I have Internet access from my office, so I can work with students during office hours on their specific pages.

- Human contact is essential. A few students formed significant professional relationships with academics and museum personnel by Internet contact. Part of what I teach is how to courteously engage professional people and how not to simply ask someone else to do their work for them.

- Keep equipment running. A close working relationship with computer services is essential for a course like this.

- Show students how to promote their own sites. Besides making professional contact, students were also contacted by a variety of people surfing the net about their museums. Once they have the beginnings of a credible museum, I have them list their museum at the school (I do this with an index page) and to add them to a variety of web indexes and search engines. Each student is encouraged to place mailboxes and other feedback mechanisms on their pages.

- Web counters count. I have students use web counters to keep track of museum attendance. Often the students are quite pleased (and surprised) at the popularity of their sites.

- Stress the importance of positive contributions to the web community. Students are impressed with the notion of the web as an interactive highway in which they can offer as well as collect information. Museum creation goes beyond the expediencies of completing a school assignment.

COURSE RESOURCES

- Syllabus: http://vc.lemoyne.edu/ant305/ant305_syl.html

- Class schedule: http://vc.lemoyne.edu/ant305/ant305_sch_le.html and http://vc.lemoyne.edu/ant305/ant305_sch_fa.html

- Sample museums (note that as students graduate they are removed from the server so all museum sites are not active): http://vc.lemoyne.edu/museum.html

- Tutorials for web page authoring: http://vc.lemoyne.edu/seminar/

- RealAudio pre-lectures: http://vc.lemoyne.edu/ant305/lectures/

- Basic support for cooperative work home page: http://bscw.gmd.de/

- Customized help files for the enclosed workspace: http://vc.lemoyne.edu/help/help_index.html

- Student self-evaluation form: http://vc.lemoyne.edu/ant305/ant305_form_self.html

- Student course evaluation form: http://vc.lemoyne.edu/ant305/ant305_form_class.html

- Student information form: http://vc.lemoyne.edu/ant305/ant305_form_bio.html

- Electronic gradebook: http://www.varedsw.com/

CONCLUSION

Web simulation, in this case the creation of a virtual museum to enhance learning in a very practical and hands-on way, has vast potential pedagogically. This particular way of conducting a class allows students a large measure of creativity as they apply practical and theoretical lessons to a concrete situation. The cost and benefit is that students must learn how to write web pages. While this takes up about a third of class time, it represents a good investment, for the pages go beyond autobiography and lists of links, the most common form of home page, to unique scholarly contributions to the intellectual climate of the Internet. At the same time, the students leave the class with a valuable skill whether or not they become professional museum personnel.

CONTACT INFORMATION

Raymond A. Bucko, S.J.
Le Moyne College
Syracuse, NY 13214
Email: bucko@maple.lemoyne.edu
WWW: http://web.lemoyne.edu/~bucko/index.html

Vignette 42 — Mystery Fossil: A Software Tool for Active Student Engagement in Introductory Anthropology Courses

John T. Omohundro and Peter S. Brouwer, SUNY, Potsdam

Mystery Fossil (written by John Omohundro and Kathleen Goodman, 1994 Research Foundation of SUNY) is a locally developed computer software package that presents students with an actual paleoanthropological problem and gives them the tools and information necessary to grapple with it. The software simulates the problem of analyzing a fossil hominid cranium, comparing it with others, and synthesizing that information with data on fossil ages and associated materials to designate and position the unknown species on the hominid phylogeny. In the process of solving this problem, students are introduced to the major fossil hominid types and competing phylogenetic models; to anatomy; and to methods of dating fossils. They become active participants in the process of discovery and argument in paleoanthropology. This exercise is intended for students in general anthropology or introductory physical anthropology.

EDUCATIONAL PHILOSOPHY

In many introductory anthropology courses, there is no laboratory component. The instructors are often cultural anthropologists who feel compelled to abbreviate the physical anthropology in the survey course because they are not well versed in this subdiscipline's methods or state of knowledge. Even in many introductory physical anthropology courses, costs or class size rule out a teaching lab. In these typical situations, students are presented with the fossil record as a fait accompli, obscuring the sense of intellectual process, or else with the grand controversies surrounding hominid evolution disconnected from any scrutiny of the key data, leaving the impression that little can be said with confidence, because methods are weak and data insufficient.

Initially, students' knowledge of the fossil record is minimal. They are not aware how anatomical form reveals functional and phylogenetic relationships. Human evolutionary stages are usually grossly stereotyped and include popular fallacies. Beginning students believe that fossil nomenclature is somehow out there in nature, fixed, with clear distinctions between hominid types and evolutionary stages.

Mystery Fossil assumes that users will be taking their first course in anthropology or physical anthropology. At the time they begin the simulation, students need have only had a week or so of class time devoted to the fossil record and paleoanthropological methods. Students will know skeletal anatomy or how to describe similarities and differences in fossils or what the functional or phylogenetic significance of these differences might be. They will know how to combine a variety of methods to bracket the age of a fossil.

The Mystery Fossil software builds on existing skills and interests of introductory students. In ten years of teaching Human Origins, we have observed that students want to handle the specimens in order to do what paleoanthropologists do. They show more interest in viewing slides and films about excavations and fossils than in listening to the instructor talk about them. They become more animated when unanswerable questions are raised than when accepted facts are presented.

The design of the software was inspired by an article Grant Wiggins published in *American Educator* (1987, Winter) titled "Creating a Thought-Provoking Curriculum." Wiggins argued that we should get students involved in "intellectual orienteering" by raising unsettling questions. These questions should 1) go to the heart of the discipline; 2) have no one obvious right answer; 3) be analytical, synthetic, and require evaluative judgment; and 4) generate "personalized" interest, because there are a variety of possible answers and modes to arrive at them. Mystery Fossil's paleoanthropological problem is certainly at the heart of the discipline. There is no right answer, either: Each of the three mystery fossils provided in the program has recently stirred controversy about its species designation and position in the human phylogeny. Comparing fossil data and synthesizing geology, anatomy, and excavation information are certainly challenging higher-order tasks, and there is more data than anyone can assimilate easily, so students must practice discrimination. Finally, following Wiggin's fourth point, students personalize the exercise because they select the data they wish to emphasize, and, to conclude, they write a defense of their decisions.

COMPUTER-ENHANCED TECHNIQUES

Computer software like Mystery Fossil provides a less expensive, more portable, more accessible, more adaptable, more personalized, and more integrated laboratory experience than most undergraduates receive in an anthropology course. Unlike a conventional fossil lab, Mystery Fossil computer software permits an unlimited number of students access to a common database of specimens. Unlike a conventional lab, the Mystery Fossil computer exercise requires virtually no investment in expensive and fragile equipment or maintenance of a special laboratory. It is perpetually available to students to use at their own pace, provided they have access to Macintosh computers. Unlike a book, the Mystery Fossil software can be readily and frequently altered to change the unknowns or edit the data. Unlike most lab packets, the Mystery Fossil contains in a single package the data to solve the problem, some analytic tools (rulers), background reference materials, a notebook, and a report generator.

Mystery Fossil simulates the problem paleoanthropologists face upon returning to their home lab facilities with a new find. The data cards accompanying the unknown fossil are equivalent to the preliminary analysis they would have conducted in their field labs and the consultants' reports submitted by geologists and dating labs. The Mystery Fossil exercise picks up at that point, demanding careful comparisons with known fossils and the synthesis of diverse information to convert this unique specimen into a useful datum of human prehistory.

Mystery Fossil permits students to appreciate how the task of comparison and synthesis of fossil data lead to the generalizations in their text. They discover that conclusions not only are based on careful observation, incomplete information, and Holmesian detection skills but also on sophisticated analytical techniques, like potassium-argon dating. Students report that having to commit themselves in an argument for the final report raises their empathy and interest in paleoanthropological controversies, because they grasp the process behind them.

Mystery Fossil's most creative attribute is its nonlinearity: Once students accept the challenge to name and to position the unknown fossil, how they exploit the data provided to solve the problem is up to them. The software permits the student to access any of its features from any other by means of on-screen navigation and a hypertext function. For example, to conduct comparisons, students can toggle between the pictures or data on the unknown fossil and a known specimen. Because this nonlinearity demands more student control, guidance for how to proceed is provided in an on-screen Help feature and discussed more thoroughly in the accompanying manual.

Mystery Fossil's most attractive feature is the high-quality images of the 11 fossil crania, presented in three views, comprising the unknowns and the known fossil hominid. The software includes tools to measure these specimens for comparison. Because the students are beginners, a glossary, anatomy chart, and dating guides provide clarification. The basic Help screens gently guide anxious beginners through the fundamentals of Macintosh computer use.

To our knowledge, from 1989 until 1998, this software package was the only one created for teaching physical anthropology to undergraduates.

MEASURED RESULTS

Prerelease versions of Mystery Fossil were tested in many ways. Most important was a test of Mystery Fossil in a Human Origins class of 100 students in fall 1989. In section one of Introduction to Human Origins, totaling 50 students, the Mystery Fossil software was assigned as a classroom lab exercise. In section two, also of 50 students, Blind Watchmaker, a computer simulation of natural selection but without paleoanthropological content, was assigned. The unit being covered at the time was the paleoanthropological method. At that point, midway through the course, there had been no discussion of paleoanthropology.

Section one had two days of lecture on evolution and natural selection to substitute for Blind Watchmaker. Section two had two days of lecture on the fossil record and paleoanthropological methods, including slide presentations, to substitute for Mystery Fossil.

Both sections spent two class periods working on their respective exercises. The authors of the software observed and coached the students in their work. None of the students had the opportunity to keep the software for homework or to study for the unit test. In future use, students would keep the software for individual study.

The unit test, held one week later, was a multiple-choice test of 50 questions, of which 13 were judged in advance to concern paleoanthropology and on which students using Mystery Fossil should outperform students using Blind Watchmaker. The results showed that students using Mystery Fossil performed better on nine of the 13 questions. They achieved 6.3% more correct answers on these questions than did section two students.

The same week of the unit exam, a student opinion survey of Mystery Fossil was conducted. In brief, students reported that by analyzing, comparing, and synthesizing, they developed an intuition for the paleoanthropological process and an appreciation for the source of the data. By looking hard at the pictures for clues and picking through the data, students learned the fossil record, anatomy, and vocabulary better than by reading the textbook. They feel emboldened after using Mystery Fossil to examine fossil crania and to make evaluative judgments about their species and phylogenetic positions, a common task for the remainder of the semester.

LESSONS LEARNED

Creating instructional software initially takes an enormous amount of time. It may require that other professional interests are set aside. In this case, when the development effort is amortized over the ten years the program has been used, it seems a reasonable investment. Mystery Fossil represents an instruction module that has proven useful in a number of courses. When Mystery Fossil is being used in a course, the students are doing all the work. The teacher is relegated to coaching, which is a good role.

Using educational technology often requires more than one coach. Assistants are useful when a large class is working with Mystery Fossil. Fortunately, upper-division students who have used the software are happy to assist. A couple are invited to roam the lab, to deal with technical problems and to help students develop research strategies—to figure out what to look for in the fossils.

It's always been our goal to teach so that alumni remember the course and its intellectual challenges 20 years later. When we speak with alumni, they most frequently mention Mystery Fossil, because they felt like they were doing anthropology with real data.

Gratifying results from course evaluations, controlled testing, and alumni remarks have motivated the lead author to take the time to upgrade the software, once in 1992 and again in 1998. This last upgrade was a collaboration with a student. When the fossil database was expanded, higher-grade color photos were added, a Windows version was developed, and the package was made available in CD-ROM format.

Developing computer software packages like Mystery Fossil can have monetary benefits. A contract has been arranged with the State University of New York to market the package. As a result, a portion of each sale returns to the anthropology department to purchase additional laboratory materials.

REFERENCE

Wiggins, G. (1987, Winter). Creating a thought-provoking curriculum. *American Educator.*

CONTACT INFORMATION

John T. Omohundro
Professor of Anthropology
SUNY, Potsdam
Potsdam, NY 13676
Email: omohunjt@northnet.org
Phone: (315) 267-2050
Fax: (315) 267-3176

Peter S. Brouwer
Email: brouweps@potsdam.edu

Vignette 43 Virtual Multimedia Laboratories and Examinations in Physical Anthropology

John Kappelman, University of Texas, Austin

Advances in computer technology and multimedia software permit instructors to significantly enhance the range of materials and exercises that are included in lecture presentations and laboratory assignments as well as evaluations of learning. This new approach to teaching integrates the processes of both learning and evaluation. Some examples of this approach in physical anthropology are presented in this vignette.

EDUCATIONAL PHILOSOPHY

One of the centerpieces of any science course is its laboratory component. Laboratory exercises permit the student to follow the steps of research design and hypothesis testing, from taking measurements to analyzing the outcome, thus providing a hands-on science experience that in the best of cases actually imitates the real work of scientists. Because there exist wide disparities in collections of osteological and fossil cast materials as well as access to living primates, it is easy to understand why the content of introductory physical anthropology laboratories varies so widely among college programs. Many schools with limited or no laboratory materials are often unable to offer any laboratory component at all, thus precluding their students from experiencing the true range of study found in this discipline.

COMPUTER-ENHANCED TECHNIQUES

One solution to limited holdings of laboratory materials is to be found in digital technology and the recent advances in computer storage hardware and multimedia software. My lab group, with the generous support of the National Science Foundation and the University of Texas, has been engaged in mastering laboratory curricula for physical anthropology on CD-ROM. This work culminated in the 1998 release of Virtual Laboratories for Physical Anthropology (Kappelman, 1998). Although the exact digitized materials in each laboratory vary by subject matter, we include a full range of 2-D images captured by video, conventional and digital photography, and flatbed scanners; 3-D objects reconstructed by computer-aided design or captured by high-resolution X-ray computed tomography and 3-D laser surface scanning; sound; and text. These multimedia materials (e.g., still images, video footage, sound, and 3-D animations) and text are mastered as laboratory exercises that 1) introduce a general observation or problem; 2) present a group of objects related to the general observation that can be studied with a model and quantified; 3) permit the collection of data; and 4) provide an assignment asking what conclusions can be drawn from the analysis and how they are related to the initial observation.

We have also posted web CD hybrid applications on the course web site. These pieces pull selected animations or images off the CD and remaster them for review and study for display using instructions posted to the web site. This approach adds utility to the CD and permits us to remaster ideas and materials literally overnight to take into account new discoveries and interpretations.

It quickly became apparent that our paper examinations were no longer adequate for evaluating student learning, because this traditional testing medium did not permit us to include the full range of multimedia materials that the students were being taught. Again, with the generous support of the National Science Foundation, we developed an easy-to-use dual platform computer program, VExams, that permits instructors to deliver interactive virtual multimedia exams and quizzes. The content of each exam is drawn from the full range of multimedia materials that an instructor uses and can include 2-D color and black-and-white images or plots, sound clips, video clips, and 3-D animations. The multimedia materials can be integrated with multiple-choice, matching, true/false, plotting, fill-in, story problem, and interactive questions.

To use the VExam program, the instructor saves the desired media in commonly used formats. Questions are saved in a simple text file format that permits the instructor to cut and paste questions from previous exams into the file. These materials are next imported into the program, and the questions and multimedia materials are linked to one another within the exam framework. The exam can mirror common hard copy exams in presenting a fixed number of questions. A second option is what is termed the interactive exam. This format can be designed to select randomly or expertly from among questions of various categories or difficulty levels to produce a unique but uniform exam for each student that is built "on the fly" and tailored to the knowledge level of each student.

The grade for each exam is calculated automatically and reported to the student immediately upon the exam's completion. Each student's responses for every question are written to separate log files, and these files can be accessed by a second program that reruns the exam for the student, displaying the student's response along with the correct answer and, if desired, an explanation of why this is the best answer. This review program is a critical step in the learning process.

We have also had good success in mastering demonstration quizzes for delivery over the web. Although students are very interested in this approach, these self-quizzes are not counted toward the final grade, because no mechanism exists to ensure that students are not helping each other. These exercises do serve an important function as review and study guides.

MEASURED RESULTS

Students are generous in letting us know what does and does not work, and the results from the use of the Virtual Laboratories for Physical Anthropology have been gratifying. First, students now have easy access to the full range of living and fossil materials that they hear about in lecture and study in lab in both 2-D and 3-D by way of the CD-ROM. If they wish to access a particular fossil skull, they simply call it up on their CD and view it in three is dimensions. Having the ability to conveniently review their materials is, they tell us, a great boon to their learning.

A second important result from this work is found in the use of the CD off the University of Texas campus. Although the CD is in its first year of use, it is receiving high marks from colleges and universities that have teaching collections that are not as complete as those at UT. The CD is helping to equalize the imbalances that exist among colleges and greatly expanding the reach of physical anthropology as one of the key science courses within the college curriculum.

We have used the raw code for virtual multimedia examinations for two years at UT and have been very pleased with the results. Students are satisfied that their efforts in learning the multimedia applications are rewarded during their evaluations. Even something as simple as seeing images from their textbook appears to jog their memories. In addition, students appreciate knowing their exam grade at the end of the exam rather than having to wait one or two weeks for the instructor to complete the grading by hand. The review program also offers much more immediate and detailed feedback on the student's performance than is generally offered by traditional paper exams. The VExams program is in its initial phases of testing both on and off the UT campus and, at this point, appears to be well received. The learning and evaluation processes are on par, because the materials that the students are learning are now the same materials on which they are tested.

LESSONS LEARNED

The most important lesson in producing multimedia-teaching applications is to produce a detailed working outline before writing the program. The basic template should be organic enough to incorporate changes.

Nothing that we have found beats an old-fashioned essay question for evaluating the student's comprehension of complex topics, and a human being remains the best tool for grading these exercises. Although we have come to rely on the virtual multimedia exams for evaluating how the student learns the bulk of the objective material that we teach, this part of the grade accounts for about 80% of any given exam. The remaining 20% of the grade is based on an essay question. Why not release students from the pressures of producing an essay in a timed setting and instead give them the opportunity to turn in their best effort? That is what we do, and the essay is both take-home and open book.

We have discovered that the student should be included as an integral part of every development process. All of our efforts have been thoroughly evaluated by our students, and their comments have served to correct what were basic problems that the developers had missed. Our upper-division students have also proven to be some of the best proofreaders and debuggers that we have. These students come to the programs with a fresh mind that is not tainted by the development process and are often able to jump right to the critical issue or problem. These teaching materials are, after all, for the students, and including this audience in the development process helps to ensure that the students will be satisfied with the final product.

ACKNOWLEDGMENTS

Thanks to the National Science Foundation (DUE-9354427 and DUE-9752326) and the University of Texas for generous support of these efforts.

REFERENCE

Kappelman, J. (1998). Virtual laboratories for physical anthropology [CD- ROM]. Belmont, CA: Wadsworth.

CONTACT INFORMATION

John Kappelman
Professor
Department of Anthropology
University of Texas, Austin
Austin, TX 78712-1086
Email: jkappelman@mail.utexas.edu
WWW:
Virtual Exams: http://www.dla.utexas.edu/depts/anthro/kappelman/vexams/vexam.html
Virtual Labs: http://www.dla.utexas.edu/depts/anthro/kappelman/vlabs/vlabs.html

Vignette 44 — Teaching MBA Students to Compete in Simulated Oligopoly Environments

Philip S. Crooke, Luke Froeb, and Steven Tschantz, Vanderbilt University

We teach MBAs how to compete by putting students into simulated competitive environments and asking them to make strategic choices. We teach the principles of competition through practice without requiring students to learn the mathematical machinery behind the models that create the simulated environment. All of the games are motivated by actual antitrust cases. This degree of realism makes it easy to sell the games to MBA students, who are ever wary of learning abstract models with little relevance to the business world.

EDUCATIONAL PHILOSOPHY

As the price of computing power has fallen, researchers have adopted computationally intensive research tools that allow them to solve new problems with increasingly complex and realistic models. In almost every branch of science, including the social sciences, new high-level languages such as Mathematica, Maple, and MatLab have radically changed the way research is done.

Unfortunately, the potential of these tools to change teaching has gone unfulfilled. The reasons for this are two-fold: First, the cost of the software and hardware necessary to use these programs is beyond the reach of most students, and second, the programs are very difficult to learn, particularly for entry-level or nontechnical students.

In response to these cost and pedagogic issues and in our search for new instructional models, faculty from the department of mathematics and the Owen Graduate School of Management developed new technology in 1995 called MathServ. MathServ uses existing web browsers, such as Netscape Communicator or Internet Explorer, as an interface to the Mathematica computational engine (the Mathematica kernel) running on a remote server. By putting a user-friendly web interface on Mathematica, instructors can use the computational power of the program for pedagogical applications at very low cost.

The web pages used in the system are typically focused on narrow tasks that permit a greater degree of control over the learning process. The instructor designs tools, exercises, or games that illustrate one particular idea or concept with an easy-to-use web interface. The student learns the concept by playing the games or using the tools to answer questions. We discuss some of the games below.

SEALED BIDDING GAME

This game is introduced in class by describing the tradeoff that bidders face when trying to decide how high to bid for an object in a sealed-bid auction. A higher bid raises the probability of winning, but it also lowers the potential profits. An optimal bid balances these two effects. The game proceeds as follows:

- Students choose the value distributions out of which they and their opponent (the computer) are drawing values.

- Students are shown a graph of the two distributions and asked to submit bids at three different values.

- The program computes expected profits at each of the three values.

- If the bids are good enough, then the game stops. Otherwise, students are asked to resubmit bids.

Students learn by trial and error how to trade off a higher probability of winning against a large margin if they do win. They develop an intuitive feel for how optimal bids change as the competitive environment changes. Students are asked to answer several questions about the results of their play. Forcing students to summarize what they have learned is an important element of the learning process. Often, they will go back and conduct experiments to ensure that their answers are correct.

SPATIAL MERGER SIMULATION

This game was motivated by an investigation of merging lumber firms in the Tahoe National Forest in 1987. Each firm had several competing mills. Students are put in the role of economists trying to predict the effects of a merger among several timber mills in a forest. They have to find by trial-and-error the most and the least anticompetitive mergers, with respect to their effect on Forest Service timber revenues. The output of the simulation is a number, showing how much revenues decline, as well as a topographical map of the forest showing where prices have risen most.

Students find that the most anticompetitive merger (from the standpoint of the Forest Service) is one where adjacent mills merge—and the least anticompetitive merger is one where distant mills merge. The analogy of a timber mill in a forest to positioning brands in product space is very easy to draw. The geographic map is analogous to a brand map, which is used in marketing to analyze product positioning. Those consumers hurt most by the merger are analogous to forest tracts close to the merging mills. This game is typically not assigned as homework, but is used in class to illustrate lectures about spatial competition.

OTHER GAMES

In another game, students are put in the role of an expert witness who must decide if a merger between two consumer goods manufacturers is anticompetitive. Given data about the characteristics of the market and the merging products, the students simulate the post-merger world and determine if the merger will result in significantly higher prices. If the products of the two merging firms are close substitutes, then price effects are large, and the expert recommends blocking the merger. This particular game is based on L'Oreal's successful acquisition of Maybelline.

L'Oreal is a higher-end product than Maybelline, and it appeals to older and higher-income consumers. There are also nonmerging products in between the products of the merging firms that keep the industry competitive—even after the merger. After running the simulation, students can see that the anticompetitive effects of the merger were very small.

Other games include analyzing a merger between defense contractors bidding on a government project and computing damages in a patent infringement case. In the latter game, students are asked to estimate how much money the plaintiff (the patent owner) would have made without the infringement by the defendant. To answer the question, students simulate the disap-

FIGURE 44.2

TIMBER AUCTION EXERCISE

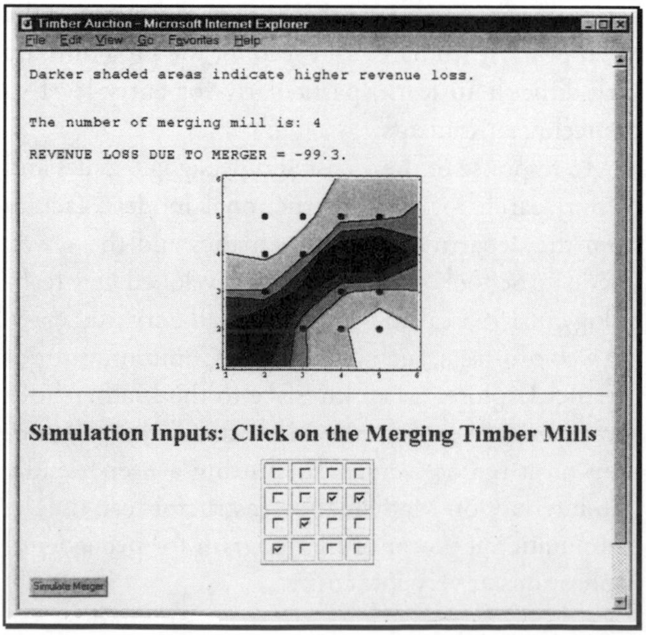

FIGURE 44.1

SEALED BIDDING EXERCISE

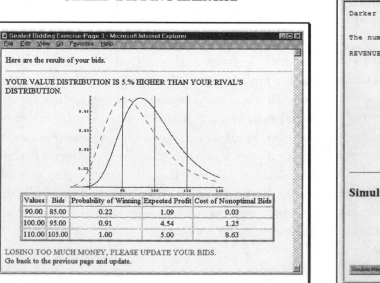

Interactive Learning

pearance of the defendant. They then determine by trial-and-error that the stronger the remaining competition, the lower the estimated damages. The game teaches students about the effects of entry and exit by a competitor.

CONCLUSION

While it seems clear to us that the technology is working, we have not developed any formal tests of its pedagogical effectiveness. Although our usage logs indicate hits from all over the world, including educational as well as commercial and government domains, the games are probably not well-developed enough to be used as stand-alone teaching tools. We find they are most effective if used in class to illustrate how firms compete or in a laboratory setting where students can ask questions of a lab assistant or professor. Before they are assigned as homework, it is important to show students how the game is played and to describe the set-

ting that motivated the game. This background puts the principles learned in a decision-making context, something that is crucial for teaching MBA students.

CONTACT INFORMATION

Philip S. Crooke, Professor of Mathematics
Vanderbilt University
Department of Mathematics
Nashville, TN 37240-0001
Email: pscrooke@math.vanderbilt.edu
http://math.vanderbilt.edu/~pscrooke/index.shtml
Phone: (615) 322-6671
Fax: (615) 343-0215

Luke Froeb
Email: luke.m.froeb@vanderbilt.edu
WWW: http://math.vanderbilt.edu/mathserv

Vignette 45 | **CyberShows: Using Information Technology to Solve a Dilemma**

Gordon E. McCray, Wake Forest University

This vignette describes an application of information technology (IT) in the core undergraduate management information systems (MIS) course in the Wayne Calloway School of Business and Accountancy at Wake Forest University. Undergraduate programs in business face the competing needs to develop in students so-called career-building skills (general skills, such as critical analysis and problem solving skills, as well as generic methods and models unique to a business discipline), while also assuring that students possess skills and knowledge in focused domains of business (such as software skills and basic accounting knowledge). The latter often represent time-sensitive knowledge and

skills. Once learned, this knowledge often is useful for only a relatively short period of time. What one learns with respect to a particular software application, for example, may be rendered useless upon the release of a new version. However, the former (critical analysis and problem solving, for example) are difficult to contemplate objectively and are not easily related to tangible benefits to a hiring firm.

Further complicating this dilemma is the fact that while many senior executives express a fundamental desire to hire students with more generalizable career-building skills, college recruiters more often seek students with far more specific skill sets. While we may praise the foresight of the senior executive, students must first progress beyond the hurdle represented by the recruiter and his or her notions of an attractive candidate. What, then, is an instructor to focus upon? One semester provides precious little time to build both these skill sets in students. Indeed, most would agree that the attention of any business course must focus upon one or the other skill set. To do otherwise would be to do neither skill set justice. Perhaps this dilemma is nowhere more pronounced than in the field of management information systems which is characterized by a sobering pace of change and rapidly expanding set of core concepts. Introductory MIS courses increasingly are difficult to design and execute.

UNDERSTANDING THE PROBLEM

To identify potential IT-based solutions to the problem I've described, I employed a simple mental exercise. I posed to myself a straightforward, if daunting, question: How would I design and execute an introductory MIS course if there were no scarcity of time, financial, or information/knowledge resources? My response highlighted two desires not currently attainable via the traditional classroom model of teaching and learning:

- Core MIS concepts would be presented, then discussed, and then explored in depth via evidence available in the practitioner press.

- Students would have extensive opportunities to apply their newfound knowledge in interactive classroom and team settings.

The primary deterrent to realizing these course characteristics was insufficient time. As with most introductory courses, students come to the course tabula rasa. Rich interaction during class meetings, therefore, is not tenable until students possess a threshold level of knowledge. Instilling this level of knowledge takes time—so much time, in fact, that little time remains with which to more meaningfully explore the topics at hand or to examine a wider set of issues (e.g., those sought by recruiters or executives).

CRAFTING A SOLUTION

As I deliberated privately the most attractive means by which to leverage IT in my quest for redefining the core MIS course, I contemplated the relative strengths of IT and instructors. Earlier applications of IT had focused upon extending the class meeting into the future, beyond the conclusion of any given classroom-based session. Most often, this is accomplished via threaded electronic discussions. This form of electronic discourse is still found efficacious by many instructors and should not be stricken from any list of feasible applications of IT to the teaching and learning process. This said, employing threaded discussions as a requirement beyond the classroom setting poses certain challenges, including:

- Fostering meaningful participation

- Evaluating the potentially large volume of contributions to the discussion

- Managing the discussions (often across multiple sections of a given course)

Seeking a greater leveraging effect for IT, the concept of extending the classroom meeting into the past was explored. Suddenly, an entirely new model for the core MIS course emerged. While IT is certainly capable of enabling group and threaded discussions and, in this way, allowing a class meeting to continue beyond the confines of the classroom, the richness with which this is done is decidedly less than that encountered in face-to-face interaction. The key concept here is interaction. When presenting material for the first time, typically there exists little interaction, save the occasional student question. When students begin exploring, applying, and debating this newfound knowledge, however, interaction abounds. Why not then allow IT to somehow perform the lecture function, thus freeing the instructor to facilitate the subsequent interactive learning during class meetings? Rather than use IT after the class meeting, students would employ IT prior to those meetings to experience a lecture that presents the basic knowledge required to engage in critical discourse.

THE CYBERSPACE TECHNIQUE

This notion of extending the class meeting into the past is now manifest as the CyberShow in the core MIS course in the Calloway School. The CyberShow is a PowerPoint slide show that is coupled with an audio recording of the course instructor unidirectionally delivering a traditional lecture. CyberShows are available from a course web site and are arranged topically. Slides are timed to advance at the appropriate point in the audio presentation. Students who experience confusion or difficulty with a concept in the CyberShow may use an on-screen control to rewind the Cyber-Show to an earlier point in the presentation and replay the presentation from that point forward. Prior to the introduction of the CyberShows, class meetings were a delicate balancing act as we sought to progress through course material at a rate neither too fast for the least knowledgeable students nor too slow for the most knowledgeable students. Students now engage in self-paced learning. This is particularly attractive in introductory MIS courses where students typically exhibit a broad range of skills relative to IT.

After experiencing the CyberShow assigned for the next class meeting, students then take an online objective quiz (typically ten to 15 questions) that is graded and recorded automatically. In this way, the instructor can gain confidence that the student has an appropriate level of knowledge prior to the next class meeting. Class meetings then proceed in three phases:

1) Students are given an opportunity to pose any questions or make any comments relative to the Cyber-Show assigned for that day's class meeting.

2) Additional topics, either related to or more advanced than those in the CyberShow, are presented by the instructor,

3) Students engage in any of a collection of interactive learning exercises, including debates, in-class case studies, simulations, and hands-on demonstrations.

The result is both greater depth of understanding of fundamental MIS issues and greater breadth of coverage of both abstract and applied MIS concepts. The aforementioned dilemma has thus been overcome. Cyber-Shows make available precious class meeting time, thereby allowing more in-depth coverage of a greater variety of topics and issues.

MEASURING SUCCESS

Anyone who has undertaken any form of computer-enhanced learning has faced, probably unsuccessfully, the challenge of determining in some objective manner, the efficacy of the IT-based change they have introduced. I strongly suspect that most academicians,

when evaluating curricular or pedagogical enhancements or changes, rely principally upon soft factors. Do students seem to have a better grasp of the relevant material? Do they seem to perform better on exercises and exams? Do I, as an instructor, seem to be addressing more material in the same amount of time without sacrificing learning outcomes? The answers to these and a host of related questions either build or diminish confidence in any form of change, IT-based or not. It is the answers to these questions that cause me to believe the CyberShow format is having impressively positive impacts on the learning outcomes of students.

IT-based pedagogical innovation, however, is a high-risk endeavor. The cost of failure is high, both economically and from the perspective of time already committed. Recognizing this, a formal study that controls for instructor, students, and content is being undertaken to more objectively determine the positive and negative consequences of the CyberShow approach. Results of that study will be made available to the public.

LESSONS LEARNED

IT-based pedagogical change is not easily achieved. The significant investment of time necessary to execute an IT-based innovation like the CyberShow model, however, tends to be a one-time investment. Maintenance of IT-based resources, CyberShows included, is much more manageable. In the case of the Cyber-Shows, the scripts for the audio recordings are preserved as word processing documents and are therefore easily updated and re-recorded as needed. Furthermore, within the library of CyberShows for the introductory MIS course, that information with a more enduring longevity is presented in CyberShows that are separate from those containing information that likely has a short "shelf life." In this way, maintainability is further enhanced.

Some have asked why simply reading a textbook is insufficient compared to the CyberShow. For some courses, the CyberShow may present little or no comparative advantage. For a field evolving as rapidly as management information systems, however, printed texts rarely are sufficient and typically require augmentation by the instructor. These texts often are criticized for their technical rather than organizational or strategic focus. The CyberShow has afforded an opportunity to package a complex body of knowledge in a highly customized manner that is reflective of highly current events and issues within the discipline.

It should be stressed that CyberShows are not employed to the exclusion of other pedagogical applications of technology. Email is used extensively to communicate with students, and discussion groups are available on an ad-hoc basis. An extensive course web site also is maintained to provide to students electronic versions of the syllabus, course-related notices, study guides, links to topically arranged relevant web-based resources, libraries of Lotus ScreenCam movies used to teach various software applications, and selected collaboration tools. In a course that is replete with IT-based resources, however, the CyberShow has had the most profound and transformative effect.

CONCLUSION

The CyberShow model of the introductory MIS course in the Calloway School has produced positive feedback, although results of a more formal study are pending. What is certain, however, is that students are exhibiting greater depths of understanding of a broader range of material. The aforementioned competing desires on the part of hiring firms are being addressed. Perhaps as importantly, students are engaged in the learning process. The CyberShows are alive, rather than passive, and are more personalized than CD-ROM textbooks. While my role certainly is not to entertain students, if IT can be employed to cause students to be more engaged in the learning process, then I feel it my duty to explore those possibilities.

CONTACT INFORMATION

Gordon E. McCray
BellSouth Mobility Technology Faculty Fellow
The Wayne Calloway School of Business
    and Accountancy
Wake Forest University
Box 7285, Reynolda Station
Winston-Salem, NC 27109-7285
Email: gmccray@wfu.edu
WWW: http://www.wfu.edu/~gmccray
Phone: (336) 758-4914
Fax: (336) 758-6133

Unanticipated Benefits from the Use of Computer Technology in a Large Introductory Course

Andrew P. Barkley, Kansas State University

After teaching upper-level courses for several years, I was presented with the opportunity to teach AGEC 120, Principles of Agricultural Economics and Agribusiness. The transition from teaching classes of 30 to 40 junior and senior majors in Agricultural Economics, to teaching over 170 freshmen, primarily non-majors, required many changes in my teaching style, assignments, and objectives. After three years of experience, I have gained insight into using technology to achieve greater efficiency and greater learning in a large introductory course.

EDUCATIONAL THEORIES

Learning economics is best accomplished through problem solving. Several years of teaching economics at the intermediate and advanced levels confirmed my belief that weekly problem sets requiring students to apply basic economic principles to real-world issues and events are crucial to the development of economic skills. Weekly assignments provide an excellent way for students to practice their problem solving skills, keep up with the course material, receive feedback from the instructor, and, if necessary, get help from either the instructor or peers to complete the problem sets and learn the necessary concepts.

In a small, required class at the upper level, I was able to keep up with these weekly assignments without much trouble, but in the larger course, the logistics became much more time-consuming than I had expected. Technology has allowed me to overcome many time-consuming activities by 1) providing course material and information over the Internet, 2) using computer presentations in the classroom, and 3) using email extensively to answer students' questions.

COMPUTER-ENHANCED TECHNIQUES AND ASSESSED OUTCOMES

Internet

In a large class, the distribution of course materials requires time. For example, extra time must be allowed for 170 students to pick up a copy of an assignment. The development of a course web site that includes the syllabus, assignments, old exams, and answer keys has made the logistics of teaching a large class much more efficient. Students have convenient access to all course materials at any time. One interesting result of this distribution method is that it shifts copying costs from the department to the students. For a large course with weekly assignments and answer keys, these costs are significant. Instructors and administrators may want to carefully consider the consequences of shifting these costs to students. Another disadvantage of this system is that it reduces the number of office visits by students, thereby reducing the opportunity to get to know them outside of the classroom.

Technology in the Classroom

Prior to teaching Principles of Agricultural Economics, I had a negative opinion of technology use in the classroom. I wondered why anyone believed that any pedagogical differences might exist among a chalkboard, an overhead projector, and a high-technology computer presentation. I also had heard negative reviews of instructors who had converted lecture material into computer presentations. Presentation technology, when used exclusively in a lecture, is not well received by students, who believe that they can read the material just as easily as have it read to them off of a screen with the lights dimmed. I had these negative perceptions before I taught in a large classroom; after the large class experience, I became a believer in the use of classroom technology.

I was fortunate to be assigned one of several high-technology classrooms at Kansas State University. After finding out that the technology would be available, I interviewed faculty, students, and administrators about how to best use it. A former student suggested that the course information, including assignment due dates, the date of the next exam, instructor's office hours, and the topics of each lecture could be presented on the large screen prior to each class period rather than on the board. This has benefited my instruction by allowing me to use the ten minutes before class to interact with students and answer questions about the course material. This may appear trivial, but I believe that setting the proper environment for a lecture is crucial to an effective presentation. Ten minutes of casual interaction with students allows the instructor to learn more about them, how they are doing, and how well they are keeping up with the material. This information can be the basis for adjustments in the content and pace of the lecture.

I soon began to include computer presentation slides for terms, concepts, and definitions. In earlier courses, I wrote this type of information on the chalkboard. I have identified three distinct advantages to using the computer technology:

1) The instructor can face the students, read the definition two or three times, and see when the students are ready to move on to the application of the economic concept. Of course, definitions are printed in the textbook and could be passed out before class, but I believe that the physical act of writing out a definition helps many students learn the concept. This may be why we continue teaching in a lecture format.

2) In a larger classroom, extra time is required to write in a large and legible fashion on the chalkboard. The technological solution provides a large screen with very clear and legible wording that the entire class can see well.

3) Adding variety to a classroom improves the attention and retention of students. One totally unanticipated positive consequence of using classroom technology is getting students' attention by altering the lighting. How does this work? I prepare four to six presentation slides per lecture at the computer in my office. I save these slides on a mainframe drive that can be accessed directly from the classroom computer. I have noticed that when I dim the lights

to show a slide, the students' attention is captured. When the lights brighten so that the chalkboard can be seen, the attention of the class is refocused.

Simply put, my experience in a large classroom suggests that a combination of chalkboard and computer slides is superior to either format alone. Computer presentations alone and leaving the lights dimmed for the entire period can lead to boredom and a perception that attending class is not necessary. Using the chalkboard alone in a large room can waste valuable time to write in a large and clear fashion. I believe that using several presentation methods results in more creative, more interesting classroom lectures that increase learning.

Email

I have been an email user for over ten years. However, it has only been recently that most students have had the ability to use email to enhance learning in the classroom. Many students are comfortable visiting the instructor during office hours to ask questions. Increasingly, many students are unable to do this: They live too far away or do not have transportation. Other students may have work or lab requirements during office hours. Lastly, some students unfortunately are apprehensive about conversing with an instructor, particularly during their first year of school. I have been excited to be able to share electronic conversations with many students who otherwise would not have asked for or received help in learning the material in Principles of Agricultural Economics.

CONCLUSION

Teaching large classes can be enhanced effectively with computer technology. My teaching experiences have transformed my view of technology from skepticism to neutrality to advocacy. The incorporation of technology into class assignments, lectures, and student/teacher interactions allows an instructor to gain efficiency in teaching tasks, such as distribution of assignments and answer keys. More importantly, it allows instructors to review their course content, teaching style, and learning objectives and upgrade them.

CONTACT INFORMATION

Andrew P. Barkley, Professor
Department of Agricultural Economics
Kansas State University
217 Waters Hall
Manhattan, KS 66506-4011
Email: barkley@ksu.edu
    or see http://www-personal.ksu.edu/~barkely
Phone: (785) 532-4426
Fax: (785) 532-6925

Vignette 47 A Computer-Enhanced Course in Microeconomics

Byron W. Brown, Michigan State University

The need for students in microeconomics to do practice problems is widely acknowledged. But printed practice problems, either from textbooks or from handouts, suffer from some serious limitations. For example, every student gets the same problems, and grading requires a substantial amount of work in itself, delaying feedback to the students. My solution to these problems has led me to create a new experimental course that includes a combination of computer-based exercises, a help room, and shortened class meeting times. In what follows, I recount the innovations in the course, report student reactions to these innovations, and present some preliminary data on student outcomes.

EDUCATIONAL THEORIES

Many years of teaching microeconomics to students of widely varying ability has convinced my colleagues and me of the importance of students doing practice problems and applications. If students don't do practice problems before the exam, they certainly won't be able to do them on the exam.

I have also become convinced of the importance of students cooperating in learning and of receiving prompt feedback on their work. Of course, there may be a fine line between cooperation and cheating. An important challenge is finding ways to promote cooperation, while at the same time preserving the integrity of students doing their own work.

AN EXPERIMENTAL COURSE IN PRINCIPLES OF MICROECONOMICS

At Michigan State University, in the fall of 1997 I offered an experimental section[1] that differed from its conventional counterparts in three ways. First, the class met only two hours per week for lecture and discussion, instead of three. Second, we created a virtual lab in which students were required to do a series of computer-based exercises written specifically for the course. Third, we set up a help room with 15 computers as a place where students could get help on the computer problems as well as on general course work.

The Economics Virtual Laboratory

In the experiment, a 320-student section met for two 50-minute sessions per week for lecture and discussion. A third credit for the course consisted of laboratory activities that were designed to occupy two hours per week on average. (At MSU, laboratory time translates into lecture/discussion time at a rate of two lab hours per lecture hour.)

The most important laboratory activity (20% of the total course credit) was a series of 25 computer-based problem sets, written by the author, called *Problems in Microeconomics* (these problems are available on the WWW at http://www.bus.msu.edu/econ/brown /pim). These Excel-based problem sets are highly interactive, give instant feedback to the students on correctness of answers, and include a randomization feature that gives each student a unique version of a problem set.

The Problem Sets

Each problem set has two parts. The first, provided to the students as printed copy or as a file in portable document format, consists of an extended story problem that describes the economic theory on the topic and a series of up to 20 questions. The second is a companion Excel workbook, provided from a web site, that must be used to answer the questions. The workbook has an interactive graphical display that shows the effects of changes in economic variables particular to a problem. Topics run from simple supply and demand to monopoly, covering almost all of the topics included in most microeconomics courses. Students do the problems when and where they wish, subject to due dates throughout the course.

When students think they have the answer to a question, they flip to an answer sheet (another spreadsheet in the same Excel workbook) and enter it in the space provided. The answer is instantly graded. The student has unlimited tries to get the answer right. I've decided to use the problems as a kind of mastery learning system[2], so to get credit for a problem set, all of the questions have to be answered correctly.

Each student gets a different version of the problems through the use of a randomization technique.[3] Because the questions are the same for all (e.g., "What's the best output for the monopolist to choose if profits are to be maximized?"), and the answers vary from student to student, cooperation is encouraged and rewarded. Answer sheets are printed out and contain the student's name and identification number.

The Help Room

We knew that if the course included required computer-based problem sets and a substantial minority of the students were inexperienced computer users, then some new and aggressive steps would be needed to make sure these users did not become overwhelmed by frustration, anger, and despair. Our answer to this problem was a student help room staffed by graduate and undergraduate teaching assistants. The room was equipped with 15 computers. All of the materials for the course were accessible from a course home page on the web, so were available from these computers as well as from over 50 public microcomputer laboratories across the MSU campus. The room was staffed during operating hours by a minimum of three assistants. As the semester progressed, the room became a popular studying place for students, as help was readily available either for the computer exercises or with other course-related questions.[4]

STUDENT EFFECTS—HOW THEY DID

The course was not part of a controlled experiment, so anything reported comparing it with other sections of the microeconomics course should at best be interpreted as suggesting a future research agenda and not as a conclusion about the efficacy of the techniques. I found enough differences from earlier sections of the same course to be worth extended comment and enough similarities with courses in other fields that used a similar innovation to suggest some hypotheses about the effects of the kind of computer-assisted instruction we used.

Figure 47.1 shows the distribution of final grades for my course in two semesters, fall 1996, one year before the experiment, and fall 1997. The fall 1996 course was taught by the same instructor in the same room, had the standard three-day-a-week schedule, but had no help room, and a different textbook. The two distributions are statistically different at the 5% level of significance.[5] With the experiment, there was an increase in both the proportion of grades of 4.0 and 0.0.

The average grade of 2.49 in 1996 rose to 2.72 in 1997, a statistically significant difference. The increase in average grades was probably due, at least in part, to how the problem sets were graded. The grading curve for the problem sets was very steep, with students losing all credit on that part of the course if a quarter of the problem sets were not turned in. But most students managed to get their problem sets completed and turned in, so a good grade for 20% of the course was for them guaranteed. For MSU's students at least, it appears that if you give them a well-defined task, most will complete it.

There is an interesting variation on this theme. In economics courses generally, women traditionally do less well than men.[6] In 1996, when the average grade was 2.49, men had a mean grade of 2.62, and women a significantly different 2.32. In the 1997 experiment, the male advantage virtually disappeared. Men had an average grade of 2.73 compared to women's 2.72. A preliminary analysis suggests that closing the gap was due mostly to the women being more successful in completing their computer problem sets. Figure 47.2 shows the distribution of the course grades in 1997 by gender. While men got somewhat more grades of 4.0, they also tended to have an edge at the bottom of the distribution.

In the 12th week of the course, we surveyed the class. We asked a series of categorical questions about the course (e.g., "If you had a choice between doing the computer exercises, and spending another hour in lecture, which would you choose?") and a series of open-ended questions that allowed the students to write a response (e.g., "Which students benefit most [or least] from the computer exercises?").

The students overwhelmingly favored the virtual lab, with 96% of the respondents saying that the computer exercises were a good substitute for the third class hour each week. When asked whether using the computer exercises as part of the course, was "overall, good for me," 91% responded positively.

LESSONS LEARNED

We learned from the survey that the most desirable aspects of the problem sets were the degree of interactivity and the hands-on aspects of learning. Many students commented that the problem sets helped them learn more quickly and that the problems related closely to materials covered in class. Not all of the comments were positive. Some students were bothered at having to get all answers correct to receive credit for a problem set.

We came away from the experiment convinced that if computers were to be an important part of instruction, then something like our help room had to be available. Regular, extended hours with staff always on hand to provide support was an important part of our success.

Getting instant feedback as part of the computer problems was also a crucial feature as was having each student get a different version of each problem. We have since observed that many successful computer innovations seem naturally to promote cooperation in learning, and this was certainly the case with our students.

FIGURE 47.1

COURSE GRADES, 1996 & 1997

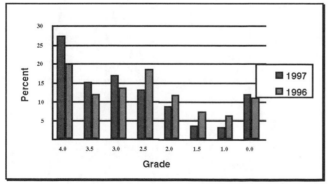

FIGURE 47.2

COURSE GRADES BY GENDER, 1997

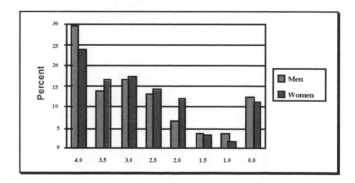

CONTACT INFORMATION

Byron W. Brown, Professor Economics
Department of Economics
Michigan State University
East Lansing, MI 48824
Email: brownb@pilot.msu.edu
Phone: (517) 355-2364
Fax: (517) 432-1068

ENDNOTES

[1] Principles of microeconomics at MSU enrolls about 2,000 students per semester. The experimental section was one of seven offered that term and enrolled in excess of 300 students. The experiment has now become institutionalized as separate sections of the principles of microeconomics course.

[2] Bloom, B. S. (1976). *Human characteristics and school learning*. New York, NY: McGraw-Hill.

[3] Entering the same student number always results in the exactly the same problems—questions and answers. This makes helping individual students easy, as the tutors can replicate exactly the same problem on another computer.

[4] Prior to setting up the experimental course, the instructors were each given a number of TAs who would each hold their own office hours. Students had to seek out and find particular TAs. The help room was a dramatic change in that students could now go to one place, over a large time block, and be assured of getting help. Service to students was vastly improved, and it turns out the help room could be staffed with fewer TAs than the earlier system.

[5] MSU's grade system has a 4.0 top grade, while grades below 2.0 are unsatisfactory. The movement toward a bimodal grade distribution was also observed in MSU's CPS 101 course reported on Vignette 19 of this volume.

[6] There is quite a bit of evidence on the higher performance of men in economics courses. Durden and Ellis found no significant effect of gender on learning, but reported this as an exception to the usual finding (see Durden, G. C., & Ellis, L. V. (1995). The effects of attendance on student learning in principles of economics. *American Economic Review*, 85(2), 339-42). Why women tend not to major in economics and do less well in economics courses has been the subject of heated debate in the profession (see Ferber, M. A., (1995). The study of economics: A feminist critique. *American Economic Review*, 85(2), 357-61).

Vignette 48 | Competitive Strategies: A Team/Case-Based Approach to Economics Education

Sheldon Sax and Michael Claudon, Middlebury College

While economics majors are given a heavy dose of traditional micro and macroeconomic theory, students typically tend to be poorly equipped to deal with situations when the traditional assumptions do not hold. The Competitive Strategies course, Economics 455, taught in spring 1998, was a case study-based, senior-level economics seminar designed to challenge students to think beyond the standard models. Assignments included readings, case studies, and a team-oriented competitive strategy analysis of a local Vermont business. (Local businesses were invited to participate under the auspices of the Addison County Development Association. Students and faculty were required to sign nondisclosure agreements with the companies in exchange for access to confidential financial information.) Former Middlebury students enrolled in the MBA program at the Tuck Business School at Dartmouth acted as mentors to the teams.

We and the 16 students met twice a week for a standard seminar and once a week for a three-hour computer lab. The computer lab aimed to introduce and to refine student technical skills using Microsoft Excel and PowerPoint software. Familiarity with both applications was required for the team presentations of their evolving strategies.

The class had a set of web pages (http://cweb.middlebury.edu:202/ec455a/), a file server directory, and an electronic discussion forum. The web pages were set up so that off-campus visitors could register with the class, leave their electronic addresses, and receive updates about course progress. The mentors at Tuck and some interested alumni participated via email. The final class activity was a trip to Dartmouth, where the four teams presented their competitive strategies for their respective local businesses to the mentors, the business principals, and interested Tuck faculty.

EDUCATIONAL THEORY

The combination of case studies, student/team presentations, and technology into the course was designed to achieve the following:

- Introduce students to the case study method and sharpen their critical reasoning skills

- Provide a real-life context to which students could apply economic theory

- Encourage team-based learning

- Develop student presentation skills, both in groups and as individuals

- Improve the technological skills of our economics majors

- Facilitate communication both on and off campus

COURSE ACTIVITIES

To meet the course objectives, a number of changes were implemented.

Computer Lab

Initially, this three-hour weekly session was used to teach students how to use the more sophisticated components of Excel and PowerPoint. Students quickly picked up these skills and showed each other and us the latest techniques they'd discovered. The lab became increasingly informal but remained highly productive. This allowed faculty to spend time with the students answering questions about assigned readings and cases; to conduct impromptu meetings with teams about the status of their business strategy project; and to sort out any technological difficulties students were having with the web site, presentations, file server, etc.

Lectures with PowerPoint

PowerPoint was used judiciously in lecture situations during the course. We found that while developing electronic lecture material could be time-consuming, the investment was worth it.

Student Team Presentations

Student presentations were very effective both pedagogically and technologically. Student public speaking skills improved with each of the four presentations required. Team PowerPoint presentations evolved to a very professional level. We were fortunate to have access to a computer lab with 100 Meg switched ethernet speed and 200 MHz Pentium II processor machines because the graphically intensive presentations required adequate processor speed and hard disk space.

Electronic Publication of Best Presentations and Papers

Some case assignments were team-based and required an in-class PowerPoint presentation of the analysis. The best presentations were made available from the course's home page.

Electronic Syllabus

The web-based syllabus enabled us to announce schedule changes and to keep information current. Notes, talking points, and summaries were available from the web site (http://cweb.middlebury.edu:2021/ec455a/resources_pages/resources_notes.asp).

Participation of Social Science Reference Librarian

Part of each team's assignment was to situate its local business in the context of regional, national, and international competition. The students had to research the type of industry, the potential competitors, and the industry structure. One of the college's reference librarians did a workshop with the class and developed a set of class-specific resources available on the Internet (http://www.middlebury.edu/~lib/classguides/ec455.html), from which students could do a substantial amount of their industry-specific research. The class research guide was available electronically from the library web pages. It included links to online databases such as Lexis/Nexus, EDGAR, etc. The involvement of the reference librarian was very helpful.

Publication of Student Résumés

Inasmuch as the class was composed of graduating seniors, each student's résumé was published in PDF (portable document format) on the class web site so that it could be viewed or downloaded by prospective employers. A number of students provided the URL to their résumé prior to job interviews and, in fact, the interviewers did access this information online.

MEASURED RESULTS

Each course at Middlebury is evaluated anonymously by students at the last class using a standard form. Student evaluations of the course were uniformly positive. Presenting with technology was mentioned by a number of students as being a valuable, lifelong skill. The students' mentors at Tuck and the Tuck faculty who viewed the team presentations were unabashedly enthusiastic and impressed with their quality. Further, the principals of the four local businesses who attended the presentations were extremely impressed with the depth of understanding that the students had acquired about their businesses and the quality of the competitive strategies that the students produced. We think that the combination of team-based learning and technology was very constructive.

Students found the workload for this course too onerous. The combination of assigned readings from the text, case studies, midterm exam, and the local business project required significantly more effort than their other courses. For the next iteration of the class, we are adjusting the workload, reducing the readings somewhat, and analyzing fewer cases.

LESSONS LEARNED

- We found that while it could be time-consuming to develop electronic lecture material, the initial investment was worthwhile. Animated graphs are a particularly effective way of presenting information. It is a big mistake, however, to project a screen full of text on the screen and then read it. PowerPoint and similar presentation software are valuable when they present material in a unique and informative way. The ease of editing and revising is a significant advantage as is the ability to make the material available to students/mentors/faculty outside of class via the web site and/or file server.

- The class rarely used electronic conferencing. In retrospect, we may have introduced too much technology at once. Participation was voluntary and, given the heavy work load that the rest of the course requirements imposed, skipping the electronic conference was one way for students to compensate. We are currently considering mandatory conference participation.

- Having both a class web site and class file server folder was redundant and required posting identical information in two locations. We thought that since students were more familiar with the file server, offering both would be an advantage and ease the transition to web-based information. It was not and seemed to confuse students. We will migrate exclusively to web-based class information.

- Team-based learning is particularly effective with technology. Inevitably, at least one student in each group is technologically sophisticated and willing to share expertise with peers.

- Students are very tempted to look only at online resources. Further, many have difficulty evaluating the quality of information that they find, particularly on the web. An industry analysis could come from an authoritative source, such as *Baron's*, or from a tenth grader's project. Involving a reference librarian with the course's research component and developing quality resources is critical. The class-specific resource page, developed by a professional librarian, ensured that the links from that page were of high quality. We will involve the reference librarian next semester to help students develop criteria by which to evaluate the quality of online information.

CONCLUSION

The students enjoyed the team approach and profited from the real-world case study on which they worked. They were more engaged with the course materials and their team projects than in previous semesters. They adapted to the technological component of the course very quickly and they seemed eager to acquire these new skills. Technology gave them tools with which to develop their analysis and present it in an effective manner.

This fall 1998 semester, we introduced new forecasting and simulation software, Crystal Ball, in addition to the Excel and PowerPoint applications. Positive responses from the students convince us that the introduction of appropriate technology can be a beneficial experience for both students and teachers.

CONTACT INFORMATION

Sheldon Sax
Director of Instructional Technology
Middlebury College
Voter Hall #204
Middlebury, VT 05753-6200
Email: Sax@middlebury.edu
WWW: http://www.middlebury.edu/~sax,
http://www.middlebury.edu/~its/IT
Phone: (802) 443-5679
Fax: (802) 443-2067

David G. Brown, Wake Forest University

The idea behind my section of our required freshman seminar is that professionals approach life through the thinking filters of their own disciplines. In all things they do, whether listening to a symphony or raising a child, economists use principles, such as cost-benefit, comparative advantage, and supply-demand. Literature professors and physicists use different principles. By learning in this required freshman seminar how an economist applies thinking filters, students gain insight and practice how to approach their other professors and get the most out of their courses.

Fifteen of us meet twice a week for one semester. All students live in wired dorms and own identical laptop computers that are connected to the campus network, or ethernet, during all classes. The class has a web page, a Lotus Notes-based electronic discussion group, and a listserv.

EDUCATIONAL PHILOSOPHY

Faced with the opportunity to supplement traditional teaching strategies with computer-based tools, I asked myself some very basic questions: What strategies have worked best for me in the past, and are there computer tools that will build on them? What are my course objectives, and how can these newly available tools enable them? What are some of my basic beliefs about how students learn, and how can they be advanced through computer enhancements? From these questions emerged a set of educational principles.

- Collaborative learning (students help each other to learn)

- Frequent student/faculty dialogue

- Timely feedback

- Trust (professor viewed as knowledgeable and sincere, views students as able and earnest)

- Application of theory (practice increases learning and retention)

- High expectations (high standards build student self-respect)

COURSE ACTIVITIES

Once I identified the principles to emphasize, I asked my early adopter colleagues to suggest computer tools that might be used to pursue them. Among the new approaches were the following:

Email

The biggest change that the computer has made possible is continuous contact with my students. Instead of only interacting twice a week when the class meets, we communicate electronically between classes. In a typical week, I exchange nine individual email messages with each of them. Many of my students continue to email after the final examination and throughout the summer. Thanks to our email group, which can send a single message simultaneously to every member of the class, students keep up with each other both during and after the course. I have also used email to invite my classes to attend a play and to join me for a short discussion afterward. In short, community is strengthened by ease of communication.

Prelecture Discussion

Often I pose a question about the reading that relates to an upcoming lecture. All class members are expected to enter the electronic discussion prior to class. By monitoring the discussion, I can not only surmise the appropriate beginning for my lecture, but also know who is doing the reading.

One-Minute, In-Class Quizzes

Typically, after lecturing for 20 minutes, I ask every member of the class to enter a one- or two-sentence summary of what has been said. Through the network, each student's answer appears on all computers. The class is then encouraged to focus on a particular answer, to fix it up, if necessary, and then to move on to another. I stress that the refined definitions are acceptable answers on exams. This transfers the mantle of expert from the textbook author to the instructor and then, crucially, to the student.

Subgroup Advice on First-Draft Papers

After a concept of the week is introduced, students write a one-page essay in which they define the concept and provide an example of its application in a recent newspaper article, usually from the Internet. This essay is submitted electronically to four classmates and a Wake Forest alumnus, a volunteer who may live anywhere. Over the next two days, the five responders suggest ways to improve the first draft, each using a different colored electronic pen. Since all responder comments appear on the original draft and are viewable by all six people, second and third responders often comment on earlier responses as well as the original. After this stage, the author has one day to revise and to submit the paper for grading. All graded papers, including my comments, are returned electronically to all members of the class, not just the author. All final papers are subsequently made available to future classes, so the level of expectation is constantly raised. My follow-up lecture on the concept under discussion usually focuses on the papers and my comments on them.

Electronic Publication of Best Papers

My personal web page provides access to the best papers on each topic.

Electronic Syllabus

By convenient hyperlinks to supplemental readings, students are encouraged to stretch beyond the minimum requirements of the course. With the electronic syllabus, assignments can be changed midcourse, and materials updated easily.

Computer Tip Talks

At the end of each class, one student reports on how he or she uses the computer to enhance learning (e.g., using the library's electronic catalog, making a PowerPoint presentation, and searching the Internet). Before leaving, each student is asked to send by email an evaluative paragraph of praise and criticism to the student lecturer. These critiques cover the content, the credibility, and the clarity of the report.

Internet Search

On several occasions, I ask students to search the Internet for resources relevant to the topic under discussion and then share their knowledge with the class. This has multiple advantages: It hones their search skills, forces them to evaluate the quality of their discoveries, and gives them a sense of independence from the text and the instructor.

MEASURED RESULTS

In comparing this course to their other courses, 100% of my students have rated their experience as average or above average on the criteria "How much have you learned in this course?" and "How much fun have you had in this course?" This is consistent with campus-wide findings, which indicate that both professors and students find the quality and character of student/faculty interaction to be substantially enhanced by universal computing.

LESSONS LEARNED

Computer-intensive teaching was new to me. Inevitably, I tried some things that didn't work well; with others, I was initially too timid. Several of these experiences are listed here.

Lectures with PowerPoint

The preparation of graphic diagrams and tables is generally very time-consuming and not particularly productive. Dimming the lights and looking away from the students to the screen is very awkward; I still use overhead transparencies and the blackboard. I am more likely to distribute copies of the PowerPoint slides in advance than to talk from the slides in class.

Threaded Conversations

Students tend to ignore poorly structured discussion groups. Asynchronous electronic discussions work best when all are expected to enter the conversation, and there is a deadline date (usually two or three days) for participation.

Short Papers and Readings

Subgroup editing works best when the original draft papers are limited to three pages, and the groups to six people. Similarly, since most students print out assigned readings that exceed ten pages, hard copy readings placed on reserve in the library still have their place. The computer screen seems to be best for shorter messages.

Limited Use of Computers in Class

The real difference in my teaching is what happens between classes, not in class, when we are all together. Providing ethernet connections to each student seat in each classroom may not have been a good investment for the university. Too much can go wrong with the network, connections, and individual computers. Even when all systems are working, many computers work slowly, particularly when they are performing the same tasks on the same network at exactly the same time. When meeting face-to-face, group discussion and lecture enhance our technology-aided communications of the past few days.

The Buddy System

When students help each other learn how to use the computer, after six weeks it is difficult to distinguish those with extensive computer experience from the neophytes.

Conclusion

My course design is a work-in-progress. The old constraints of time and place seem not to matter as much. Students are taking more responsibility for their own learning. I'm experiencing conversations without lapses between classes and without endings at each semester and the delight of longer conversations with my students. We are all risking new ways of thinking. There is little chance that I will ever be comfortable teaching without using the computer as a basic tool for increasing communication.

Contact Information

David G. Brown, Vice President and Dean
International Center for Computer-Enhanced
    Learning
Professor of Economics
Wake Forest University
P. O. Box 7328, Reynolda Station
Winston-Salem, NC 27109
Email: brown@wfu.edu
WWW: http://www.wfu.edu/~brown
Phone: (336) 758-4878
Fax: (336) 758-4875

Shared Field Experience in Teacher Education

Timothy J. Schwob, SUNY, Potsdam

The students in an elementary science methods course for preservice K-6 teachers used electronic communications to exchange lesson plan assignments and to share course information with each other, field experience sponsor teachers, and the course instructor. The provost's office at SUNY, Potsdam provided funding for participating sponsor teachers to secure Internet accounts with local service providers. This vignette describes the components of the course and an analysis of the effectiveness of technology in improving student communication and prepared lessons.

EDUCATIONAL THEORIES

Each course in a college student's career should demonstrate the "Seven Principles for Good Practice" as developed by Chickering and Gamson (1987). The use of technology explicitly addresses three of those principles: good practice encourages contacts between students and faculty, gives prompt feedback, and communicates high expectations.

The effectiveness of teacher preparation courses is greatly enhanced when theory is tested by practice. The ability of preprofessional teachers to translate methods-course learning into public school classroom presentations is considered crucial to their success. Lessons written by a college student for delivery to young children can only benefit from the consistent feedback of practicing professionals.

The elementary teacher preparation program at SUNY, Potsdam requires that students spend time in the public school classroom prior to their final student-teaching semester. In the science methods course described here, students register for a concurrent practicum, which pairs them with an exemplary elementary grade-level teacher. These teachers are chosen for their expertise in pedagogy as well as their comfort level with technology. The students spend one morning per week for ten weeks with their sponsor teacher. Each student is required to present at least three full-class lessons in the public school classroom.

Whenever teams of professionals, separated by the geography of a rural area, are expected to work together, clear communication among all parties is of paramount importance. The Internet and the ability to send and receive email are extremely valuable tools to facilitate information sharing. What follows is a description of a science methods course that has benefited from rapid and easily accessed Internet communication.

COMPUTER-ENHANCED TECHNIQUES

To be certain that each of the team members—college student, course instructor, and public school sponsor teacher—is current with both course activities and expectations, the instructor maintains a web site. From the course home page, links are available to the course outline, descriptions of all assignments, interesting science teaching and learning web sites, names and email addresses of all class members and sponsor teachers, and the current and past weeks' class activities. In this way, the public school teachers, many of whom now have both school and home Internet access, can be aware of what the students are learning on campus and encourage them to implement their newly learned teaching strategies in the public school classroom.

The main purpose of the practicum attached to the methods course is for the students to gain experience in planning and delivering lessons to young children. To maximize effectiveness and ensure appropriateness, the course instructor and sponsor teacher must both review the lessons prior to planned delivery. In the past, this necessitated the physical passage of paper copies of each plan back and forth, first to the course instructor, then to the sponsor teacher. Since all three members of the team rarely had time together to collaboratively critique the plans, the process was very cumbersome, inefficient, and often ineffective.

Using email as the medium of discourse has not only expedited the process of lesson plan development but has also improved the product. The student sends the first draft to the course instructor, who reviews it and makes suggestions for improvement. Because formatting options are limited in the email program presently used, suggestions are given in upper case. Other, more sophisticated software would allow more options, but they are not universally available to either the college students or the sponsor teachers. This draft is returned to the student electronically, usually within 24 hours. At the same time, a copy of the draft with the instructor's suggestions is also sent to the sponsor teacher.

The student makes the suggested improvements and submits a second draft. Often this draft with minor corrections is sufficiently complete to forward to the sponsor teacher for additional comments. What was once a two-week process involving mail or personal delivery of the drafts, now can occur in less than five days. Each member of the team is aware of the evolution of each lesson, which minimizes miscommunication.

MEASURED RESULTS

At the end of the school year, each teacher who was successful in accessing her/his account reported that the ability to communicate directly with the course instructor and students and to access course information electronically was valuable. On a 0–3 scale (Didn't do, Disagree, Neutral, and Agree), the participating sponsors gave an average value of 2.9 in response to the question, "I felt the student's work was improved because of the ability to communicate (share lesson plans, etc.) electronically." The ability to communicate with the instructor earned a 3.0, and the ability to communicate with the students warranted a 2.9. Clearly, the sponsor teachers felt the experience was worthwhile.

The course instructor saw a marked improvement in the quality of the lesson plans as the semester progressed. They think that because the student received rapid and extensive feedback, their efforts to produce a higher quality product increased.

What is not conclusive is the value to the sponsor teacher of having course information available. The average score for this item was 2.4—not really high enough to show strong support. Perhaps its main value is simply to support the environment in which shared communication is considered important and worthwhile.

LESSONS LEARNED

For a project such as this to be a success, the following must be in place:

- Each sponsor teacher must have ready access to the Internet either at home or at school.

- Each college student must have the same ready access. The SUNY, Potsdam campus is completely networked, both in computer labs and residence halls.

- The Internet service provider must be reliable and conscientious. We made the decision at the outset that our campus did not have the personnel resources to troubleshoot problems that might arise with sponsor teacher communication. Hence, contracts were arranged with local providers.

- All participants must develop the habit of checking the course web site and their email often and responding quickly.

The ability to share work and messages asynchronously has clearly improved the quality of the lessons produced by the college students in the practicum. Additionally, useful student contacts with faculty have increased, feedback has been rapid and frequent, and the high expectations for the final product have been communicated, as called for in the Seven Principles for Good Practice.

As we move into our second year using electronic communication, we have made the following changes:

- Most sponsor teachers now have their own account either at home or at school and are becoming more comfortable with email. As the need arises, we will be offering short instruction to develop that comfort level further.

- Each student is required to submit all lesson plans electronically, and corrected copies are automatically forwarded to sponsor teachers.

- The choice of Internet service provider is left up to the sponsor teacher, which removes the course instructor from responsibility for technical problems with email and web page access.

- The sponsor teachers and students are requested to check the course web page weekly to be sure that all are aware of both course activities and assignments.

We are confident that with more students and faculty connected, the quality of student work will improve.

REFERENCE

Chickering, A. W., & Gamson, Z. F. (1987). Seven principles for good practice in undergraduate education, *AAHE Bulletin, 39* (7), 3-7.

CONTACT INFORMATION

Timothy J. Schwob
Associate Professor of Teacher Education
SUNY, Potsdam
304 Satterlee Hall
Pottsdam, NY 13676-2294
Email: Schwobtj@potsdam.edu
Phone: (315) 267-2504
Fax: (315) 267-2474

 **Interactive Multimedia in an Integrated Course in Science, Education, and Technology**

Angelo Collins, Vanderbilt University

Integration is a hot term in public school education today. Elementary teachers are encouraged to design units that integrate science, mathematics, language arts, social studies, and other school subjects. However, undergraduate course work typically fails to provide models of integrated instruction for prospective teachers. Most often, faculty in the college of arts and sciences teach their disciplines while faculty in the college of education teach about teaching those disciplines. Frequently, students take discipline-based courses before courses in pedagogy. In an attempt to provide an integrated learning experience, we taught a course for prospective elementary teachers that wove together content in science, education, and technology. Computer technology was essential in both instructional design and development and in improved communication.

When the course was first offered, four instructors, a graduate student, and six prospective elementary teachers met daily from nine to three for five weeks. During May 1997, three instructors and a teaching assistant met with ten students on a similar time schedule. Students earned four credits in laboratory science, two credits in science teaching methods, and met the state and national requirements for technology for teachers.

The course focused on cystic fibrosis (CF). Topics included the biology, genetics, molecular biology, symptoms, treatment, and ethical issues associated with the disorder. Aspects of teaching science included subject matter, inquiry, application, assessment, and organization. The course was designed around the students' production of an interactive multimedia program on CD-ROM for teaching about CF.

IDEAS BEHIND THE COURSE DESIGN

The design and delivery of the course were influenced by three concepts in learning and instruction: transformation, critical event, and reflection. Transformation is rooted in Lee Shulman's (1987) work on pedagogical content knowledge (PCK): the idea that masterful teachers have deep understanding of their subject matter, and hold this knowledge in ways that can be used to provide students with opportunities to learn it. One stage in the process of acquiring PCK Shulman calls transformation: the reorganization of discipline understanding into useful forms. The production of a CD-ROM was included in the course so students would be required to make transformations.

The term "critical event" emerges from contemporary learning theories, such as situated cognition (e.g., Brown et al., 1989), cognitive apprenticeship (e.g., Collins et al., 1991), and anchored instruction (CTGV, 1990). According to these theories, students attain understanding when learning activities are organized around tasks that require the application of knowledge from various points of view. Such tasks do not have a single correct answer but provide multiple ways for students to demonstrate they have attained learning goals. In the course, the critical task was the multimedia program on CD. In year one, the class produced "Billie's Story," a CD for middle school students. In year two, the CD contained three approaches to teaching about CF, one each for early elementary students, middle school students, and the public.

Contemporary learning theories also support metacognition, which occurs when learners reflect on what it is that they are learning and how they are learning it. To support such reflection, students were required to write reflective journals, which were maintained on a server.

COURSE ACTIVITIES

Each class day included instruction in science, education, and technology. Much of class time was spent designing and developing the CD. In addition, students visited the CF clinic, interviewed both healthcare providers and patients, did science laboratory activities, visited the news archives, and spent time in public school classrooms. Coursework was iterative; when students tried to express complex science ideas

for the future user of their CD, they had to return to the science ideas for clarification and deeper understanding.

The CD

We chose HyperStudio to produce the interactive multimedia program. Students had to master a number of computer skills: word processing, audio recording, scanning, drawing, animation, researching using the World Wide Web (WWW), video compression, and linking components. The students also had to develop screen-design skills. We all listened to Sally Cystic and Frank Fibrosis tell nonreaders that cystic fibrosis sounds like 65 roses as one group developed a program for young children. We all watched in amazement as a student-designed animation was used to explain the functioning of the sodium channel to adults.

The production of the CD provided the context for discussions about levels of scientific language appropriate for the target audience, about the advantages and disadvantages of different illustrations, and about the possible sequences for the presentation of ideas. The production of the CD provided reasons to discuss issues of curriculum design and implementation as well as to develop understandings of science content.

Computers and Communication

To enhance communication among class members, we designated a course folder on a dedicated server. The science, teaching, and technology syllabi were posted in the folder and on a course web page. Students also prepared reflections every other day in response to thought-provoking questions, which were submitted to the computer-based folder in a section restricted to the faculty. Each faculty member read the student reflections and prepared a response. Since the CD production was done in groups, the written communication with individual students provided a balance in instruction. Everyone commented about how the expertise and values of each faculty member made these computer-based discussions both personal and rich.

Requirements

While the production of the CD provided the students opportunities to exceed state requirements in technology for teacher licensure in some areas, such as program design using HyperStudio, other requirements were not addressed. Therefore, students did an assignment about grading and contacting parents that required the use of a spreadsheet, database, and mail merge.

MEASURED RESULTS

The science instructor was committed to using assessments similar to those used in other science courses in the college of arts and science. He created a traditional test of multiple choice and short answer questions. He chose questions from existing MCAT study exams, AP exams, and on-file exams from molecular biology courses for biology majors. It is with great pride that we report that none of the students, elementary education majors, scored below an A- on the science exam either year. It is amusing to report that after the science instructor returned the exam papers, he commented that all of the students had missed a certain question. One student pointed out that the answer he had expected was from their 1994 textbook, but more recent and accurate information was found on the web. She shared the URL.

Working alone, each of the education instructors analyzed the CD for evidence that the pedagogical criteria had been met. We then compared our professional judgments. We found that not only had all the criteria been met by each student, but there was a sophistication in the work that neither of us had previously seen.

There are several other indicators of the success of the course. The students were eager to display their work, and so we held an open house in a computer laboratory. Faculty and students from arts and science, education, and medicine, university and school administrators, local teachers, and parents attended. Students answered questions on science content, pedagogy, and instructional technology with ease and accuracy. Over a period of several months, the CD was displayed at a number of education meetings, and students were still able to talk about their work. In fall 1997, the students presented a poster session on the CD at the 11th Annual North American Cystic Fibrosis Conference. Not only was their presentation well received, an international drug company inquired into the possibility of purchasing the CD for distribution. Since that was not our intention, the opportunity was declined.

LESSONS LEARNED

We learned that the production of an interactive multimedia program that required accurate scientific understanding applied in a pedagogically correct manner promotes knowledge transformation and reflection. We learned other lessons not directly related to the use of computers. While some of these lessons are described here, further information on the course can be found in an article in the *Journal of Science Teacher Education* (Collins, Bercaw, Gary, Palmeri, Altman, & Singer-Gabella, in press).

Cost

The design and implementation of this integrated course is expensive in terms of time and personnel. We offered the course during "Maymester," when students were not enrolled in other courses. Although the course met no longer than required for the credits earned, because sessions met all day, every day, with no other classes and no days in between for students to do assignments or for faculty to revise plans, the experience was intense. A great amount of out-of-class time was required of students, most it spent in the computer lab. This meant that a faculty member, graduate student, or staff member had to be available at night and on weekends.

In addition, three faculty members, one each in science, education, and technology, were needed to staff the course. These faculty and others involved faculty and a teaching assistant met almost weekly the semester before the course was held and daily the week before the class. Further, these faculty made the commitment to attend all sessions every day. This is a lot of faculty time for a few students, a commitment the university was willing to make to explore issues of collaboration and integration.

Obviously, Peabody College of Vanderbilt University has well-equipped computer facilities for students to use for CD production. Scanning and videocompression equipment, multiple computers with adequate memory, speed, and Internet capabilities, as well as flat surfaces and storage were readily available in a single place.

Collaboration

Universities are organized around colleges and departments. A lot of faculty time was spent on organizational activities, such as how to register for a course earning some credit in each of two colleges. Beyond organizational issues, we quickly found that different colleges and departments have different norms. This was most evident on issues of assignments, group work, grading, and what is appropriate use of faculty time.

CONCLUSION

While the course was not taught during May 1998 because of shifting faculty responsibilities, the use of the computer for interactive multimedia program production has influenced assignments in several courses in both science and education and has had an impact on development work with practicing teachers.

ACKNOWLEDGMENTS

Other instructors who contributed to the success of the course include Todd Gary, Amy Palmeri, Jan Altman, Marcy Singer-Gabella, Lynne Bercaw, Tamara Altman, and K. K. Gaston.

REFERENCES

Brown, J. S., Collins, A., & Duguid, P. (1989). Situated cognition and the culture of learning. *Educational Researcher, 18* (1), 2-42.

Cognition and Technology Group at Vanderbilt. (1990). Anchored instruction and its relationship to situated cognition. *Educational Researcher, 19* (6), 2-10.

Collins, A., Bercaw, L., Gary, T., Palmeri, A., Altman, J., & Singer-Gabella, M. (in press). Good intentions are not enough: A story of collaboration in science education and technology. *Journal of Science Teacher Education.*

Collins, A., Brown, J. S., & Holum, A. (1991, Winter). Cognitive apprenticeship: Making thinking visible. *American Educator,* 6-46.

Shulman, L. S. (1987). Knowledge and teaching: Foundations of the new reform. *Harvard Educational Review, 57* (1), 1-22.

CONTACT INFORMATION

Angelo Collins, Associate Professor
Peabody College of Vanderbilt University
GPC Box 330
Nashville, TN 37203
Email: angelo.collins@vanderbilt.edu
Phone: (615) 322-8091
Fax: (615) 322-8999

Sarah E. Irvine, American University

Uses of Technology in Education is a three-credit course for preservice teachers, designed to train future teachers on how to incorporate computer-based technology in the K-12 classroom. When I first joined the faculty at American University in Fall 1995, the course had been taught exclusively by adjuncts, and very little of it had to do with the educational uses of technology. Today, students in the course use an online discussion and are trained to design instructional web sites and multimedia software, to assess educational programs for learning attributes, and to make informed decisions on hardware and software for classrooms and schools.

EDUCATIONAL THEORIES

According to the National Center for Education Statistics (NCES) March 1998 Issue Brief, approximately 78% of all public schools have some access to the Internet. The report indicates that one challenge to Internet use in schools is time for, and access to, professional development for teachers and administrators. To help teachers better use technology as an instructional tool, teacher educators in colleges and universities must rethink their courses to provide training and hands-on experience (Cradler & Parish, 1995). Faculty modeling the use of technology by integrating computers and the Internet into the curriculum is an ideal method for preparing teachers (Thomas, Larson, Clift, & Levin, 1996).

In addition to the need to prepare future teachers to use computers and networks because of the influx of technology in schools and classrooms, teacher education institutions like American University are also being persuaded to use technology by accrediting agencies. The National Council for Accreditation of Teacher Education (NCATE) has incorporated technology into standards for teacher accreditation. For example, one standard in the area of Content Studies for Initial Teacher Preparation expects candidates to "complete a sequence of courses and/or experiences to develop an understanding of the structure, skills, core concepts, ideas, values, facts, methods of inquiry, and

uses of technology for the subjects they plan to teach" (NCATE, 1997). The International Society for Technology in Education (ISTE) and the International Technology Education Association (ITEA), two professional organizations in the area of educational technology, have devised technology standards for all preservice. Important elements of these standards include demonstrating strategies for the educational use of electronic networks, such as the Internet, interpreting knowledge about computers, and illustrating the effective use of computers in classrooms (Wetzel, 1992). These standards inform much of what I do in my course.

COURSE ACTIVITIES

Online Discussion

My discussion group is a required, graded component of the course. During the first few weeks of class, I spend class time teaching the facilitation process. Each week, a student posts a question, which facilitates a discussion that has to do with an issue in education and/or technology. Students respond and are graded as follows:

- One point = post a comment in response to the issue of the week

- Two points = post a comment and provide your opinion of the topic under discussion

- Three points = post a comment, provide your opinion, and provide examples from your own course-related readings

- Four points = post a comment, provide your opinion, provide examples from your own course-related readings, and provide a meaningful basis for further discussion

This system encourages students to connect issues such as free speech on the Internet, professional development for teachers, tenure for faculty, and Microsoft's court battles, to the technical applications we use in class. Often the discussions are heated, and students avail themselves of the opportunity to get into the theoretical underpinnings of the course more often than in regular discussion. The framework for their remarks doesn't discourage the immediate, gut response that a student might have to another's opinion. I find that after a few weeks, students really begin to converse about the important issues in educational and technology. I appreciate the fact that this simple tool allows me to get to know what they are thinking about topics about which they will have to make decisions in their own classrooms.

CD-ROM on Technology

The course I teach is project-based. I teach web design, software evaluation, multimedia authoring, and hardware decision making. Over the years, I found that I was sharing many of the same programs that I downloaded off the Internet and passing out dozens of disks. I finally decided to put all these applications and sample projects in one place, so I've developed and produced a CD-ROM that I pass out in the beginning of the course. I've added my PowerPoint presentations from course lectures, sample projects created by children, and simple, step-by-step instructions for the basic computer tasks that students need to know to complete the assigned projects such as how to scan a photograph for use on a web page and how to create an image map. The CD also contains many demos of educational software that I've collected over the years, so that these teachers-in-training can have an opportunity to play with some of the popular programs that kids are using in classrooms, such as Jump Start Kindergarten and Reader Rabbit.

For the instructional web design part of the course, I created a web site that teaches the HTML editor that is included on the CD. The web site is on the CD as well, so students who don't have a connection to the Internet at home can access the instruction and create their own sites. I've found that each semester the CD allows us to spend class time on more advanced technical skills, and I find I can refer students to specific sections of the web page or the HyperStudio stack to answer common questions. I think it is important that I have created the presentations and instructional material contained in the CD, because it is matched to how I teach and present information in class.

Lab-Based Teaching

Although I present lectures and engage in in-class discussions, about 50% of class time is dedicated to teaching how to use technology. The class is typically held one evening a week for two-and-a-half hours. Some class meetings are entirely lecture and discussion, and I use the computers to bring up a web page or to demonstrate an application that illustrates the topic under discussion, but the students don't use the computers. However, some class meetings are entirely hands-on, and I spend my time training the students to use an application, such as Netscape Composer, HyperStudio, or Macromedia Director. We switch from Windows computers to Macintosh computers, depending on the application we are using, but every week we are in a lab.

Three Challenges to Lab-Based Teaching

1) There are simply not enough computer labs on campus. During the weeks that our time in class is spent in discussion or lecture, we don't need to be in the lab, and a classroom with a connection to the network and presentation hardware would be a better space for teaching. Without the computer monitors in the way, I would be better able to engage my students and see their faces. I know that students would be less tempted to check their email or surf the web when they get distracted, and another class could be using the valuable lab space.

On the other hand, it is important that we get into the lab when necessary. Extra time in the lab is hard to schedule at the last minute. Since I am very careful to attend to the needs of my students, I might change the plan to spend more time showing them how to do something, rather than engage in a lecture about why to do something. My class might be the only class that some students will take with any hands-on training, and I feel committed to giving these teachers-in-training the chance to try it themselves before trying it in their classrooms.

2) It requires individualized attention. When I am training students to use an application, I first show them what we are going to do, then I have them do it along with me, and then I have them do it themselves. I lose some students at this second step. They get too far ahead or too far behind or too far off course, and I have to go over to their machines and help them get back in step. Sometimes a quarter or even half of the students are not with me, and I either have to start over or come around and get each one of them back on track. With a large class, I can usually get other students to help out, but it isn't really fair to make them attend to their neighbors while they both get behind. A lab assistant would be great but isn't realistic in our department. As much as I can anticipate problems, I include step-by-step instructions on the CD. Often, I teach smaller parts in class and then stay later to help the students who need it.

3) The computers that I use to train the students during class are not set up the same way as those the students have at home. For example, some students are more comfortable with Internet Explorer and Microsoft Publisher than Netscape Navigator and Netscape Composer. When we are working on web page design, they get started with Publisher or another HTML editor, and then they have questions about how to do something that I've shown them. I have to download the program myself or, in some cases, go on house calls to dorm rooms or offices to help students work through a problem. Although I give the students samples of Netscape and other programs on the CD, I don't feel that I can require them to use an application when they can do the same thing with their own programs. If I want to maintain that the course is about using technology for educational purposes and not a course on Netscape or HyperStudio, then it benefits me in the long run to encourage my students to use what they have.

LESSONS LEARNED

When it is 10:30 p.m., and I'm sitting in a dorm room trying to help a student align images on a web page, I might be a little resistant to learning at all. I should have learned to tell the students to figure it out for themselves or to call the technical support hotline. I should have learned to demand that the students use the programs I show them in class. I should have learned that I can't stand Microsoft Publisher.

What I have learned is that teaching with technology is time-consuming and can be frustrating. I've also learned that this is time well-spent, and students are proud of their work. I know that I have been better able to encourage students to make real connections to the content of the course as well as to each other through online discussion. I feel that I'm better preparing the next century of students by teaching their teachers today.

REFERENCES

Cradler, J., & Parish, E. (1995). *Telecommunications and technology in education: What have we learned by research and experience?* San Francisco, CA: WestEd Regional Laboratory.

National Council for Accreditation of Teacher Education (NCATE). (1997). *Technology and the new professional teacher: Preparing for the 21st century.* Washington, DC: NCATE.

National Center for Educational Statistics. (1998, March). *Internet access in public schools.* Washington, DC: United States Department of Education.

Thomas, L., Larson, A., Clift, R., & Levin, J. (1996). Integrating technology in teacher education programs: Lessons from the Teaching Teleapprenticeships Project. *Action in Teacher Education, 17* (4), 1-8.

Wetzel, K. (1992). Models for achieving computer competencies in preservice education. In D. Carey, R. Carey, D. A. Willis, & J. Willis (Eds.), *Technology and Teacher Education Annual.* Charlottesville, VA: AACE.

CONTACT INFORMATION

Sarah E. Irvine, Assistant Professor
American University
4400 Massachusetts Avenue, NW
Washington, DC 20016-8030
email: sirvine@american.edu
Phone: (202) 885-3714
Fax: (202) 885-1187

Vignette 53 Information Technology and Learning

Al Rudnitsky, Smith College

Information Technology and Learning is a course about how to employ technology to enhance the teaching of any subject matter. Students who are interested in becoming teachers and students who are interested in how technology can affect thinking and learning take the class.

Information Technology and Learning began 15 years ago as a course named Computers in Education. My original intention was to introduce prospective teachers to the educational applications of computers. Early in the 1980s, most educational applications were drill-and-practice oriented, and computers were a rarity in most public schools. At the same time, most of the college students taking the course had little familiarity with computers. In fact, most were downright phobic about computers and had drawn on every conceivable strategy to avoid them. Workshops were offered about how to use word processors, but, as far as academic or in-depth experience, introductory computer science was students' only choice. Thus, students who had avoided computers until reaching college were likely to continue to do so. This course was de-

signed as a gentle way for beginners to learn about computers. While some students may not have found the going as gentle as advertised, most persevered in the course and emerged considerably more skilled, less mystified, and frequently excited about computers.

Computers in Education had two points of emphasis. One, grounded in cognitive science, examined what we know about teaching and learning and how computers could be employed effectively in educational settings. We did a lot of reading and talking about computers and how they could and should be used. The second point of emphasis was actually using computers. This included critical examination of educational software, the use of basic tools, such as word processing and databases, and the LOGO computer language. Consistent with a cognitive orientation toward teaching and learning, having students employ the computer as a tool was presented as the most effective way to use computers in education. The LOGO computer language was a major course focus because it immersed students in new ways of thinking, let them see and participate in what, at one level, computers are doing behind the scene, and allowed them to experience the computer's potential as a means to help students become better problem solvers.

The course has evolved over the years, due largely to experience teaching the course but also to important changes that have taken place, including the rapid development of the Internet as an information resource, the wide availability of powerful multimedia computers, and the fact that many more students enter the course with computer literacy. Experience has led me to focus more on learning and using applications and less on talking about using these applications. It has become increasingly clear that talk about why and how to use technology is largely pointless when students do not have first-hand experience in its use.

I tell students at the beginning of Information Technology and Learning that this is a four-credit opportunity to learn about computers and about themselves as learners. I repeat for several weeks that the course does not happen during scheduled class meetings but rather when students are working on the computer. Students cannot do well in this course by coming to class and being attentive. They must put in the work. At the same time, I guarantee them a good grade if they make an honest effort. Students keep a journal tracking and reflecting on their work. This journal is used as the basis for several assessments during the semester.

COURSE DESCRIPTION

Students learn a variety of things in the course:

- How to use a multimedia authoring program. They must design and complete a project over the course of the semester. The project must be grounded in a content area, be well designed, and must exploit the medium by exploring its topic in an interesting and nonlinear manner.

- How to create web pages. They create a personal home page. In addition, I form and assign groups of students to K-12 classrooms. Working with the classroom teacher, they design and produce a curriculum web site that supports and enhances something the class is studying.

- The LOGO computer language and a variety of other support applications for drawing, graphic

representation, and working with images, sound, and video.

- Principles underlying effective learning can be brought into play through these technology applications. The main message is that the best use of computers in education is as a tool, probably the most powerful our culture has yet devised, where students are active agents. This notion of the learner being in charge is something we discuss with regularity.

- Computers allow students to create cultures of collaboration, where ideas and expertise are freely shared. Creating products for an audience other than the teacher promotes a level of authenticity that typical schoolwork does not, requiring much more thought and editorial work and leading to a more meaningful grasp of the material.

Teachers often get to see students and student thinking in an entirely new light—one that can have a profound impact on the teacher's assessment of a student's capabilities.

Computers can enhance the possibilities for reflection on one's own learning and problem-solving processes and the opportunity to learn self-regulatory strategies.

MEASURED RESULTS

I ask students for an assessment of progress about midway through the course. A number of comments have appeared consistently. One that always amuses me is that, early in the course, many students perceive themselves to be behind everyone else. I point out that this is not possible, which prompts students to take a closer look at what they and others know. We have a 12-station computer lab devoted to the course and located in the building housing the department of education and child study. Students, without a great deal of encouragement, soon begin doing most of their work here. This is the entry to the class's collaborative culture and is an essential feature of the course. The widely held conception that computers and computing is asocial (or even antisocial) and that using a computer leads one to become a lonely nerd is shattered. Work on computers is intensely social. Students recognize the importance of practice. While sometimes thinking they understand something when they leave class, having to apply it in their work gives them a much clearer conception of what they do and do not know. The need to consider the structure of knowledge as they design their projects is something that almost all students become aware of. Students, to varying degrees, find learning the computer applications difficult and often frustrating. They confront personal theories of learning that turn out to suggest that learning should be easy, nonproblematic, and painless. What a bizarre notion, especially for people who are going to go on to teach. I believe the cumulative impact of these insights about learning, gained through experience rather than reading an educational psychology text, are the most important course outcomes for prospective teachers.

LESSONS LEARNED

Since Information Technology and Learning is about teaching and learning with technology, I always keep students up to date on my experience teaching the course. I am intensely aware of what and how students are learning and that they represent a wildly diverse range of abilities, background knowledge, and approaches to learning. Most college courses, certainly those with enrollments of more than 25 students, isolate the instructor. The instructor might know if an individual is in deep trouble, if for example, the student has either attended an office hour or did poorly on some assignment or exam. The instructor may have some hunches about students who are doing well. But exactly what the students are experiencing, what they are having difficulty or success with, is largely invisible. Using information technology in the classroom does for me just what I promise future teachers it can do for them.

CONTACT INFORMATION

Al Rudnitsky
Professor of Education and Child Study
Smith College
Northampton, MA 01063
Email: Arudnits@smith.edu
WWW: www.smith.edu/edc333
Fax: (413) 585-3268

Electronic Conferencing and International Political Economy

Jeffrey Cason, Middlebury College

In the process of integrating technology into the classroom, I have experimented with a number of different techniques in a variety of political science courses. These have included placing all course materials on the web, including discussion and reading questions; requiring students to post their papers on the web; developing a web resources section on a web-based syllabus; and incorporating electronic discussion into the class. This last technique—incorporating electronic discussion—has proven the most effective in promoting extra learning and intellectual stretching on the part of students. After using it in several courses and refining my approach, I found it to be very effective in my intermediate-level course on International Political Economy, taught during the spring semester of 1998.

EDUCATIONAL THEORIES

The main goals in using electronic discussion in my classes are 1) to encourage students to engage classroom issues outside the classroom, and 2) to give students who might otherwise be shy a chance to participate in discussion.

With the first goal, my hope was to make the education process more extensive, to encourage students to think more deeply and thoroughly about the issues that they were confronting in the class. With the second goal, I face a classroom in which, at best, perhaps half of the students participate regularly in class discussion. Other students, outside of class, have told me that they feel intimidated by the smarter students, and they don't think as quickly as the more vocal students. In the International Political Economy course, I hoped to use electronic discussion to bring more of these students into the loop, with the hope that, through it, they would eventually feel more comfortable speaking in class.

COMPUTER-ENHANCED TECHNIQUES

Over the last three semesters, I included electronic discussion in the class. Some students participated regularly in this discussion, while others rebelled against it. For PS304, I decided to offer students an option: participate regularly in electronic discussion or write an additional paper.

The first week of class, students were trained by a member of the college's instructional technology group in the use of electronic discussion. Middlebury has adopted a web-based electronic conferencing system called Motet. This has proven an easy-to-learn and easy-to-use conferencing system that meets the demands of my class discussion. Because Middlebury is a mixed-platform environment, Motet works well on Mac, Windows, and UNIX machines. Student computers already have a web browser installed, so we need no additional software. Students are taught how to log onto the conferencing system, find their conference, and read and post messages. The class orientation takes about 25-30 minutes.

In general, I let the electronic discussion be a place for students without much direct intervention from me. To create the feel of a small group, I divided the class into two groups of ten and posted the same question to each group. Fewer participants makes it easier to follow the thread of the discussion. Roughly once a week, I threw out a question for discussion, often following up on something that had come out during a class discussion or a reading. I did not ask factual questions or "What did so-and-so say about the rise of free trade in the 19th century?" but rather "Is free trade a viable strategy for developing countries? Why or why not?" This more open-ended questioning led to engaging discussion. Generally, however, I tended to stay out of the student discussion, to encourage informality in their exchange.

MEASURED RESULTS

There were no comparative quantitative measures used to assess how well the incorporation of electronic discussion worked. However, I have observed some substantial changes. First, the goal of encouraging greater participation was realized for many students. Around ten of 20 students participated on a regular basis during class time. Four participated in electronic discussion and demonstrated that they were grasping the material quite successfully, which I would not have known otherwise.

In addition, especially near the end of the class, students were using the electronic discussion in a debating style, canvassing one another for ideas as they prepared for the final exam. Opposing views were represented in the reading, and students ended up taking sides in the electronic discussion, which led to spirited debate. It struck me that through the electronic discussion they were engaging with the course material more than they might otherwise.

LESSONS LEARNED

- Students must be required to post regularly, and it must factor into their grade (in my case, 10%).

- Alternative assignments generally do not work; only one student chose to do the alternative assignment. If expectations are clear at the beginning of class, there is no need for an alternative.

- Participation should be evaluated regularly during the semester. When I first started using electronic discussion, I made the mistake of telling students they would be evaluated at the end of class. Since they had to have two postings a week, some of them waited until the eighth or ninth week to begin posting, which defeated the purpose of encouraging the students to engage with class material outside of class. Now, I tell the students that they will be evaluated every three weeks. This encourages regular participation and gets students into the swing of electronic discussion, which they tend to like once they get over the hump of figuring it out.

- The emphasis for this electronic discussion should be on informality. Students are used to informal communication with email, so to the extent that it can be made an extension of their email practices, the more willing they are to engage in discussion. I have found it necessary to remind them at certain points during the class that this informality is essential and that it is largely their space for communication about the class.

CONCLUSION

I have found that the use of electronic discussion can significantly enhance both the breadth and depth of discussion outside class meeting times. However, as with most teaching techniques, a process of refinement is required to find the best mix of required participation, discussion topics, and monitoring. Not only is careful planning on the introduction of technology required, constant tweaking is necessary to maximize its effectiveness in a particular course. Given the success of the electronic discussion in the International Political Economy course, I plan to continue to use web-based conferencing in future classes and expect that with the help of student feedback and thoughtful assessment and adjustment, I can continue to improve the pedagogical value of this technology.

CONTACT INFORMATION

Jeffrey Cason, Assistant Professor
Political Science
Middlebury College
Middlebury, VT 05753
Email: cason@middlebury.edu
Phone: (802) 443-5154
Fax: (802) 443-2050

 **Threads as an Alternative to the Paper Quizzes**

John R. Galvin, Tufts University

With the advent of the Internet, dynamic discussions among groups of people separated by temporal and geographic boundaries have become commonplace. Within the university environment, web-based educational tools designed specifically for course work have recently been introduced. Dean John R. Galvin of the Fletcher School of Law and Diplomacy at Tufts University has begun using a web-based educational tool that supports discussion threads in his popular graduate level course on international leadership and management. Discussion threads can be thought of as a series of related electronically posted comments, questions, and answers organized by subject. Responses can be added to existing threads at any point, and new threads can be started at any time. Thus, existing threads can be dynamically lengthened, thickened, and woven into a virtual tapestry of ideas captured on a web site in a clickable format. The use of threaded discussions (hereafter referred to as threads) have allowed the evolution of a new kind of class assignment that can complement or replace the quiz. Using threads allows quiz answers to be transformed from static responses into dynamic ones. Learning can be furthered by threads because they allow for flexible exchange of ideas between student and student, and professor and student. Responses, comments, questions, and insights can be captured quickly, previewed privately, and disseminated publicly. Progress toward desired learning outcomes can then be monitored and guided. Threads offer an exciting alternative to the paper quiz and showed an overall positive reaction from approximately four out of five students.

THREADS AS QUIZZES?

Tests today must be vehicles for helping students learn, providing feedback about what materials students are finding difficult and why. Most of the improvements that technology offers have been seen in large-scale aptitude and skill testing. Results are available sooner, questions can include activities—such as drafting architectural designs—and data on student performance is immediately ready for analysis.

But what about that great assessment workhorse, the traditional paper quiz? How can it be transformed to address today's assessment goals? Our experience suggests that threads, a simple technology, can bolster the value of the paper quiz.

THREADS AS AN EDUCATIONAL EXERCISE

I have used a threads approach to assess students' conceptual simultaneous understanding of the competing needs between leadership and management roles and how to exercise both roles effectively. The exercise was based on an excerpt from John Kotter's book, *A Force for Change* (Kotter, 1990), in Dean John R. Galvin's graduate-level international leadership and management course. Traditionally, an instructor might motivate students to investigate these concepts by quizzes. However, Kotter's work is complex. Threads offer the added learning benefit of rethinking, reflection, and exposure to many different points of view. These processes promote the complex appreciation of rich ideas.

The assignment required students first to comment on Kotter's work then to comment on ideas proposed by peers, and, finally, to create a group point of view. It took place over three weeks. Periodically, the instructor and teacher's assistant reviewed the discussions and introduced comments and suggestions.

STUDENT REACTIONS TO THREADED DISCUSSIONS

Students' reactions to the use of discussion threads were monitored with a Likert scale survey after they completed the three-week threads assignment. Overall, students were very enthusiastic. Of those surveyed, 75% reported that they had never used threads before, indicating that the decision to use this tool risked rejection. Despite this possibility, nearly all students participated in the exercise, and more than 80% found it both useful and enjoyable.

When asked to describe properties of the discussions they found most useful, most respondents indicated that it provided flexible and easy access to information and team members, facilitated expression of ideas, and allowed for reflection prior to additional threaded discussion responses. Sixteen students remarked that the discussion threads page helped to promote teamwork within their groups and allowed flexible access to information.

When asked what they disliked about the discussion threads, the responses indicated that technical problems and lack of experience produced a frustration that interfered with their enjoyment or use. Others wished for features that could provide additional control of the discussion thread environment.

LESSONS LEARNED

Our data suggest that the move from quizzes to threads will not be difficult for most students, even for those with little familiarity with the technology. A crosstab analysis demonstrated that prior experience with discussion threads compared favorably with present student experience in this course. The analysis explicitly showed a moderately positive, statistically significant association reported for "liking" (Kendall's Tau, 0.56, 95% confidence interval, 0.33 – 0.78) their current experience as compared to students' prior experience. The analysis also revealed a moderately positive, statistically significant association between finding the current experience "useful" (Kendall's Tau, 0.60, 95% confidence interval, 0.36 – 0.84) as compared to prior experience. We used StatXact 3 for Windows, Statistical Software for Exact Nonparametric Inference published by Cytel Software Corporation, 1995. Web-based applications may have advanced information technology to the point where learning curves for usability barely exist. Unfortunately, without a more thorough assessment, it is harder to conclude with certainty that a student acquired a deeper appreciation of Kotter's work.

Despite not having completed an assessment, learning appears not to have been compromised. Student answers did not suggest a decline in understanding. Some student responses seemed to grow in sophistication as the assignment progressed. Though no grades were assigned, each student response was the equal to an answer on a quiz and could have been assigned a grade. The idea, however, was to shift the burden of assessment onto the students themselves. Students judged the merits of their ideas under the observation of the instructor and teaching assistant. Threads thus provide a powerful way in which technology and assessment can serve education.

Our experiment suggests that more research is needed to isolate the learning effects of threads. If students can learn to grade themselves, threads will replace the quiz as a staple of both assessment and motivation in education. In addition, it is recommended that content analysis of threads be investigated to determine standards for measuring quality in support of assessment.

REFERENCE

Kotter, J. A. (1990). *A force for change: How leadership differs from management.* New York, NY: Free Press.

CONTACT INFORMATION

John R. Galvin, Dean
The Fletcher School of Law and Diplomacy
Tufts University
Medford, MA 02155-5555
Email: Jgalvin@emerald.tufts.edu
WWW: www.tufts.edu/fletcher
Phone: (617) 627-3050
Fax: (617) 627-3508

Vignette 56 International Students in the World of US Technology

Leslie Opp-Beckman, University of Oregon

INTRODUCTION

Students at the University of Oregon's American English Institute (AEI) are working to improve their language skills and to attain a variety of personal and academic goals. Many are preparing to take the Test of English as a Foreign Language (TOEFL), on which they need to achieve a certain minimum score that will give them entrance to a US institution of higher learning; some are expanding current job opportunities or making career changes; and all are striving to fit into a culture and an environment that differ from their own.

I teach one or more elective courses for my department that center on the use of computers in a US academic setting. Students are grouped by two criteria: their skill level in English and their level of expertise with computers. Depending on enrollment, we typically offer one or more sections in Computer Basics for Low-Level English, Computer Basics for Intermediate/Advanced-Level English, and Advanced Computer Skills for Intermediate/Advanced-Level English.

All classes are diverse in terms of the students' age, gender, and primary language background. There are typically 15 to 20 students per class each ten-week term, and classes meet once a week for two hours in a computer lab. The goals for students enrolled in this course are as follows.

- Academic: to prepare students for credit-bearing coursework in a wired university setting. The material includes, but is not limited to, handling a personal Internet account for email and web page authoring; knowledge about, and use of, online university library facilities and other sources of help for technology-based problems or questions; and familiarity with, and appropriate use of, university labs.

Once students have adequate language skills and a basic technology foundation, they can freely participate in numerous workshops offered through the University of Oregon's award-winning computing center and Knight Library on topics ranging from web page authoring to Photoshop and from operating system

trouble-shooting for microcomputers to UNIX commands (cf. "Workshops" at http://cc.uoregon.edu/ or http://libweb.uoregon.edu/).

- Linguistic: to improve skills in the target language, in this case, US English. All aspects of this course are conducted in English. Technology is the focus topic, and all language skills are integrated (speaking, listening, reading, writing).

- Cultural: to facilitate acclimation to various aspects of US culture in technology-specific settings including encounters that occur both face-to-face (e.g., asking for help from a lab assistant) and online (e.g., US email netiquette).

- Affective: to remove barriers that inhibit the acquisition and use of technology-related skills. Training varies from student to student and from group to group. A typical beginning-of-term survey, for example, might reveal the need to increase student confidence in using computers and to develop self-help strategies in approaching new situations with computers. Experience has shown that students who are motivated to learn and who take charge of their own learning are ultimately more successful in, and satisfied with, their educational experience.

IDEAS BEHIND THE COURSE DESIGN

Courses are conducted according to overall student level; information from students' individual needs assessments at the beginning of each term (previous experience, personal goals, perceived needs, etc.); and the current state of technology. Students who enter AEI bring a wide range of experience in technology. Computer support courses are offered primarily to students with the least experience in computer technology in order to help them succeed in their academic coursework. Additionally, computer technology is made available to help bridge the physical gap of being far from home. A combination of good Internet connections and a well-supported language lab allows international students to access up-to-the-minute news from their home countries, listen to audio broadcasts and files, view real-time and recent satellite transmissions, exchange non-Roman script email messages, and chat online in non-Roman scripts (see Yamada Language Lab at http://babel.uoregon.edu/).

We cover basic survival skills in a number of areas.

- Hardware: the names and functions of the various parts, how the mouse works, how the CPU turns on and shuts off, etc.

- Operating system: how to save files and create folders, how to select a printer, how to install software, how to retrieve an email attachment, etc.

- Software: keyboarding, word processing, and language skill-specific software (reading, vocabulary, pronunciation, spelling, etc.) is integrated into core AEI courses and is generally not covered in the elective courses. Elective course programs include email (NCSA Telnet and Pine), web browser (Netscape), and basic graphic software (digital camera, image/text scanner, GraphicConverter and/or Kid Pix). Web authoring, database, and spreadsheet software are introduced according to student interest and needs.

- Servers: definition and how some function at this institution, how to back up files to the departmental server, and how to download public domain software for University of Oregon students and faculty, etc.

Other factors should be considered beyond the sheer mechanics of hardware and software. For example, what are the roles of the student and the instructor in this type of small, lab-based classroom? In the US, international students must learn to be part of a system where they act on their own behalf in a self-motivating and self-actualizing manner. In the AEI computer courses, they must learn to interact with instructors who function more as facilitators or resource specialists, instead of as omniscient sage-on-the-stage lecturers. Students explore technology from the framework that asks, "How can I use it to make me more efficient?"

AEI computer courses are taught in a content-based framework with technology as the overarching theme. It is an ideal dual-immersion environment because students are acquiring knowledge and skills in English and in technology simultaneously through the direct use of both. They complete weekly miniprojects and a final term project. Students frequently pair up or work cooperatively in small groups, and every class participant is seen as having something to offer. In some cases, it will be some particular technological skill, but creativity, a willingness to share, a good eye for graphics, and top-notch researching skills are also recognized. As the class leader, I am challenged to work very hard to keep pace with everyone's enthusiasm and questions as well as the fast-paced changes in technology.

COURSE ACTIVITIES (COMPUTER-ENHANCED TECHNIQUES)

A typical class begins in a circle, with students facing away from their computers. We quickly review the previous week's topic along with a plan for the current week. I briefly demonstrate or explain new concepts, assign a task or series of tasks, but most of our time is devoted to hands-on work. Every effort is made to incorporate high-interest materials and activities, to assign tasks that will have real-life meaning, to introduce new concepts at the point of need and to use an exploratory rather than a button pushing, lock-step format. An open-ended question related to the day's activities is often posed as food for thought. At the end of class, we return to our circle and debrief, share announcements, and hash over the food for thought answers

Whenever possible, student work is displayed on the overhead projector or on a bulletin board, so they can share ideas and receive recognition. Students are encouraged to communicate with each other and instructors outside of class through email and various asynchronic discussion modes.

MEASURED RESULTS

International students have consistently given this course very high ratings. It is one of the few electives we offer in multiple sections every term and one for which there is such high demand that we have to turn students away due to lack of lab availability. No matter what the time of day, starting as early as 8 a.m. and as late as 4 p.m. on a Friday, students consistently attend and participate in earnest. They tell us that it has a positive effect on their ability to survive in today's wired US learning institutions, and that it makes them competitive in job markets in their home countries. A small percentage of students come back to volunteer and to mentor other students during class time, and another handful go on to work in our lab as paid assistants. Their dual expertise in multiple languages and technology pays off in a very real sense.

LESSONS LEARNED

In my mind, the constant challenge and the many opportunities to learn are some of the best things about being involved in educational endeavors emphasize technology. It is important to keep in touch with and learn from fellow technology specialists and educators, both on and off campus. We have made the following observations.

1) Flexibility in setting up course offerings is important. Every term presents new challenges as a new group of international students comes in with different expectations and varying levels of expertise in language and technology. We have learned to set up lab space for three courses and then to determine exactly which three computer courses to give once we see our population.

2) We need more instructors who can teach computer courses. It's a constant effort to recruit teachers who are willing and able to learn the technology and who develop the confidence to teach it. Instructors tend to be young faculty members with less seniority. No sooner do they feel comfortable in this role than they are gone.

3) As the demand for computer courses has increased, we have expanded outside our departmental lab into other labs on campus. This presents unique opportunities and challenges. Students appreciate the exposure to additional facilities. However, instructors become even more uncomfortable when things go wrong far from home. One solution has been to pay a lab assistant to accompany the faculty member and help out during class. This seems to work fairly well.

4) To eliminate some repetition and to avoid the stressful beginning and end-of-term periods, I would like to restructure computer meeting times

in the future. Instead of 20 hours spread over ten weeks (once a week), I would like to try meeting twice a week during weeks three to seven. I predict that students would retain more information between class meetings and benefit from having more free time when they are first settling in and later finishing up the term.

5) This ten-week course has been successfully adapted to our shorter four-week special summer courses over the past three years. The project's format differs somewhat in that students publish their online projects on our departmental web site instead of through their individual student accounts. This tends to make more HTML coding work on the faculty/administrative end but makes the most of the students' short time in Eugene.

6) Success with our face-to-face ten-week and summer four-week courses has enabled AEI to develop distance-education courses that are tailored to meet specific groups' needs. This is an area we would like to expand.

CONCLUSION

Many hours are given over to attending workshops and experimenting with unstable and sometimes frustrating technology. However, I feel that the time I am investing in trying to enhance students' quality of education through technology is well-spent. Whether or not we use technology, the courses that involve face-to-face communication continue to be the most rewarding for all concerned. In cases where that is not possible, the online distance education alternative has been an excellent substitute.

See http://cc.uoregon.edu/ or
http://libweb.uoregon.edu/
http://babel.uoregon.edu/
http://darkwing.uoregon.edu/~leslieob/
http://darkwing.uoregon.edu/~aei/sanno98me
    mories.html
http://darkwing.uoregon.edu/~aei/senshu98
    projects.html
http://darkwing.uoregon.edu/f98senshu.html

CONTACT INFORMATION

Leslie Opp-Beckman
Technology Coordinator
University of Oregon
American English Institute
107 Pacific
Eugene, OR 97403-5212
Email: leslieob@oregon.uoregon.edu
http://darkwing.uoregon.edu/~leslieob/
Phone: (541) 346-3945
Fax: (541) 346-3917

 **From Analog to Digital: Teaching About Criminal Sentencing with Technology**

Kent E. Portney, Steve Cohen, and Sal Soraci, Tufts University; and Jerry Goldman, Northwestern University

Teaching undergraduate students about criminal sentencing—about how and why criminal defendants receive the sanctions they do—is a difficult task. The problem is rooted in the fact that each student comes into class with preconceived ideas concerning variability: what causes it and whether or not it is acceptable. Why is criminal sentencing, particularly the issue of explaining variation in criminal sentences, so difficult to teach? One of the primary reasons is the fundamental drive in all people to reduce unpredictability. Rather than tolerate unpredictability, most people will attribute causes to events. There is comfort in having attributed causes to events, even if the causes are wrong (i.e., have no empirical validity), are appropriate only in certain idiosyncratic settings, tell only part of a story, or are ideologically driven.

EDUCATIONAL PHILOSOPHY

What does this fundamental drive to reduce unpredictability matter for those trying to teach criminal justice sentencing? It matters because most students typically begin a course having had some exposure to the basic problem of variability in sentencing decisions. Whether through the media, secondary education, or personal experiences, most students have some idea that fairness in sentencing is elusive. It is difficult to imagine a student with no concept of variability in sentencing. When asked to do so, most students can readily recite examples of criminal cases where they believe the defendants were treated unfairly.

Most students with exposure to sentencing issues will spontaneously attribute causes to the sentencing variability in an effort to reduce the unpredictability. In most, if not all cases, these causes will have some legitimacy. However, the causes attributed are likely to include simple-minded reactions or incomplete explanations. Students often attribute virtually all variation in sentencing to a single cause, such as racism, gender bias, political corruption, judges who are too liberal or soft on crime or too tough on criminals, inequality of wealth or income, incompetence, or other single factors. One reason it is easy for students to quickly attribute these causes to sentencing variability is that the real agents of the causes, namely the judges and judicial system, are external to the student. According to the fundamental attribution error in social psychology, it would be more difficult to attribute and rely on causes like racism or incompetence if students themselves were the agents. It is clearly difficult to see yourself or your peers as racists or incompetents, but it is easy to see others this way.

As is abundantly demonstrated in the literature on criminal sentencing, these causes do not tell the whole story. Factors like theories of criminal sanctions—deterrence, retribution, rehabilitation, and incapacitation—certainly play a complex role in decisions. However, faced with the need to attribute causes and reduce unpredictability, naive attributions are handy. Without the attributions, students are faced with the difficult task of tolerating unpredictable behavior. As they craft teaching methods and instructional designs, teachers must consider the kinds of beliefs and ideas that occupy student's minds.

Naive beliefs present challenges to teachers when they try to help students replace ideas that are inconsistent with formal, theoretical notions or simply help them build on their prior understanding. The instructional goal in teaching criminal sentencing is not to replace naive beliefs like bias and/or incompetence, for they certainly have a legitimate place in any network of understanding about sentencing. Incompetence, racial and gender bias, political corruption, and so on do exist. Rather, the goal is to extend and reconfigure each student's network of ideas and beliefs to include additional factors.

Research on generative learning suggests a way to help students reconfigure their beliefs. Students who generate their own responses to open-ended queries tend to remember them better than when the responses are provided to them. This has been shown to be a robust empirical phenomenon that occurs across a wide range of learning contexts. In some sense, this can be seen as support for active learning.

Related research suggests that the order of the information is important. For instance, telling students that the house became smaller because the sun came out followed by the word "igloo" results in much better memory than mentioning "igloo" prior to giving subjects the sentence. This suggests an unusual instructional design: Start by creating ambiguity by providing an ambiguous, incomprehensible context, have the student actively engage in resolving the ambiguity, and superior learning occurs. While it may be best for students to resolve the confusion on their own, superior learning also occurs when the confusing sentence is proposed first, and the key concept is subsequently revealed. This is important, since education often does not permit enough time for students to resolve as many puzzles as we would like.

We believe this kind of learning process is essential if students are really going to broaden their understanding of sentencing. Simply telling students that factors like deterrence or retribution influence sentencing decisions will not help most appeal to these ideas when confronted with issues of criminal sentencing. Students may be able to recite them on a test, but they do not seem to avail themselves of these explanations when critically reviewing controversial decisions. Students must first appreciate the limited application of their preconceived ideas.

COURSE STRATEGY

To take advantage of what we know about the generative learning effect, we devised a four-step instructional intervention.

1) Introduce students to the topic of variation in sentencing. This can be done with traditional methods—lectures or readings from texts or other written sources.

2) Have students play the role of judge in sentencing simulations. This can be done through a variety of techniques, although as we discuss later, the multimedia approach has distinct advantages over paper-and-pencil simulations or simple roleplaying. To facilitate Step 3, the simulation must not only establish the extent to which there is variability in the

sentences students render; it must also yield a compelling explanation why these variations exist. We conduct the simulation using an experimental design that systematically varies the characteristics of the cases that we offer as explanations.

3) Confront students with their own sentencing behavior, and challenge the class to rationalize/explain the results. When the students render their sentences, these sentences must be recorded, tallied, and summarized for presentation to the whole class. In other words, there must be a way to hold a mirror up to the students to show them what they produced. This process essentially causes the confusion that the generation effect requires.

4) Teach theories of sentencing. Once students come to recognize the limits of their explanations, they are open to new and more complete explanations. Exposure to theories of sentencing and the literature positing alternative explanations offers students a way to resolve their confusion.

Simulation

Simulation/role play works as follows. Each student in a class plays the role of sentencing judge and renders sentences for the same set of cases (defendants). When all students have had a chance to play judge, the instructor tallies the sentences for the class and presents the results. When students see the enormous variability among sentences that they themselves produced, we expect their naive beliefs to weaken. These beliefs suddenly have a real limitation. Simulation results force students either to see themselves as biased, racist, or incompetent, or to look for an expanded set of beliefs around which to structure their thinking about sentencing. Once students' naive beliefs are challenged and naive causes are seen as inadequate, students may be in a better position to develop a more complex appreciation of criminal justice sentencing.

To examine whether the technology-based intervention seems to work, we simulated roleplaying in two different forms. In one, we developed case files that contained written materials describing each of six different criminal felony cases. In the other, we created a multimedia simulation experience where students would feel as if they were actually presiding over court proceedings. In this simulation, called Crime and Punishment, students sit at a computer and sentence six

cases that are composites of actual cases. The simulation contains an array of documents typically available to sentencing judges and presents the relevant actors— the prosecutor, defense lawyer, defendant, and victim—in full-motion video. The student gets the feeling of walking into the courthouse, passing through the metal detector, greeting court personnel, and entering chambers. Once in chambers, the student picks up a court docket and folder and walks into the courtroom. Upon hearing "All rise," the student proceeds to the judge's bench. The docket is placed on the desktop, and the student can select a case by clicking on any one of the six on the docket. At this point, something that looks like a standard paper file opens, revealing two court documents describing the case at hand on one side and a presentence investigation report on the other. By clicking on either document, the student can read it. When ready, the student can view a sentencing hearing by clicking on the desktop gavel. The sentencing hearing consists of full-motion video of the prosecutor explaining the case and making a sentence recommendation, the defense lawyer presenting mitigating circumstances, and the defendant making a brief statement. After the student digests the case materials, he or she proceeds to render a sentence. Within the constraints imposed by the governing criminal statutes in the case, students have full control over the severity and type of sentence to be imposed.

The user first encounters an armed robbery case. It serves as an anchor and, therefore, was created with no variables (i.e., all students see the exact same case). The remaining five cases—possession of drugs with intent to distribute, armed robbery, grand larceny shoplifting, and sexual assault on a minor—are made accessible to the student through the court docket. Thus, the multimedia application is, from the outset, considerably more interactive than is its paper-and-pencil counterpart.

Because the simulation is delivered to students over the Internet, we are able to vary characteristics of the cases in systematic ways. Instructors can vary the race, gender, appearance, or affect of the defendant. The instructor can also control whether or not the victim will make a statement. By allowing only one of these characteristics to vary and holding everything else constant, we can isolate the effect of that variable on the sentences that the students render. For example, we can vary the gender of the defendant and hold everything else constant. We do this by simply inserting a different video image into the courtroom scene while keeping the rest of the visual array constant. For classes that are sufficiently large, the simulation allows the instructor to vary more than one characteristic simultaneously, such as the race and the gender of the defendant. In classroom experiments, simulations were implemented where only race and gender were varied, while all other characteristics were held constant. Again, because the simulation was delivered via the Internet, Step 3 in the instructional intervention—reporting the results to the class—was relatively easy since the aggregation of the data from all participating students was automated.

We also created paper versions of each of the cases found in the multimedia simulations. All of the information contained in the multimedia simulations, except the visual elements, was reduced to paper. The same experimental design was used, where the race and gender of the defendant were systematically varied. Preparation of four versions of each of the six cases was a considerably greater challenge than with the multimedia simulation. Logistically, aggregation and analysis of the resulting data for all students was much more labor-intensive than with the multimedia simulation, because each student's sentences had to be hand-coded and keyed into the computer.

ASSESSMENT

We set out to determine whether students do, in fact, seem to learn more from using this instructional intervention. Three political science classes at Tufts and Northwestern Universities were used in this assessment.

Students in classes 2 and 3 were exposed to the same materials as those in class 1 plus the instructional intervention. As part of this intervention, students who used a simulation (role-play) were confronted with the following results after they all had a chance to participate in the exercises:

- Summary measures of their sentencing behavior (class means and standard deviations)

- Histograms of sentencing distributions for the entire class

- Extreme sentences and the written justifications

After the course's sections on their respective treatment of issues of criminal sentencing were completed, students were administered a questionnaire to develop specific information about what they might have learned. Three different measures were used. We asked students to explain how a judge could be justified in sentencing an African-American man to a longer prison term than a white man in order to stem the tide of drug crimes in a neighborhood. The problem is designed to evoke reference to racism as an explanation or an answer of deterrence or both. We asked students to describe the actual level of intracourt variability in

FIGURE 57.1

COMPARISON OF THREE POLITICAL SCIENCE CLASSES

CLASS 1	CLASS 2	CLASS 3
No simulation	**CD-ROM-based simulation**	**Paper-based simulation**
Control class, using traditional lectures and reading to teach variability in sentencing. This included extensive reference to empirical studies and opportunities for students to analyze data from actual felony cases.	A class using a CD-ROM multimedia simulation that presented sentencing hearings and allowed students to play the role of judge and sentence convicted felons in six cases involving different crimes	A class using paper-based simulations where the cases were identical to those included in the multimedia counterpart

criminal sentencing, using a five-point Likert scale. We also had students sentence two cases, one of sexual assault, the other of grand larceny. These cases were different from the cases incorporated into the role-play simulations.

We also assessed how comparable the three classes were and how the CD-based simulation results would compare to the paper-based results. Students found the CD and paper simulations equally realistic and typically took about two hours to complete the assignments. We had a clear a priori reason to believe the students in the three classes were comparable, but we opted to administer questions to provide specific evidence. These questions asked students to report on a variety of factors we thought might conceivably affect any intergroup differences in the assessment criteria, including differences in SAT scores, grade-point averages, baseline knowledge of the judicial system, familial socioeconomic status, and others, and no differences were discerned.

The comparisons among the three classes showed distinct patterns of difference. The data show that only 14% of students in the control group cited deterrence as a possible cause for the sentence disparity. In other words, for 86%, deterrence did not come readily to mind as an explanation for the sentencing scenario. But when exposed to the instructional intervention, deterrence became a useful concept for 20% of the students participating in the paper-based simulation and for 33% using the CD-based simulation. There was a similar effect in students' ability to appreciate what a difficult problem fairness in sentencing really is. Only 13% of the students reported that they considered the level of variability as "acceptable," while 23% of the CD-based simulation students and 43% of the paper-based simulation students reported the level of variability to be "acceptable." We expected to see the instructional intervention produce reduced variability compared to the control group. When we examined the standard deviations of the prison sentences for the larceny case, both the CD-based simulation and the paper-based simulation show lower standard deviations without affecting the mean sentence. Thus, the intervention seems to have influenced students who might have given sentences at either the high or low ends of the permissible range to opt for middle range sentences. This pattern is not evident in the assault case, however.

Those students in classes using the simulations demonstrated an effect due to the intervention, regardless of the media used to deliver it. There is more unacceptable variation and greater reliance on punishment theory when confronted with the most stimulating exercises. The data also reveal striking similarities between paper and multimedia simulations. This suggests that any simulation has merit over no simulation. The comparisons also suggest that variation in some kinds of cases (sexual assault) may be more difficult to reduce than in other cases.

CONCLUSION

We expect that the learning effects from the instructional intervention, particularly using the multimedia approach, may well be greater for students who have lower verbal aptitude. The more difficulty students have learning from more traditional sources, such as books or research articles, the more likely they will experience improvement as a result of the instructional intervention. We also expect that the relative advantages of the multimedia-based simulation will be substantially greater for students whose reading comprehension is challenged. This expectation makes the results reported here all the more remarkable, since the assessment was conducted with the participation of students at two colleges where verbal aptitudes are likely to be higher than those at many other colleges.

Although the multimedia role-playing simulation did not produce across-the-board learning improvements, it is clear that using such technology-based simulations is considerably easier than paper-and-pencil alternatives. Preparing four or more paper-based versions of each criminal case is a tedious task that most instructors would not have the time nor resources to do. Furthermore, the collection, aggregation, and analysis of the results—the sentences students render—adds considerable time to the process. The beauty of the multimedia-based simulation is that these administrative processes have been automated, and the time and energy that would have been devoted to more mundane tasks can be spent preparing interpretations of the results. The multimedia approach is much more likely to be used than its paper-and-pencil counterpart.

The design of the instructional intervention was heavily informed by a particular conception of belief networks and conceptual change. We are planning future research designed to assess a range of alternative instructional intervention designs based on other belief networks in order to examine how broad-based this approach is.

CONTACT INFORMATION

Kent E. Portney
Department of Political Science
Tufts University
Medford, MA 02155-5555
Email: Kportney@tufts.edu

WWW: http://ase.tufts.edu/polsci/fac
    _staf/pfportne.html
Phone: (617) 627-3465
Fax: (617) 627-3660

Steve Cohen
Email: scohen@tufts.edu,

Jerry Goldman
Email: j-goldman@nwu.edu

Sal Soraci
Email: ssoraci@tufts.edu

 **Psychology and the Arts**

Sam C. Carrier, Oberlin College

After an extended stint in administration, I resumed active teaching in 1996-97. My administrative work had included responsibility for the archives, art museum, computing center, and the library system. Leading these academic support operations made me acutely aware of not only the costs but also the exciting educational possibilities enabled by the information technology revolution. By the end of my administrative service, a high-end workstation had more processing power than the computing facilities for the entire campus at the time I left the faculty.

How best to put information technology to work in my own teaching? Fortunately, I had a sabbatical leave to become reacquainted with the subject matter of psychology and to prepare new courses. During the leave, I asked myself some basic questions about pedagogy and, in particular, how computer technology could be brought to bear on teaching and learning.

EDUCATIONAL THEORIES

Early on, I established several design principles and goals. Foremost was the idea that courses would take full advantage of the campus network: I shall neither distribute, nor receive, paper. This implied that courses would have web sites, not syllabi. Second, I would use presentation software for class sessions rather than slides or an overhead projector. Third, I would use professional-level software and encourage my students to do likewise. Fourth, I would have students work in groups. While alumni reported considerable satisfaction with many facets of their Oberlin education (ability to think clearly and critically, command of fact and theory, research and writing skills), they frequently mentioned their lack of experience in working as a member of a team. Finally, the overarching goals for my commitment to information technology were 1) to stimulate student learning through hands-on experiences and interactivity, and 2) to improve students' communication skills by insisting that documents be more than words double-spaced on paper.

COURSE DESCRIPTION: PSYCHOLOGY AND THE ARTS

Aimed at students whose primary interests lie in the visual arts and music (Oberlin's Conservatory of Music enrolls about 525 students), this course was designed to explore the psychological processes involved in the arts and included topics such as neural and behavioral systems prerequisite for art, creation of art, the psychology of performance practice and technique, and the observer's response to art.

The web site contained links to the syllabus, instructions for individual and group projects, template forms for the web-based quizzes, contact information, and a help section. Clean in design, it was a model. Enrollment was large for an Oberlin course, well over 100.

The class, to be taught in the new high-tech classroom with recently installed video projection equipment and first-class stereo sound, would begin with a Director-based multimedia presentation designed to stimulate student interest and to show off the reborn professor's technology chops. Being ever cautious, two days before classes were to begin I decided to preview this lovingly created and thoroughly debugged extravaganza in the classroom. Unsurprisingly, the test failed. The components were speaking in tongues. Much tweaking later, all was in harmony.

Finally, the first day of class, equipment connected with cables galore, software loaded, a group of eager students waiting—the confident instructor strode to the podium, double-clicked the application. Great graphics appeared, but there was no sound. Where, oh where, was that beautiful Pink Floyd? At least the network connection to the web site worked so I could review the syllabus.

The regular classroom presentations went better. They certainly took a long time to construct—outline the topic, find and scan the images, type the text, place on layers, add a transition or two just for fun. Sometimes they were ready a day ahead. Sometimes an hour ahead. Often minutes ahead. Many presentations were a pale shadow of their conception.

Following each class, the presentations were placed on the college's server. This approach enabled students to obtain the materials at any time. Lectures would no longer be a means for transferring information from the instructor's notes to the students' notebooks.

The forms-based quizzes were uploaded to the web site two hours before they were due. They included multiple choice and true/false questions based on the assigned readings. Students could take them from any networked computer. Immediately upon submission, a grading script evaluated the responses and provided immediate feedback about which answers were right and which wrong. The quizzes were not well received, but at Oberlin, objective tests never are.

The course included two individual lab exercises. The first, written in Director, is a demonstration of the perceptual phenomenon known as simultaneous contrast—the intensity of the background against which a test stimulus is presented influences the apparent brightness of that stimulus. Students download the application and an Excel data analysis template from the course server on the Oberlin network. They run the demonstration, enter the data in the Excel spreadsheet, append their own analyses and conclusions, and copy their work to the course's drop box on the server.

The second lab exercise involved looking carefully at an object in the Allen Memorial Art Museum, describing how some perceptual process operates while viewing the work and comparing an electronic image of the work to the real object. Students select works from the about 40 for which digital images are available on the course server. After viewing the work through the eyes of an experimental psychologist—that is, as a visual stimulus independent of its iconography, trying to understand what perceptual principles are operating—students prepare a short document that incorporates the digital image, describes and discusses several perceptual mechanisms at work, and indicates how the digital image differs from the original work of art. This report is then deposited in the course drop box.

Group projects replaced the traditional term paper. Students were assigned to groups of four or five and encouraged to select a topic from a set I had developed or to develop one of their own. Three documents were required, all in HTML format, and due about a month apart: 1) a prospectus, defining the topic and proposing a work plan; 2) a progress report, presenting interim work; and 3) a final report. While several groups included students with some HTML experience, many did not. I therefore spent one class session on HTML basics, demonstrating simple mark-up syntax. Students were generally surprised to learn how easy it was to prepare a document for the web. For the most part, they were delighted to see their work posted—a tangible and public presentation for their parents and friends to see.

As the semester progressed, documents clearly improved, both in substance and design. Several final products went beyond web pages (e.g., a videotape about the creation of a work of art and a rather sophisticated CD-ROM about performance practice).

The course evaluations reflected mixed student views. Some were less than enthusiastic about the material. They wanted more about art and the psychodynamics of the artist and less about the biobehavioral perspective. Others resented the intrusion of technology; after 40 years, C. P. Snow's two cultures remained. There were enough appreciative comments, however, to reinforce my belief that information technology could be useful in the craft of teaching.

LESSONS LEARNED

As an early adopter, I faced obstacles—some technological (there were many, many things to learn about scanning, color resolution of monitors and projectors, setting up the development and presentation machines to be identical, quickly reconfiguring the system just before class in a multiuser classroom), some pedagogical (how many text and graphic slides to fit in 50 minutes, when not to use some newly learned effect), some born of sheer fatigue. As the semester progressed, the technology did begin to recede, and the content moved to the foreground. Lessons were learned, partly by trial and error, partly by reading manuals, partly by consulting computing center staff. It was harder than I ever imagined, but fun and richly rewarding.

In the fall of 1998, the course was taught for the third time. It retained most of the features of version 1.0, but with many of the bugs eliminated, significant improvements, and some fresh ideas.

There is still a web site instead of a printed syllabus (see http://www.oberlin.edu/~scarrier/Courses /Psych_108/Intro.html). I now tell students how to print the web pages, if they must. With the aid of a student, the site was redesigned both conceptually and graphically. It now is more dynamic, with the opening page containing a section titled "updates and announcements"—a means of reminding students of due dates for assignments and exams, a feature that they greatly appreciate.

The web-based quizzes have been replaced with more traditional hour examinations. I considered adapting web forms for short answer and essays but have adopted the traditional blue book on the grounds that exams themselves are stressful enough, so why impose technology just so that I can have the students' answers in machine readable form? In this case, students' convenience here outweighs my inconvenience.

Virtually all the presentations are routinely modified each year, with perhaps 25% being substantially recast—adding new text but particularly including new graphics as I find suitable color images to replace those previously presented in black and white. I continue to learn about scanning and images—color balancing, brightness and contrast control, and image compression.

Both laboratory exercises and the group project remain, with only minor modification. Here students learn useful skills: how to use the network, the basics of web page construction, incorporating images into documents, rudimentary data collection and analysis, working in teams.

CONCLUSION

For me, teaching this way is exhilarating. Despite the challenges, frustrations, and long hours, I enjoy my work. The students appear not to suffer unduly, and many seem to appreciate the still relatively unusual format.

In the absence of a controlled experiment (and despite my training, I'm not prepared to undertake one— not for lack of time or will, but because I would mightily resist teaching without the technology), its impact on actual student learning is difficult to assess. I think it helps, but I can't really be sure.

It also remains unclear how much weight the administration gives to course development, particularly technological innovation, in salary review. However, using the technology has at least one tangible benefit —my machine is upgraded every other year.

CONTACT INFORMATION

Sam C. Carrier, Associate Professor of Psychology
Oberlin College
70 North Professor Street
Oberlin, OH 44074-1090
Email: sam.carrier@oberlin.edu
Phone: (440) 775-8170
Fax: (440) 775-8356

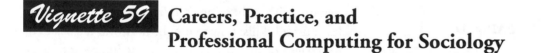

Vignette 59 Careers, Practice, and Professional Computing for Sociology

Raymond A. Bucko, Le Moyne College

COURSE GOALS AND STRATEGY

This course provides a basic introduction to the profession of sociology. It is generally taught in the second year of the program to encourage students to consider their professional interest in the discipline early and to make positive moves to formulate and fulfill career goals. During the 1997–1998 semester, we expanded the course to include web literacy as part of the curriculum. It was geared to the profession and designed to teach students how to contribute to the web community and how to present themselves professionally using both an enclosed workspace and a home page on the World Wide Web.

We attempted to integrate the goals of electronic communications and career literacy. Assignments on career planning were carried out through asynchronous conversations on the Basic Support for Coopera-

tive Work (BSCW) program, and career goals were presented with appropriate professional links on each student's web page.

COURSE ACTIVITIES

- Students interact with the faculty through email. They may also ask questions and make comments in selected discussion areas on the workspace. The goal here is to enhance communications between students and professors, to accustom them to using electronic communication, and to show them the possibilities for professional communications through direct email and mailing lists (listservs).

- The course meets two days a week. One is devoted to computer literacy and the other to professional development. We are careful not to present two

186

different courses by integrating assignments in the professional development lectures into the workspace and the web.

- Assignments for workspace and web publishing activities are hyptertexted to instructions specifically designed for students to help them with each activity. We wanted to prevent the print-out syndrome and accustom them to using the computer for the entire assignment. Students can work at their own pace (within limits), learn how to read instructions and carry out complex tasks, and keep from falling behind.

- Students create a professional résumé and present it on either the workspace or their home pages.

- Students who have more computer experience are encouraged to help students with less. Students who act as tutors receive class credit.

- Students have an online syllabus to consult, and assignments are linked to the syllabus. Each student is notified by email whenever an updated version of the syllabus is uploaded to the web. Students are assured that the number of assignments will not be increased. Updates are intended to clarify assignments.

- Each week, a web page or electronic portfolio of the week is presented to the entire class to give a concrete demonstration of effective web communications and presentation, and students can visit each other's web sites through an index page.

MEASURED RESULTS

The standard course evaluation forms used at Le Moyne were issued to each student. Students evaluated each of the two professors on separate forms. Generally, students were satisfied with the course, and it compared favorably with other sociology courses as well as college-wide. While some students struggled with the computer aspects of the course, they were universally convinced that this was an important aspect of professional preparation.

LESSONS LEARNED

Dr. Kelly and I taught this course twice. We climbed quite a learning curve with regard to effective motiva-

tion of students. The first time we taught the course, students put off most of the computer work to the last minute, which resulted in getting tasks done rather than acquiring web publishing literacy.

This course was also effective for teaching faculty computing literacy. One professor was quite literate, while the other was new on the web. The first time the course was given, the less literate faculty member took the course along with the students. The faculty member's direct learning experience and perceptive comments helped strengthen the course the second semester.

The following are specific points learned from this course:

- Keep students working through almost weekly assignments but allow flexibility for those who have a steeper curve to climb.

- Integrate all elements of the course. Because the computer assignments were geared to learning about the profession, students were more motivated and interested. Rather than simply creating a home page, they created online professional portfolios that served as future reference for career choices.

- Stress the fact that the Internet can be interactive. We required that students make some Internet contribution which they generally accomplished by indexing professional sites.

- Be specific about the quantity of material to be presented electronically. Unfortunately, some students are satisfied with the minimum; if three graphics per Internet page are required, then three are submitted. However, vague requirements for web page and workspace assignments result in poor work or late submissions.

- Encourage students to work together. Some students are very literate, while others have a steep curve to climb. Students are very good at instructing one another informally. The good students should not be overburdened, however.

- Use extensive help files. As students asked questions and ran into difficulties, we continually updated and created new web page help files. Students were rewarded for asking questions.

- Use office hours to help students up the curve. Scheduling periodic assignments with flexible but specific deadlines encourages students to come for help long before the semester ends.

- For the computer aspect of the class, give short verbal instructions and point students to help pages to reinforce the lessons. Students go blank if an instructor gives a series of complicated instructions. This is particularly true for students lower on the learning curve.

- Keep in mind that this is learning enhancement. Students respond well to goal-oriented assignments and enjoy seeing results on the workspace or on their web pages, particularly when results are hard earned.

COURSE RESOURCES

Because Le Moyne College uses very long file names, it is often difficult for students to accurately type out specific addresses for pages and/or resources. We compensate for this with a home page for our Virtual Classroom that can be found at: http://vc.lemoyne.edu/.

Unfortunately, we post courses there only for the current semester. The following are the URLs for resources mentioned in the vignette.

- Syllabus: http://www.lemoyne.edu/academic _afairs/departments/sociology_anthropology/buck o/soc200_s.html

- Basic Support for Cooperative Work Home Page: http://bscw.gmd.de/

- Sample computing assignment: http://www .lemoyne.edu/academic_affairs/departments/soci-ology_anthropology/bucko/comp_03.html

- Customized help files for the enclosed workspace: http://vc.lemoyne.edu/help/help_index.html

- Help files for HTML publishing geared to Le Moyne College's computing facilities: http://vc .lemoyne.edu/seminar/

CONCLUSION

This course is aimed at giving students a professional direction as they continue in our major. Combining web literacy with professional literacy has allowed students to access rich areas of information as well as to make themselves accessible professionally. The expertise our students gain allows them to quickly adapt to most other computer-involved courses offered. It seems clear that one-day computing seminars are not effective in teaching literacy to our students. Ultimately, this responsibility falls on individual departments. If this literacy is not used throughout the curriculum, however, it becomes a pointless exercise.

CONTACT INFORMATION

Raymond A. Bucko, S.J.
Le Moyne College
Syracuse, NY 13214
Email: bucko@maple.lemoyne.edu
WWW: http://web.lemoyne.edu/~bucko/index.html

Robert Kelly, Co-Professor
Email: kellyrf@maple.lemoyne.edu
WWW: http://web.lemoyne.edu/~kellyrf/

Vignette 60 Multimedia Courseware in a Social Sciences Methods and Statistics Class

Carolee Larsen, Millsaps College

As an instructor of a social science methods and statistics course, I was frustrated by the limitations imposed by a text- and overhead transparency-based teaching format. I wanted to find ways to make the class more interactive and engaging, and I wanted to be able to animate certain statistical concepts to better demonstrate the principles behind them. The opportunity for realizing these goals came in 1997 through summerlong workshop at Millsaps College. Based upon a workshop which had been funded by the W. M. Keck Foundation, the workshop was organized to train selected faculty in software packages and HTML so they could design multimedia courseware to be used in their courses. In this workshop, I began to design and create components of my course, including statistics tutorials, a web-based statistics resource page. I also adopted an easy-to-use statistics package that comes with a workbook and textbook.

EDUCATIONAL PRINCIPLES

A course like methods and statistics requires students to immerse themselves in the material and requires the instructor to find innovative ways to help students make sense of the material. I was dissatisfied with the textbook-based approach that was the way I learned statistics and used to use in my teaching of the course. The course was revised with the following educational principles in mind.

- Multiple styles of learning should be addressed. Not all students learn best by reading a text and listening to lectures. The computer-enhanced course can better present material to appeal to a variety of learning styles.

- Active learning promotes understanding and retention.

- Relevant assignments and activities spark student interest and motivation.

- Course materials should be easily accessed outside

of class to encourage students' immersion in the study of the subject area.

- Students should be able to get instant feedback on how well they understand the material.

COMPUTER-BASED TEACHING MATERIALS AND ACTIVITIES

The following computer-based materials and assignments comprised the core of the course.

Interactive Tutorials

I designed several interactive tutorials using Macromedia's Authorware software. Authorware is an icon-based authoring tool that allows the user to design interactive tutorials, quizzes, and demonstrations, with no previous knowledge of programming. Graphics, video clips, sound, and animation are incorporated easily into the Authorware project, thus enabling the designer to address a variety of learning styles. The Authorware projects are web-deployable, enabling students to use them off-campus. The tutorials I designed illustrated several descriptive statistics and different forms of graphical representation using animation and built-in quizzes. I found that for many students, specific concepts are difficult to understand when presented in text form. The animated tutorials let students see exactly how the data are manipulated when making graphs and frequency tables, or finding the mean, median, and mode. The tutorials also contain several self-tests for students to check their understanding of the concepts as they advance through the tutorials.

Interactive Online Quizzes

To provide students with self-assessment opportunities that gave instant performance feedback, I designed several quizzes using Authorware that students could take in preparation for the exams. These were posted on the web.

PowerPoint Presentations

Each lecture was accompanied by a PowerPoint presentation. The presentations contained important definitions and step-by-step instructions on how to work formulae or design research. The PowerPoint presentations were posted on the web for students to reference outside of class. Because the presentations were available on the web, students were able to listen more attentively knowing that what they saw did not need to be feverishly copied down. Some days when the lecture was especially technical, I distributed PowerPoint handouts to students on which they could take notes.

Hypertext Handouts and Class Notes

I placed notes I used and handouts I made for the class on the web. These included a glossary of statistical terms with links to related concepts.

Hypertext Syllabus

A hypertext syllabus contained links to the tutorials as well as links to hypertext notes and PowerPoint lectures. The syllabus provided everything the student needed to reinforce his or her understanding of the lectures. It contained materials that reinforced the lectures and helped with completion of assignments and preparation for exams.

Integrated Textbook and Software Package

Students completed weekly homework using Micro-Case Corporation's *Methods in the Social Sciences* that comes packaged with a workbook and student version of the company's data analysis system. The package is affordably priced and enables students to statistically analyze data and interpret the results. The data sets provide real data from several sources, and the homework assignments ask students to explore relevant social issues statistically. Students not only learned to analyze data on a computer, but also were motivated by the germane and timely social issues they explored through the homework assignments.

The Internet as a Teaching Tool

I used the Internet to supply real data for class projects, exams, and lectures. I maintained a web page with links to many data sources (many of which are governmental). My hope in doing this was to have students see that valuable and usable data are available at no cost on the Internet. They also gained experience in cleaning the data and compiling it into forms that are usable in statistical analysis.

MEASURED RESULTS

I looked at outcomes of using computer-based materials in two ways: student evaluations and test performance.

FIGURE 60.1

STUDENT EVALUATIONS

QUESTION	MEAN	STANDARD DEVIATION
The tutorials were helpful in my learning the concepts	4.714	.561
The tutorials helped me study for the tests	4.571	.811
The tutorials were easy to use	4.714	.463
The course web page was useful	4.476	.602
The PowerPoint presentations were beneficial to my learning the material	4.476	.680
The online quizzes were helpful in preparing for the tests	4.600	.598
N=21		

Student Evaluations

I issued an anonymous questionnaire to the class at midterm, after they completed the section of the course that used the statistics tutorials. I did not wait until the end of the course to evaluate these materials because I wanted students' experiences to be fresh in their minds as they provided evaluation. The mean scores to key questions are reported in Figure 60.1. On a scale of 1 to 5, five reflects strong agreement with the statement.

These results show that students were generally very satisfied with their experiences using the multimedia resources (tutorials, PowerPoint presentations, and hypertext documents) for the class. They found the resources user friendly and beneficial to their learning of the course material.

Test Performance

I used a quasi-experimental design to explore changes in student performance on tests that could be attributed to the multimedia resources (MR). I compared the previous year's class's performance on a statistics test (in 1996, n=28) with the scores on a comparable test from the class that used multimedia resources (1997, n=21). The mean improvement in test scores was 17.7 points over the previous year's class: The mean exam score for the quasi-experimental group was 82.2, compared with 64.5 for the previous group that was subjected to "traditional" instructional methods.

The histogram reveals a distinct shift in the shape of the score distribution after the multimedia resources were introduced into the curriculum. Whereas before the multimedia resources were used, most of the previous class's students scored in the under-70 ranges, after multimedia resources were introduced, student scores shifted towards the over-70 ranges. This suggests that the type of student who did not respond positively to traditional methods of teaching statistics and research methods was helped by the multimedia tutorials and presentations.

LESSONS LEARNED

Technical Support and Resources

A course like the one outlined above requires much technical support and sufficient numbers of computers for student use. Fortunately, Millsaps provided the technical support and has significantly increased the availability of PCs over the last few years. A course such as this is best conducted in a lecture room equipped with a PC which is connected to a projector. While ideal, this setup is very expensive. Alternatives to this are a portable PC cart or a classroom PC with a large monitor classroom.

Plan for Equipment Failure

Infrequently I would experience equipment failure or network problems at times when I had a computer-based presentation planned. I learned that it is important to have a backup plan or alternative version of the presentation on hand. For example, PowerPoint presentations can easily be printed as overhead transparencies.

FIGURE 60.2

COMPARISON OF TEST SCORES

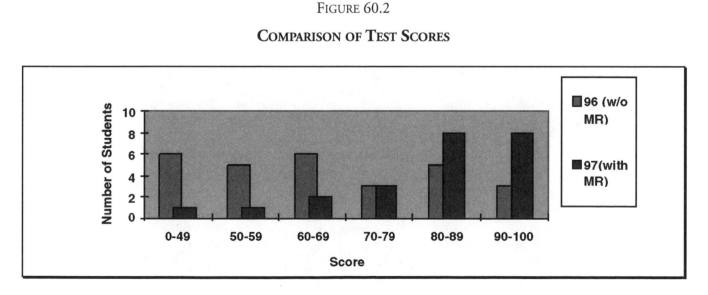

PowerPoint Presentations

While students liked the availability of the PowerPoint presentations online, and most liked having them as part of the lectures them in class, some students did not like being in a darkened room during lecture. Also, I found the presentations limited the spontaneity in lectures. Because of their size, some students had difficulty viewing them over the Internet by modem (but there was no problem with viewing them over the school's T1 connection).

Time Consumption

Building a course like this from scratch requires a large amount of time. The Authorware materials take many hours to build, and the PowerPoint presentations take considerable time and planning. However, once in place it is an easy and time-efficient course to maintain.

Technophobia

For a small minority of students, the idea of relying so heavily on computers for a class was terrifying. While most of these overcame their initial aversion to technology, one or two did not. For them the class was a negative experience.

CONCLUSION

I consider this course to be a success in achieving the goals I set for it. Students were more engaged in the material than when I taught the class in the traditional manner; test performance improved largely because of the multimedia components of the course; and students developed computer skills that will carry over to other classes, as well as the workplace or graduate school.

CONTACT INFORMATION

Carolee Larsen
Assistant Professor of Sociology
Millsaps College
1701 N. State Street
Jackson, MS 39210
Email: LARSECA@millsaps.edu
WWW:http://www.millsaps.edu/www/socio/caro.htm,
Home Page for Methods and Statistics: http://www
    .millsaps.edu/WWW/socio/methstat.htm
Phone: (601) 974-1386
Fax: (601) 974-1397

Women's Studies 241:
Feminist Approaches to Science and Technology

Donna Heiland and Janet M. Gray, Vassar College

Women's Studies 241, Feminist Approaches to Science and Technology, began as a special topics course in the women's studies program and is now a regular part of the curriculum, crosslisted with the science, technology, and society program. Team-taught by Janet Gray of the psychology department and Donna Heiland of the English department, this course questions the principles by which scientific authority is constructed as well as the ways in which the sciences frame questions and generate answers. It looks at science as discourse and as practice and is at all times informed by a concern with gender as both a factor in and product of these activities.

IDEAS BEHIND THE COURSE DESIGN

This course had its genesis in a conversation about Donna Haraway's "Manifesto for Cyborgs" (Haraway, 1991) during which Professors Gray and Heiland realized that they were both deeply engaged by this most difficult of essays. They had both understood it to be raising issues crucial to their disciplines but had read the essay very differently from each other. This concrete acknowledgment that the sciences and humanities have basic questions in common but that their methods generate different approaches and answers led Gray and Heiland to propose teaching together. FAST—as students call it—was the result.

The course addresses issues of theory, praxis, and their relationship to each other through its specific focus on representations and roles of women in science and technology, devoting some time to historical study, but focusing primarily on studying contemporary issues relevant to women living in a highly technological world. The syllabus breaks down into two major sections. The first looks at how women figure in, and are figured by, the world of science, and the second looks at those same issues in relation to technology. Readings come from the natural sciences, the history and sociology of science, philosophy, semiotics, literature, and film.

COURSE ACTIVITIES

Small class sizes—11 students in 1994 and 18 in 1996—guaranteed that Gray and Heiland could work closely with their students. Relatively frequent meetings—two 75-minute discussions a week plus one two-hour lab session—ensured them adequate time to work through ideas in a variety of ways. The 75-minute discussion sessions took a variety of forms, ranging from relatively open-ended conversations to collaborative work in groups to short, formal presentations of demanding material. The aim in these classes was always to engage the day's readings in a way that was at once open and rigorous. Lab sessions were planned in a more experimental spirit and ranged from the dissection of sheeps' brains in an effort to understand how brain structure and function bear on gender development, the viewing of films, and workshops on the semiotics of advertising in the field of technology. Most important, however, lab time provided students with a chance to work—individually, but in a group setting—with electronic technologies.

Perhaps because their decentered narratives embodied the very ideas that Gray and Heiland were discussing in class, hypertexts interested them most. The fact that Gray and Heiland were both hypertext neophytes the first time they taught the course decentered the classroom even more, pushing those students who were really interested in hypertext to learn from others in and even outside the class and finally to become expert not just in hypertext but also in the newly emerging World Wide Web. Gray and Heiland also experimented with real-time online discussions in our lab sessions that ran concurrently with face-to-face discussion in the classroom. As students took on one role after another in the virtual space opened to them, their questions about the nature of human subjectivity, its relationship to the body, and whether human subjects need bodies at all took on an urgency they did not have before.

By the time Gray and Heiland taught the course a second time, they had learned that one of the most helpful things they could do, both to further class discussion and to foster a sense of community, would be to have students generate hypertexts, then exchange and comment on each other's work, all during one lab session. They asked students to argue in a specifically gendered voice about matters of public policy, such as health care or genetic engineering. What it might mean to speak as a man or as a woman was thus foregrounded in the assignment. While the technology allowed that it might not be essential to identity, the frequency with which students relied on parody to convey masculinity or femininity suggested the difficulty of escaping gender stereotypes. Students found ways to understand both the theoretical issues fueling the course and the nature of their relationships.

Finally, both years that Gray and Heiland taught the course, electronic writing which might include written text, visual images, graphics or sound, was always an option for students, and many students chose to produce hypertexts rather than traditional papers.

MEASURED RESULTS

Hypertext became for many students a way of exploring hitherto unperceived relationships between ideas and disciplines, and the fact that some students became sufficiently expert in that technology to instruct not only their peers but their instructors speaks to the independent thought sparked by this course. Once students understood that hypertext's exposure of the contingency of narrative forms correlated with all that the course had to say about questioning the structures of knowledge and authority generated by scientific discourses, they were able to produce work of astonishing originality. Sandra Harding's "strong objectivity" (Harding, 1991), Donna Haraway's "situated knowledge" (Haraway, 1991), and even Jacques Derrida's arguably more radical assertion that "the center is not the center" all provided students with theoretical tools for understanding why the decentered structure of a hypertext was the appropriate medium in which to question, for example, the gendered assumptions behind current thinking about obstetrics and gynecology.

Indeed, the student who wrote her final paper on just this topic brought a similar methodology to bear on her thesis the next year, turning her attention to community-based treatment of AIDS patients and moving easily between hypertext work in Storyspace to creating a web site for her work. After she graduated, she continued this web work with community mental health activists in Nicaragua.

LESSONS LEARNED

Professors Gray and Heiland feel certain that when they next teach this course, they will not only talk about technology in ways that reflect the most recent scholarship, but that they will also use technology to extend that discussion in ways they have not yet tried, perhaps including hypermail discussions, classes built around Internet resources, and collaborative construction of a course web site. More importantly, in considering their discussion and use of technology in teaching FAST, Gray and Heiland now see the course as a product of its historical moment. Feminist studies of science have proliferated since they first taught the course in 1994, even as technological literacy among Vassar faculty and students and the use of technology in the classroom has become increasingly common. In much the same way that students in the course learned to see that knowledge of a subject is never absolute but always situated in a specific context, the two professors became strongly aware of how their circumstances have energized what they teach. Technology helps us situate our lives in a community of learners and teachers and enhances the intimacy and energy of our classrooms.

REFERENCES

Haraway, D. J. (1991). *Simians, cyborgs, and women: The reinvention of nature.* New York, NY: Routledge.

Harding, S. (1991). *Whose science? Whose knowledge? Thinking from women's lives.* Ithaca, NY: Cornell University Press.

CONTACT INFORMATION

Janet M. Gray, Professor
Department of Psychology
Vassar College
Box 246, Vassar C.
Poughkeepsie, NY 12604
Email: grayj@vassar.edu
http://depts.vassar.edu/~psych/FacultyPages/gray.html
Phone: (914) 437-7378
Fax: (914) 437-7538

Vignette 62 Going the Distance: Webbing a Hospitality Cost-Controls Course

Rebecca Gould, Kansas State University

Three statements guide my course development both on campus and at a distance. These statements provide the impetus to get beyond what I call the students' just-sitting-there syndrome. McKeachie (1994) said, "I only lecture when it will do more good than harm." "You learn to do by doing" is the motto at Texas Women's University. "The classroom model is approaching the sale by date" (Daniel, 1997). The traditional lecture no longer engages the students in the learning process, especially when they are bombarded by the hijinks of MTV, electronic gizmos, hand-held computers, or the Internet. It is unlikely that we will be able to maintain the interest of the current generation with just chalk and a blackboard.

Active learning must to be a part of course development. There are hundreds of articles and books written on the subject (Bean, 1996; Johnson, Johnson, & Smith, 1991; Silberman, 1996). Enhance interactivity

and you have an engaged, committed, learning community of students. In distance courses, interactivity does not have to be extensive or involve a difficult programming language. Interactivity can be as simple as email messages or a threaded message board or a once-a-week chat (referred to as a discussion room) with the students.

While teaching scholars debate the quality of distance education, they should consider that the quality of a distance course must be greater because of the world audience. These principles are fundamental to course development: the centrality of the learner, interactivity, and quality.

IDEAS BEHIND THE COURSE DESIGN

HRIMD 422, Cost Controls in Hospitality Operations, was reengineered for distance learning because of the appeal to both our hospitality and dietetics students. To survive in their future careers, graduates of these programs must understand numbers (ratios, variances, profit-and-loss statements, etc.) that are important for the success of a lodging or food service property. Course development began with a concern for how to teach numbers via distance and how to measure students' understanding of the numbers. Further, students must know where the numbers come from and what they mean in day-to-day operations.

Another part of course development was to avoid simply transforming cost-control lectures to web notes. Modules are written with word processing software or in PowerPoint slides. Each topic includes concepts covered, a review of the terminology, practice problems, and answers. In the assignment part of the module, the student applies the information covered in the topic by completing a case study or solving more problems. This time there are no answers. All assignments are then emailed or faxed.

LESSONS LEARNED

Before webbing any course, consider your goals and teaching philosophy. Decide whether the course is strictly asynchronous, partially synchronous, and/or cohort-based. These decisions might make a difference in interactivity, the types and number of projects assigned, and your ability to manage the course and students.

There is no cookbook to design web-based courses. Read, read, read, and learn from the trials of other distance course architects. Some reading suggestions to enhance your understanding of distance include *T.H.E. Journal, The American Journal of Distance Education,* and *Distance Learning Converge.* Attend every lecture by faculty who have developed courses for distance. Some of these are provided on the web, such as http://www.adec.edu/workshops/main.html. Try the latest innovations in distance technology.

Develop the course in many modes (i.e., Acrobat Reader, PowerPoint, word processing software, and audio streaming). The students stay engaged when varying formats are used. Use approachable language. Make the material interesting with graphs, charts, clip art, and colored text. Use links frequently. Have some fun with the material—interject humor.

Web course development takes a lot of time. Every lesson prepared for distance requires twice as much time as a lesson prepared for the classroom. There are many issues to work out electronically, including how students best will understand a formula or the best way to depict this case study or how students be able to email this spreadsheet.

Basic benefits of the distance class are the reevaluation of current teaching methods, reaching the student who often is silent in the resident class, and the ability to assess learning quickly. Distance education forces a teacher to rethink the how, the what, and the why of information delivery. Efficiency, simplification, and reorganization occur. You will throw away your legal pad notes. As Janet Poley, President and CEO of A*DEC noted, an instructor can't "just bolt in technology" (Poley, 1998). If planned correctly, the distance course can serve both resident and distance instruction purposes, perhaps with minor modifications. Those students who may never speak up in a classroom provide some profound statements via distance.

Another benefit of distance education is the ability to detect problems at an earlier stage. When students email an attached spreadsheet, it is easy to detect if they understand how the numbers were derived. One recent spreadsheet submission contained all numbers and no formulas. When the student was confronted with this fact, the reply was, "I just don't understand how to use a spreadsheet." Additional distance tutoring occurred.

EVALUATION OF THE COST-CONTROLS COURSE

Courses must be evaluated in both formal and informal ways by students, peers, and administration. Informally, I receive emails about modules from students. I look at the number of questions received and determine where confusion exists in an assignment or a topic. I also make the changes as soon as possible, before the email is deleted.

Ask the students periodically what is working. Ask during a chat discussion. I recently tried the latter and was amazed at students' ability to vent frustrations regarding some aspects of distance education and then to marvel at the spreadsheets they completed. Try an online, nongraded exam to see if students understand the material.

Before putting a module on the web, review the content and assignments with a peer or a computer programmer. This second opinion is valuable feedback for continuous improvement.

CONCLUSION

There is a very real need for distance education classes for students pursuing first degrees, advanced degrees, and engaging in lifelong learning. The rewards are worth the time, resources, and dollars invested. The connectivity to students, the opportunity to rethink the teaching and learning process, the ability to learn numerous technologies, and the opportunity to change, change, change keep a faculty member fluid.

REFERENCES

The American Journal of Distance Education. http://www.cde.psu.edu/ACSDE/Jour.html.

Bean, J. C. (1996). *Engaging ideas: The professor's guide to integrating writing, critical thinking, and active learning in the classroom.* San Francisco, CA: Jossey-Bass.

Daniel, J. S. (1997, July/August). Why universities need technology strategies. *Change, 29* (4), 11-17.

Distance Learning Converge. Sacramento, CA: Republic Inc. http://www.convergemag.com.

Johnson, D. W., Johnson R. T., & Smith, K. A. (1991). *Active learning: Cooperation in the college classroom.* Edina, MN: Interaction.

McKeachie, W. J. (1994). *Teaching tips: Strategies, research, and theory for college and university teachers* (9th ed.). Boston, MA: D.C. Heath.

Poley, J. (1998, November). Focusing the distance blur. Presentation to faculty of Kansas State University.

Silberman, B. (1996). *Active learning 101: Strategies to teach any subject.* Boston, MA: Allyn and Bacon.

T.H.E. Journal. http://www.thejournal.com.

CONTACT INFORMATION

Rebecca Gould
Associate Professor
Kansas State University
103 Justin Hall, HRIMD
College of Human Ecology
Manhattan, KS 66506-1404
Email: gould@humec.ksu.edu
WWW: www.ksu.edu/humec/hrimd/main.htm, http://www.dce.ksu.edu/, *T.H.E. Journal,* http://www.thejournal.com.
Phone: (785) 532-2207
Fax: (785) 532-5522

FINE ARTS

Donald R. Sexauer, East Carolina University

IDEAS BEHIND THE COURSE DESIGN

Art 1020 is a beginning drawing class for incoming freshman. The basic concepts related to creating visual images, especially drawing, are necessary to all areas of the visual arts. If I can reach a small group in their first year in art school, then I feel that by the time I see them in my printmaking classes, they will have a good foundation for the visual creation of their ideas.

During the first 30 years of my experience teaching this course, all the drawing concepts were taught using static visuals (slides), drawing demonstrations that could be rather long and on occasion made it difficult to maintain the students' attention. What's more, words could never really explain a visual concept.

I was introduced to the computer in the late 1970s and was immediately intrigued by this tool's quick and efficient problem solving. With the introduction of the application Hyperwriter, I found a way to deal with information nonlinearly. The application had some very modest graphics capabilities, and this initiated my first venture in using the computer to present drawing concepts in my drawing classes.

The web opened more possibilities. In the past several years, I have moved all of my course-related work (text and graphics) to web sites that I manage. There are several advantages to using the web:

- The concepts are easier to explain.

- Web technology allows for delivery either from a hard disk or a server.

- Students have the problem requirements and my presentations as a resource that they can access at anytime.

COURSE ACTIVITIES

At our first class meeting, the students are given a single sheet of paper. The sheet contains a graphic representation of the drawing course's web site and the Universal Resource Locators (URLs) for the art course home page and my home page. The first class period is spent explaining how the web browser works, how to identify hot links on a page, how to copy and paste information into other applications, and how to print out the information.

Communication via Email

Students who have trouble with the assigned problem, questions about concepts taught in class, or difficulty using the new technologies contact me via email for help.

Each Major Problem to Be Covered Is Assigned a Separate Page

At the beginning of the semester, all of the web pages for the course are ADummy@ pages without any information related directly to the specific problem. These pages are updated with relevant information only after the problem has been presented in class. Once the web page has been opened, it stays open for the remainder of the semester.

Material Can Be Continuously Reviewed

The students' ability to review the various problems as often as necessary aids the learning process.

MEASURED RESULTS

I teach each section of beginning drawing using the web site either on my hard disk or on the server. It is used as a presentation tool in the studio-classroom and is also available as a resource for further study. In the past three years, only a few students have complained about using the web site as a resource to gather information related to a specific problem. In all cases, the complaints were directed at the technology: difficulty in accessing a computer, browser problems, or fear of the new technologies.

LESSONS LEARNED

With the exception of the first meeting with the students where I explain how to use the web browser, I do not teach the students how the technology works. I use the technology as a tool to teach concepts related to our drawing problems.

I repeat the presentation on occasion when I find the students are having difficulty grasping any of these concepts.

CONCLUSIONS

The new tools have made it easier to present concepts that in the past were difficult or at times almost impossible to make clear. The content of my web site is always being enriched as I introduce new ways to examine a concept and find the graphic means to make the concept more clearly understood.

CONTACT INFORMATION

Donald R. Sexauer
Professor
School of Art
East Carolina University
Jenkins Fine Arts Complex
5th Street
Greenville, NC 27858-4353
Email: Sexauerd@mail.ecu.edu
WWW: http://personal.ecu.edu/sexauerd/sexauer.htm,
http://ecuvax.cis.ecu.edu/~arsexaue/linkdraw.htm
Phone: (252) 328-6665

Andrea Wollensak, Connecticut College

The design studies courses at Connecticut College focus on understanding visual information systems in a variety of forms and media. Advanced Design Studies concentrates on the paradigm shift from linear information to nonlinear language structures. Issues of identity, place, and perception are examined as metaphors for new media. Much of the coursework identifies multiple ways in which new media have influenced how we think, work, live, and learn. Students develop an understanding of the expanding boundaries of design that includes related fields in electronic communications, interface design, and virtual environments.

COURSE DESCRIPTION

This course investigates the practice of design as well as some of the issues affecting the design discipline. Explorations are project-based and include research, required readings, and writing that critically address the discipline. New and traditional media are used throughout the semester. Building on a previous course (Design Studies 209), continued study in both two- and three-dimensional spaces are explored. Specific projects involve complex typographic studies, time-based electronic works, new forms of publication, and examination of the cultural implications of the production of objects and images. The course is structured primarily for individual projects, although group projects are possible with the electronic journal web site.

Students at Connecticut College have access to relevant visual software and the Internet. The design studies area of the art department has a web site that lists course requirements, project statements, student projects, other links in the design discipline, and information on graduate programs. Additional office hours are conducted online with discussion groups. The classroom environment operates as a studio space, where students practice the ideas presented in lectures. Students work in the classroom and an adjacent computer lab that has Macintosh and PC platform workstations with scanners, digital cameras, printers, Zip drives, and networking to other campus labs. The upper-level design class focuses on the changing nature of information and the way it is received and understood by its audience. Students learn how to learn; they take responsibility for the process in an ever-changing field of media and communication. Collaborative learning, open exchange between students, and prompt evaluation of projects are strategies that work successfully with the integration of technologies in the classroom.

Design studies courses focus on a learning-by-doing classroom structure, where the student is introduced to visual problem solving through lectures and multimedia presentations. Individual and group projects allow the student to design, refine, and implement ideas related to the topic. In the doing stage, students develop basic hand-eye coordination in page layout and image programs, followed by more sophisticated skills with the introduction of three-dimensional drawing and modeling programs. Writing is used as a means of conceptual and expressive development.

Communication
Contact with students is both in-person and online. I set up office hours outside of class time for students to meet with me to discuss class projects and readings, and I also have online office hours, which allow students to ask questions or raise issues.

Sketchbook
The sketchbook is used to develop reflexive thinking. It is a space for students to reflect on the class readings, design viewing, in-class discussions, and design projects during the semester. It is used for all research, sketching, notetaking, and general documentation.

Electronic Syllabus
All project descriptions and required readings are online as are a bibliography and links to other sites, allowing students to explore the broader domain of the discipline.

In-Class Group Exercises

This part of the course introduces the computer as a tool for sketching, drawing, and refining ideas in the design process. Students work in small groups at computer workstations on short visual metaphor projects that familiarize them with the software.

Electronic Journal

Electronically created in-class exercises and individual sketches are saved into student files in a class folder on the server. Bimonthly, I access the in-progress files and provide feedback in the form of a grade or written comments, a process that both saves time and encourages students to use the electronic tools.

Computer-Enhanced Course Projects

The computer is one of the primary tools used for visualizing information in design studies. My challenge as an educator is to seamlessly implement technology into existing teaching strategies in the studio. The issues I address improve communication between students and myself, encourage the process of design through sketching and documentation using an electronic sketchbook, promote group learning through computer exercises, and implement major projects using the computer as a tool for development and refinement of the finished work.

I have introduced a few projects in the last few years that brought together design students from different schools. The McLuhan Probes course brought together Nova Scotia College of Art and Design (NSCAD) students with Connecticut College students to create visual messages related to Marshall McLuhan's media theories. The finished works are online at http://www.mcluhan.ca. Students gained experience communicating and collaborating at a distance, being dependent on and responsible to others with project deadlines, and learning communicative and visual technologies.

THE McLUHAN PROBES: A COLLABORATIVE PROJECT WITH NSCAD

The Herbert Marshall McLuhan Foundation's goal in making McLuhan's short written observations, or probes, available for this project is to reactivate interest in McLuhan among the younger generation. Many of the probes have a prophetic quality, as McLuhan's ideas anticipated many current major news events. The McLuhan Probes project tries to identify some of these ideas and link them to images from recent events. This project introduces students to time-based and interface design as they create a written and visual animated narrative responding to a selection of readings by McLuhan. Students learn how to construct clear directional signals in a nonlinear environment and are responsible for the design of the sign that signifies the action as well as the action itself.

Elements required in the document include digital images, a McLuhan quote, and the student's response to it. The interface incorporates two different navigation paradigms as well as a page for the user to respond to the work.

MEASURED RESULTS

Reports by students at the end of the semester affirm the contemporary aesthetic, technological, and practical applications of the course material. They mention looking forward to applying their understanding of design in the professional environment of summer jobs and internships. Students in Advanced Design Studies 310 are enthusiastic about electronic interactivity and find information sharing an exciting and accessible process.

LESSONS LEARNED

I find it is helpful to recognize that students today are well versed in media technologies by the time they arrive on campus and therefore easily connect with information distributed through this medium. Some technologies used as teaching tools are listed below.

Lectures Using the Internet and CD-ROM as the Visual Form, Replacing 35 mm Slides

Slide presentations have been the most accessible form of visual analysis outside of viewing actual works. In the last few years, I have been introducing interactive CD-ROMs and specific Internet sites relevant to the class project. The interactivity of the visual form makes for an engaging learning experience. One example I incorporate as an interactive learning tool is "Understanding Media," a CD-ROM on Marshall McLuhan that includes video clips of his lectures, visuals, sound, and text that meld together to make a cohesive presentation of his theories on media communication.

Electronic Communications outside of Class
The introduction of online office hours, in addition to regularly scheduled office hours, encourages students to use email on a regular basis. This expanded communication helps integrate the course into other parts of the students' day by maintaining a dialog about ideas and issues in design studies.

CONCLUSION

The use of multimedia for instruction, the Internet for communication, and software for visualizing ideas results in a transformative and valuable experience for the student and teacher. The interactive component encourages lateral thinking by providing ideas in different media. My experiences with computer-enhanced learning in the Advanced Design Studies 310 course have positively integrated pedagogy and practice. Students implement the computer in their own process of making visual communication in a hands-on, technology-enhanced learning environment.

CONTACT INFORMATION
Andrea Wollensak
Associate Professor of Studio Art
Connecticut College
270 Mohegan Avenue
New London, CT 06320
Email: Ajwol@conncoll.edu
WWW: http://www.conncoll.edu
Phone: (860) 439-2748
Fax: (860) 439-5339

Charles S. Rhyne, Reed College

INTRODUCTION

This vignette describes four assignments involving high-quality, high-resolution computer images developed for three different courses at Reed College. One assignment (The Reconstruction of the Ancient Buddhist Site at Sanchi, Central India) was developed for an advanced seminar, Art History and Conservation. The second assignment (The Architecture of the Getty Center, Los Angeles) was developed for an intermediate level course, History of Modern Architecture. The third and fourth assignments (A Pair of Japanese Nam Ban Screens at the Portland Art Museum and The Totem Poles of Haida Artist Robert Davidson) were developed for Introduction to the History of Art.

IDEAS BEHIND COURSE DESIGN

The primary educational idea behind these assignments has been basic to my teaching of art history for over three decades at Reed College. Although this idea does not depend on computer use, it has been enhanced and extended by the possibility of digitizing images at high resolution and making the high-quality images available on institutional servers and the World Wide Web. My primary instructional presupposition is that the number and quality of published images of most works of art and architecture are inadequate for anything approaching in-depth research, including student projects. Whenever possible, original works of art are used for student projects. However, only a small percentage of the world's art is available even in New York or Paris, and we therefore rely heavily on images. Most commonly, teachers and students use illustrations in books, but these are almost never adequate for architecture or sculpture and rarely allow the type of close examination desirable for most paintings. To provide for this lack, many instructors take slides of the works of art they use in their own research and teaching. Over the years, many art historians have developed large personal slide collections because these have

proven necessary for their work. In many cases, instructors have used these slides only for personal research and lectures. In other cases, the slides have been added to institutional slide collections and made available for students' projects.

The advantages that digital images, computer display, and network availability add to traditional photographic techniques are well known (for further details, see Rhyne, 1996). When photographs or slides are scanned, they can more easily be straightened, cropped, and adjusted for contrast and clarity. Properly stored and copied when necessary because of new digital formats, they can be more permanent than color slides. Large, high-quality monitors, increasingly available at colleges and universities, are more convenient for an individual viewing digital images of high-quality color slides than looking at slides through a loupe or in individual projection booths. Unlike the use of slide projectors, computer-displayed digital images may remain on view for long periods of time without fading the slides. With two or more large, high-quality monitors, students can more easily make comparisons and zoom in to examine details. Putting images on an institutional network allows many students to view the same assignment at the same time. Putting images on the World Wide Web allows students at other institutions to study the same images. Even in those few cases where an adequate number of high-quality images is available in books, multiple copies of such books may be too costly for institutional libraries to purchase.

COMPUTER-ENHANCED TECHNIQUES

For these assignments, 35 mm color slides were taken by the instructor with Fujichrome and Ektachrome film, 100 ASA, using a Canon A-1 camera with Cannon marco lens FD 50 mm and Cannon zoom lens FD80-200 mm, all handheld. Slides were scanned onto Kodak Photo CD discs by LUNA Imaging, Venice California, and Wy'east Color, Portland, Oregon. The thumbnails and 1024 × 1526 resolution images were then adjusted using Adobe Photoshop 4.0. Because these images are being studied as evidence, I make no adjustments to separate parts of any image.

Three of the assignments were studied by students on two side-by-side, 21-inch Nokia Multigraph 445X monitors operated by a Power Mac 7500/100. For these three assignments, the computer was not connected to the institutional server, and students were not allowed to copy the images, avoiding copyright problems. Students studied the images two students at a time, signing up for half-hour slots.

One of the assignments, Architecture of the Getty Center, Los Angeles, was expanded and posted on the World Wide Web (www.reed.edu/gettyarchitecture or http://web.reed.edu/academic/departments/art/getty/). This web site was designed cooperatively with Greg Haun, a Reed College graduate, artist, and author of *Photoshop Collage Techniques* (1997).

ASSESSED OUTCOMES

I made a point of discussing with the students, both in and outside of class, whether or not they found the assignments more helpful than comparable assignments that were not dependent on digital images and, if so, in what ways. I also asked them whether there were ways they felt the assignments could be improved. In one case, I asked two especially capable and interested students to write up their impressions. Their statements have been published in an article, "Student Evaluation of the Usefulness of Computer Images in Art History and Related Disciplines" (Rhyne, 1997). While it is obvious that even high-quality computer images cannot substitute for study of the original works of art, there are certain benefits. For example, comparing the work of art to many related images and to text descriptions while writing a paper is more convenient at one's home institution than returning to the museum when one wishes to examine and reexamine visual details.

Critics often make the mistake of criticizing digital images for being less accurate than original works of art. Of course, this is true of digital images, but it is also true of illustrations in books. In research and teaching and in students' projects, computer images substitute primarily for illustrations published in books. Here, with the exception of a few masterpieces that have been lavishly reproduced, it is possible to make available, for any subject, many more large, high-quality digital images than can ever be afforded in print publication. This is clearly the main advantage of computer images over published illustrations. This advantage applies dramatically to art history but also to other disciplines that study images as evidence, such as astronomy, biology, and medicine and, increasingly, anthropology and social history.

For the web site "Architecture of the Getty Center, Los Angeles," I have received enthusiastic email messages from viewers in the United States, Europe, and Asia. The site has not been advertised outside of a few professional societies but receives about 1,000 visits per month and is used by several architecture schools. Responses nearly always comment on the high quality of the images. US viewers often comment on the speed with which even the high-quality images appear, while those in Europe sometimes comment on how slowly they appear. Occasionally, specialists in stone or landscaping suggest additional images in their area of expertise.

LESSONS LEARNED

In nearly every way, actual production and use of these high-quality digital image assignments reinforced my previous, nondigital practice and confirmed my expectation of the advantages of digital images and the Internet. In addition, examination of web sites that include images of works of art and architecture has clarified my understanding of the characteristics that are important for any research images posted on the Internet (see Rhyne, 1997).

The Internet offers immense new possibilities for research and teaching using high-quality digital images. Under a grant from the Northwest Academic Computer Consortium, I am now developing additional web sites, each an attempt to demonstrate a different use of high-quality digital images for research and teaching.

ACKNOWLEDGMENTS

Funding for development of these assignments was provided by grants to Reed College from the Andrew W. Mellon and Charles E. Culpeper Foundations. The assignments were developed by the instructor.

REFERENCES

Haun, G. (1997). *Photoshop collage techniques.* Indianapolis, IN: Hayden Books.

Rhyne, C. S. (1996). Computer images for research, teaching, and publication in art history and related disciplines. *Visual Resources, 12,* 19-51.

Rhyne, C. S. (1997). Images as evidence in art history and related disciplines (347-361). In D. Bearman & J. Trant (Eds.), *Museums and the web 97: Selected papers.* Pittsburgh, PA: Archives and Museum Informatics.

Rhyne, C. S. (1997). Student evaluations of the usefulness of computer images in art history and related disciplines. *Visual Resources, 12,* 67-81.

CONTACT INFORMATION

Charles S. Rhyne
Professor Emeritus, Art History
Reed College
3203 SE Woodstock Blvd.
Portland, OR 97202-8199
Email: Charles.rhyne@reed.edu
Phone: (503) 771-1112 ext. 7469
Fax: (503) 788-6691

Vignette 66 Artifact: An Interactive Software Program for the Survey of Art History

Eva R. Hoffman, Tufts University

How do we bring the history of the visual arts to life and make it relevant to today's students? This is the challenge of our two-part survey of the history of world art called Art, Ritual, and Culture and Art, Politics, and Culture. With enrollments of approximately 100 to 150, students receive a basic (and sometimes their only) education in art history. In the survey course, students discover the field and go on to pursue art history as a major.

Electronic technology has greatly enhanced the range of teaching and learning in these survey courses and encourages thinking and dialogue among students as well as help them make effective use of their time. We have used technology in three ways:

- A web page, containing the course syllabus, readings, and assignments, with appropriate updates.

- A listserv, Artichat, provides the forum for student questions and discussions, a necessary component in a large lecture course. A focus question is posted on Artichat before each weekly recitation.

- A database of images and an interactive software program, ARTIFACT, the most innovative electronic component of the course and the focus of this essay.

The technology is currently being developed in a web-based format and is available on any campus computer with Internet access. With consideration for issues of copyrighted images, we have restricted access to ARTIFACT to computers on the Tufts campus.

PEDAGOGY AND CONTRIBUTION OF ELECTRONIC TECHNOLOGY

In our introductory surveys, we are committed to exploring a wide range of monuments and themes of world art and architecture, extending well beyond the traditional textbook canon. Unfortunately, the lack of availability of all the images shown in the lectures and recitation has presented a constant challenge. There are no facilities for slide study on campus. This is particularly frustrating to students in a course where the visual images comprise the data of study.

ARTIFACT, our database of images and text, has helped us address this challenge in three ways.

1) *Access.* Using ARTIFACT, it has been possible, for the first time, to make all the images shown in our introductory surveys readily accessible for study.

2) *Customization of course and complex mix of visual material.* ARTIFACT has also made it possible to tailor material to meet the specialized and singular needs of the survey course. Our course integrates a complex mix of visual material simply unavailable in any single textbook. The material is brought together in our team-taught environment involving the entire faculty of the department of art history, with faculty members lecturing on their specialties, resulting in an individualized, customized course. The value of customized courses becomes especially striking where specialists in unusual areas of art history make unique contributions to the survey. For example, in our survey courses, we not only have specialists in African, East Asian, and Islamic art, but also an expert in Armenian art, Professor Lucy Der Manuelian, whose material can now be fully integrated into the curriculum rather than appended to the course as an interesting sidelight. The uniform use of digitized material allows for the equal presentation of all material, preventing the privileging of any area over any other.

3) *Linking Images from a Variety of Historical and Cultural Contexts.* Beyond the availability of the visual images as a reference tool, the software provides an interactive learning environment where students can develop skills, such as looking at images critically and making connections and comparisons that allow them to transcend traditional religious, cultural, historic, and geographic boundaries. Six

representations of divinity, for example, can be juxtaposed at the same time for comparative study. The pedagogical exercises encourage user participation, placing the students in an active rather than passive role. So that, for example, the students may study preselected images, or they may select the comparative images of divinity themselves. Such exercises engage students in an interactive learning experience, involving a higher level of thinking and understanding. Furthermore, we believe that the availability of the material in an innovative format will make the study of art more accessible and exciting to all learners and not just those adept at memorizing the textbook.

In sum, ARTIFACT offers ways of learning unavailable in other media both by providing access to material not readily available in any single book and by exploring familiar material from a new point of view.

CONTENTS OF ARTIFACT: THE BASIC DATABASE

The ARTIFACT database contains over 1,800 images and is always being expanded. It includes images from Stone Age caves to the 1990s in Africa, India, Western and Eastern Asia (notably the Middle East, China, and Japan), Europe, and the Americas.

Links to Other Databases

We are currently developing a web-based program that is available to students on campus with Internet access regardless of platform. The program uses a web-based slide database already in place for our slide collection and is being developed by the same programmer who designed that database. In the web-based version, the program will be linked to many other databases and web sites, considerably expanding the range of teaching and learning. In addition to inserting images into specific lectures in their courses, instructors may also direct students to visit cyberspace exhibitions pertinent to their course. Furthermore, we expect students will be encouraged to conduct research and to gather information on these works and exhibitions. The web-version will also contain a frame or shell to provide instructors with a flexible template and methodological tool by which to structure material. For example, instructors will be able to insert additional images, modify images, and create links with other web-based digitized materials.

Interactive Functions

ARTIFACT uses three interactive functions:

1) *Search engine:* Allows for search by lecture number, artist, period, style, and subject.

2) *Practice section:* Contains matching, flashcards, and comparisons. This component contains exercises for review of images and allows students to make cross-cultural comparisons. For example, a Gothic cathedral, Byzantine church, Islamic mosque, and Jewish synagogue may all be explored on the screen at the same time in order to compare the forms and functions of religious architecture. A component under development will allow students to share information with other class members and to solve problems and to draw conclusions collectively.

3) *Interactive study guide:* Basic text for reference includes a guide for visual analysis, glossary with visual examples of architectural terms, artistic techniques, iconography, and a timeline. This component can be customized to suit the needs of the user's course. The study guide is currently under development and will be made fully interactive, with illustrations and demonstrations of entries.

New Function

"Big Ideas" is a function that will contain case studies by scholars involving a range of interpretative strategies, such as style, iconography, feminism, orientalism, social history, and reception. Students will generate image sequences and construct their own interpretive essays on such topics as architecture and ritual spaces, the life of a city, the relationship between art and the real world, art and the body, and art and propaganda. The images will assist in formulating arguments and providing evidence. We also intend to provide links for new research on these topics and links to specialized collections of relevant images.

INTERDISCIPLINARY FOCUS

We have already begun to adapt the ARTIFACT frame for use in some of our other art history courses and could adapt it for courses in other departments. The program lends itself to disciplines such as anthropology, arts, humanities, and languages, where slides of visual images are routinely integrated into the curriculum. By benefiting these other users, this project may serve as an excellent mechanism and model for integrated, inclusive, interdisciplinary study.

MEASURED RESULTS

Students have been polled to determine how they have used the program. Responses have been generally favorable. The major benefits offered by ARTIFACT involve access to materials and interactive activities requiring detailed analysis and increased depth processing. Some improved performance on exams was noted by both students and teaching assistants.

LESSONS LEARNED

Production of Quality Technology Requires a Group Effort

ARTIFACT is the result of efforts of a dedicated and skilled team. Director Eva Hoffman is an assistant professor of art history and coordinator for FAH 001 and 002; technical consultant and designer Christine Cavalier is our departmental photographer; database manager Pamela Krupanski is our curator of slides; and programmer Mark Wong is a B.S. candidate in the department of civil engineering, Tufts University. Steven Cohen of Academic Computing served as technical advisor. The project has received financial aid from Tufts University grants.

The Medium of the Present Can Be Used Effectively

The medium of the present can be effectively harnessed to teach the art and culture of the past. The electronic technology component attracts students to take the survey course who might otherwise be hesitant.

The Equipment Must Be Reliable

The benefits of computer instruction occur only if transmission and equipment are reliable. Our change to a web-based version was undertaken, in part, to achieve greater reliability.

Proofreading Is Critical

Material produced in electronic format must be proof-read as carefully as hard copy. Material disseminated with errors will be learned with errors.

Not All Web Sites Are Equal

It is necessary to evaluate web sites critically and to teach students how to do so.

Computer Instruction Cannot Substitute for Classroom Instruction

The lectures and recitations provide the key for how to use the visual images in the database.

CONCLUSION

The use of computer technology has provided a flexible system for designing a customized survey course. Through its connection to links on the web, it extends the material, offering a truly comprehensive course that is limited neither by page capacity nor by the accessibility of images. It presents all material on a level playing field. Obscure works, which receive little or no attention in the textbooks, are here given the same space as the most celebrated works. ARTIFACT has helped our course to define itself beyond the limitations of the textbook model as an inclusive course of the history of world art.

CONTACT INFORMATION

Eva R. Hoffman
Assistant Professor of Art History
Tufts University
11 Talbot Avenue
Medford, MA 02155
Email: ehoffman@emerald.tufts.edu
WWW: www.ase.tufts.edu/art/AHwelcome.html,
www.artifact.tufts.edu
Phone: (617) 627-5287
Fax: (617) 627-3890

Ed Epping, Williams College

A version of this course has been offered as an independent study with five students. The course described below will be offered for the first time to campus-wide registration in the 1999–2000 academic year.

ENVISIONING INFORMATION ARTS 200 LEVEL

In a culture, local and global, that presents and receives its data on two-dimensional surfaces (paper and computer monitor), it is imperative that we recognize the critical relationship between how information appears and what it means. Information and its presentation manifest design challenges. The organization of complex, dynamic, and multidimensional layers requires an attention to the detail of the data's appearance, while maintaining an overview of its meaning.

Edward R. Tufte's book, *Envisioning Information,* (Tufte, 1990) offers diverse representations in image, word, and number that explore the limits of their medium and expose the exacting requirements of the data presented. Examples from the Chapin Rare Book Library, selected web sites, and interactive CD-ROMs will serve the class as primary reference study materials. Projects for the course will include both works on paper (two- and three-dimensional) and computer-generated imagery (printed and monitor-display). Guest lectures on typography, numeric statistical analyses and their presentation, cartography, and graphic design will supplement studio work using, among other software applications, Macromedia Freehand, Macromedia Director, Adobe Photoshop, and Adobe Pagemaker. This course assumes only that the student is comfortable working with a computer. Enrollment is limited to the number of computer workstations available for dedicated course use but will not exceed 16.

EDUCATIONAL PHILOSOPHY

Content, for me, is a measurement of all data presented; this includes the underlying structure of its as-sembly, the textual and numeric information attached to that architecture, and the graphic ways it is revealed. The weakness of most communication is directly connected to the fact that these arenas of assembly are segregated and placed in a hierarchical, privileged position.

At Williams, each student can examine the complexities of art and better understand the qualities and conditions in which art, the sciences, humanities, and social sciences are entwined within contemporary and historical cultures. To become a maker of images, a devisor of meaning, each student must examine and comprehend issues that exist beyond the studio. There must be an opportunity to compare, analyze, experience, and experiment with the ideological possibilities argued in other disciplines. We build meaning by comparing things. The more important and extensive the comparisons, the richer the opportunities to explore the content that has shaped our visual cultures.

I suspect I am not alone in witnessing an alarming number of student-produced web-site designs that are poorly organized and visually confusing. At Williams, we teach the students a great deal of information, but rarely do we teach them specific structures for envisioning all types of information.

This course will rely on technology in two ways: using the web and published CDs as a resource for design study, looking at the words, images, and numbers, and their relationship to the information. We will use software applications to make printed, projected, and monitor displays. The course will emphasize how computer technology offers unique design problems while recognizing that their solution may be found through the study of other technologies and their limits. Charting a season's hunt on a cave wall in southern France demonstrates the successful transfer of data through technology.

This course does not assume any programming experience but expects students to be comfortable working with the computer. I will provide them with basic instruction in the software applications, and I will seek technological counsel from student TAs and guest presentations. The 16 students will often work in teams of two, but there will be individual projects that require large commitments of the resources.

COMPUTER-ENHANCED TECHNIQUES

Beginning Assignment

Produce a web site for a glass of water using the following parameters:

- A banner or headline that introduces the page and its content; typically a single word or few words that announce the content of the page (e.g., newspaper headline).

- No more than three images (photographs, drawings, and diagrams) that incorporate the conditions and the qualities of a glass of water.

- No more than two paragraphs that define or detail the contents of the page about the glass of water. These paragraphs may be fictions, factual data, and computational measurements; the text to which they refer may be found or invented.

- No more than two marginal notes that elaborate on some data in the body of the text or could serve as a caption for the selected images.

- A signature that identifies the maker of the image.

An Advanced Assignment (Later in Term)

Build a web site that is socially complex using the following parameters:

- The primary content of the site is the dispersal of information regarding HIV and AIDS.

- The primary clients are people who are unfamiliar with a PC environment, not necessarily literate, and do not consider English their primary language.

Steps in the process include:

1) Discover all existing sites on the dispersal of HIV and AIDS information; construct a detailed analysis of the form and content and make a presentation/critique.

2) Determine the best means of getting information across without relying on words.

3) Determine the complexities of presenting this information in ways that are familiar to the language culture selected.

4) Decipher the role of animation and graphic files that are successful substitutes for textual language.

5) Develop all this data in a package that might be complemented by hard copy; the web, after all, is not in every barrio around the world.

MEASURED RESULTS

Since the full course, Envisioning Information, has yet to be offered, my results are limited to the five students with whom I worked in an independent study. Here, the results from the first assignment were unbelievably wonderful. The simplicity of the assignment let the students build something very complex and multilayered. Learning that simple content, with limits, could easily be expanded indirectly taught students that the presentation of complex data can easily become confusing if over-elaborated.

Employing animated graphics, one student built an intriguing site that examined the glass half-empty/glass half-full metaphor. Each choice revealed an expanded architecture that continued to weave deeper into the meanings of this simple ideology.

LESSONS LEARNED

I learned that studying the history of graphic design is critical to the contemporary computer application. The importance of design in a 14th-century manuscript, a 17th-century anatomy book, a late 19th-century investigation of algebra, and a 20th-century collaboration between an artist and writer clearly demonstrates the breadth of form and content relations. New technology should study all technologies that preceded it and incorporate their strengths.

REFERENCE

Tufte, E. R. (1990). *Envisioning information.* Cheshire, CT: Graphics Press.

Ed Epping, Professor of Art
Williams College
1097 Main Street
Williamstown, MA 01267
Email: eepping@williams.edu

Vignette 68 CD-ROMs in a Modern Architecture Course

M. David Samson, Worcester Polytechnic Institute

The curriculum innovations described in this vignette use a multimedia computer laboratory donated by the Worcester Polytechnic Institute's class of 1956 and installed on campus during the summer of 1997. I first used the lab in my architectural history survey course, Topics in 19th- and 20th-Century Architecture, to add new material, increase interactive learning, and present complex topics more effectively. The seven-week course presents the development of modern architecture as a shift in both buildings' appearance and in fundamental ideas about architecture's nature and use. By holding two class meetings in the media lab, structured around class use of CD-ROMs on modern architecture, and through homework assignments based on those CD-ROMs, I made more kinds of documentation on architecture available to students and more effectively showed them the connections between buildings and ideas.

PRINCIPLES OF THE COURSE REDESIGN

Like other art history courses at the 2000 level at WPI, Topics in 19th- and 20th-Century Architecture is a 50-student slide-lecture course. I came to believe that the slide lecture was an inadequate educational strategy for teaching architectural history. While slides may suggest a building's shape and surface decoration, they cannot always convey a full sense of its space and mass, relation to its location, or symbolic significance. Although I could take the class to visit a few buildings for a real-life experience that slides do not provide, the campus neighborhood has no significant examples of modern architecture. The unusually brief term also makes it hard to cover any topic in depth. My sense that students found long, detailed lectures more tedious than helpful told me that loading more slides and verbiage into standard-format lecture classes would be a poor strategy. I needed a teaching tool that could present a quickly accessible range of pictures, plans, and data, both in and out of class.

I also found the standard format unhelpful in conveying the ideas behind modernism. More than most artistic styles, functionalist modernism depended on its pioneers' intellectual convictions about architecture. The flat roofs and top-heavy overhangs of a great building by Le Corbusier, for example, are not always attractive or explicable with reference to architectural styles before modernism. To gain a full historical perspective of the architect's achievement, it is necessary to know the concepts Le Corbusier had in mind. This can be conveyed in slide-lecture format only in rather dull ways. I needed a teaching tool that would help students make quick, memorable connections between the evolving style of modernism and the convictions and theories that drove it.

Finally, after several years of watching students' eyes glaze over during long lecture sessions, I wanted a teaching method that would let them be active and not passive learners. Yet because Socratic dialogue about slides or readings might slow down a large class too much, I needed a method that would carry a lot of information in itself.

EDUCATIONAL PHILOSOPHY

My teaching philosophy can be summed up as follows: *Students of art (including architectural history) must be enabled to experience the art object (or building) as fully as possible, yet they must also understand that every art object is the vehicle of ideas—about society, about the artist's vision, about art itself.*

When I was offered the chance to participate in the new WPI media lab, I decided that the best way to enact my philosophy within the architecture class's format was to have the students use CD-ROMs on architectural history. CD-ROMs would not only expose the student to material not available in textbooks or lectures, they would let the student actively put different materials together. A combination of teaching with the CD and assigning independent exercises on it let me turn the student loose to learn, while still keeping course material focused.

DESIGN AND IMPLEMENTATION OF THE COMPUTER COMPONENT

One CD-ROM of the type I wanted to use was already on the market. This was *The Frank Lloyd Wright Companion,* designed by William Allin Storrer (Storrer, 1996) and modeled after his guidebook of the same title (Storrer, 1993). The CD lists every executed building by the most important architect of the century. Each building entry accesses a text describing the commission, ground plans, photos, and, in some cases, video walk-throughs; they are cross-referenced by

Wright's style phases, building types, and location. This CD replaced a videotape guide to Wright's work that was no longer available to the class and contained information and pictures that I did not have either in the tape or slide collections.

Working with a computer science major, I designed another CD-ROM, *The Heroic Period of Modern Architecture,* on the styles, buildings, and concepts of European modernism in its period of development, 1890–1933. We organized the CD in three main sections. First was a stylistic overview, with text explaining the origins and chief characteristics of modern styles, such as art nouveau and functionalism. Second was a glossary of modernist theory, explaining such key concepts as "revealed structure," "architecture as abstract space," "social architecture," prefabrication, and so on. Finally, there was a selection of pictures of significant modernist buildings and projects. The sections were interconnected through hypertext links.

It was a condition of my participation in the class of 1956's media lab project that I hold classes in the new media lab. This was done twice. In the lecture class before each session, I laid out some of the topics to be covered in a preliminary way. Before the lab session with the Wright CD-ROM, I lectured on Wright's early development and showed a videotape of his Oak Park house and studio, which he used as a laboratory for architectural effects. In the following media lab session, I broke the class into search groups and gave them each a question to be answered from the CD-ROM. Each group had 20 minutes on individual networked PC terminals to find an answer. At the end, a representative of each group projected its answer on a screen that is connected to my monitor. After the exercises, I put some of the images from the Heroic Period CD on the master screen and asked the class to compare them to the Wright images they had just seen. Because of a large class enrollment and limited lab space, the class did this exercise in two one-hour sections. We continued comparing Wright's work to European modernism in the next regular class, using both regular slides and a CD-ROM-equipped terminal with projection screen.

Before the next lab session, I sent out via email a list of tasks and questions that the students were to answer by using the Heroic Period CD in the lab in their own time. These questions asked the students to use the hypertext links to connect buildings with ideas as well as to become familiar with modernism's landmark buildings. Students came to the media lab with their answers, which they both demonstrated to the class on the master monitor and turned in as hard copy. We discussed the various possible answers and, in following lecture classes, looked at the changes in architecture and society that made them possible.

RESULTS

The curriculum changes that computers made possible had to be made quickly because of the terms of the gift. There was not much time to make changes to the rest of the syllabus or my evaluation methods to complement the new CD-ROM component. As of yet, I have no solid quantitative measure of how the CD-ROMs affected class performance. I can say that final exam discussions of 1920s radical modern architecture, especially the theories behind it, are usually painfully wrong and that I noticed far fewer bad discussions of the topic during the final examination. I conclude that the hypertext exercises linking buildings, styles, and theories did some good. It may also be the case that my prose in the CD-ROM captions was clearer and more to the point than the textbook's. In the area of class morale, one of the course evaluation sheets commented on how much the student appreciated the use of different kinds of teaching media, so that the boredom of slide lecture after slide lecture was avoided.

LESSONS LEARNED

The only aspect of using the lab I disliked was that it was too small for my class. In addition to doubling students up on terminals, I had to break the two-hour class into two one-hour periods. These were just long enough for the students to do what I wanted them to do, but I would have liked the option of longer lab classes.

I was a little dissatisfied with the CD-ROM on European modernism, because the program my student employee designed had smallish pictures and fewer hypertext links than I wanted. I did not have time to secure all the copyright permissions I needed for WPI's Instructional Media Services to scan images onto the CD-ROM. I was limited to images from sources published by Rizzoli, fortunately a publisher of many high-quality architecture books. Still, the CD was a very useful supplement to the textbook and helpful background for the lectures.

Both the students and I enjoyed using the media lab. It was a completely positive addition to the curriculum. I am convinced that as I become better at manipulating and designing programs, the connections I want students to gain from their computerized surfaces will work even faster and more memorably.

REFERENCES

Samson, M. D., & Jalbert, K. (1997). The meanings of modern architecture [CD-ROM]. Worcester, MA: Worcester Polytechnic Institute, Instructional Media Center.

Storrer, W. A. (1993). *The Frank Lloyd Wright Companion.* Chicago, IL: University of Chicago Press.

Storrer, W. A. (1996). The Frank Lloyd Wright Companion: The interactive multimedia reference on the architecture of Frank Lloyd Wright [CD-ROM, version 1.2]. West Chicago, IL: Prairie Multimedia.

CONTACT INFORMATION

M. David Samson
Associate Professor of Art History
Worcester Polytechnic Institute
Humanities and Arts Department
100 Institute Road
Worcester, MA 01609-2280
Email: Samson@wpi.edu
Phone: (508) 831-5370
Fax: (508) 831-5932

Kathryn Rohe, University of Virginia

When I began my digital archive project, the university's drama department had more than 1,000 pieces of historic clothing stored in its basement. The oldest garments date roughly from 1800. Occasionally, someone dug through the piles in search of a costume for a student production, but the greatest activity was the settling of dust. Designed in part to properly preserve these relics and in part to bring students more directly into the process of research and scholarship, my digital archive has grown to include some 40 dresses, and 15 or so are added each semester.

The Costume Museum Archive web site is divided into three frames. The left lists each dress with a hot link to its documentation. The large, center frame displays the garment, and the right side features the student's qualitative analysis of it. Analyses typically include discussion of historical factors, such as the Art Deco movement and the Great Depression, that influence not only lives, but also design, materials, and ornamentation. Sketches and drawings from the period also are included in the analyses.

IDEAS BEHIND THE COURSE DESIGN

Exploit Departmental Resources
The department held a large, untapped resource which had been amassed through donations to a sizable collection of antique clothing. No formal records or catalogues about the clothing exist, and I sought to preserve them and to publish the collection.

Engage Students More Directly in Scholarship
By giving students the chance to handle, conserve, and research historic artifacts, I expose students to an unusual kind of primary research. By having their work published on the web, students understand that their efforts are not exercises in a vacuum. These experiences foster a deep, early interest in the subject matter.

Give Students Opportunity for in-Depth Learning
The goal in most survey courses is to cover a vast amount of material with little in-depth attention given to any particular issue. I wanted to provide students with a hands-on experience that would create a lasting impression.

Create Collaborative Learning between Faculty and Students
I work with students individually as they conserve and photograph the garments. The additional one-on-one time provides the opportunity for fuller discussions of students' findings and the general context of their work.

COURSE ACTIVITIES

Artifact Conservation and Digital Archive
During the first few days of the course, students select the garment they will handle, conserve, photograph, and research for their final project. Each project includes a full photograph of the garment (some of which are filmed in QuickTime video and can be manipulated by viewers) and an essay about the clothing, its original use, and a commentary on the social, cultural, and artistic conditions at the time of its creation. Throughout the semester, students work with staff from the university library's digital imaging center. Technical staff help them to assemble the data, digitize photographs and other artwork, and provide design advice. I have adapted class lectures to focus students' attention on matters essential for success on their project, which accounts for 40% of their final grades.

MEASURED RESULTS

Although I have not gathered quantitative assessments of the project's pedagogical effectiveness, several anecdotal factors weigh heavily in its favor. Students seem more interested in the subject matter, are more apt to do thorough research, and produce higher quality final reports, all of which are integrated into the web site. At the end of the course, students are in command of issues in costume design.

LESSONS LEARNED

- Partnerships with technical experts can be professionally satisfying and extraordinarily effective. Faculty need not be fluent in the technology used to enhance their teaching, but they must know their limits and know where to turn for advice and assistance. My reliance on technical staff from the university library's digital imaging center required extensive planning and advance coordination.

- Students must be given ample time and help to process the new information, especially the technical matter. I found that some of my students did not possess fundamental technical skills and were faced with the completely unfamiliar prospect of using the web to publish their work.

CONCLUSION

I have made an important contribution to the drama department and the university by creating the digital archive with my students. The project gives me more purposeful, one-on-one time with students and allows me to participate in their discoveries. It also organizes, analyzes, and makes available for use an astonishing collection of antique costumes.

CONTACT INFORMATION

Kathryn Rohe
Associate Professor of Drama
University of Virginia
Culbreth Road
Charlottesville, VA 22903-2434
Email: kmr3c@virginia.edu
WWW: http://cti.virginia.edu/~kmr3c/docs
/costumes.html

Vignette 70   Curriculum Development in Music Education

Peter R. Webster, Northwestern University

Developing solid curriculum in music education for public schools is not always a major focus for the busy music educator. Often, music teachers are caught up in the day-to-day pressures of preparing concerts, teaching large numbers of elementary children, or performing other tasks for their specific schools. Rarely do they have time to consider the entire program in their districts and how the total curriculum functions. A graduate-level course, Curriculum Development in Music Education offers an opportunity to consider the larger picture. Students are required to think about how their own specialties (band, chorus, orchestra, classroom, or private instruction) fit into a whole curriculum for a K-12 school system.

EDUCATIONAL PHILOSOPHY AND STRUCTURE OF THE COURSE

Like many teachers who believe in constructivism as an educational philosophy, I am always seeking to enhance cooperative learning and to encourage class dialog as well as creative and critical thinking. I try to remove myself as a professor at key moments in the course and allow the students to teach themselves by having them share their project assignments. I design the course around a series of readings and four projects that relate the readings to the individual's teaching context. Each involves such technology as PowerPoint presentations, school web sites, and videotapes of school settings.

The Electronic Yarnball

The electronic yarnball assignment usually comes toward the middle of my course and is based on a series of readings about historically successful curricular initiatives in music education. I begin by dividing the class into groups of four. The goal is for each group to write a paper cooperatively by using a central server in the computer lab that records their writing. Each student must prepare three or four pages of text on the topic independent of the others and also react to the writings of their colleagues. Timing is critical in this assignment. Students must be prepared to add their part of the electronic yarnball on a specified day.

Here is how it works: I set up folders on the computer lab server on Monday. Each folder contains ideas about the curriculum initiative, usually written in a descriptive format. For example, in one folder, I might describe the Manhattanville Curriculum Project in music education and its importance in encouraging creative thinking in music. In this text file, I might embed URLs for web sites that bolster my point or include other media, such as pictures, diagrams, or links to sound files. I document all my work with references from class readings or other sources. Depending on the size of the class, I might create three or four of these folders with initiatives or perhaps the same one if I want the whole class to write about the same thing.

Next, students are preassigned days to come to the lab, read the paper, and make contributions. Their work must be completed by the end of the assigned day. Although they come prepared to add their own text, media, and references, they must also explore and digest what is already said and be prepared to spend time responding to it. For this reason, I advise students to come in the morning, read the material, revise their prepared material, and then return with a new version by the end of the day. As a last step in this process, I create a simple HTML document that represents the full paper, and we read the work from the class web site and discuss it as a full class.

Assessed Outcomes

This is not a complicated use of technology, but it is effective. I can assess the graduate student's ability to prepare materials based on the readings and on personal experience. In addition, I can assess each student's ability to think critically and to respond constructively. The ability to add media, such as pictures, diagrams, remote web sites, and sound and video files, to one continuously developing document, is an excellent approach that matches my philosophical goals for the course.

Student assessment of the assignment is very high. Course evaluations suggest that this is a unique and interesting assignment. Most report that the initial idea of the electronic yarnball seemed silly and unproductive but that the final result was very different. There is generally a lot of support for the use of the technology, and many report that they intend to try the same idea in their own teaching in public school.

My assessment of the quality of the papers varies with each team and class, but most of the time, I am very pleased with the result. If I use the same topic for the entire class, I am always struck by both the differences and similarities each paper takes as the project is spun out in time. The class learns a great deal from reading each paper in its entirety. Graduates of the class report later that this experience was the most rewarding of the class.

Lessons Learned

One difficulty with this practice is the different experiences students have, depending on when they add to the paper. The person first to respond is challenged less by the responding element but must supply creative and meaningful material for the paper to succeed. Students who respond late are rewarded by the amount of material but also risk having their prepared remarks already addressed by earlier students. In some ways, these difficulties balance, but each student is challenged in a different way, which might result in inequity. A solution might be to give a second assignment with the same structure and invert the students' order, but I have yet to try this approach myself.

I believe that newer technology provides many opportunities for changing the way we ask our students to think and to write. Cooperative writing is often difficult and unproductive when students work together at the same time (synchronously). The simple idea of a cooperative project that allows each student to add content with media support and react to previous work—all done independently (asynchronously) in a timed fashion—seems to work well for me.

CONTACT INFORMATION

Peter R. Webster
John Beattie Professor of Music
    Education/Technology
School of Music
Northwestern University
Evanston, IL 60093
Email: Pwebster@nwu.edu
WWW: http://pubweb.acns.nwu.edu/~webster
Phone: (847) 491-5740
Fax: (847) 491-5260

Vignette 71   Creating and Using Multiple Media in an Online Course

Maurice Wright, Temple University

Computers in Musical Applications is a required course for music students and an elective for students from other disciplines, satisfying a core curriculum requirement in science and technology. The course had been offered in a traditional format for five years when the opportunity arose to redesign the course for online delivery.

I wanted to use the new format to explain accurately and dramatically the concepts underlying digital encoding, recording, and synthesis of musical sound. I also wanted to address some recurring problems: the inability of some students to select and use appropriate mathematical formulas to solve problems, difficulties with lecture comprehension by students for whom English was a second language, an occasional shortage of informed lab instructors, and schedule conflicts for busy music performance students.

CONSTRUCTING THE COURSE

Guided by instinct and previous experience, I developed a short list of design criteria:

- The course would emphasize broadly applicable concepts and not focus on specific computer programs.

- The course material would be as engaging as possible, using whimsy, metaphor, and multiple modes of communication.

- The laboratory assignments would be self-contained and self-guided.

- The course delivery would be asynchronous.

Using these criteria, I developed four sets of materials:

- Ten short lectures as movies recorded on CD-ROM

- An orientation, course schedule, and ten tutorials for Internet delivery

- A revision of the paper text that I had written and used for several years in the course

- Ten laboratory assignments using Dale Venneman's *SoundHandle* program and prerecorded soundfiles also recorded on CD-ROM

The Movies

Lasting ten minutes or less, the movies are full of facts and metaphors for the topic of study. They introduce each week's topic and provide a collection of graphics that are also used in the course web pages. At the time the course was introduced, the transmission of movies over the web was impractical, and the CD-ROM was a convenient and reliable alternative.

I decided that the movies, sounds, software, and extra material should be made to fit on a single CD-ROM. Some of the taped lectures were scripted, some were extemporaneous, and others were a mixture. The extemporaneous lectures took much longer to edit and required the insertion of voice-over recordings to cover blunders and non sequiturs. The scripted lectures were easier to edit, and the structure of the movies is simpler, but eye contact was lost when I looked down to read. The taped lecture defined the form of the movie. Still images, animation, and other video sequences were added as necessary to explain a point, present information in another form, or to cover an error in the taping. Many of the animated sequences were created during the editing process, using transition and motion effects in software. The recorded voice from the video was augmented with sound effects, occasional music, and extra voices. The next step after editing was compression. Finally, the component parts of the movie were archived and disk space freed for the next movie.

Simple procedures work reliably. An inexpensive VHS camcorder can provide crisp 320-by-240 images and can be used to digitize stills. I set up the tripod next to my computer and focused the camera on a small easel illuminated with a 75-watt, incandescent desk lamp. I could capture a single frame, process it, and save it for use in the movie or the web pages. Software editing systems offer a dazzling list of filters, transitions, and motion effects, yet the simple cut is still one of the most powerful effects and inexpensive in processing time and memory use. A long, slow, cross fade produces a complex sequence of images that don't compress terribly well and take a long time to process.

The Tutorials

The gateway to the course is a web site containing orientation information and a list of weekly assignments. A tutorial reviews and develops material from the textbook reading and the movie. There are five virtual tutors, designed to counter cultural stereotypes and to appeal to the diverse interests and backgrounds of the students.

Each tutor is introduced with a short narrative description. The first tutor, the Cup-Bearer, treats the student like a king. The image of an ancient figure carrying a drink of wine emphasizes the ceremonial and potentially pleasant experience of learning. The second tutor is alleged to be one of Lord Byron's daughters, Ada Lovelace, but the image is from a book in the public domain, a collection of women's fashions. Lord Byron's daughter evokes a romantic image, and her stance with hand on hip suggests an assertive personality. This tutor sometimes antagonizes the students, exhorting them to work quickly so as not to waste her time. The third tutor might appeal to those students who feel overwhelmed or frightened by the course content. A talking fish is perhaps the ultimate nonchallenging figure, and Herbie the Talking Fish takes the lead with some of the most complicated quantitative material in the course: digital sampling theory and filter theory. The fourth tutor is a parody of an expert. Replete with deerstalker, spectacles, and mustache, Claude the Detective leads the students down digressing paths. The goal was to make students aware of the pertinence of quantitative detail to the solution of practical problems and to reason carefully.

LESSONS LEARNED

Course grades were computed using examinations from the traditional form of the course but with new laboratory reports. The grade distribution was similar in both the online and face-to-face formats, but based on conversations with self-selected students, I believe there may be significant differences between the two formats. Procrastination posed a problem for the online student and in some cases for the instructor as well. Try as I might to reserve hours to work at a computer for the course, my schedule tends to fill up with face-to-face appointments, performances, meetings, and other events. The flood of lab reports at the end of the semester was daunting and requires a remedy that may compromise the asynchronous design criteria.

Although I wish to believe that most of my students were honest and hardworking, I would sometimes find the erroneous calculations and unusual phrasing in work submitted by different students. The line between cooperative study and brazen cheating is drawn finer by the email facility, where my comments on a student's lab report could be remailed, printed, or otherwise circulated without my knowledge. Greater automation of the laboratory process to provide randomly different data might improve the process.

Online instruction is clearly inappropriate for some. Two students sought me out separately to tell me essentially the same story: They felt unable to function without a group meeting with the instructor and the other students. Both students had immense difficulty passing the course and were emotionally distraught as a result. They characterized themselves as good students with excellent academic records. Indeed, they had been publicly recognized by the music faculty for their achievements. Both students were very gregarious and popular. It was clear to me that they were unable to function academically without a social interaction, and I resolved always to offer at least one face-to-face section of the course per year.

Those students who liked the class were extremely enthusiastic about the online format. Several wanted to buy the CD-ROM, which had been loaned to registered students. Others took it home during their semester breaks to show their friends and family. Students for whom English was a second language would watch the movies slowly, stopping to replay complicated phrases and take notes or printing dozens of pages of tutorials on which they could underline sections for review in an office appointment. The number of students who continued to an advanced course in digital sound synthesis rose by 400% from the previous years of face-to-face instruction.

I would argue that online instruction has value but is fundamentally different from gregarious instruction. I do not believe that email, listservs, and static web pages offer as many modes of presentation as a class lecture and that online classes must compensate through other devices.

REFERENCE

Venneman, D. *SoundHandle* (version 1.0.3). [software program available from freeware of dvenneman@get.com].

CONTACT INFORMATION

Maurice Wright
Laura Carnell Professor of Music
Esther Boyer College of Music
Temple University
Philadelphia, PA 19122
Email: Wright@astro.ocis.temple.edu
WWW: http://www.music.temple.edu/~maurice
Phone: (215) 204-8016
Fax: (215) 204-5528

Maud Hickey, Northwestern University

Teaching Composition in the Schools, a course required for junior and senior music education majors, examines the practical and research literature on teaching composition in the schools, analyzes the design of curricular materials, and requires students to compose using traditional and electronic means. In addition, students interact on a regular basis with public school students via an Internet composition collaboration project titled MICNet! (Musical Internet Connections).

This course is unique in two ways. First, few, if any, colleges or universities require music education majors to take a course about teaching composition in the schools. We require such a course at Northwestern because of our strong belief in the need for creative music-making in music classrooms, as opposed to just recreation or performance. The composition and improvisation of music has long been ignored in typical public school music classrooms and reserved for only the professional composers or "jazzers." With research pointing to the importance of creative music activities, along with the advent of the National Standards in Music Education, which require abilities in music composition and improvisation, we find music teachers must learn how to employ these methods in the classroom.

The second unique aspect of this course is that our undergraduates interact with public school children, their teachers, and a professional composer via a web site in an Internet music composition collaboration and exchange. The philosophy, goals, and actual practice of MICNet! (http://collaboratory.acns .nwu.edu/micnet/) are described in the following sections.

MICNET! PHILOSOPHY

At the composition or improvisation level, the computer, along with simple software, a synthesizer, and MIDI protocol, provide an instant palette from which to create, mold, edit, and organize sounds into musical compositions. Children as young as six and seven years of age are able to create original compositions using these tools. This constructive approach to learning and interacting with music provides enhanced musical experiences for children of all ages.

When it comes to taking advantage of technological tools in education, however, music teachers lag far behind those in the sciences and math. While music technology provides tools that make composition for children more accessible than it has ever been, teachers are unaware of these resources or simply afraid to use them. In our teacher-training program, we have the responsibility to teach future teachers these technologies so that it will be easy for them to infuse creative music composition into their teaching.

The solution is to expose preservice teachers to these technologies and to real students and teachers who are using them. The Internet learning environment can inform present and future teachers about the possibilities of music composition with students as well as link teachers, students, and a composer to create an exciting and interactive learning environment.

The MICNet! project was launched at the start of the spring quarter in conjunction with the Teaching Composition in the Schools class. The goals of MICNet! are the following:

- To connect K-12 music students and their teachers with college preservice music education majors and a professional composer to collaborate on music composition

- To facilitate creative composition skills as a supplement to traditional music instruction by integrating computers and MIDI technology into the curriculum

- To help future as well as current music teachers use technology/MIDI in music composition teaching

- To develop and to share curriculum units for technology/composition in conjunction with existing music curricula

- To gather research related to Internet music learning

MICNet! in Action

Using the World Wide Web, music students from the 12 public schools that volunteered to be a part of MICNet! (a mixture of elementary through high school levels) submitted musical compositions in MIDI file format to a central database. Students could submit compositions whenever they were ready, and there were no specific lessons or rules given; each classroom teacher decided. Once compositions are submitted to the database, they appear along with information about the composition on a web page at the MICNet! web site. At that point, other students, teachers, our resident professional composer (Dana Wilson from Ithaca College was hired using grant moneys), and the university music education students can download the MIDI files, listen to them, make changes if necessary, and provide feedback to the student composers via uploaded submissions to the web site. This ongoing dialogue and exchange continued throughout the spring quarter.

The 18 university students in Teaching Composition in the Schools were required to provide feedback to the student composers on at least four occasions over the span of the ten-week course. In class, we discussed the compositions that were submitted and also wrote lesson plan ideas for the school music teachers and their classes.

Measured Results

The information shared was beneficial to all. As the project moved on, it became apparent that our university students were learning how to give feedback. This growth and success was evident in the dialogues from the university students, as well as the feedback from the students at the end of the course. The public school teachers all expressed positive feedback regarding their students' experiences. The students who submitted files were able to get feedback from multiple listeners and also to hear compositions from peers outside their own classrooms. For the entire ten-week spring quarter, a total of 25 MIDI file compositions were submitted by public school students, and approximately 102 comments were exchanged among the university students, public school teachers, and Dana Wilson.

The ubiquitous and simple nature of the web page format made the technology simple to use. MIDI files via the QuickTime plug-in are small and easy to manipulate. Any school teacher with web site access and a desire to share student work is welcome to join. In addition, we hope that MICNet! will become a clearinghouse for composition lesson ideas shared by the professional composer, teachers, and university music education students and that it becomes a helpful database for any music teacher who might need materials for teaching music composition.

Lessons Learned

Due to the wide-open structure of the project (i.e., no forced dialogue or rules about responding, etc.), we found that the public school students who originally submitted compositions never responded to those who wrote comments. Often comments would contain questions or suggestions for the composers, but not one student composer wrote back or resubmitted their MIDI files based on these comments and suggestions. The university students felt they needed that feedback in order to know if their voices were heard. In a telementoring one-on-one situation, this would be less of a problem since the public school student would feel more of a direct relationship with a university student and, hence, be more inclined to respond. The teachers who responded felt that the main problem was time for the public school students. Apart from submitting their files and reading their comments, there was little or no time to revise or respond. As the project continues, the goal is to improve in this area.

Contact Information

Maud Hickey
Assistant Professor of Music Education
    and Technology
School of Music
Northwestern University
711 Elgin Road
Evanston, IL 60208
Email: mhickey@nwu.edu
WWW:
http://www.nwu.edu/musicschool/people/faculty
    /mus_ed/mus_ed.html#hickey
Phone: (847) 467-4726
Fax: (847) 491-5260

Literature, Languages, Writing, and Humanities

Pompeii as Urban Laboratory

John J. Dobbins, University of Virginia

The Pompeii Forum Project is a web site that I originally created as a repository for my archeological research and comprises information about my interdisciplinary field work in Pompeii. The web site combines scholarship from the fields of mechanical engineering, art history, architecture, and urban studies. It is well established and for several years has featured a rich array of images, essays, and CAD-rendered depictions of structures as they might have looked before destruction.

Long a popular site for students and interested laypersons, the Pompeii Forum Project web site was not initially designed for instructional purposes; its audience was other scholars, but the site was broadened so that I could use it to teach art history to undergraduates.

Ideas behind the Course Design

My courses involve intensive examination of an archeological field site thousands of miles away from the grounds of the University of Virginia. Although I encourage students to visit Pompeii, and several students work with me there during the summer months, I also recognize the need to bring the primary materials of research closer to students in the classroom.

Deep, hands-on learning through research is commonplace in the sciences, but it is more challenging to design these experiences for students in the humanities. Bringing students more directly into the research process is of prime importance to me. Imbedded in that notion are the following objectives:

Deepen Students' Understanding of the Subject Matter and Research Process
When students can see the evidence clearly, they can better visualize three-dimensional relationships and

comprehend the historical change and personal ambition inscribed in the physical contours, arrangements, and details of the buildings. The web-based exercises are designed to supplement in-class work, allowing students not only to discuss particular features of the field site at Pompeii but also to abstract from these concrete examples.

Engage Students More Directly in Scholarship
I am certain that the exercises I developed require students to assimilate visual and textual information and to create their own scholarly narratives. Other exercises use the Socratic method to challenge students to see complexities in images and constructs and to reason through problems systematically.

Foster a Collaborative Learning Relationship between Instructors and Students
By pulling students directly into my own research, I involve them at a high level in a scholarly project. The web-based exercises allow students to act as researchers, which fosters greater collegiality between students and teachers and blurs traditional distinctions between them and their work.

Course Activities

Case Studies
I created interactive, web-based tutorials that guide students through viewing and interpreting a Roman wall painting and Latin building inscriptions. Using the Socratic method as a core design principle, I built the tutorial so that students first see the work intact, are given a certain amount of information about it, and then are asked a series of questions. The questions and

corresponding visual assessments grow increasingly complex and challenging throughout the exercise.

Silent Video

My colleagues and I made several narrated videos of the forum, several houses, the Forum Baths, and 1997 excavations. These included tripod setups and steady-cam walk-throughs. We also made a silent video, a non-narrated walk-through of the House of Pansa. Once students have learned about the Pompeian house and have viewed the narrated videos of the House of Faun and the House of Vettii, they view the silent video out of class and write their own narration. One or more of the student narrations is presented in class.

QuickTime Virtual Reality

In 1998, some of my colleagues and I shot several QuickTime Virtual Reality (QTVR) nodes. In this process, a 35 mm camera is attached to a calibrated tripod that is set up at some critical or interesting point (an intersection, a street, atrium of a house, garden, etc.) Eighteen frames are exposed as the cameraperson rotates the camera through 360 degrees (i.e., one frame for every 20 degrees). This allows for considerable overlap between frames. The developed negatives are scanned and stitched together electronically to provide a seamless 360-degree view from the node, or setup point. These are non-narrated images which, like the silent video, may be used as stand-alone study aids or may serve as the basis of student analysis and/or narration.

Digitized Slides

I compiled a visual database of slides of Pompeii both for my use during class and by students independently. Although this element of the project was among the simplest to design and implement, it is highly useful to and popular among students, who appreciate the ready access to resources not otherwise available to them.

MEASURED RESULTS

Early anecdotal responses from testing some of the new course materials with students at a local private high school and with students at the University of Virginia rated the material very highly in terms of its organizational clarity, level of instruction, and graphic presentation.

I have designed several ways to solicit evaluations of the new materials from University of Virginia students and from faculty and students elsewhere. For example, I've created the case study of the Latin inscriptions so that students' responses to the questions posed on the web site are directed back to me. This will help me gauge the pedagogical effectiveness of the new tools.

LESSONS LEARNED

Developing the scripts and exercises proved more time-consuming than originally planned, and staying ahead of the student programmers who were working for me was challenging. Remaining flexible enough to seize the opportunity to develop new ideas and, in some cases, to abandon original ones was important. Thinking through the equipment necessary to exploit the new material was essential. While field testing an exercise at a local school, I discovered that some of the monitors in the school's computer laboratory did not produce images of sufficient resolution to allow the students to pursue the exercise.

CONCLUSION

Developing instructional technologies is neither easy nor inexpensive. Invariably, the process takes longer than hoped, and even the most enthusiastic devotees of technology are, from time to time, left wondering about its usefulness. In the end, however, little doubt remains—classroom discussions are more robust, students' knowledge is deeper, and student/faculty relationships are richer.

CONTACT INFORMATION

John J. Dobbins, Professor
Classical Art & Archaeology
McIntire Department of Art
Fayerweather Hall
University of Virginia
Charlottesville, VA 22903
Email: Dobbins@virginia.edu
WWW: http://pompeii.virginia.edu
Phone: (804) 924-6128
Fax: (804) 924-3647

Collaborating on Technology and American Frontiers

Hugh A. Blackmer, Washington and Lee University

Ideas for courses often have diverse purposes and origins, but this one may set a record. It began when I was moving books into the new science library and found a nearly complete run of the *Journal of the Franklin Institute,* starting in 1826. What a shame, I thought, that nobody uses this resource, one of the first American journals of popular science and other useful arts. Other 19th-century gems came to light, fragments of a history of inquiry and ingenuity which built the nation, and I started to explore the library's 19th-century resources and consider how they might be made more accessible, fitted into courses, and how students and faculty could be encouraged to explore these riches.

At more or less the same time, I began to work on a proposal for geographic information systems (GIS) capability for the library, aimed at raising awareness of the utility of spatial information in a broad range of disciplines. The GIS scheme (funded by a small Mellon grant from Associated Colleges of the South) is organized around development of a regional map database and Internet map server centering on the area of western-central Virginia where Washington and Lee is located. The intention is to gather and interrelate historical and contemporary maps, including geological, biological, and archeological, genealogical, and local history data. ArcView's hyperlink capabilities make it practical to connect spatial data with texts and images.

Another campus connection led me to a nascent project on the iron industry in this part of Virginia, combining the interests, data sources, and talents of a group geologists, chemists, metalsmiths, archeologists, foresters, and historians. Clearly, both 19th-century library resources and 20th-century GIS capabilities apply to this initiative and provide an opportunity for me, as an anthropologist and science librarian, to combine my own long-term interests in technological history and regional studies with my more recent web-based work in information access.

EDUCATIONAL THEORY

In exploring means to encourage cooperation among computing services, the media center, the library, and teaching faculty, I had a discussion with John Blackburn, director of the library's media center, about two interlinked problems: 1) how to use new technologies to inspire students to take control of their own educations, and 2) how to get faculty interested in using the new possibilities in their teaching. We agreed that student commitment must rest on a sense of personal worth in what they do and that any uses of new technology in the classroom must have the practical difficulties straightened out before any but the most adventurous faculty are likely to adopt them.

COURSE DESCRIPTION

Out of this came a plan to collaborate on a seminar course in the history of American technology, for which the output form and a primary medium for student participation would be web pages instead of conventional papers. There are several reasons for this approach:

- escape from papers written only to please the professor

- the pride, responsibility, and engagement that an essentially public project engenders

- the possibility of an audience for student work

- the chance to develop presentation skills, including multimedia as a testbed for teaching web skills

- the possibility of a permanent record, upon which others can build

- my conviction that the best way to improve the quality of the web is to participate in the creation of quality

Broadening the audience to other students and all sorts of anonymous web denizens should promote personal responsibility, including intellectual responsibility in matters of citation and attribution, and might help to move undergraduate efforts away from imitating traditional models of scholarly communication toward modalities that communicate personal engagement, enthusiasm, and originality. We want student work to be more fulfilling in ways that conventional academic papers rarely are, and some of us want something even more subversive—making undergraduate scholarship respectable by giving it a voice and promoting collaboration between students and faculty, and perhaps extramural individuals and groups as well.

On the technical side, cooperation from university computing and the library made a computer-training classroom available for the multimedia portion of the course. The media-center director will assist with teaching the necessary skills. Techniques developed for this course and the difficulties overcome should provide a model for other faculty and a technical basis for extension of the overall design to other courses.

History of Technology is a quintessentially interdisciplinary subject, connecting the technical and scientific with the social and cultural; it is much concerned with the consequences of technical innovation. The course description sketches the flexibility we intend:

> Technology deals with materials, processes, energy transformations, mechanisms, the taming of physical forces, and the domestication of biological systems. As people adopt new machines and techniques, their relationships to one another and to their surroundings change. This course focuses upon American technological frontiers and examines the technical background and social and cultural implications of a broad range of evolving technologies. A cross-disciplinary seminar with a media lab component, the course will include selected readings, library exploration, and class and World Wide Web presentations. Three credits.

Students choose one or more of the following for their course projects: a technology, a decade or an era, a frontier, a region, a person (author, inventor, artist, etc.), or an industry. They will use university library re-

sources as the primary basis for exploring the consequences of technological change. Starting points (an illustration, a text, a specific event) matter less than the connections that explorers make and the adventures they have as they pursue implications.

The general metaphor of the frontier appeals to us as an organizing theme, both for its inclusiveness and its implication of evolutionary development. While spatial frontiers are the most obvious example, we also mean to suggest past and present technological frontiers and arenas of social and cultural implication, such as infectious diseases, miniaturization, domestic architecture, free verse, fertility, precision, deafness, and so on.

A number of faculty have expressed interest in sitting in on the course, probably as much for its novel subject matter as for the multimedia approach. We anticipate that we as instructors will learn a great deal about the practicalities of teaching the integration of multimedia resources. Most important, we hope that creative use of the web will enhance learning and give students a taste for research and writing for an audience.

CONTACT INFORMATION

Hugh Blackmer, Science Librarian
Washington and Lee University
Lexington, VA 24450
Email: blackmer.h@wlu.edu
Phone: (540) 463-8647
Fax: (540) 463-8963
Further details can be found at:

- http://www.wlu.edu/~hblackme/technol/ (links to various course-related pages)

- http://www.wlu.edu/~hblackme/technol/iron.html (links to iron-working pages)

- http://www.wlu.edu/~hblackme/giswork/ (links to GIS project pages)

- http://madison.wlu.edu/~blackmerh/technol/ (links to course page)

Vignette 75 Adapting to a Digital Culture: Technical Writing in a Networked Classroom

Michael R. Moore, University of Arizona

The field of technical writing is being transformed as corporations, government agencies, and publishers increasingly design and place information and product documentation online. Technical writers are no longer responsible only for generating print manuals, instructions, and proposals, but also are designing interactive web sites, writing software documentation, and producing usability tests and studies.

The pilot section of technical writing I'm teaching is in a networked classroom. The course is traditionally taught with an emphasis on the rhetorical situation of creating a text: recognizing that rhetoric is an action and is inextricably linked with a writer's and organization's ethos and an audience's needs.

IDEAS BEHIND THE COURSE DESIGN

I've incorporated four major elements into the course:

1) practical document design

2) theories of technical communication and technology

3) usability testing

4) critical self-reflection

Practical Document Design

Using networked computers in the course helps facilitate the exchange of documents during the drafting, revising, and design stages. These activities highlight the collaborative nature of document design (Schriver, 1997) and the critical thinking required to collaboratively produce HTML documents (Norton, Segaard, & Duin, 1997).

Students work together in teams of two to four to create collaborative semester projects. Groups are designated according to academic majors and interests, so that, ideally, each group has a member who has identified his or her strengths:

• leadership (project management)

• writing and editing

• marketing

• computer skills

Group members are responsible for designating one person to manage their communications portfolio throughout the semester. Each group provides ongoing progress reports, trip and interview reports, memos, and activity logs. Some of these documents are transmitted via email to me directly, and others are posted to the course listserv. Print documents undergo at least one revision, and each group is evaluated as a whole according to the grading criteria. Some groups have elected one person to produce and revise all the documents, while others share those responsibilities. Each document is evaluated according to readability, choice of typography, rhetorical effectiveness, and the quality of information. For some of the longer documents, groups have the option of putting their work online and providing me with a URL. Some documents are created in class with two or three students in front of a computer negotiating the design and phrasing, while others are submitted in finished form at the beginning of class.

In addition to emphasizing the skills needed to design a readable and rhetorically effective document, I've incorporated readings on the ethics of documents design to increase critical awareness of the ways designers manipulate information (Dragga, 1996; Moore, 1992). This is particularly relevant when discussing online documentation and other Internet issues, since credibility and authority are crucial features in the exchange of information.

Theories of Technical Communication and Technology

One of the more pressing pedagogical concerns addressed in technical writing networked environments and in an expanding digital culture is visual literacy (Brasseur, 1997). Students in my course practice (in their own projects) incorporating text with graphics, but we also consider the visual aspect of hypertext design, which has proven to be an excellent collaborative problem solving activity.

In addition, by incorporating visual literacy exercises in a technical writing course, students become more adept at communicating interface-design issues with a professional, organizational team that may contain computer programmers and technical and scientific members. We also analyze user interfaces found in software from Microsoft Word to popular WYSIWYG editors, and we discuss how those elements often shape us as writers (Selfe & Selfe, 1994).

In terms of writing activities, I'm experimenting with a process we're calling web site iterations, in which students make copies of their web pages throughout the semester and analyze their progress in designing their sites: layout, typography, colors, tone, graphics, and overall usability. This exercise is designed to yoke together a view that all writing is recursive, with the fact that emerging electronic platforms are not designed for and thus do not encourage revising or tracking changes in drafts. At the end of the semester, students will have copies (index1.html, index2.html, index3.html, etc.) of the stages of their web site and these iterations serve as records of the design process.

Usability Testing

Students are introduced to the basic principles of Human-Computer Interaction, and then compare and discuss contemporary approaches to usability testing: contextual analysis, ethnographic study and field observation, and focus groups. In groups, students then select a product (software, web site, or ergonomic device) for testing, design a test that incorporates representative tasks, select representative users, and observe the user/participants completing a series of tasks. The groups then analyze their observation data and write a report with the product's design team as the audience.

In addition to online documentation and formal report writing, students gain experience in creating timely and effective correspondence and working with actual designers and systems administrators. More importantly, the project allows students to analyze computer interfaces, sets of instructions, and other forms of technology, while acting as an advocate for an end-user.

Critical Self Reflection

I ask students to reflect on the ways in which technology has affected them as students, in their nonacademic lives, and in the lives of their parents. Some scholars argue that technology serves to de-skill workers via standardizing training (Apple, 1997) and that we must recognize technology not as a neutral tool, but as a system of beliefs and values. This is a helpful approach. Students are able to analyze the reasons they are being trained to learn certain kinds of writing, use particular brands of software, and learn different professional discourse conventions. Other critics suggest that if we are training students to inhabit virtual cyberworlds where they will create text and meaning for others, we should be encouraging them to inquire into issues of identity and power. In each of these cases, we're using technology to critically analyze technology.

Finally, I encourage students to pursue service-learning projects for their collaborative semester work that will allow them to combine the fundamentals of technical writing in networked environments with a community-oriented project (Bowdon & Wurr, 1998).

The hands-on experience of designing real-world documents, combined with active participation in the community in which they live, is a practical and responsible application of what they're learning, where they're learning it.

One group is redesigning a web site for the local chapter of American Friends Service Committee, a nonprofit organization committed to social justice, peace, and humanitarian service. Another group has created a program, Grandparent Buddies, which will bring together fourth-graders from a local school with residents of a home for the elderly; the two groups will write autobiographies together and engage in other literacy activities. This project group is also creating web site and online materials that will publicize their work and help homes for the elderly and elementary schools develop their own similar programs.

LESSONS LEARNED

Issues of student access to computers remains a universal problem. Not all students own computers; not all students' schedules allow for consistent access to campus labs. This is an ongoing concern when developing curricula and assignments that require out-of-class access.

Though this course is a pilot project, all indications are that the level of engaged collaboration rises in networked environments. This doesn't mean that all collaborations are flawlessly effective, or that all group members share the exact same vision of a project. Rather, we concentrate on effective strategies for collaboration including intercultural concerns, accommodating varying levels of computer literacies, and solving real-world project management problems.

Students engage the creation of text much more actively in a computer classroom than they do under the more traditional take-home-the-instructor's-comments-and-rewrite paradigm. Students seem to spend more time writing and revising documents than they do in a traditional classroom (Albers, 1997).

Teaching in a networked classroom does have a decentering effect: Students are engaged with their texts, their computers, and their peers rather than listening to me lecture. Some students know more than I do about certain software capabilities and are often willing to suggest alternative approaches to problems. Students are also working in an environment (networked, team-based) that they are likely to find themselves in when they pursue nonacademic, professional situations.

References

Albers, M. J. (1997). Peer evaluation in technical communication courses: Pedagogical implications for the computer-based classroom. Paper presented at the 1997 SCMLA Annual Conference, Dallas, TX.

Apple, M. (1997). The new technology: Is it part of the solution, or part of the problem in education? In G. E. Hawisher & C. L. Selfe (Eds.), *Literacy, technology, and society: Confronting the issues.* Upper Saddle River, NJ: Prentice-Hall.

Bowdon, M., & Wurr, A. (1998). Service-learning in composition.<http://w3.arizona.edu/~guide/sl/>

Brasseur, L. (1997). Visual literacy in the computer age. In S. Selber (Ed.), *Computers and technical communication: Pedagogical and programmatic perspectives.* Greenwich, CT: Ablex.

Dragga, S. (1996). Is this ethical? A survey of opinion on principles and practices of document design. *Technical Communication*, 1, 38.

Moore, P. (1992). When politeness is fatal: Technical communication and the Challenger accident. *Journal of Business and Technical Communication*, 3, 269-92.

Norton, D. W., Segaard, M., & Duin, A. H. (1997). The HTML decision-making report: Preparing students for the information age workforce. *Computers and Composition*, 14, 377-94.

Schriver, K. (1997). *Dynamics in document design.* New York, NY: Wiley.

Selfe, C., & Selfe, R. (1994). The politics of the interface: Power and its exercise in electronic contact zones. *College Composition and Communication*, 4, 480-504.

Selfe, C., & Selfe, R. (1996). Writing as democratic social action in a technological world: Politicizing and inhabiting virtual landscapes. In A. H. Duin & C. J. Hansen (Eds.), *Nonacademic writing.* Mahwah, NJ: Lawrence Erlbaum.

Contact Information

Michael R. Moore
Graduate Associate Instructor
University of Arizona
445 Modern Languages
Tucson, AZ 85721
Email: Moore@u.arizona.edu
WWW: http://www.u.arizona.edu/~moore,
http://www.u.arizona.edu/ic/moore/308/project_criteria.html
Phone: (520) 621-1836

Vignette 76 — Problem-Posing Learning in the Computer Writing Classroom

Linda S. Bergmann and Lucas P. Niiler, University of Missouri, Rolla

According to the policy statement of the University of Missouri, Rolla (UMR) English department, "English 60 (Writing and Research) has three main goals: 1) to improve the students' competency in the techniques of research writing, 2) to improve their abilities to read and analyze various kinds of primary and secondary research materials, and 3) to require them to write research papers of a quality that suffices in school and the work place."

Expected student outcomes for this course include the capacity to write "research papers that contain an identifiable thesis that is intelligently and coherently developed with sufficient supporting details based on the use of sources," to demonstrate "abilities to locate, select, and analyze source material" and to integrate "research information into research writing involving the accurate and consistent use of a standard system of documentation, which includes notes and bibliographies." Students are also expected to learn how to use our university library for reference and to avoid plagiarism. Sections of English 60 are limited to 25 students and meet for three hours a week.

For the past two semesters, several professors have taught sections of English 60 partially or totally in UMR's Center for Writing Technologies. The center, equipped with 25 computers on a local network with access to the campus-wide network, offers a working environment where students can both conduct research and produce written products (not only the research papers on which the course focuses, but also web sites, hypertexts, and presentation graphics). The following vignette describes two faculty members' uses of this classroom and other computer applications to 1) achieve the goals and outcomes established by English department policy, and 2) foster the problem posing, collaborative pedagogy that we both endorse.

EDUCATIONAL THEORIES

We share a teaching philosophy that favors student-centered learning and collaboration among students and between students and teacher. We have been influenced by Paolo Freire's *Pedagogy of the Oppressed,* in which he advocates problem-posing education. Freire argues that for students to really learn, teachers must shift from the roles of authoritarian enforcer and knowledge bank to the roles of co-searcher, facilitator, and participant in dialogue. As Cynthia Selfe suggests (Selfe, 1989) literacy (and, thereby, authority) must be repeatedly redefined in light of computer access and our students' often impressive computer expertise.

Our computer-enhanced sections of the research writing course apply these ideas by assigning open-ended projects that encourage students to develop their own research interests, and we require substantial work with computer-based sources of information, such as libraries, newsgroups, chatrooms, the World Wide Web, and professional discussion lists and their archives. Because we encourage students to develop expertise in areas other than ours, and because neither students nor faculty have exhaustive experience in using the emerging electronic sources and tools, we naturally take on the roles of collaborators and fellow-researchers. Computer access lowers the barriers of time, space, and rank that conventionally separate students from faculty, letting us share knowledge and develop expertise as the semester progresses.

COURSE ACTIVITIES

The Daedalus Integrated Writing Environment (DIWE)

Daedalus software is designed to facilitate a process approach to writing; it sequences the work into several steps that can be followed from beginning to end or in any order. Students build their written assignments piece-by-piece, from generating ideas to drafting, revising, and final editing. DIWE provides prompts for brainstorming paper topics; offers word processing; allows students to revise their work via prompts and electronic exchange of papers; creates an in-class chatroom for electronic discussions; includes a mail function for posting papers, assignments, and messages within the class; and features a bibliography database from which MLA and APA references can be formatted automatically.

We have used all of these functions in our sections of English 60. Dr. Niiler finds the brainstorming prompts particularly valuable because they can be easily modified for a particular course or writing project. The revision prompts, also easily modified, allow self-evaluation and directed peer critique of writing in progress and reinforce our insistence that revision is a crucial step in the writing process. The bibliography function takes the guesswork out of preparing Works Cited pages, although we need to clarify personal preferences for Internet citations, because of the uneven way publishing information is presented at many web sites.

The in-class chat function called Interchange enriches ancillary discussion. We have found that electronic discussion often facilitates interaction among students who seldom participate in oral discussions, which accords with observations recorded on the Daedalus faculty discussion list. Participation in Interchange discussions requires that students write constantly for the greater portion of a class period. Faculty can archive, print, and mail transcripts of electronic discussions. These transcripts enable us to assess both the quality and quantity of students' participation and allow students to incorporate this informal discourse into formal writing projects. Sometimes these discussions are passed along to people outside the class; for example, to faculty interested in redesigning their own courses for use in the computer classroom. To bring closure to Interchange discussions of course readings, which can range widely over the topic, Dr. Bergmann assigns one or more students to write a summary of each discussion, which is posted to the class discussion list before the next session.

Email

We know that email eliminates the traditional barriers of time and space that confine many teacher/student and student/student exchanges to the classroom or office hours. Students are free to ask questions of both instructors and classmates at any time, day or night, via private email or section discussion lists. Email fills an important need in classes like ours, where students direct much of their own research projects through fre-

quent conferences. Electronic conferencing, moreover, frees class time for group discussions, lectures, and presentations. Email also plays a rich and rewarding role in student research and can help eliminate the perceived barriers between the classroom and the real world. Often students email sources at web sites they visit during the course of their research; they ask follow-up questions, request further information, even begin correspondence. Some of Dr. Bergmann's students lurk on professional or academic lists and consult list archives. Last semester in Dr. Niiler's class, a student emailed a query to his congressman and received not only a quick electronic response, but also a package of previously inaccessible government documents.

Internet Applications

The Internet is a vital component of our sections of English 60. Not only do students have ready access to the net throughout campus and in their dorms, apartments, and homes, but the UMR library is completely online. To go to the library, then, means clicking on the library home page, through which students have quick and easy access to the catalog of the UMR library, the entire University of Missouri system, and other college and university collections statewide, as well as to interlibrary loan, online databases, bibliographies, encyclopedias, and other reference tools. In fact, we no longer take the students to the library to learn how to do reference work; the librarian comes to our electronic classroom, and we access the library from there. As students conduct Internet-based research (including both traditional academic sources and web sites, chatrooms, newsgroups, MOOS, etc.), they must learn and practice critical thinking. They learn to assess the credibility of the material and to distinguish academic sources from the commercial, governmental, and personal. At a time when net publishing is growing exponentially, we teach and practice the traditional higher-level thinking skills of analysis, evaluation, and synthesis.

Peer Research and Editing Groups

Students engage in considerable independent learning and writing based on the expertise they develop and share with the class. We look at independent learning and collaboration as complementary aspects of the writing and learning processes. Computer applications facilitate the peer groups that are vital to this work. Students communicate by email and in subdivided Interchange conferences. They exchange drafts of their work-in-progress electronically, give presentations with computer-generated materials, and distribute progress reports to peer groups and, eventually, to the entire class. The computer technology creates opportunities for students to collaborate by testing and sharing research interests. They develop a real, as compared to theoretical, sense of writing to an audience, and they learn from that audience's response. We encourage students to point each other toward additional sources of information on the web and in electronic bibliographies, to help each other master the conventions of report writing, and to constructively evaluate written drafts and oral presentations. This collaborative approach teaches students that how they present their research is often as important as what they discover. Students learn that good researchers have a responsibility to communicate clearly to both general and specialized audiences.

MEASURED RESULTS

While we have used aspects of computer technology in several different classes, fall semester 1998 was the first semester in which we conducted English 60 sections fully committed to, and designed for, this electronic environment.

In a mid-semester survey, conducted after the first research assignment was submitted and graded, students were asked to evaluate how working in the computer classroom affected their research. We focused on several key areas of the research process: locating, selecting, and analyzing source materials; documentation; library resources; comprehension of research materials; and improvement in writing research papers. A total of 54 students from three sections were asked to evaluate each of these areas, using a scale of one (poor) to five (excellent). The questions and measured results follow:

- How much has classroom access to the World Wide Web helped you develop the ability to locate, select, and analyze source material? 90% answered with a 3 (average) or above.

- How much has using the computer writing classroom helped you learn and maintain a consistent documentation style (MLA, APA, etc.)? 88% answered with a 3 (average) or above.

- How much has using the computer classroom helped you learn to use the UMR library resources? 90% answered with a 3 (average) or above.

- How much has using the computer classroom helped you improve your ability to understand research materials? 82% answered with a 3 (average) or above.

- How much has using the computer classroom improved your writing so far? 90% answered with a 3 (average) or above.

- Would you like to use this software/write on the computer again? 88% of our students replied, "Yes."

We expect to conduct a more complete survey in the future. We will compare grades and dropout rates in the computer-enhanced sections to those in regular sections and try to obtain some comparative student satisfaction data as well.

LESSONS LEARNED

Student Adaptability

This approach to teaching research writing provides an alternative to the traditional top-down, lecture-based instructional methods familiar to many students. There is both promise and peril here: promise, in the sense that many students flourish in such a classroom environment and learn not only about their area of research but also about taking responsibility for their own education. Through defining problems, sketching out a method of solving them, critically examining the sources of solutions, and learning to present their findings, students learn how knowledge is created and disseminated and hone crucial skills in research and communication that they can apply to other courses and their careers. The peril: Some students are unwilling or unable to assume this responsibility. Faculty must be very clear about our expectations and flexible in our approaches to the opportunities technology fosters.

Power Shift

When our students log on, much of our authority as rule-enforcers, lecturers, or, as Freire puts it, knowledge banks, evaporates. This adjustment constitutes a shift of power in the classroom, a move from hierarchy to collegiality, which can be uncomfortable at times to both students and faculty. We place ourselves at a considerable disadvantage by inviting students to explore open-ended topics, as we cannot guarantee expertise in disciplines other than our own, even though we can provide writing expertise and experience in methods for effective, efficient research. Faculty must carefully plan for students to develop research and writing skills and must establish clear criteria for evaluating student projects.

REFERENCES

Freire, P. (1970). *Pedagogy of the oppressed*. New York, NY: Seabury Press.

Selfe, C. (1989). Redefining literacy: The multilayered grammar of computers. In G. H. Hawisher & C. L. Selfe (Eds.), *Critical perspectives on computers and composition instruction*. New York, NY: Teachers College.

CONTACT INFORMATION

Linda S. Bergman, Associate Professor
English Department
Director of Writing Across the Curriculum Program
University of Missouri, Rolla
1870 Miner Circle, Department of English
Rolla, MO 65409
Email: bergmann@umr.edu
Phone: (573) 341-4685
Fax: (573) 341-4600

Lucas Niiler
Email: niiler@umr.edu

Vignette 77 English 101: Hypermedia/Phanopoeia

Michael Joyce, Vassar College

ENGLISH 101, Hypermedia/Phanopoeia, explores the relationships of word and image in the literature of a post-alphabetic age. I offer this freshman course through the English department. Hypermedia/Phanopoeia is a course about what we see when we read and what we read when we see within electronic textuality. Reading from disk-based and web hypertexts as well as printed texts ranging from Blake's *Marriage of Heaven and Hell* to *Passionate Journey,* the woodblock novel of Frans Masereel, to graphic novels and contemporary print fiction incorporating images, students realize that word and image have been shifting places throughout history.

IDEAS BEHIND THE COURSE DESIGN

As institutions like ours and disciplines like English reconsider the importance of human community in a new media age, they illuminate comfortably habituated spaces: places of wood and marble, weaving and canvas, voice and gesture, fragrance and depth. The light we shine upon ourselves projects a representation of us that we sometimes do not recognize. The new media reflect our human spaces and quotidian concerns in a surface of dazzling flatness and constant linearity. This course asks students to consider the tradition of various literacies in which our understanding of the verbal text and its relationship to visual and verbal images measures our understanding of the value of human embodiment and community. Students use new media to un-

COURSE ACTIVITIES

Literally in the midst of a MOO session discussing N. Katherine Hayles's essay, "Virtual Bodies and Flickening Signifiers" (Hayle, 1999) with my students, I received email from Hayles regarding these issues. This course is less enhanced than enacted within computer environments. It takes place in a computer classroom where students meet for both face-to-face and synchronous virtual discussions and collaborative reading and writing of hypermedia. A class hypermail list extends discussion outside the time and space of class meetings and represents a rich web resource for student writing. Storyspace, a hypertext system for readers and writers, serves as an editorial environment for both web discourse and traditional papers. Joyce frequently has students engage in a synchronous computer discussion of class issues at the same time as they are having an oral discussion of the texts under consideration, which are often hypertextual or otherwise dynamic. Students are encouraged to weave the computer discussions ("down under," as they frequently characterize them) with the ongoing discussions "up" in the classroom. Similarly, students weave online discussions with segments of text and image, whether electronic texts or digitized print and images, into hypertexts that also incorporate contributions from mail lists, web sites, and email with other students and professors, distant critics and theorists, and even, on occasion, authors of the texts under study.

MEASURED RESULTS

Students in this course go on to further inquiry into the theory of hypertextuality in my advanced course, to making interactive films and videos in a film department course, to cultural criticism of emerging media and genres in English; philosophy; science, technology, and society; and women's studies courses. The course enjoys high ratings in the standard evaluations that all courses at Vassar undergo. Graduates who began their academic careers with this course already play important roles in the new media industry. Anecdotal evidence suggests that students are better able to under-

stand and to produce scholarly and professional discourses and to consider ideas through particular inquiry into a variety of disciplines and interdisciplinary programs. More importantly, however, these students integrate their understanding of these issues throughout the curriculum and beyond: in graduate school creating hypertext papers and senior theses and web sites, but also acting as informed social and cultural critics, theorists, and practitioners.

LESSONS LEARNED

The chief lesson learned is that the course isn't about things that work but about understanding how computer-based environments help learners and teachers understand and represent the work of culture and literacies, including new media. The course is a series of constant adjustments, intellectual as well as technological. Because all computer technologies, including the Internet and the World Wide Web, are unstable as yet in comparison to the stability and calm of face-to-face human discourse and print-based reading and writing, repeated successes in the course have involved using the stability of institutionalized discourse as a lens into the emergence of a new age whose name we may never know and whose form we can barely decipher, but whose connections to the continuity of human history we embody and represent.

REFERENCE

Hayles, N. K. (1999). Virtual bodies and flickening signifiers. In N. K. Hayles, *How we became posthuman: Virtual bodies in cybernetics, literature, and infomatics*. Chicago, IL: University of Chicago.

CONTACT INFORMATION

Michael Joyce
Associate Professor of English
Vassar College
Poughkeepsie, NY 12604-0360
Email: mijoyce@vassar.edu
http://iberia.vassar.edu/~mijoyce
Phone: (914) 437-5941
Fax: (914) 437-7578

Synchronous and Nonsynchronous Exchange in Basic and Advanced English Classes

Mark A. Wollaeger, Vanderbilt University

As director of college writing, I wanted our beginning writers to develop a keener sense of audience and a more critical relationship to assigned reading; as a teacher of advanced literature classes, I wanted students to remain engaged with course materials throughout the week. Since I have always considered assigned writing an extension of classroom discussion, I hoped to draw more students into classroom conversations. In 1996, I began experimenting with synchronous and nonsynchronous computer-mediated exchange, using collaborative writing software in a networked computer lab for my composition class and web-based conferencing software for an English honors seminar.

With all dormitories hardwired, students have relatively easy access to networked computers, most from their rooms. Although use of the computer lab is currently limited owing to the number of disciplines competing for time, use for computer-assisted writing instruction has nonetheless expanded over the past few years to include 15 to 17 writing-intensive sections each semester as well as one course in women's studies. Many more classes make extensive use of email.

ASSUMPTIONS GUIDING IMPLEMENTATION

Early in my Vanderbilt career, I found that our students, while very bright, often were reluctant to disagree openly with one another in class. In response, I started to experiment with intensive collaboration in small groups, followed by plenary discussions. New computer tools were becoming available on campus at this time, and I soon discovered that many of the principles governing computer-assisted writing mesh with those governing collaborative learning and writing across the curriculum (WAC). The following apply to all three:

- Writing should be integrated into the everyday activity of the class, not pushed to the periphery.

- Good writing typically emerges from real communication situations.

- Good writing emerges from specific ideas generated from within class exchange.

- Student writing should build on what they know instead of recapitulating what the teacher knows and has already told them.

- Collaborative learning works: Peers effectively motivate and educate one another.

Other principles relate more specifically to computer-assisted instruction (CAI):

- Quiet students will be drawn into discussion by computer-mediated exchange.

- Students in computer-assisted writing classes write more than those in the traditional classroom.

- CAI adds the stability and carefulness of written discourse to the dynamic of classroom exchange.

- CAI creates new ways for students to work in collaborative groups and receive quick and detailed written feedback from peers and instructors.

- CAI encourages active learning.

The convergence of CAI, WAC, and collaborative learning suggested new ways to address old problems: How can we teach young writers to understand writing as a process, as the production of, rather than the display of, knowledge? What might help young college writers write for a real audience—the community of their peers—instead of for an imaginary audience that elicits artificial academese? In what follows, I first describe how CAI worked in basic composition and then in my advanced honors class. My conclusions bear on both kinds of course.

COURSE ACTIVITIES: BASIC COMPOSITION

My composition class met three days a week; nine classes over the semester used the Daedalus Integrated Writing Environment (DIWE) in a networked computer lab. When the pilot program expanded, I set minimum lab usage for Monday/Wednesday/Friday classes (seven to eight sessions per semester) and Tuesday/Thursday classes (five to six per semester) in order to make the computer sessions an integral part of the class. I used DIWE and email for several purposes:

Invention

Most basic writers devote too little time to invention. To address this problem, I sometimes had students do an invention sequence in which the computer offers prompts I programmed in advance. In a 50-minute class, students can respond effectively, I discovered, to approximately five to seven prompts, ranging from "What are you trying to accomplish with this essay?" to "Divide your topic into three subtopics" and "Arrange these subtopics in order of importance and justify your arrangement." Students can print out their work or leave it on the server. After they became acclimated to the program, I required them to do these outside of class, reserving the lab for collaborative activities. Sometimes I jump-started the writing process by moving students from a prompt sequence into a real-time chat module where they would exchange thoughts in small groups, cutting and pasting materials from their previous exercises into their messages where appropriate. This intensive exchange often led to ideas for papers. Students could also switch into another small group to practice writing their way into new discourse communities.

Recursive Use of Transcripts

All exchanges in DIWE's synchronous chat module are automatically saved and archived on the server and can be accessed or printed out by students and teachers over the semester. The growing archive became a valuable resource. I often brought sample exchanges into the next class to model how to pull a thesis claim from the flow of discussion or to underscore an important point that otherwise might slip away unrecognized. Students generated paper ideas from reading the transcripts, and when writing arguments, they often quoted one another. Early in the semester, I required students to use the archives because I discovered that options left dangling too often remain dangling. Later in the semester, students sought material from the transcripts on their own.

Peer Review and Revision

Students could exchange essays and, guided by specific prompts, write out peer reviews or go into the chat module in order to discuss their papers. With printed peer reviews and/or transcripts in hand, students left the lab already having taken the first step toward a true revision—reseeing their writing through their classmates' eyes.

Email

I encouraged students to email me their thesis statements before writing, and I was able to respond effectively to most messages in less than two minutes. These exchanges never supplanted scheduled face-to-face conferences—nor would I wish them to—but they provided quick responses and saved me a great deal of time. I also warned my students that I would check my email only during "cyber office hours" and that sending messages at 3 a.m. would succeed only in reminding me how late I used to stay up in college.

MEASURED RESULTS

Assessing writing improvement is notoriously difficult, and CAI does not ease the problem. I found that 1) my students developed a better sense of audience by writing back and forth to one another in real communication situations; 2) students became more actively engaged with course materials by writing informally about them on the computer; 3) this active engagement enabled more students to find good starting points for their essays; 4) more students participated in class exchanges—it's virtually impossible to remain silent when a transcript is forming before your eyes!—and they were more likely to engage with each other productively; and 5) students developed a heightened sense of writing as a process. The extra writing students do in CAI is, admittedly, informal, but the best way to improve writing is by writing more, and regular writing of any kind makes formal writing easier to do.

COURSE ACTIVITIES: ENGLISH HONORS CLASS

For my advanced undergraduate literature class, I used CAI primarily to promote more focused engagement with course materials. Challenging and unfamiliar materials—modernist literature and contextual materials, including paintings, ethnographies, sculpture, and philosophical and psychological treatises—required students to develop a high tolerance for conceptual uncertainty as they learned to make connections between diverse cultural productions. In-class discussion helped a great deal, of course, but the class met once a week for two-and-a-half hours, making continuity difficult, and the complex texts raised more issues than could be dealt with during class. Moreover, students daunted by the conceptual fluency of their more vocal classmates tended to fall silent, relying on the rest of us to generate the intellectual heat. CAI helped in the following ways:

Pre- and Post-Class Discussion

Early in the semester, I posted discussion questions in our conferencing software (Allaire Forums), and students posted responses at least one day before class. I required students to reenter the forum after class within 48 hours and, in light of the intervening class discussion, complicate and extend our in-class exchanges. Then we would repeat the process. Once we were in rhythm, I assigned students to post the opening questions. The software allows nested responses, so various threads can be developed simultaneously without disrupting the exchange. Students could also initiate their own threads, independent of the initial discussion questions. Early in the semester, I found that one student had created a thread entitled "What Is Art?" Virtually the entire class participated in it, teaching me a lot about my students' fundamental assumptions. Reading their postings throughout the semester, I was able to eavesdrop on the learning process and craft my lesson plans accordingly. Students were fascinated to hear regularly from everyone in the class for the first time.

Web Pages

On the course syllaweb, I placed updated assignments and bibliographic entries as well as hyperlinks to our conferencing forums, course reserves, the library catalog, and a wonderful humanities database, the Voice of the Shuttle. For the first of three essays, I asked those who wrote the two best to email them to me as attachments, and I placed them and a selection of good moments from other essays on our web pages as models; I also annotated them in red to show what made them good. Finally, online, I posted important handouts distributed in class.

MEASURE RESULTS

Students indicated in evaluations that computer-mediated exchanges knit together course materials with a thoroughness and complexity they had seldom experienced. All students participated, and in subsequent face-to-face discussions, I could draw out the more reticent by asking them to elaborate their postings. Regular posting requirements also meant that fewer students fell behind in their reading. Not only did I know more about what my students were thinking, I also learned how they were thinking: how they were reacting to the elusive ironies of Conrad, the opacities of Joyce, or the subtle, indirect discourse of Woolf. A spillover effect from the computer forums became evident in both my introductory and advanced classes, making for more inclusive, substantive, and focused classroom discussion.

LESSONS LEARNED

As a neophyte, I learned many things about CAI, including the following:

- If you plan to meet in a computer lab, you must have a good reason to bring everyone together in the same place at the same time. Solitary computer tasks can take place asynchronously outside of class.

- Synchronous exchange in a chat module is most productive when 1) students first go through a prompt sequence that highlights important features of the texts or issues you wish to discuss; otherwise, the conversation too quickly runs off-course or loses textual grounding; and 2) the instructor makes the first posting in each group to start the exchange.

- Asynchronous exchange, like all CAI, must feel like an integral part of the course, or students won't take it seriously. Assign a separate participation grade for computer exchange.

- Asynchronous exchange requires that students have a clear sense of what they are to do and how often they are to do it. You provide the structure, which they can modify, and they enter it.

- Have a partner in the computer lab the first time you teach. Otherwise, when small technical glitches occur, and they always do, you'll be frantically putting out little fires all over the room. Enlist the help of techno-literate students as well.

CONCLUSION

CAI has provided many new ways to elicit productive critical thinking and has become indispensable to my pedagogy, but potential problems exist. One student told me that while she could walk away from other classes, mine tended to follow her into her networked room, "haunting her." Now, to some degree, this is a professorial fantasy come true: The classroom walls are tumbling down. Yet without quite saying so, my student also implied the course was becoming invasive, and I realized that if we all were simply to add regular asynchronous exchange to our courses without altering the rest of the syllabus, students would be overwhelmed. Posting responses after reading and taking notes takes time, and without cutting back other requirements, we risk souring the digital age experience for many students. For me, the tradeoff between assigning a little less reading and requiring more out-of-class exchange is a good one. They may not read quite as much, but they read more deeply.

CONTACT INFORMATION

Mark A. Wollaeger
Director, College Writing Program
Vanderbilt University
Department of English
P. O. Box 1654, St B
Nashville, TN 37235
Email: Mark.wollaeger@vanderbilt.edu
www.vanderbilt.edu/ans/english/mwollaeger
      /index.htm
Phone: (615) 322-6527
Fax: (615) 343-8028

 **Web-Based Resources in a Traditional Literature Course**

Gail B. Sherman, Reed College

During the summer and fall of 1997, I expanded, modified, and used a previously existing web page for the English junior seminar to enable students to make better use of its resources available there and to integrate it more closely into class projects. Teaching third-year English majors whose computer literacy ranged from typist to technogeek, I had to make materials easily accessible to allow students at all levels to develop their skills and, perhaps most difficult, to avoid overwhelming students in an already demanding course.

EDUCATIONAL THEORY

My choice of resources and assignments grew out of the pedagogical aims of the course. First and foremost, this course (in versions taught by several faculty members in different terms) helps students develop a sophisticated grasp of critical theory, canon formation, and research methods. In my version, we read authors from Ovid to Toni Morrison with additional literary theory and critical reading. The course invites students to work in a range of periods, including texts by Chaucer, Milton, Fielding, and Mary Shelley. Beyond the heavy reading load, students work independently and in groups to write an annotated bibliography on a text of their choice, a discursive critical history, and a substantial critical essay building on their research. In addition to the usual library resources, the materials I use to support this course range from databases on the classical world to bibliographies of living authors.

I added materials to the web page and designed web-based assignments for the course with three aims in mind: 1) to define inquiries that would be inherently interesting and that would reinforce an approach to the text under discussion; 2) to introduce skills that would be useful in student research; and 3) to allow appropriate choices for students of varying experience with computers. Web assignments included a mini-report posted to a course folder, with each student reading one or more.

Underlying my development of the web page and the web-based assignments are the same principles that underlie all my teaching. Perhaps the most important is the firm conviction that we all learn best when we are active participants in learning and in designing some of the tools we use to explore and define materials and to research questions. Second is my belief that intellectual growth requires both individual work and group work, as well as a variety of forums in which to present it. Finally, since levels of sophistication vary from student to student, I believe any course should ideally be structured so that it enables growth for all students.

COURSE DESCRIPTION

To accompany each text we read in the course and writing assignments, I designed research and writing assignments that introduced students to one or more features of the web page and other technological resources. In general, I have found that students are happy to invest time and energy in learning to use new technology if the benefits are clear, immediate, and integrally related to the goals of the course. Just as they would not be interested in performing writing exercises unrelated to their projects, so they are justifiably interested only in finding ways to use technology that augment their engagement and productivity in the specific issues, materials, and goals of the course.

The syllabus was only available as a web page, to encourage students use their Internet browser. A mailing list and course folder supplemented the web page, offering quick and convenient communication with the class and a shared site for posting reports and work in progress for the shared term project. Students checked out a web assignment from the weekly syllabus; read a general introduction to the variety of possible approaches; and chose one, including reading articles on the web, searching a text to discover a thematic focus, discovering background on the author, or devising a web search to find more materials on the text under study. Each student wrote a brief report on the results of the web work, posted it, and read at least one other student's report.

RESULTS

I will continue and will encourage others to use Internet-based resources in teaching, in part because of some surprising results. More students completed their research in a timely way, with excellent content. Including the use of electronic resources from the outset may have acclimated students quickly to the idea of exploring further resources on class materials and helped them structure their time in ways that allowed for the major commitment to research and writing necessary later in the term. Since the assignments sent students to resources that encouraged and then required independent exploration, the web-based assignments may also have helped them break down a project into smaller steps. Class discussions were enriched by student references to questions, ideas, and information gleaned from the web-based resources.

In addition to reinforcing and developing research and work habits, what did the web-based resources add to the course? The web page introduced students to inherently valuable resources: online bibliographies, journals, documents, and literary texts; access to visual art materials; and online discussion groups on scholarly topics in students' areas of interest. Students were able to read unpublished translations of medieval legal cases in conjunction with Chaucer's "Wife of Bath's Tale." One student found a forthcoming article, emailed the author, and was sent a preprint, a possibility usually only available to scholars who know each other's work. Students were able to view Hogarth prints online during their reading of Fielding's *Joseph Andrews*. Finally, the students all reported that they used electronic resources in their research, whereas in the past some students relied exclusively on print resources. I had fewer complaints about being unable to find books or get copies of articles in time. Introducing web-based resources early in the term helped students develop competence in electronically based research methods they had to use to complete their final papers.

LESSONS LEARNED

As I continue to develop my use of web-based and other technology in my teaching, I hope to address more fully some of the challenges I discovered in this project. First and foremost is the issue of my own facility with electronic media. I found it relatively more difficult to adapt materials on the web than in print format or on the course folder; I expect such skills will increase as I gain more experience. Reed also makes available student assistants for web page development, without which I would not have had the courage to embark on this project. Next in importance is a continuing effort to integrate web-based resources with other course materials and to bring them into the classroom. Reed has classrooms equipped to project computer images. However, I see the primary benefit of web pages and web-based resources as offering students benefits in their independent work and their work outside the classroom, rather than in it, where discussion is crucial.

With the support of my invaluable student assistant, Kim Oldenburg, I was able successfully to integrate web-based resources into my teaching. I found using web-based resources in a traditional course time-saving and task-enlivening, both for me and the students. As I discovered, web-based resources can augment the multiple technologies we already use in teaching, from books to email. I look forward to serving as a friendly resource to other faculty members beginning to make use of web-based resources in teaching.

CONTACT INFORMATION

Gail B. Sherman
Professor, English & Humanities
Reed College
Portland, OR 97202-8190
Email: Gail.sherman@reed.edu
WWW: http://web.reed.edu/academic
/departments/english/courses/English301/
Phone: (503) 771-1112

Vignette 80 Documentary Technologies

Shawn James Rosenheim, Williams College

COURSE DESCRIPTION

Documentary Technologies is a seminar investigating the ways that new media technologies simultaneously ground and undermine notions of the real in contemporary culture. Combining critical reading and viewing photographs, documentary films, medical imaging, net documents, and home video with workshops in image production, the course examines how conventional photography, audio recording, and their digital elaborations are affecting our understanding and narration of the world. Topics include media recycling and culture jamming; the loss of referentiality; changing thresholds of evidence; and strategies for responding to the global media archive. Requirements for the course include short essays, individual exercises in image manipulation, and a final hypermedia essay combining visual and textual elements. Although there are no formal prerequisites for the course, which is cross-listed in English and Studio Art, experience with web design, film history, or video is a plus.

This course grows out of a seminar on nonfiction film that I've taught for nine years, during which time the proliferation of digital technologies has altered the very idea of documentary or nonfiction recording. I've expanded the earlier course into two separate classes. Documentary Fictions is now a more traditional genre course, while Documentary Technologies will wrestle with the cultural implications of contemporary developments in the production and consumption of images. Because the course combines critical writing with media workshops, students will now be able to move beyond merely paraphrasing visual evidence in their texts into quoting the films or videos they discuss verbatim, through the use of reproduced stills, embedded audio files, or digitized video clips. The use of digital editing suites like Media 100 will also allow students to re-edit existing films in order to articulate formal, rhetorical, or narrative patterns implicit in the original work. Most dramatically, students will also be able to combine materials from diverse sources into hypermedia essays that will make use of visual and spatial dynamics not available to traditionally written essays.

Course assignments should be flexible enough to suit students from widely varied backgrounds. I have arranged with the Office of Information Technology and the art department to offer students instruction in scanning, HTML design, Director, Sound Edit, and nonlinear digital video editing. Not all students will need to learn identical skills; at a minimum, however, students will be required to do the following computer-based exercises:

- Construct a false image. The result of this project should be a single image constructed from scanned or captured images, combined and altered using Photoshop.

- Recreate a cinematic space. Create a simple walk-through of a cinematic space, from a movie of the student's choice, using Virtus Walkthrough.

- Re-edit a sequence from an existing documentary in order to change its logic, rhetoric, and use of evidence, using Sound Edit or Media 100.

For the final project, students will construct either a hypermedia web essay combining navigational elements, photographs, and sound and image files, or they will create a short audio or video documentary, using Sound Edit or Media 100.

LESSONS LEARNED

Based on the work students have done for me in Documentary Fictions, I expect that the computer-based exercises in Documentary Technologies will highlight three themes.

- Producing digital objects is intensely time-consuming. This is a simple point, but one often lost on humanities students whose attempts at cultural theorizing are often unconstrained by knowledge of how the objects of their interest are produced. I want my students to experience the difficulty of building intention and argument into these new, often increasingly dispersed artifacts.

- The explosion of documentary technologies means that the lines between documentation and interpretation or between fact and fiction are more porous than ever. The process of re-editing an existing film makes it stunningly clear that there is no natural or uninflected way of telling a story, and that all visual materials involve rhetoric, argumentation, and manipulation.

- Finally, the relative ease with which students can learn to manipulate and reconstruct documentary film, video, and audio raises serious epistemological, aesthetic, and ethical questions. What happens to notions of property, intellectual creativity, and authorization in a culture in which there is no firm original? What happens when students can re-edit a film so smoothly that viewers might never know it had been altered? How do we handle questions of evidence and proof when we can no longer trust the evidence of our eyes?

CONTACT INFORMATION

Shawn James Rosenheim
Associate Professor of English
Williams College
Stetson Hall
Williamstown, MA 01267
Email: Shawn.j.rosenheim@williams.edu
Phone: (413) 597-2363
Fax: (413) 597-4032

Vignette 81 — Using a Template to Teach French Holocaust Literature

Patrick Henry, Whitman College

I can still vividly recall my initial skepticism when asked to participate in a computerized learning project at Middlebury College in the summer of 1996. I used email on a daily basis, but that was the extent of my computer literacy. "You will learn some new techniques in language teaching," I was told repeatedly when I expressed reluctance to travel 3,000 miles for nothing. As a matter of fact, I didn't learn a single new technique in language teaching, but I did acquire a magnificent tool for teaching literature—the template.

EDUCATIONAL THEORIES

As a French literature teacher, my task is always the same: to teach students how to read the great literary masterpieces written in French. I follow the traditional explication de texte method, which comes down to a very close reading illuminating the richness of a text. My belief in this method (in opposition to lecturing to students about literature) is linked to my logically prior belief that my job is to teach students how to read. To do so, we have to read the text together. It is my specific role to seek out any and all means to bring the text to life, to make it both comprehensible and meaningful for my students.

At Middlebury College, I learned that the creation of a template could greatly enhance my traditional method of close reading. By using clips from documentaries, films, and interviews, I could supplement texts used in class and make them and their historical setting come to life in new, dramatic fashion.

COMPUTER-ENHANCED TECHNIQUES

After watching the expert team of teachers and lab technicians at the Mellon Workshop at Middlebury College, I decided to create a template on the Holocaust, which is the final segment (four class periods) of my French Civilization through Literature course. On my return from Middlebury, I spent 80 hours viewing films, documentaries, and interviews that all dealt with the Holocaust, most of which concerned the Holocaust in France under the Vichy régime. With the help of Gary Esarey, the director of Whitman's Language Learning Center, and Piers Barry, his student assistant, we were able to create a template that would profoundly enhance my teaching of this period.

The first two texts on the template are written by survivors of Auschwitz, Charlotte Delbo and Elie Wiesel. By splicing together various parts of Claude Lanzmann's *Shoah*, we were able to begin the template with a 45-second train ride into the very station where both Delbo and Wiesel arrived in Auschwitz—Birkenau. The students have already read the two works, but when the lights go out, and we move into hell together, the impact is visible. The video brings the students to the text in a new and very powerful way.

The centerpiece of the template, however, concerns the third text, a sermon delivered by a Protestant pacifist pastor, who inspired a rescue mission that saved 5,000 refugees from the Nazis. This text is preceded on the template by another train ride into a village, Le Chambon-sur-Lignon, that was dedicated to hiding Jews and other targets of Nazi hatred. The train ride is taken from Pierre Sauvage's *Weapons of the Spirit*, a brilliant documentary on the rescue mission in Le Chambon-sur-Lignon. There are several other clips from this documentary that present the general history of Vichy France and interviews with people who were part of the rescue mission. One other clip, taken from Carol Rittner's, *The Courage to Care*, also highlights the moral strength of rescuers during the Holocaust.

Up to this point, the template has been used to supplement the texts, to confirm their veracity. It soon occurred to me that I could use the template to resist the text, to question it, and to force the students to think critically at the moral level. To do so, I inserted two extraordinary clips. The first, drawn from a very recent French film, *La Colline aux Mille Enfants,* is a dialogue between the pastor and a young Jewish woman who, although thankful for all that has been done for her in the village, says that she is now going to join the violent resistance in order to "exterminate the Nazis." The second is drawn from the PBS video, *Facing Evil*. Oddly enough, this is a clip of Phillip Hallie, the author of *Lest Innocent Blood Be Shed*, the book that first

told the story of the village, eight years after its publication. Now he explains, "Something in my heart resents the village. They didn't stop Hitler. They did nothing to stop Hitler. It took decent murderers like me to do so."

During the fourth and final class period, we discuss a series of excerpts from Saint-Exupéry's *Terre des Hommes*, all of which deal with the idea of community. During the two years that I have used the template, this has been the best class of the semester, with real debate about the value and limitations of nonviolence and the nature of community. There can be no doubt that the computer-enhanced techniques are responsible for the passion of student involvement.

MEASURED RESULTS

- On the last two final exams, I gave students a choice of questions. Every student in the class chose to respond to the question on the Holocaust. They not only referred to clips on the template, but their answers showed that the clips enabled them to understand better the ethical nature of the literature they read.

- The evaluations of the class were excellent each time, and about 75% indicated that the most engaging and meaningful part of the course was the part on the Holocaust. It is certainly not an accident that in this portion of the course the template was central to their learning experience.

- About half the students told me either in person or on their evaluations that they went to the lab on their own and viewed the template a second time.

LESSONS LEARNED

Only one lesson has been learned. My template is a magnificent teaching tool that helps to illuminate texts and their historical context. The template is there whenever I want it; no more trips to the audio/visual center each time I want to show a clip. Everything that I have included is permanently on the template unless I choose to delete it. The template is, therefore, a work in progress that I can always adjust and enrich as new, relevant materials become available.

I have made one other less ambitious template for

the same course. During the medieval section of the class, we read a poem entitled "Monoceros" (The Unicorn). It is the only text that the students read in Old French. The template has a complete glossary for every word in the poem. If students don't know the meaning of a word, all they have to do is highlight it, and the word appears on the screen in modern French. There are also four places in the poem where the students can highlight a word and listen to and watch four individual 45-second clips on the unicorn tapestries, each one explicating a different aspect of the mythology and theology of the hunt, which is the subject of the poem in question.

I intend to create several other templates for this course and my 16th-century French literature course. All of the ones I currently have in mind will be on poems that we study and their relationship to the music and the paintings of the period during which they were composed.

REFERENCES

Hallie, P. (1979). *Lest innocent blood be shed: The story of the village of Le Chambon and how goodness happened there.* New York, NY: Harper & Row.

Moyers, W. (1987). Facing evil [video]. New York, NY: PBS.

CONTACT INFORMATION

Patrick Henry
Professor of French
Whitman College
345 Boyer Avenue
Walla Walla, WA 99362-2083
Email: henrypg@whitman.edu
Phone: (509) 527-5254 (5248)
Fax: (509) 527-5039

Vignette 82 A Revolutionary Literature

Wilda Anderson, Johns Hopkins University

EDUCATIONAL ISSUES

The primary goal of this course was to put the much-touted idea of electronic reserve lists to the test. It was structured around the fact that the work on the French Revolution exists in many layers, each succeeding layer of writing referring back to those in the preceding layers, in what can be called cascades of direct and indirect references. I had always wanted to show the students how succeeding generations use the work of their predecessors, one of the most important issues in literary analysis or intellectual history, of which the Revolution is a striking example, but it was impractical. Most of the materials I wanted to use are out of print or exist only in manuscript form in France. Some were engravings and paintings or songs. I knew what I wanted

to teach, but using normal printed materials or even a library plus purchased texts, the cost would have been prohibitive and the relating of the materials to each other logistically unwieldy within a semester or within class time. Then it struck me that hypertext provides an ideal structure for organizing and making available literary research materials because it is similar to an archive.

The digital knowledge center staff of the Milton S. Eisenhower Library and the university's lawyer agreed to work with me to solve the problems of copyright access, either by accessing public domain digital editions already available on the web or by establishing tight security around the web site. We digitized at least 1,000 pages and about 50 graphic images into HTML format so that they could be linked to the texts already online and to a few critical articles related to the primary texts. These were all linked to the relevant pictures and to my lecture notes or other secondary materials that I wanted to use, including an online glossary of revolutionary terms and names. I also wanted to see if students study and think in ways they might not with paper copies. Roger Chartier of the Ecole des Hautes Etudes en Sciences Sociales in Paris, who invented the field of the history of the book, was interested in seeing if the students' reading experience would be substantially different when they read texts in electronic formats. Using a small laptop with ethernet connection and a projector, the class was held entirely electronically. After a brief period of resistance, the students found that the advantages of the hyperlinked format outweighed the disadvantages, and what was to have been a one-semester course was, by their request, extended to a full year. I quote one student, "This was not a course. The web site created a research environment, and we have just begun to explore its potential."

This was more than I had hoped. The students read much more acutely now that they understood, via the structured but easily modified body of materials, how all archives work in the humanistic disciplines: They are not shelves of paper, but the virtual structure created when scholars read and then link texts in their memories. Archives are active, not passive, intellectual spaces. To quote the same student, "Now I see that libraries are really exciting places." The students learned how to do research, evaluate their own insights, and use them to choose what subsequent texts were relevant to extend their insights. They learned what can only be learned through experience, not through explanation: how to develop good intellectual judgment. My response to Roger Chartier's challenge is, therefore, somewhat unexpected: The students learned to read more quickly and better, and their sense of intellectual adventure was awakened much more quickly.

One of the most interesting results of this course, to my mind, is how eager the students were to move from passively receiving knowledge to actively delving. It has long been difficult, even grueling, in the humanities to introduce students to the research experience, yet it is the sine qua non of their cultural education.

My other goal was to run a writing-intensive course that would not sacrifice intellectual content.

We have noticed, as has everyone else in the humanities, that most of the students coming in simply cannot write a competent essay. Bluntly put, students who cannot write cannot think. Yet teaching students to write is a time-consuming task that requires a good deal more direct interaction than is usually possible in a content-oriented seminar, no matter how small. In our department, we have tried to remedy this situation in the language courses and in the introductory literacy survey. This has been insufficient, so that students coming into the literature classes are held back by their inability to make sustained, articulate, analytic arguments, yet the class time must be spent on the literary and cultural materials that are the subject of the course.

I wanted to see if it would be practical to use computers to teach writing asynchronously, leaving class time for intellectual discussion. As incoming students are increasingly at ease with computers, I decided to take advantage of the new software available to increase the students' direct faculty contact. The Milton S. Eisenhower Library's digital knowledge center immediately chose a courseware program, WebCT, and adapted it to my needs. We set up a secure web site for the course that had as one component a hypertext-linked database of the students' papers, my comments on them, their rewrites, my further comments, and so on. The students were able to see but not to modify each other's papers and comments. There was a small bulletin board where the students posted questions to me and to the others in the class, so that the discussion and correction/editing experience was carried on completely after hours. We developed together a set of online writing tools (explication de texte outlines, a small dictionary of poetic terms, examples of successful and less successful essays, all linked to the relevant parts of the outlines, and to some explanatory diagrams). This was quite simple to set up and more successful than I had expected. Students improved their writing in one semester as much as they normally do in about two semesters. I also found that it took me approximately half as long to correct their papers online, and that I was able to give them more complex and useful feedback: For example, besides providing spelling or stylistic corrections and intellectual commentary, I could link problematic passages in their papers to the passages in the primary texts that they needed to either reconsider or review, link them to the writing tools they needed to consult, or to each other's papers when one of them had had notable success resolving a particular problem. In other words, it was much easier to focus on process.

The second semester, we extended the reach of the course two steps further. First, the students were involved in developing the archive themselves. Second, they requested an initiation into the mechanics, esthetics, and rhetoric of web site construction, and they each carried out complementary exercises on a single subject: They were responsible for developing a small archive of their own and investigating the rhetorical peculiarities of presenting serious intellectual analysis in an accompanying web site. To this end, we developed a short but intensive introduction to web structure, to OCR, and to Adobe Photoshop. We also drew up a small cinema component to the course both to extend the archive and to introduce the disciplinary conventions of the esthetic judgment of visual materials. We constructed, as a group with the digital knowledge center, a small overview, empirically derived, of rhetorical constraints as they apply to the successful online presentation of various types of information and the tools for a web-writing component to complement the print-writing component we developed last semester.

LESSONS LEARNED

To my surprise, after two weeks, the students stopped printing out the texts, as the paper format could not reproduce the hypertext archive structure. They ended up preferring the online texts.

This was not a canned course that could be exported. The digital environment provided a particularly supple space for on-site activity. I could rapidly adapt and shift the contents and structure to accommodate the changing interests of the students. I could quickly add or subtract components as I foresaw the students' needing new tools or new directions to explore or as I discovered new things or developed new ideas myself.

An essential part of this course, obviously, has been that it has been increasingly a team effort. The direct knowledge center staff set up the course structure and modified it according to the very idiosyncratic needs of a non-English language and multi-goal humanities course. Second, the staff used their astute perceptions of the epistemological goals of my course and of the complementary possibilities offered by the digital environment to drive the course well beyond what I initially had imagined. In a very real sense, they were co-teachers and co-researchers. I would not say that we were producing an interdisciplinary experience for the students but that we were involved, at however small a scale, in redefining the discipline in which I work—a cultural discipline—to adapt its form of analysis to the changes occurring at the moment in our larger cultural environment. I personally find this to be a very laudable structure, as it not only develops successful courses but also demonstrates on a daily basis the ongoing and increasing interdependence of humanists on their particular laboratory environment the modern library.

A quick take on costs: My course was supported by a Kenan grant of about $2,300. I had not guessed what the real costs would be. The sum turned out to be sufficient. I bought some specialized software (Adobe Photoshop and PageMill, and an OCR program), but the scanning was the greatest cost, both in time and money: It had to be done by someone who could train the OCR software to recognize 17th- and 18th-century French fonts and other types of nonmodern archival materials. I would estimate that at least 400 hours should be allocated to scan materials for a good-sized course.

The course didn't take long to set up, but the time to digitize the materials was enormous. As much as possible should be done ahead of time, which I would estimate should have been at least two months for my course. During the semester, it is reasonable to expect to spend about five hours a week to digitize and upload new things as they come up.

CONTACT INFORMATION

Wilda Anderson, Professor of French
The Johns Hopkins University
Charles & 34th Streets
Baltimore, MD 21218
Email: Me@diderot.fre.jhu.edu
Phone: (410) 516-7227
Fax: (410) 516-5358

Vignette 83 A Cross-Cultural, Web-Based Approach to Developing Students' Understanding of a Foreign Culture

Gilberte Furstenberg and Shoggy Waryn,
Massachusetts Institute of Technology

INTRODUCTION

One common assumption in the field of foreign language instruction is that when we teach language, we also teach culture. All of us teachers of a foreign language automatically associate those two words and see ourselves as teaching language and culture. Yet, more often than not, we give priority to the teaching of the language itself—its syntax, its forms, and its communicative uses. Culture is seldom integrated into the teaching of the language and even more rarely comes to the forefront.

In our global world, however, the understanding of another culture is becoming crucial. We need to know and understand the different cultural value systems that shape our respective thoughts and actions if we are going to communicate effectively across cultures. Language teachers have a key role to play in that domain and therefore need to find ways to better integrate the teaching of culture in our language classes.

This has never been an easy task for language teachers: Culture is the traditional domain of anthropologists, and we have been trained in the area of language and literature, not culture. In addition, teaching culture—particularly in the sense of behaviors, attitudes, and values—is extremely difficult, since these are very elusive, often abstract, implicit, and essentially invisible notions.

The challenge was to find a tool and an approach. The CULTURA project, designed and based at MIT and funded by the National Endowment for the Humanities, has allowed us to experiment with a new way of bringing culture to the forefront of a language learning class.

HOW THIS PROJECT CAME TO BE

Having spent several years developing multimedia applications for the teaching of French, we became increasingly aware of one powerful feature of interactive technologies: their capacity to bring forward and connect different types of materials. The sheer process of juxtaposition allows variations that would otherwise stay buried and undiscovered to emerge and be revealed.

For instance, the comparison of interview segments where several people use the same word—*travailler,* let's say—allows us to discover, then to analyze how that word can take on different meanings for different people, which in turns leads us to try and understand the reasons behind these variations. Close analysis of several segments in a film, where people use the same speech act (greetings or asking for a favor) allows variations to become visible and enables us to analyze the different factors that come into play, such as the relationship between the people (friend/colleague/boss, etc.), the general context, the very nature of the request, etc. This approach seemed to us full of promise for developing our students' understanding of another culture and led us to the notion of cultural comparisons.

What CULTURA offers is a cross-cultural approach which has students from two different cultures—in our case American and French students—observe, analyze, and compare similar materials from their respective cultures. This approach, we felt, would allow them to start seeing by themselves the differences as well as similarities. It would provide them with the unprecedented ability to identify underlying connotations, various attitudes toward events or situations, or concepts. It would constitute the first step toward deciphering and understanding why these differences exist and what they may reveal and signify.

The tool that best serves our purposes is the World Wide Web, as it allows us to bring together and juxtapose a large variety of materials from both French and American cultures. These materials can then, thanks to the Internet, be analyzed in a cross-cultural perspective by American and French students together. This unique, comparative, cross-cultural approach for gradually constructing knowledge of other values, attitudes, and beliefs, in an ever-enlarging construction of the foreign culture, is what CULTURA is all about.

CONTENT AND MECHANICS OF THE COURSE

The project involves 30 MIT students in third-semester intermediate French classes to work simultaneously (both inside and outside the classroom) with 30 French students taking English classes at the Institut National des Télécommunications (INT). Students follow a process that unfolds along a series of steps designed to introduce them to more complex artifacts and to larger domains of inquiry.

In the first stage, our MIT students and the INT students answer (outside of class) a series of identical questionnaires, designed by us to activate and ascertain basic cultural differences toward such topics as family relations, power structures, work, etc. Each student is asked to respond in a spontaneous manner and in his or her own native language. The use of native language in all web communication is an essential component of CULTURA, as all cultural nuances can only be fully expressed in one's native language. One such questionnaire is based upon word associations (What other words do you associate with the following ones? ex: freedom; politeness; etc.); another one is based upon definitions (Please finish the following sentences: ex: A good neighbor is someone . . .); and the last one upon specific situations (How do you react to the following hypothetical situation? ex: You see a mother in a supermarket slap her child). Both American and French students submit their answers on the web. These answers are then collected and processed to create easy-to-read web tables, with the French and American responses appearing side by side.

A few days later, both sets of students are asked to read the answers, look up unknown vocabulary items, and start to analyze the various responses, first on their own outside of class, then in class. With the help of the teacher, they are asked to make observations and then to form initial hypotheses about the reasons for the differences they have just noticed. Outside of class, students then post their remarks on the web via a discussion forum in which they share their observations with their transatlantic partners and query them for clarification, more cultural information, and more in-depth understanding of the differences they have observed.

We felt it necessary also to give students access to comparative statistics and opinion polls from each country, so as to place the knowledge they gain from each other's observations and remarks in a much broader socio-cultural context. A national opinion poll about what qualities most French parents want to instill in their children, for instance, will lead American students to make connections between the subjective remarks of their French peers and the more objective polls. It allows them to see whether the remarks made by the French students reflect the broader context or not, which then in turns leads them to ask more probing questions from each other. And vice versa.

In the second stage of the project, both the MIT students and the INT students start working together on another type of material. Outside of class, they screen the French and American version of the same film to which they will apply the same cross-cultural methodology (we are currently working with the film *Trois Hommes et un Couffin* and its American remake, *Three Men and a Baby*). Students are asked to compare corresponding scenes and specific themes in both films. Through this close analysis and the accompanying web discussions, they discover new topics and explore, among others, the different cultural modes in which a same story can be told, while using similar elements such as humor, suspense, discourse, or gestures in diverse ways. In addition, the CULTURA site gives students access to an increasing array and variety of other related comparative information, such as French and American reviews of the films, press articles, historical documents, cross-cultural texts, and literary texts. These are accessible on their own and will soon be linked through a search engine, allowing students to make newer and finer connections and view their findings with a different and broader lens.

In the final stage, students and their instructors will be free to choose their materials and tailor their next activities based upon their interests. The highly flexible structure of the site will allow the project to constantly evolve and incorporate new materials and ideas.

In terms of the mechanics of the course, students work both in and outside of class. Outside of class, they answer the questionnaires, watch and analyze the films, read articles, and communicate with their French partners. They are always asked to bring their findings to the class. The classroom thus becomes the place where discoveries, insights, ideas, are brought together, confronted, and discussed. It is the place where students start developing out of that mosaic of information—

with the help of the teacher, their own classmates, and their French partners—their own web of interpretations and an overall, global understanding of the other culture: how it works, what it is based on, and why it functions the way it does.

CURRENT ASSESSMENT

We are currently in the third semester of experimenting with CULTURA, and the outcomes are extremely promising. The process is working exactly as we had anticipated and has even surpassed our own expectations. We were ourselves surprised at how revealing the answers to the questionnaires were and how strikingly indicative they were of underlying cultural attitudes. For instance, to the question: What is, to you, a well-behaved child (un enfant bien-élevé in French), students in our classes noticed that French answers would tend to emphasize the notion of politeness over any other, whereas the word polite did not appear once on the American side. Students then discovered by looking at responses to other questionnaires—where the notion of politeness would appear—that the very concept of politeness differs in both cultures: In the French frame of reference, politeness is essentially of a social nature (acknowledging someone's presence, saying thank you, etc.), whereas to American students, someone being polite is respecting other people's feelings.

The importance placed on feelings in American culture clearly came out in many different instances and contexts. Whereas the French tend to view a good boss, a good doctor, even a good parent as someone competent above all (a good parent to the French students is someone who overwhelmingly éduque bien ses enfants, namely instills values), a good parent on the American side is above all someone who loves his/her children unconditionally.

Students in our classes also noticed other types of differences, namely that the French would tend to be more confrontational in their reactions. For instance, whereas a number of French students would tell a guest (in an often sarcastic way) that they didn't appreciate him or her going to the refrigerator without asking for permission, the American students who thought it rude as well tended to think it and not express it (perhaps for fear of offending the other).

One of the most positive aspects of this initial experience for our students, besides their newly acquired ability to actually see the emergence of cultural patterns, is the very immediacy of the experience. Students are not told how the French tend to think and see things, but they are able to discover for and by themselves some traits of French cultural attitudes. They are right in the thick of it. Culture is unmediated and is apprehended in a dynamic way through direct contact with the other culture. This type of discovery invariably leads students to become progressively more aware and insightful of their own diverse cultural assumptions and the use of their own language.

What we increasingly found is that as we discuss cultural traits, we inevitably go back to the language itself—that the study of the culture always brings us back to the study of the language. In analyzing the responses to the questionnaires, the language of the films, the written texts and exchanges on the forums, we invariably pay close attention to the different ways in which ideas are expressed in one language versus the other—the use of slang, the amount (or lack) of negative expressions, the use of objective versus subjective statements, abstract notions versus concrete examples.

Even though the students are writing on the web in their native language, the discussions in the MIT classrooms are always entirely in French, and our students have the added benefit of using as a base for discussions a very rich, dynamic language—that used by the French students of today. By working with an authentic linguistic database, students are constantly learning new vocabulary and current expressions. They are also able to discover that the same words don't necessarily have the same meanings or cover the same reality, that words may exist in one language but have no equivalent in the other, etc. A new dimension to the study of vocabulary opens up.

Grammar also enters into the picture, and we find that we increasingly base our study of grammar on the materials on the web. For instance, looking at the responses to Un bon voisin est quelqu'un qui (A good neighbor is one who)..., leads us to naturally study the relative pronoun, and our examples are increasingly taken from the French students' responses and observations on the forums. Likewise, when French students express how they would react if a guest whom they don't know well, helps himself/herself in the refrigerator (saying such things as je le lui fais remarquer, je lui demande, je lui en veux...etc.), we then work on the object pronouns. Culture and language have become truly one through the study of culture itself.

LESSONS LEARNED

We have learned that, in order for such a project to be successful, some key elements need to be present:

- A very close collaboration with the foreign partners is absolutely essential. Everything needs to be clarified and shared: goals; pedagogical approaches; issues such as different schedules, different (often culturally based) work expectations, different priorities (the INT students initially resisting, for instance, the notion of writing on the web in French, because they wanted to practice their English). Such collaboration, as well as a shared commitment on the part of all instructors, is essential.

We also became more convinced than ever of the crucial role of the teacher. A fairly commonly held view is that when technology is concerned, the teacher's role is peripheral. It has become increasingly clear to us, however, that his or her role is absolutely central. Students initially do need help and guidance in comparing and analyzing the materials; otherwise, they tend either to skim the surface, get lost in details, or stop halfway. Students need to be guided in the different ways of doing cross-cultural analysis: to separate the common traits from the unique ones, to see what words/concepts often recur on one side but rarely on the other, to look for emerging patterns, to identify what words reflect what concepts, to unearth specific cultural references, to figure out what the equivalent of the English word such as caring might be in French, etc.

Our responsibility as teachers is to orchestrate everything, to coach the students, guide them, provide them with specific tasks, encourage them to pursue discussions on the forums as far as possible and expand as much as they can their knowledge through the reading and analysis of various other materials and texts. We need to encourage them to constantly make connections between newly discussed topics and earlier ones, so that they keep questioning and refining their understanding of the other culture. We need to help our students along that continuous process.

We also learned that we need to provide regular and concrete benchmarks along the way to help students get a better grasp of where they stand in their journey to a better understanding of the foreign culture. This is an area we are currently working on, trying to find suitable ways of helping our students measure their progress along that road.

CONCLUSION

We are very optimistic about the new approach CULTURA epitomizes, as we find it ideally suited for learning about another culture in a foreign language class. It has allowed us to create a new pedagogy which is no longer based just upon readings (by the student) or talks (by the teacher) about the differences between American or French cultures. Thanks to this approach and the web, culture is no longer reduced to a series of facts about the other country, but is built upon a dynamic, interactive process that involves interactions with multiple materials—raw or mediated—and multiple partners—learners, teachers, other students, other teachers and experts. Culture is no longer an abstract notion but becomes both a personal and a shared experience—shared not just with other students in the class, but with other people on the other side of the World Wide Web line.

We are continuing our work to make CULTURA available to other schools, including high schools. Students at The Ohio State University, for instance, will be integrating it on a large scale in their intermediate French classes next year, and we expect the project to be more and more widely used as time goes on. We are also interested in making our methodology available for other languages.

CONTACT INFORMATION

Gilberte Furstenberg
Senior Lecturer in French
Rm. 14N-423
Massachusetts Institute of Technology
Cambridge, MA 02139-4307
Email: gfursten@mit.edu
WWW: http://web.mit.edu/fll/www/people
    /GilberteFurstenberg.html
Phone: (617) 253-3067
Fax: (617) 258-6189

Vignette 84 Using Technology to Increase Writing

Franziska Lys, Northwestern University

The upper-level German course described here was offered in the winter quarter 1997–98. There were 18 students enrolled, and the class met three times a week for 50 minutes.

EDUCATIONAL THEORY

One of Northwestern University's goals is to provide students with an excellent education in writing, analytical thinking, and creative expression. However, a study of course descriptions by Ken Seeskin, director of the Center for the Writing Arts, had shown that only 14% of the A-level and B-level courses surveyed and 34% of the C-level ones had an important writing component as part of the teaching, learning, and evaluation process. When the McCormick Fellows of the Searle Center for Teaching Excellence met during the fall quarter, 1997, their discussion focused on the various possibilities for increasing writing in the undergraduate curriculum. Writing as a tool for self-expression is a critical skill for any student to master, but it needs nurturing and constant practice in either the first language or in a foreign language. The class project described here represents an attempt to get students to develop their writing, analytical thinking, and creative expression in a foreign language through the use of technology.

Students majoring or minoring in German are required to take a third-year and a fourth-year grammar and composition class in German. The focus in these classes had traditionally been on reviewing grammar concepts, which were then practiced in various exercises. To shift the emphasis away from practicing grammar toward developing students' writing skills, the German department had recently redesigned both composition classes. Today, grammar is treated as only one component in the process of developing writing, and the syllabus contains many activities geared toward the process of writing. The emphasis in the third-year composition class today is on developing various genres. Students write about six distinct compositions during the quarter, each dealing with a different topic

and writing style. In order to distinguish the fourth-year writing experience from a composition class on the earlier level, I was searching for a writing project that would emphasize the process of writing and revising and give students an incentive to work on one piece over a longer period of time.

COURSE DESCRIPTION: USING TECHNOLOGY TO TEACH WRITING

My goal in designing this class was to foster writing, analytical thinking skills, and creative expression in students learning German by getting them to develop their writing over a longer period of time, including researching, writing and revising, and presenting information. In order to achieve this goal, I set certain guidelines:

Topics
The writing topics would not be assigned by the instructor but would be chosen by students to ensure that students really wanted to write about the topics. However, the topics had to require a fair amount of independent research over an extended period of time.

Format
The writing project format had to inspire students to continue writing and encourage them to revise their first, second, and possibly third drafts. Students would be taught to see their writing as an organic whole with a definite structure. Furthermore, the format had to allow students to share their writing with other members of the class; evaluating, criticizing, and presenting ideas to an audience at any stage of writing was part of the strategy to learn from each other.

The name of the project was *die das Leben schrieb* (stories written by life or life stories). The students had to find a German-speaking person on campus or in the community with an interesting life story to tell. They then had to interview their subjects over the next ten weeks, at least once a week, and create an illustrated book of their life stories, all in German. This illustrated book had to be written, designed, and published as a web project. For the web pages, students had to work with color and fonts and link each part of the project so that a reader could easily navigate the pages. Furthermore, students had to combine the text with navigational elements such as links to relevant Internet sites which would illustrate their subject history and image files, like scanned photographs and pictures made with a digital camera.

The course demanded that the students master quite a lot of technology. Since this was a course to teach German grammar and writing, only a minimal amount of class time could be devoted to teaching the necessary technological tools. The basic technology for writing and illustrating a web page was taught in five half-hour sessions distributed over the ten weeks of the course. The content of these sessions is shown in Figure 84.1.

MEASURED RESULTS

The incorporation of technology has made an incredible difference in this class. This difference can be measured not only in the amount and quality of writing produced, but in the enthusiasm students showed toward their assignment. As one student put it, "The Internet project was the highlight of the class." It was particularly gratifying to see that students were constantly revising, rereading, adjusting; what at first seemed appropriate for a first chapter was rewritten several times based on how the project unfolded. Students wanted to revise their work because 1) the assignments were short enough to do regular revisions, 2) there was constant positive feedback from peers and from the teacher, and 3) the projects were on the web, accessible to others. One student wrote, "I think the idea of interviewing someone and writing one part per week is great. Weekly assignments are much less overwhelming than one big composition." The topics the students chose were all very enga ging and showed a genuine concern for the life experiences of other human beings. There was another dimension to this project that I had not foreseen.

Because the collecting of information and writing involved collaboration with another person, these collaborators or volunteers became mentors to the students. They were genuinely interested in their progress, and students shared their projects over the Internet sometimes on a weekly basis. The collaborators often gave advice on the structure of the project, corrected factual information, and shared pictures from their personal photo albums so that they could be scanned in and become part of the report.

LESSONS LEARNED

Although few students had prior knowledge about writing web pages, most of them acquired the necessary skills to handle the basic technology quite easily. The biggest problem was the posting of pages on a server and the linking of documents and images. Extra office hours were offered to those with special problems or needs. Still, I believe there was a general feeling that what the students learned was useful beyond learning how to write in German, and, therefore, students were willing to struggle through some of the technology parts. One of the students wrote in the final evaluation, "I loved the Internet project. It's a great way to force us to write in German, and it teaches us a valuable skill for the future."

CONTACT INFORMATION

Franziska Lys
College Lecturer
Northwestern University
Kresge Hall 113, Department of German
Evanston, IL 60208-2203
Email: flys@nwu.edu
WWW:http://www.german.nwu.edu/lys
    /franziska.html,
http://www.german.nwu.edu/c91projects/index.html
Phone: (847) 491-8298
Fax: (847) 491-3877

FIGURE 84.1

WRITING TASK/TECHNOLOGY SKILL

WRITING	TECHNOLOGY
Week 1 Brainstorm in class about possible topics.	**Week 1**
Week 2 Find interview partner and conduct initial interview. Report to class.	**Week 2**
Week 3 Write first chapter, hand in, revise, post.	**Week 3** Introduction to HTML and Claris Home Page. Design title page document and text document. Link the two documents. Post documents on server.
Week 4 Write second chapter, hand in, revise, post. Share project with one other student and revise text and design based on discussion.	**Week 4** Introduction to page design: background colors, text colors, fonts, and tables.
Week 5 Write third chapter, hand in, revise, post. Write a short biography about yourself, link with picture and post.	**Week 5** Introduction to the digital camera: take picture of other students for biography and post-process in Photoshop. Link image to text.
Week 6 Write fourth chapter, hand in, revise, post. Share project with one other student and revise text and design based on discussion.	**Week 6** Introduction to scanning: scan picture, post process in Photoshop, and link to text.
Week 7 Write fifth chapter, hand in, revise, post.	**Week 7** Introduction to the web. Search for, find, and evaluate relevant background web pages. Create links to other websites.
Week 8 Write sixth chapter, hand in, revise, post. Share project with one other student and revise text and design based on discussion.	**Week 8**
Week 9 Write seventh chapter, hand in, revise, post. Discuss project with instructor. Instructor makes final corrections and suggestions.	**Week 9**
Week 10 Make final revisions and post project by middle of the week. Find a partner in the class. Read his/her project and prepare a short critique. Present your project to the whole class.	**Week 10**

Vignette 85 — Introducing Multimedia Materials in Intermediate Spanish, or How I Learned to Love Technology

Nancy Saporta Sternbach, Smith College

I am not what you would call a techie. On the contrary, I came late to the computing arena and only because I realized that I was making my life harder by not entering. I do, however, have extensive experience and demonstrated results in language teaching. When I was approached by the director of our cutting-edge multimedia laboratory about getting some materials into the Spanish curriculum, I couldn't resist.

Here was the problem: In my intermediate conversation and composition class, I could concentrate on the traditional skills of reading, writing, and speaking. I could even make more time for listening comprehension, but there was not much I could do to help students make the transition from the language classroom to real-life situations; i.e., understanding native speakers at normal speed.

I was not a newcomer to using multimedia materials. I introduced video, video clips, Spanish radio, Spanish television, songs, and many other audio materials to my classes throughout the 1980s. What was missing was a way for students to access native speech on their own and work with specific exercises whose sole purpose was to assist them in understanding it without taking away their own joy of discovery.

At about the time that my frustration increased, I discovered a laser disk from Spanish television, made for and by native speakers in real-life situations. With the assistance of the technical staff, we were able to isolate segments and post a series of exercises to accompany them that, when completed, would require the student to have engaged fully and interactively in the language.

EDUCATIONAL THEORY

I was interested in having the students learn to take risks in the language, to use the material that they knew in order to create new language. In some instances, the material showed body language instead of dialogue. Students were invited to make educated guesses about these gestures to teach them that language is more language is more than a string of words but rather cultural contexts, body language, tone, and expression. Even episodes that were extremely difficult for them to understand were useful in that students had to draw on their own vocabulary to describe their sense of the tone.

Course Description

Each video lesson that I prepared had two components: 1) listening comprehension with dictionary and transcription, and 2) exercises based on it. Each assignment had its own pedagogical goal, and these varied with the material. They ranged from guided compositions, cultural critiques or comparisons, and grammatical uses, such as converting adjectives to verbs.

RESULTS

Instead of waiting for the professor to correct their work, the students were able to get immediate feedback on their comprehension. The computer-assisted exercises congratulated them when they got the right answer and asked them to try again when they didn't. The most dramatic example of this technique was accomplished through a guided dictation prepared by the lab technician, Joann Carlson. An extremely difficult video segment was made intelligible by the use of this guided dictation. After a number of tries, students were able to access the correct answer. Student response to the material was extremely positive. Even those students who, at the beginning of the semester, showed some computer phobia were totally convinced of the worth of these exercises by the end of the term. To be able to understand real material and respond to it in a variety of ways became an exciting and challenging part of the semester for them. In-class evaluations revealed that they considered this the best part of the course.

LESSONS LEARNED

Class Time

As much as I share wonderment about what we can accomplish with computers, I do not believe in the fantasy that they can replace real teachers. For this, the lab was essential, since these exercises were done outside of class. I do, however, spend one day a week during the semester teaching in our electronic classroom. There I am able to respond to individual questions about the video and clear up any misunderstandings that might have occurred in that week's work. This is the time that I set aside to discuss specific episodes.

Evaluating Use

I am currently using these exercises in my intermediate conversation class and have been doing so since 1993. To say that the integration of this material radically altered my course is an understatement. I will go so far as to say that it has altered the curriculum in my department. After having redesigned our first-year course to include a video and having redone this one, we then evaluated our second-year course. What has become obvious is that when one of the courses in a curriculum changes so completely, it requires reflection about all the others: How will they fit into the sequence of language learning?

CONTACT INFORMATION

Nancy Saporta Sternbach
Department of Spanish and Portuguese
Smith College
Northampton, MA 01063
Email: Nsternba@sophia.smith.edu
Phone: (413) 585-3459
Fax: (413) 585-3415

Vignette 86 — Implementing Chat Software in the Foreign-Language Curriculum: The Case of RTA

Robert J. Blake, David W. Fahy, and Richard F. Walters,
University of California, Davis

Learning to speak a second language is an intensive and time-consuming process, taking normally about five years to reach functional fluency. Difficult writing systems, like Japanese, exacerbate the process. Going to the region(s) where the target language is spoken and immersing oneself in the language and culture remains the preferred—but also most expensive—method of acquiring competence in another language. For those unable to do this, how can we increase meaningful contact with, and interactions in the target language, the main mechanisms for nurturing second-language acquisition?

Research has demonstrated the importance to language learning of oral interactions with native speakers that require the negotiation of meaning (Hatch, 1978; Long, 1980; Holliday, 1993). The same benefits appear to accrue in the interactions among nonnative language learners as well (Pica, 1994; Gass & Varonis, 1994). Could technological advances allow the instructor to extend these benefits beyond the spatial and temporal limits of the classroom?

This report describes the implementation of a network-based communication, or chat program, into intermediate Spanish and Japanese language courses at UC, Davis, using a package we have developed called Remote Technical Assistance (RTA). RTA permits synchronous transfers of text, sound, and graphics and provides a collaborative writing tool, TEXTPAD. (For more information on RTA, see the RTA home page: http://escher.cs.ucdavis.edu.)

EDUCATION THEORY

One frustrating aspect of acquiring a second language is the relatively long period when students communicate in a degenerate code described as interlanguage, an in-between linguistic state where they repeatedly make mistakes and borrow structures from their native language. How do students liberate themselves from the interlanguage quagmire and truly attain fluency? Research suggests that they must first realize their mistakes (Schmidt, 1990). When working in pairs to solve a real communication task, students typically "push-down" from the discourse of the task to negotiate problems in meaning (i.e., lexical, grammatical, and phonological confusions). These negotiation events result in the correction of specific mistakes and promote the evolution of their interlanguage toward the target (Pellettieri, in press).

In this project, we hypothesize that these types of negotiation events constitute the principal stimulus for language acquisition and the gradual remediation of interlanguage. If this metalinguistic awareness comes about by working in pairs or groups, we postulated that network-based communication would facilitate this process just like the to face-to-face negotiations in the classroom. Our pilot project, in spring 1998, confirmed our expectations, but the proof can be seen only in a close examination of the transcripts and not in the results of the more standardized proficiency tests and attitudinal surveys.

COURSE DESCRIPTION

In spring quarter 1998, an intermediate Spanish and a Japanese class of 25 each worked in pairs once a week for six weeks using the RTA chat program to communicate synchronically with their partners. The pairs were to accomplish tasks similar to those listed below, though the specifics differed slightly by language. The results from the language measures were then compared with a control class that did passive lab with no interaction.

Tasks

Introductions. Develop a personality profile of your partner; summarize the profile in writing using the collaborative writing tool, TEXTPAD.

Drawings. Identify the drawing that doesn't fit in a group of four, where each partner can see only two of four drawings; then develop a rationale for these choices and summarize in writing using TEXTPAD.

Calendars. Share the activities from two different personal calendars and identify the events the two people did in common. Develop a story in the past tense about those common activities using TEXTPAD.

Apartments. Find an apartment in Madrid by sharing different sets of web ads and radically different personal preferences for the ideal living conditions; summarize the results using TEXTPAD.

Of these four tasks, only the first implied an open-ended solution; tasks two to four were closed in that they guided students toward a single solution, although not all answers would be the same. We also predicted that the closed tasks would stimulate more negotiation events because the tasks' meanings had to be fully understood to be solved.

The Chat Tool, RTA

The Remote Technical Assistance (RTA) package was conceived approximately three years ago, with a goal of enhancing learning in all modes of instruction. In 1996, we received support from the University of California Office of the President to experiment with RTA between the UC, Davis and UC, Berkeley campuses. These experiments were less than satisfactory: Network communication failures and other technical bugs caused many problems as did unpredictable support from Berkeley technical staff. The tasks were incompletely defined by the instructors, and they were not fully understood by the students. Because of the client-server design, which monitored all traffic, it was possible to detect and to correct most of the technical problems that interfered with student communication, so that by fall 1997, the package was reasonably robust. In 1997, we received support from the Education Department's Fund for Improvement of Post-Secondary Education (FIPSE).

RTA was first designed as a platform-independent, multimedia tool to enhance human interactions. Interaction was envisaged as including either synchronous, live chats between pairs or groups, or asynchronous messaging. Both would support complex messages. The process was monitored by a server-manager that routed all communication and stored whatever had to be saved for subsequent use or analysis. Sound and images could be transmitted and saved as needed (i.e., because voice messages were not telephonic, they could be replayed).

Early in the research, the need for foreign language character sets was addressed. RTA now supports Spanish, Russian, and Japanese character sets on multiple computer platforms, mainly PC and Macintosh, and could easily be adapted to accommodate other character sets. Language input for each was based on keyboard adaptations widely used in each language, minimizing the amount of learning specific to RTA interaction.

MEASURED RESULTS

FIPSE requires extensive evaluation, both formative (evaluating the process) and summative (evaluating the results). We were fortunate to have a consultant who is expert in the design of evaluation measures, and, with his help, we developed pre- and postquestionnaires, attitude surveys, and other written instruments that test language proficiency.

By the start of the spring quarter, we were ready to test the new course content using RTA. Two sections of each course (intermediate Japanese and intermediate Spanish) were selected, one for control, the other for RTA. An electronic pretest was administered; the students in the treatment group were paired and received four tasks requiring close interaction in the target language. At the end of the course, student performances on standardized tests were compared, and attitudinal posttests administered, again electronically.

The results of this study showed no perceived significant difference in test scores. The electronic tests proved to be a mistake, since few students in the control groups bothered to answer them, skewing those results to a probable bias in favor of the more electronically adept. Students were uniformly highly enthusiastic about the RTA-mediated experience. We believe that we would probably note a significant difference in cultural acclimation to the second language over a longer period of time (terms at UC, Davis are ten weeks long with a one-week final exam period), but we also recognize a real problem in measuring this type of

skill and subtle changes in the students' interlanguage. We did find that the stored conversations between students offered a wealth of material suitable for analysis of negotiated breakthroughs in understanding.

Contrary to fears that conversations among nonnative language learners will only reinforce the substandard forms of their interlanguage (Kern, 1995), the dyad work with RTA shows that students actively correct and teach themselves when performing closed tasks in a network-based communication environment. Approximately 75% of these corrections consisted of lexical confusions, as illustrated in the following transcript of a negotiation event in Spanish between person A and person B:

A: *Cuales son en común?*
 (What are in common?)

B: *como se dice comun en igles? no comprehende*
 (How do you say "common" in English?. . . no understand)

A: *común es cuando algo y una otra algo son el mismo; entiendes mi explicacion?*
 ("Common" is when something and another thing are the same; do you understand my explanation?)

B: *si, gracias. . . .*
 (Yes, thank you.)

The students involved in the Spanish project also corrected each other's grammar mistakes.

A: *la o el país?*
 (Is it "la" or "el" for the word "country")

B: *pais es masculino*
 ("Country" is a masculine word.)

A: *sí?*
 (Yeah?)

B: *ok*
 (Ok.)

A: *pero, usamos era o fue?*
 (But, do we use the imperfect or preterite of "to be"?)

A: *Fue un día llena*
 (Preterite fue. It was a full day.)

B: *creo que fue porque todo occure en el pasado*
 (I think preterite fue because it all occurs in the past.)

B: *y fue un dia y no un serie de dias*
   (And it was one day and not a series of days.)

A: *esta bien, ok?*
   (All right?)

B: *sí*
   (Yes.)

CONCLUSIONS

The results show that network-based communication in conjunction with a closed-task curriculum does allow language learners to raise their metalinguistic awareness and, consequently, promotes acquisition of the target language. In some cases, chat communication permits many students to interact more freely than in the often anxiety-charged oral classroom. The RTA log files allow instructors to observe students' interlanguage progress and to provide positive feedback.

We also found that standardized proficiency measures and questionnaires shed little light on the students' successes because of the highly process-oriented nature of the prolonged interlanguage phase. Further testing will have to be based on long observation. Future implementations of RTA in the foreign-language curriculum will include interactions between native speakers and language learners as well.

REFERENCES

Gass, S., & Varonis, E. (1994). Input, interaction, and second language production. *Studies in Second Language Acquisition, 16,* 283-302.

Hatch, E. (1978). Acquisition of syntax in a second language. In J. Richards (Ed.), *Understanding second and foreign language learning: Issues and approaches.* Rowley, MA: Newbury House.

Holliday, L. (1993). *NS Syntactic modifications in NS-NSS negotiation as input data for second language acquisition of syntax.* Unpublished doctoral dissertation, University of Pennsylvania, Philadelphia, PA.

Kern, R. (1995). Restructuring classroom interaction with networked computers: Effects on quantity and characteristics of language production. *Modern Language Journal, 79,* 457-76.

Long, M. (1980). *Input, interaction, and second language acquisition.* Unpublished doctoral dissertation, University of California, Los Angeles, California.

Pellettieri, J. (In press). Negotiation in cyberspace: The role of chatting in the development of grammatical competence. In M. Warschauer & R. Kern (Eds.), *Network-based language teaching: Concepts and practice.* New York, NY: Cambridge University Press.

Pica, T. (1994). Research on negotiation: What does it reveal about second-language learning conditions, processes, and outcomes? *Language Learning, 44,* 493-527.

Schmidt, R. (1990). The role of consciousness in second language acquisition. *Applied Linguistics, 11,* 219-58.

RTA was developed entirely on the UC, Davis campus and is the property of the Regents of the University of California. We wish to make it available without charge to not-for-profit educational institutions, and we have already negotiated several licenses with universities and colleges in the United States and Australia. We welcome opportunities to work collaboratively with other interested institutions. See http://escher.cs.ucdavis.edu/.

We gratefully acknowledge the University of California and the UC Office of the President (IAPIF grant), the Fund for Improvement of Post-Secondary Education (FIPSE), and the Apple Corporation for their support of this research.

CONTACT INFORMATION

Robert J. Blake, Professor of Spanish, Director of SLAI
Department of Spanish and Classics
University of California, Davis
One Shields Avenue
Davis, CA 95616-8635
Email: rjblake@ucdavis.edu
Phone: (530) 752-1052
Fax: (530) 752-2184

Contact Dr. Walters for RTA questions (email walters@cs.ucdavis.edu) or Dr. Blake for questions concerning the language experiment (rjblake@ucdavis.edu).

 **Enhancing the Study of Foreign Language with Technology: A CD-ROM and Companion Web Site for First-Year French**

Carl S. Blyth, University of Texas, Austin

EDUCATIONAL THEORIES

Generations of students who attempted to learn a foreign language by practicing grammar drills and parroting dialogues rarely, if ever, gained the ability to use the foreign language for real communication. Instead, these students mainly learned how to take grammar tests and repeat dialogues, not particularly useful skills outside the foreign language classroom. After finally understanding that drills don't lead to skills, foreign language teachers began to change their methods. Today, foreign language educators emphasize communication in the classroom, that is, the use of the foreign language to encode personal meaning. When language is taught for communicative purposes, students view grammar in a very different light—as a tool to be employed in the creation of meaningful messages. Computers have come to play an important role in the new communicative methods by giving students opportunities to practice their language skills in online communication with native speakers.

In keeping with the tenets of communicative language teaching, I wanted to oblige our beginning French students to interact virtually with the people, places, and artifacts of the French-speaking world. I also wanted to improve the textbook we were using for the course by integrating its presentation of grammar, vocabulary, and culture in an interactive format that would facilitate a student's self-paced study and review. As coordinator of lower division French (the first four semesters), I was determined to use computer technology to achieve four specific goals for the beginning French curriculum at the University of Texas at Austin:

1) implementation of a more communicative and learner-centered pedagogy

2) enhancement of students' foreign language skills

3) creation of flexible materials for different learning styles

4) enrichment of the intellectual and cultural content of the curriculum

COMPUTER-ENHANCED TECHNIQUES

In order to achieve these pedagogical and curricular goals, a group of French professors teamed with a computer programmer to develop a CD-ROM and a companion web site. The CD-ROM, called *Parallèles Interactive,* is essentially a multimedia French textbook. The program includes 170 interactive computer screens linked to over 150 French language web sites.

The Internet activities that our team developed help our students to interact with French speakers and to learn more about their world. As a result, our students no longer view French as a bunch of grammar rules but as a legitimate tool for cross-cultural communication. Technology has enabled us to teach French in a way that has never before been possible.

The second objective—to enhance students' foreign language skills—has also been uniquely facilitated by technology. Analog audio and video are no match for today's digitally based instructional materials. The benefits of simultaneous, random access to audio, image, and text files are obvious to foreign language students: no more tedious rewinding and fast forwarding. Today, our students simply click on a French phrase to hear it pronounced by a native speaker and then click again to record themselves. In fact, with the new technology, students are able to pinpoint and remediate their own comprehension and pronunciation problems and take greater control of their learning.

Our third goal was to produce instructional tools that would be equally effective regardless of learning style. We wanted to incorporate various modes of learning into the curriculum—sequential, relational, and creative. To that end, we developed Internet grammar exercises that are easily navigable instructional sequences. Less linear is the CD-ROM. We created this multimedia tool to help students explore grammatical and lexical relationships through hypermedia links. Finally, we built Internet activities that emphasize personal creativity. These open-ended communicative activities help students synthesize the knowledge learned in the sequential and relational modes.

Our final pedagogical goal—the enrichment of the intellectual and cultural content of the course—has been tremendously enhanced by the CD and its web links. The inclusion of authentic written, graphic, and aural documents from the Internet makes our students more aware of cultural similarities and differences between French-speaking countries and the United States.

Another crucial aspect of our methodology has been the establishment of a cycle of research and development as a means of continuous improvement. While we conceived of the CD-ROM in terms of pedagogical goals, we designed it to facilitate a research goal: to understand how students make use of multimedia as a tool to learn foreign language. To explore student use of our CD, we included as part of the program itself a tracking device which generates a mouse-click report, thus demonstrating how the student navigates the program. Thanks to the insights that we gleaned from the student data, we have made many improvements to the program.

MEASURED RESULTS

In order to discern the impact of the computer-enhanced curriculum, we undertook a semester-long study that included tests on various language skills: listening comprehension, speaking, reading, and grammatical knowledge. In all areas, students enrolled in the computer-enhanced sections scored better than students enrolled in the noncomputer sections. In fact, there was a statistically significant difference in grades favoring the students enrolled in the computer-enhanced courses. Surveys also indicated a significant difference in motivation and attitudes. Students enrolled in the computer-enhanced curriculum reported higher levels of satisfaction with the course and frequently wrote on their course evaluations that the computer lab was the most helpful and interesting part of the course.

Besides improved student language skills and better attitudes, the computer-enhanced curriculum has had other measurable results:

- French enrollments, which have been in precipitous decline nationally, have rebounded since instituting the new curriculum.

- Students demonstrate a greater breadth of cultural knowledge about the French-speaking world.

- Instructors have been generally enthusiastic of the computer-enhanced curriculum because it has reduced teaching loads while improving student performance.

- The graduate student instructors have become more competitive in an increasingly tight market thanks to improved computer skills and increased knowledge of Computer Assisted Language Learning (CALL).

- Course materials are more accessible on the Internet.

LESSONS LEARNED

The first lesson we learned from this project concerns the nature of multimedia and the process of designing educational software. The development of multimedia programs is inherently collaborative and interdisciplinary. Most academics are socialized to work within their own disciplines and may be unaccustomed to working with experts in other fields. Technology development, however, requires a team with various expertise: content-area expertise, technical, and pedagogical expertise. Implementation requires just as much teamwork as product development. Technology in education raises very real financial, logistical, and technical concerns that can be addressed only by a team of administrators, instructional staff, and technical experts working together.

The second lesson from this project concerns the nature of learning in a multimedia environment. Anyone who has reservations about the educational potential of computer-assisted instruction should observe our students working independently and in small groups. Every student is actively engaged during the class period. Students come in, sit down, and get to work. They set their own agenda, and they stay on task.

The third lesson is to build pedagogical research into computer development projects; research and development go hand-in-hand. What we learned from analyzing data (student surveys, think-aloud protocols, mouse-click reports) not only helped us improve the final versions of the computer materials but also helped us find the most effective ways to use the materials in our courses.

CONTACT INFORMATION

Carl S. Blyth, Assistant Professor
French Linguistics
Department of French and Italian
University of Texas, Austin
Austin, TX 78712-1197
Email: cblyth@mail.utexas.edu
Phone: (512) 471-5531
Fax: (512) 471-8492

Vignette 88 New Conversations: Web-Based Forums in Spanish Civilization and Culture

Jeffrey C. Barnett, Washington and Lee University

Many argue that true learning takes place when the student actively incorporates and uses concepts in contrast to receiving information passively. This is perhaps true in all disciplines but especially in foreign language courses, which stress linguistic as well as conceptual development. In my interdisciplinary culture courses, I stress that students must be aware of the equal demands on communication and content. Although I attempt to follow this approach, unfortunately, I often find myself having to choose between devoting sufficient time to both the introduction of new concepts and their application.

There are typically 20 students in my Spanish Civilization and Culture course. All have completed at least intermediate Spanish, most are majors, and many have studied abroad. Freshmen and sophomores have direct network connections in their dormitory rooms, while others have access to the web through the various networked campus computer labs. All are familiar with navigating the web, and some have composed their own web pages.

IDEAS BEHIND THE COURSE DESIGN

I believe that the more removed the professor is from discussion, the more actively the student takes responsibility for learning. My role is that of moderator. Obviously, the communicative approach does not do away with the professor's responsibility to spark discussion with appropriate questions, lead the students to a deeper level, and clarify or correct errors. Nevertheless, I sought to avoid the traditional, passive approach of reception, retrieval, regurgitation, and recall. To make the student a more active participant, I asked myself a series of questions:

- What are the students saying?
- How are they saying it?
- How often?
- Who's talking?

These questions led to the following objectives:

- increase the quality of discussion
- increase the quantity of discussion
- refocus the direction of discussion

COURSE ACTIVITIES

To accomplish these goals, I incorporated a number of web-based activities throughout the course, including my own texts, other readings on the web, useful links, and exercises. The most successful of these, exclusively addressed here, was a web-based discussion forum made available through the HTML template program, WebCourse in a Box (WCB). Unlike many of the older newsgroups or listservers, web-based forums tend to be more friendly and familiar to students. For example, previously visited sites appear in a different color; I can use the Find command to count student entries; multimedia attachments are easily entered; it is URL-aware; and so forth. The students and I have found the WCB forum's visual organization its greatest strength. The message list serves as a chronological and thematic index by displaying the subject title and its threads. This allows the students to select with ease the topic they want to respond to or, more importantly, at what level of the thread they wish to enter the discussion. There are also a number of features that allow the professor to customize the forum (e.g., the inclusion of date stamps).

The students' assignment was very specific and achievable. Each had to read all of the new entries before class and post at least two original responses a week. The students could start a new topic, follow up on a previous one, pose a question, clarify or confirm, offer rebuttal, and so forth. They had complete liberty to organize the discussion as they saw meaningful. Almost all of the students found the forum so much fun that they invariably went well beyond the minimum requirements and, in fact, doubled the number of entries I had expected over the course of the semester.

MEASURED RESULTS

Based on student evaluations and critiques from colleagues both on campus and off, my impressions were confirmed regarding the many benefits of the web-based forum. Peer and student observations typically addressed the following six areas.

Discussion

I was looking for and achieved controlled chaos, meaning that everyone felt free to interject his or her own ideas at will. Although the comments were not submitted simultaneously in real time, the message list gives the impression that the whole class is sharing ideas at once. In previous years, I felt that I alone was engaging a single student at a time, often overlooking someone who might have had a good idea, allowing some to monopolize conversation and others blend into anonymity.

Communication as a Review Tool

Although my main goal was to remove the direct and limited professor-to-student type of query, I nevertheless found the WCB helpful as a review tool. In these instances, I would post one question to which all were required to respond. It was generally a unit review question that took the place of a quiz. More importantly, when it came time to review for the midterm and final exams, the entire class had access to a fellow student's answer.

Prolongation of Previous Discussion

The web forum undoubtedly extends our conversation beyond the classroom. Shortly into the semester, I sought the students' reactions to the forum. Although not meant as a complaint, one responded, "It's like having two classes now." I stressed to the students, however, that I preferred to see it as one continuous class instead of 24 Tuesday–Thursday sessions. Essentially, that is what the forum provided. It brought the material together as a course in contrast to disjointed class sessions. Follow-up questions and comments summarized the topic before we moved on. It gave the material continuity.

Anticipation of the Next Discussion

I found the forum useful to continue the previous class. It also helped me to anticipate the upcoming meeting in two special ways. First, it allowed me to preview and guide classroom discussion by proposing questions at an opportune moment. Previously, when I would hand out discussion questions along with the assignment, I always felt that the students did not read the text critically and only prepared the part that corresponded to the questions. Withholding the questions until class time did not give the student sufficient time to prepare a thoughtful response. The forum alleviated this conflict by allowing me to post questions the morning of class; more specifically, after the assignment had been completed yet before the students arrived. In this way, the students could foresee the direction of the in-class discussion and prepare their ideas, yet it still forced them to complete the reading thoroughly. The forum also helped me anticipate the student reaction to a given assignment. Since I had a clearer understanding of their views and opinions, I could make critical adjustments. For example, some readings that in my opinion were intriguing elicited few comments, whereas others that I judged to be somewhat straightforward evoked a wide scope of controversy ranging from gender views to ideological differences. I would have probably missed this opportunity, if not for the forum. Furthermore, when we hit a lull and no one volunteered to comment, I knew that they had something to say, because I always brought a printed copy of the archive with me to class. I could then call on a specific student to restate and expound on his premise. This decreased my frustration with silence and made better use of class time.

Interactive Potential

Perhaps the most obvious advantage of the web-based forum is its capacity for interactivity. As we discuss a particular topic, I can incorporate meaningful multimedia attachments. In one case, for example, I attached an image of a Spanish Civil War poster, asked the students to arrive at their own conclusions, and then we invited an expert from Spain to join in the discussion. The students often use the forum to share the addresses of interesting sites that they have found on the web independently.

Archive of Discussion

Finally, the forum provides an archive of thoughts in a chronological and thematic order that will help me the following semester in several ways. I can use the forum to remind myself of pertinent comments made previously, or if I choose to make it available to the students, they can compare their thoughts to those in previous semesters. Regardless, it provides continuity from one semester to the next.

LESSONS LEARNED

For subsequent success, I have altered or kept various concerns in mind.

Incorporation

Incorporate the forum as an integral part of a web-based class. In previous courses, with fewer computerized assignments, students were not motivated to go to the web often enough. It was seen as a tedious, supplemental activity. In this case, however, the students were obligated to visit our class page to get the assignments, obtain the readings, and check for important messages. As several students observed, since they were already on the class page, it made it easy to go ahead and add a comment or surf the responses while there.

Assignment

Be specific in demands and yet promote creativity. At first, some students were unsure about the type of comments they should make. Over the course of the semester, as they emulated their classmates, this problem was alleviated. Initially, however, it is important that they understand exactly what is expected of them.

Accessibility

Freshmen and some sophomores were online more frequently than upperclassmen, since their dormitory rooms are networked. Although our campus has numerous computers available 24 hours a day, still some upperclass students felt imposed on when they had to return to campus or stay after class to enter their responses. Accessibility (as relative as that term may be) is a major concern and will have a direct impact on how successful the forum will be.

Size and Speed of the Forum

Maximize speed by keeping individual fora small. If students find the forum cumbersome, they tend to respond less often. This was true for the upperclass students who were using a modem but less of a concern for the freshmen with direct network connections in their rooms. This problem can be alleviated by creating multiple fora (by topic, unit, or other chronological divisions).

Type of Forum

Choose the friendliest forum that best suits the needs of your class. In previous attempts, I had been dissatisfied with listservers and newsgroups. Some were troublesome from a technological aspect. Others, such as chatrooms and unmoderated discussion groups, did not reinforce our topics and, in fact, proved a distraction from our goals.

CONCLUSIONS

While the conclusions I draw here refer to my first experiment with the WCB forum in Spanish Civilization and Culture, I have since had equal success in three other courses: Hispanic Cinema, a senior seminar, and Spanish-American Civilization and Culture. The privacy of writing in one's own space at one's own pace has proven to be a step towards more formal writing and advanced conversational skills. More importantly, through greater quality and quantity of discussion, the students have taken an active role in creating a profound learning experience.

CONTACT INFORMATION

Jeffrey C. Barnett, Associate Professor
Department of Romance Languages
Washington and Lee University
Lexington, VA 24450
Email: barmett.j@wlu.edu
http://madison.wlu.edu/~barnettj/
Phone: (540) 463-8950
Fax: (540) 463-8479

Vignette 89 Latin American Culture, a Movie Lab, and a Professor

Angel A. Rivera, Worcester Polytechnic Institute

GENERAL BACKGROUND

Topics in Latin American Culture is a relatively recent addition to our course selection at Worcester Polytechnic Institute, as is the entire Spanish program. In 1997, WPI received an internal grant to design and build a multimedia, multipurpose language and communication center to enhance the teaching of several topics. We now informally call it the Movie Lab.

Latin American culture and civilization is a topic traditionally taught in a conventional classroom, involving long hours of lecturing and notetaking. However, in the past few years, improvements in the World Wide Web and the development of new software and faster computers have created possibilities for new approaches. Topics in Latin American Culture is an experimental course, taught now for the second time, which integrates computer technologies, Latin American culture, and the Spanish language.

My background is not related to computer technologies: I have been a professor of Spanish and researcher of Latin American and Caribbean literatures for many years. After accepting a teaching position at Worcester Polytechnic Institute, a university oriented toward the teaching of science and engineering, I became more interested in the use of technology in the classroom. My background and knowledge related to computers was, and still is, just a bit beyond basic. On the other hand, most of my students were fully knowledgeable about computer-related technologies and topics.

IDEAS BEHIND THE COURSE DESIGN

It is my experience that a course about culture and civilization should be based on developing oral and written communication skills to allow students to continue their acquisition and refinement of the target language (Spanish, in this case). The target language should be learned in an environment where students are encouraged to express their own ideas as early as possible. This approach promotes active communication and interaction by using small group activities, and the language acquired is authentic and creatively used. The classroom should be considered a window where students can practice what they have been learning.

WPI's academic year is divided into four terms of seven weeks each. This compressed time frame leaves the language/culture professor with the dilemma of deciding how to balance history, culture, and language proficiency. Following the experience of colleagues in other areas, I intuited that a multimedia language communication center could help with this monumental task.

COMPUTER-ENHANCED TECHNIQUES

The multimedia center helped me to deal with the general and the specific objectives of the course. The general course objectives were to develop a general knowledge about the many Latin American countries and cultures; to recognize that cultural identity (related to race, gender, age, religion, etc.) affects the way that people behave; to realize that to communicate effectively with people from other cultures one should understand inherited cultural connotations; and to develop the ability to evaluate crude generalizations or stereotypes about a culture.

The specific goals were to analyze and to study several aspects of Latin American cultures: indigenous heritage; topics about racial confrontation and syncretism; female participation in Latin America's culture and history; internal and external immigration patterns; art, literature, music and their importance in the development of a cultural identity; topics related to political, social, and cultural independence and interdependence; and forces behind tradition and change. We also wanted to improve and refine language skills already acquired.

To accomplish these goals, I divided the possibilities of the Movie Lab in two main areas or questions:

1) What could I do with the computers? 2) What could the students accomplish with the computers in relation to Latin America? I decided to meet with the students at the Movie Lab during most of the semester and used the conventional classroom for an occasional group discussion or for testing. I decided to enhance short periods of lecturing by using Asymetrix Tool-Book and PowerPoint.

Asymetrix ToolBook is quite helpful in developing lecture material about topics like geography and geopolitics. With both programs, anyone can create and design presentations or lecturing material. One can even prepare small drill sections about country location or identification.

PowerPoint is also a good tool for developing lectures. Using this program, I developed several lectures about specific topics, such as pre-Columbian or pre-Hispanic cultures, Sor Juana Inés de la Cruz, independence movements, etc. One of the most appealing features of this program is the possibility of not only projecting a text on a screen but also adding multiple effects like scrolling slowly from the left side to the center of the screen. One can add photos or maps to the presentation while lecturing or sound files for individual practice and review

I also constructed World Wide Web pages to present maps and to question the students about capitals, main geographical features, etc. The WWW allowed me to post all sorts of information about the course, including the syllabus, topics for research, maps, reviews, questions, and, best of all, the pages created by the students. See http://www.wpi.edu/~arivera.

A big component of this course was to develop two research projects pertinent to Latin American cultures. The topic had to be approved by the professor, and the class was divided into teams of three or four students per team. The first project was to interview a person from Latin America. The interview, approximately 1,000 words long, focused on general topics, but students could use probing questions to find information about a more specific topic that they later developed in the second project.

In the second project, students were supposed to research a topic related to the country of origin of the interviewee. Students were given several options, which were posted on the web at http:// www.wpi.edu/ ~arivera/temas.html. Instead of turning in the project in a traditional paper format, the students were required to create a web page to which they posted both projects. This way, everyone in the class had access to other teams' web pages or projects. They included photos, audio files, the interview, the researched topic, links related to the topic, comments about those links, and an annotated bibliography. The students were required to do a brief oral presentation or introduction to their web pages. The pages were to be evaluated according to the precision and relevance of the information presented, accuracy and proficiency in the use of Spanish, and the creativity and organization of the page. The oral presentation was considered part of the grade evaluation. One of the main activities required for the students was to review and study one of the web pages created by fellow teams. Students were tested on the information presented on those pages. (For a complete description of the project see the course syllabus: http://www.wpi.edu /~arivera/cult2.html.)

Some of the programs used for the creation of web pages were FrontPage and Microsoft Word. To see the results of the pages created by the students, see http://www.wpi.edu/~arivera/cursode.html.

MEASURED RESULTS

In all the categories of WPI's "Student Evaluation of Course/Lab or Conference Instructor," the evaluations for this experimental course showed that 94% in one section and 95% on the other agreed or strongly agreed with the course objectives, organization of the course material, and method of delivery. Many of the students found working with computers, the WWW, and Latin American culture and civilization challenging and interesting. Students were asked what they particularly liked about the course or lab, and some responded:

> "I like the web page projects the best. They made the research more fun, and it was interesting to see what other people did for their web pages."

> "I liked that we did work on the web, and I also liked that I learned a lot about the culture of Latin America."

> "The multimedia factor in this course really got me involved with what I had to learn. Not only did it make the class more exciting, I also felt very interested in learning the subject."

My personal observation is that students, after being exposed to multiple sources of knowledge in the Movie Lab (videos, web pages, music lectures, books, etc.) seemed to master topics that traditionally have been difficult to grasp. The question and answer sections that followed every student's presentation indicated that this was true.

LESSONS LEARNED

- Lectures with PowerPoint. This is one of the most useful tools for lecturing. It is fun, easy to use, and visually stimulating.

- ToolBox. This program is good, but mastery requires time.

- Email. This is an important tool for communicating with the students outside of the class.

- Student teams. When dividing the students in teams, be sure to have at least one person per team who is familiar with the Internet and the creation of web pages. This is not something difficult today, since most of our students have had some kind of exposure to this technology.

- The professor may have to set some time apart to conduct a training session. A better option is to contact a qualified person at your institution to do this kind of training.

- Some minor notes about the technology.

  * You need to become quickly acquainted with the technology available at your school.

  * Always schedule your visits to the facilities in advance.

  * Find who are the key persons to talk to when developing this course.

  * Warn the person who keeps the UNIX (or similar system) accounts for the students about this project. He or she may have to increase the students' quotas or available space for the creation of web pages.

  * Always do trial runs before a presentation. Equipment can often fail on you.

- Web pages
  * Be sure to state clearly your expectations about the creation of web pages. Provide guidelines.
  * Indicate how the students will be evaluated.
  * Advise the students to test what they are doing continuously.
  * Strongly encourage your students to back up their files.
  * Ask the students to turn in a printout of the posted pages on the World Wide Web. This will help you to criticize and correct the pages.
  * Choose some samples of the pages for future consultation or demonstration.
  * Collect all the addresses of the web pages created by the students and distribute them.
  * Quiz the students on the content of the pages created by other teams.
- Get release time. This is an important component when designing a new course of this complexity or dealing with new technologies. You will need to get some release time when preparing the files for the course or becoming acquainted with new computer technology or software. This is very time-consuming.
- The idea of using a blackboard should not be abandoned, but with a projector and a computer the blackboard can be replaced by Microsoft Word and the projector itself.
- The use of video clips and audio files on the World Wide Web is more complex because it involves authors' rights.

CONCLUSION

After experiencing this type of teaching, I do not think that I would like to teach this course again without using computer technology and the information available on the Internet. When used in a controlled and supervised manner, it gives power to the student. Well used, it can be an excellent teaching aid or learning tool. Also, I found that the students' essays are not flat anymore; suddenly, with the power of HTML, their essays branched out in multiple directions. All this effort made teaching and essay-grading more interesting and rewarding.

CONTACT INFORMATION

Angel A. Rivera
Assistant Professor of Spanish
Worcester Polytechnic Institute
Department of Humanities and Arts
100 Institute Road
Worcester, MA 01609-2280
Email: Arivera@wpi.edu
WWW: http://www.wpi.edu/~arivera/cursode.html

For a complete description of the project see the course syllabus at http://www.wpi.edu/~arivera/cult2.html.
Phone: (508) 831-5779
Fax: (508) 831-5932

Vignette 90 Poetry in Motion: The Rilke Project

Joan Keck Campbell, Dartmouth College

The low-intermediate level of language instruction is pivotal for both student and instructor. It is the level at which many students decide whether they will further their language study, taking more advanced literature and culture courses, or stop once they have completed the required language sequence. Consequently, the instructor is obliged to show students the full range of possibilities should they pursue their language study. Students must be moved by something in the sound, literature, or culture of the target language to find motivation for further study.

EDUCATIONAL THEORIES

In my low-intermediate German course at Dartmouth College (German 3), I wanted poetry to move my students and show them the expressive beauty of the German language. But they were stuck, many students finding poetry inaccessible because they couldn't feel, see, and hear it. My students had to move beyond their low-intermediate proficiency level, their less than optimal affective filters, their lack of experience with literary methodology, and their resistance to poetry in general. In their academic setting, students tend to fixate on finding out what the poem means, often missing the rhythm, sound, and imagery of the poem.

I wanted my students to be moved by poetry, so for this unit, I chose poetry that moved: three of Rainer Maria Rilke's *Dingedichte* (Thing Poems) in which he uses sounds, repetition, and meter to evoke an image of the thing—here, a carousel, a fountain, and a panther. I had poems that could move, but I needed a protected space in which they could move and be heard. I found this on the World Wide Web.

Two basic premises underlie my teaching of poetry. First, poetry must be heard. To study poetry without listening to it is like studying a symphony with only the score. Secondly, poetry is about perception. Because perception is individual, students should have a protected space in which to explore it by themselves before entering into a public discussion.

I set five specific goals for our study of Rilke:

1) To allow students to experience and to be moved by the Rilke poems, making use of not only their intellect, but also their senses of hearing and sight on a much more rudimentary level

2) To lower students' affective filters by providing them with a safe, protected space where they can experiment with literary methodology, explore the poems, and ask content and vocabulary questions in private

3) To dispense with time-consuming explanatory activities (questions like: "What are we supposed to read? What does this word mean? Why is this word in this case?") before class began, so that we could commence immediately with discussion

4) To enter the classroom with an understanding of the students' perspectives: who was enthused by the material and who was resistant, thus making me a better facilitator of classroom discussion

5) To facilitate frequent reading of, and listening to, the three poems.

COMPUTER-ENHANCED TECHNIQUES USED

I decided on the following parameters for the Rilke site. Here students can do the following:

• Read the poems in German or English. Since the poems are linguistically complicated, students at the intermediate-low level benefit from referencing the works in both languages. This feature also facilitates interesting discussions about translating poetry.

• Hear the poems in German or English. As I mentioned earlier, to be understood, a poem must be heard. Intermediate-low language students must hear a poem read well by a proficient speaker to understand its rhyme and meter. We were most fortunate to have Professor Walter Arndt donate both his own thoughtful translations and spoken interpretations of the Rilke poems.

- See a QuickTime video of the poems' subjects while hearing the poems read in German or English. This QuickTime feature provides both visual and auditory stimuli and gives students some sense of what Rilke may have experienced as he observed his poetic subjects and explored their inner rhythm.

- Engage in a dialogue about these poems in a chat space. The Rilke chat space guides students through a series of directed questions designed to prepare them for classroom discussions of the poems and their translations. Questions cover such topics as:

  * narrative perspective

  * translation (English versus German version)

  * recitation of the poem

  * general discussion forum

  * site feedback (issues around working with literature in a multimedia environment)

- Check the meaning of key words in a glossary section. This feature, partnered with the translations of the poems, aids comprehension.

At the outset, I simply give my students the Rilke URL and explain the above features to them. I make no statements about how they should navigate the site or the order and language in which they should read the poems. It is my intent to put the students in charge of their learning experience and give them the tools with which they can develop their own method for exploring literature. The Rilke site is like the prop room in a theater: Students go in and choose those props they need to negotiate the meaning of the text.

MEASURED RESULTS

The use of computer technology in this poetry unit allows me to create opportunities for my students that they simply could not have were they limited to traditional classroom interaction. The Rilke site creates a protected space for them where they encounter poetry on their own terms and find what methods work best for them. This prepares language students for the next level of instruction at which they analyze literary texts independently. As a result, students feel more competent when discussing literature and, in fact, a higher percentage of them now continue on to literature and culture courses.

The combination of presenting Rilke's *Dingedichte* in a multimedia environment and providing students with a chat space in which they can formulate their thoughts at their own pace before engaging in pubic dialogue results in a significant lowering of the affective filter. The written discourse practice in the chat space carries over into classroom discussions. Having tried out their ideas in written form, students are more confident about presenting their perspectives in public. Because I also participate in the Rilke chat, my opportunity for dialogue with students is no longer limited to class time. With my improved sense of student perspectives, I can now be more proactive in lowering the class's affective filter. Drawing usually reticent students into class discussions is much easier when I can make specific reference to their chat comments and use these as a springboard. Less reticent students are also apt to take greater linguistic risks in the chat space than they would in graded essays, thus stretching the bounds of their language abilities as well. Because the students can ask content questions before class, we are able to clear up any misunderstandings before they occur

The most striking result of the Rilke site is, for me, however, one that defies traditional educational measurement. This is the emotional bond that my students form both with Rilke's works and with Professor Walter Arndt. Because using the World Wide Web so streamlines the class pedagogy, our unit on Rilke also includes time for a classroom visit by Walter Arndt. My students can meet him, shake his hand, and hear in person the voice that is their channel to Rilke. Through Walter Arndt, many of my students have found their own connection to German language and literature. This is a result I cannot measure in numbers of course registrants or increased test scores, but it is something that I can see in their faces. It is something I can hear in their chat responses to questions on Walter's reading of the poems.

LESSONS LEARNED

Both my students and I have learned invaluable lessons from our encounters with Rilke's poetry and were moved—my students, to continue their study of the German language, and me, to explore more possibilities in instructional technology. I will briefly outline some of the most important lessons learned and those I would most like to share with colleagues interested in exploring the possibilities of instructional technology.

- Put people and pedagogy first. From the very outset, pedagogy and the needs of my students were in command. The Rilke site was not driven by the technology but by my desire to move my students. The presentation of Rilke in a multimedia environment facilitates a very personal connection between my students, Rilke, and his translator. Using the computer makes this first contact with German poetry a very personalized, individual encounter.

- Don't go it alone. I could never have designed and executed the Rilke site by myself. I availed myself of all the computing talent I could find and developed a close working relationship with Dartmouth's multimedia specialist, Sarah Horton, who lent assistance at every step. It was this combination of pedagogy and technology that made the site such a fruitful venture.

- Don't box yourself in. A multimedia project is very labor-intensive. To ensure that the time and effort invested pay off, one should undertake projects that can be used in a variety of settings for a variety of purposes. Because I set very few parameters for student navigation of the Rilke site, it can be used not only by my language students but also by literature seminars and by students studying translation or the impact of multimedia on culture.

Just as the navigation of such a site should be open-ended, so too should the technical design be dynamic enough to allow for future change. As more students use the site, it is natural to notice features that need change. A site should be constructed so that these changes are accomplished smoothly. There are some elements of the Rilke site that I would change in the future. To minimize the clicking and scrolling students have to do, I would like to have the glossary of terms appear as hypertext pop-up windows within each poem.

I would encourage students to be open to new academic possibilities. Transferring subject matter to a multimedia environment often allows the instructor to sneak in subject matter for which students mistakenly believe they have no aptitude. For example, students might have little interest in poetry per se, but if it is presented on the World Wide Web, then they find it acceptable. Here, I would cite the comments of one student who remarked, "I didn't understand the poetry in general at all—I am a biologist—but I find the portrayal of the fountain interesting . . . quiet within itself, talking quietly . . ." She went on to make this and other very insightful comments. She had already begun to box herself in academically. The Rilke site helped her emerge from her corner.

CONCLUSION

Working on the Rilke site was one of the most challenging and rewarding ventures of my career. It allowed me to move my students and to spark in them a deepened interest in German language, literature, and culture. This multimedia environment also facilitates the formation of a very personal and individual bond to the material. Students are not limited to one classroom encounter with Rilke or with Walter Arndt but can access and listen to the materials as often as they wish. One student reported listening to the poems 24 times. Another returned to the site a year after she had completed German 3 and began to study the poetry again.

Such experiences make students active and engaged participants in the learning process. Clearly, the multimedia environment plays a central role in this. We as educational professionals need to do more to foster such intimate contact with course material and move our students along the path to being lifelong learners.

CONTACT INFORMATION

Joan Keck Campbell
Senior Lecturer
Department of German Studies
6084 Dartmouth Hall
Dartmouth College
Hanover, NH 03755
Email: joan.campbell@dartmouth.edu
WWW: http://www.dartmouth.edu/~germ3/rilke
Phone: (603) 646-2711
Fax: (603) 646-1474

Vignette 91 The Application of New Information Technologies to an Antarctica and Falklands/Malvinas Negotiation and Mediation Simulation

Jack Child, American University

This project applied new information technologies to the teaching of a series of six negotiation and mediation role-playing simulations set in three time frames and two geographic locations. The time frames are historical, recent, and future, as follows:

	ANTARCTICA	FALKLANDS/ MALVINAS
Historical:	The 1959 Treaty	Prior to 1982
Recent:	Madrid Protocol (1991)	The War (Apr–Jun 1982)
Future:	Discovery of Oil (2045)	Mid-21st Century

The Falklands/Malvinas simulations are dyadic, between the United Kingdom and Argentina, although other actors, such as the islands' local inhabitants (the Kelpers), the United States, and several Latin American nations are also involved. This simulation also includes a number of mediators, such as the Secretary-General of the United Nations, the president of a Latin American nation, and the United States secretary of state. The Antarctic negotiation is multilateral, with up to 50 nations involved, as well as several conservation organizations and commercial firms.

THE NEW INFORMATION TECHNOLOGIES

The new technologies applied to these simulations were the personal computer and its CD-ROM capability linked to several pieces of software.

The software used in this project were Macintosh packages, although equivalent software exists for MS-DOS IBM computers. The principal software packages we used were the following:

- Filemaker, a database (program) employed mainly for the bibliography, since it permits easy sorting and rearranging of large quantities of files (almost 4,000 entries)

- Microsoft Word, a conventional word processing program used for the monograph on negotiation, the chronology, and the instructions for the simulations

- Scantastic and Microscan scanning software that, when used in conjunction with the appropriate hardware, permitted the digitizing of documents, photographs, and slides

- Photoshop, a graphic manipulation software package

- Macromedia Director, a sophisticated multimedia software package that integrates all of these items into a visual presentation. This presentation can be made interactive using hot buttons and hypertext, which permit the user to move around the program either in the linear direction set out by the author or to whatever section is of interest.

To summarize, the key advantage provided by these new technologies is that a very large amount of textual and visual material can be placed on a small disk and duplicated so that each student can have the whole package. The contents of the disk can also be placed on the World Wide Web or distributed commercially.

THE PRODUCT

We produced two CD-ROM disks, one for Antarctica and one for the Falklands/Malvinas. The various elements can be downloaded and printed as desired. Each disk includes the following items:

- **Two extensive bibliographies.** The one dealing generally with negotiation and mediation contains about 600 items, while the combined Antarctica and Falklands/Malvinas one runs to over 3,000 items. The majority are in English, although a significant number are in Spanish and some in Portuguese. The materials are also available in Spanish.

- **A monograph on negotiation** prepared as an introduction to general and theoretical approaches to mediation and negotiation. The monograph concludes with a checklist, which the student uses to analyze in writing the negotiation being simulated. The number of possible questions and the detail with which they are answered can easily make this part equivalent to a short term paper.

- **Several thousand pages of documents and other materials in the public domain.** These are organized into general materials available to all players and packets of materials for each specific actor in the simulation.

- **Background readings.** Some of these were written by the principal investigator, and some are government documents or other materials in the public domain.

- **The interactive multimedia presentation.** This combines text, visuals, mapmaking exercises, and questions to provide background information for the two simulations.

- **Instructions for the role-playing simulation.** These take the student and the instructor from the materials listed above to the actual classroom simulation. Each student is assigned a role, either as a country, an organizational representative, or a historical figure.

THE SIMULATIONS

The six simulations provided more than enough materials for a 14-week semester. It was decided to use the first simulation in each geographic setting in a passive analytical mode, which involved doing readings and answering questions that were drawn from the "Introduction to Negotiation" checklists. This approach provided a useful historical base from which to move on to the four active role-playing simulations. Of the four, the two that occurred in recent time frames (for Antarctica, the 1991 Madrid Environmental Protocol, and for the Falklands/Malvinas, the 1982 War) were the most constraining, since the players were asked to take positions and make statements that were reasonably close to what actually happened. Feedback from students indicated that while they learned from this process, they felt they could not fully use their creativity.

Their creativity was turned loose in the two simulations set in the future, when student role-players were told they could apply any approach to the negotiation and mediation process. Students could caucus in their group or negotiate and mediate with other players. For the Antarctic simulation, the setting involved the discovery in the year 2045 of a large oil field on the Antarctic Peninsula, which is especially delicate, since claims by Argentina, Chile, and Great Britain overlap. For the Malvinas/Falklands simulation, the historical setting was in the middle of the 21st century, when joint development of fishing and oil resources between Argentina and Great Britain, initiated on the basis of a real 1995 agreement, began to break down over a number of issues, not the least of which was the push for political independence by a very rich group of islanders, who had greatly profited from oil royalties and the sale of fishing licenses.

MEASURED RESULTS

The full simulations mentioned in the last paragraph were carried out in a semester course at American University in the fall 1996 semester in English and the fall 1997 semester in Spanish. An abbreviated version was used in a two-week portion of a general education course at the same university in English in the fall 1996, spring 1997, fall 1997, and spring 1998 semesters in English and the fall 1998 semester in Spanish. The language teaching element, which supplements the negotiation/mediation component, involves parallel Spanish and English screens with the same visual elements. Students running the program in Spanish who have problems with the language can get an instant translation by clicking on a hot button.

At each stage, students were asked to provide written feedback on the negotiation/mediation simulations and the value of the new technologies. The results have been almost uniformly positive, identifying confusing areas and technical difficulties and generating many suggestions for improvements.

Simulations have a long history of effective employment in the study and teaching of international relations and peacemaking/peacekeeping. Positive evaluations confirm that this is an effective method of teaching. The addition of the computer to the simulations has given students access to a very large amount of textual and visual information that would not otherwise be easily available. While it is true that the textual material could have been provided in a binder or book, the sheer volume would make this unwieldy and prohibitively expensive. Putting it on library reserve would not be an attractive option. Having it digitized and available on a floppy or CD-ROM is an ideal solution.

The presentation of the visual material in an interactive program would be possible in a classroom via slide lectures, but these would be linear and interactive only in a very limited sense. Once presented, the instructor would probably not be able or willing to present them a second or third time for students who might be absent or wish to review the material. The CD-ROM can be made available to each student to view again and again.

At American University, each course is evaluated anonymously by each student. These numerical evaluations become public knowledge after the course is finished and all grades are turned in. The student questionnaire includes some 21 standard questions. The most relevant question is extracted here for the fall 1996 and fall 1997 versions of the Antarctica and Falklands/Malvinas course which used the computer-based materials described here, and for the spring 1995 version, which did not.

SPRING 1995	FALL 1996	FALL 1997
(No computer)	(Computer)	(Computer)

Question 14, "Course overall" rating:

5.53/6.00	5.71/6.00	5.89/6.00

(Max rating: 6.00)

CONCLUSION

The test of the computer-based negotiation/mediation simulation has yielded very positive results. For the instructor, it has been an opportunity to be more creative and use a fresh and stimulating pedagogical approach. Student reaction has also been gratifying and suggests that this type of instruction is a welcome change and provides the factual basis for the higher-order interactions experienced in class after the computer portions are completed.

CONTACT INFORMATION

Jack Child
Center for Teaching Excellence
American University
4400 Massachusetts Avenue, NW
Washington, DC 20016-8045
Email: jchild@american.edu
Phone: (202) 885-2385
Fax: (202) 885-1076

Mark C. Taylor, Williams College

COURSE DESIGN

In the fall of 1992, Esa Saarinen, professor of philosophy at the University of Helsinki, and I conducted the first semester-long global seminar using teleconferencing technology. Ten students from Helsinki and ten from Williams College met once a week for two hours in a real-time, audio-video exchange. The course, which was titled "Imagologies," explored the philosophical presuppositions and implications of emerging information and telematic technologies. In addition to the weekly seminar sessions, students participated in extensive out-of-class email discussions. While the course was enormously successful, when we required a term paper at the end of the semester, students objected. They correctly insisted that the logic of the technologies we were using and the issues we were discussing was at odds with traditional papers.

In the years following this seminar, I experimented with various ways of developing writing assignments that would be more imaginative and better suited to electronic technology. I finally decided that I would replace term papers with multimedia hypertexts. I eventually developed a course named "Cyberscapes" that consists of more-or-less traditional classes devoted to the discussion of philosophers and cultural critics, ranging from Nietzsche and Heidegger to Derrida and Baudrillard, as well as a media lab where students learn how to work with multimedia. The aim is to bring together theory and practice by theorizing what we are practicing and practicing what we are theorizing.

COURSE ACTIVITIES

Since the college does not have resources adequate to deliver the technical instruction necessary for this course, I have worked with advanced undergraduates to develop laboratory materials and procedures. These student assistants conduct weekly labs where they teach their fellow students how to use Photoshop, Sound Edit, and Director. Throughout the semester, students are given specific assignments that require mastery of technical skills. This process culminates in the development of a multimedia hypertextual analysis of issues we explore in our class discussions.

In addition to this work in the media lab, I also use technology in the classroom. While most of the discussions are devoted to written texts, some of the assignments involve the critical assessment of web sites. During the last several class sessions, students are required to present their work-in-progress for criticism and suggestions. Finally, throughout the semester, students must participate in an online conference discussion.

MEASURED RESULTS

In measuring the results of this experimental course, students' response and performance as well as the quality of the course must be considered. Students who have taken the course have consistently appreciated the opportunity to explore important ideas in new ways. They realize that they must find different ways to write and to think. The quality of the multimedia work they do is simply remarkable. As new students come to college with more skills, the work improves each year. Students are also keenly aware that the skills they acquire in this course are very useful after they leave college. Many who have taken Cyberscapes are now working in emerging technologies. The course, which obviously is itself a work-in-process, has improved each year. At the end of each semester, I meet with my student assistants to discuss ways to improve the labs. Since technology is always changing, we must make constant adjustments.

LESSONS LEARNED

New Literacies
My experience of teaching and creating a multimedia CD-ROM of my own have convinced me that digital culture requires new literacies. Work in multimedia does not involve doing what we have always done differently but doing something different from what we

have previously done. Students must learn to weave together audio, visual, and verbal materials to create coherent texts and persuasive arguments.

Collaboration

During the first three years I taught this course, each student had to prepare an individual project. It has become apparent, however, that these new media lend themselves to collaborative work. I have, therefore, changed my strategy and now have students work in groups of four to five. While many have found the transition from individual to group work difficult, the quality of the projects has improved considerably.

Time Requirements

This course takes an enormous amount of time for both the instructor and students. Mastering difficult texts and acquiring new technical skills make the demands of this course considerably heavier than most other classes. In spite of the commitment required, the popularity and enrollment of the course continue to grow. Having started with 18 students, this year the class unexpectedly jumped to 41.

Class Size

Given the demands of the course and the limitation of resources, this class should admit no more than 20 students. In addition to the work involved for the instructor and teaching assistants, hardware and software costs increase quickly.

CONCLUSIONS

I am convinced that it is very important for colleges and universities to continue to explore new ways of using developing technologies in teaching and research.

This is a particular challenge for the arts and humanities. In an effort to provide support for faculty members who are moving into new areas, Williams College has created a new Center for Technology in the Arts and Humanities. This center serves as a research and development studio with state-of-the-art hardware and software. A fellowship program provides support for resident faculty and student collaborators. Workshops and demonstrations throughout the year are designed to introduce the faculty to current work being done in a variety of areas.

It is obvious that young people raised with computers will continue to demand new ways of delivering education. The training of most faculty members has not prepared them to meet the challenges students are posing. All too often, faculty and administrators tend to resist change and to insist on outdated techniques and approaches. If the arts and humanities are to have a future in the digital age, we must find new ways to probe old questions.

CONTACT INFORMATION

Mark C. Taylor
Director, Center for Technology in the
    Arts and Humanities
Stetson Hall
Williams College
Williamstown, MA 01267
Mark.C.Taylor@williams.edu
WWW: www.williams.edu/mtaylor,
    www.williams.edu/ctah
Phone: (413) 597-2370
Fax: (413) 597-4222

Vignette 93 Jerusalem: The City and Its People

Roger Brooks, Connecticut College

Jerusalem is a city that brings together the multiple disciplines of religious studies: history of religions, anthropology, archeology, comparative religion, politics, and (a host of) others. Yet most students of Judaism, Christianity, or Islam have never been to the city, nor can they anticipate a study tour in Israel, though such trips make ideal conclusions to a semester's study. Despite the prohibitive expense, over recent years I have found that my students do reach out to the web for a variety of images and depictions of the modern city—depictions that proliferate especially now, in the wake of Jerusalem's 3,000th anniversary.

The simple assumption with which this seminar begins comes from students themselves: Place matters. Students have shown that by visiting the site, even if the visit is virtual, they garner better insights into the texts they read, the rituals they study, and the symbols they unravel and explain. Computing technology enables us to use the city itself as a classroom and to enhance more traditional studies with virtual fieldwork.

COURSE DESCRIPTION

Learning takes place in the process of analyzing data, not merely describing it. Yet much of the material available on the web, whether official Israeli tourist information, sites edited and produced by religious groups, or photographic essays designed to give the feel of touring Jerusalem, is descriptive. Students find themselves inundated with raw data, that rarely have been subject to academic categorization, presentation, or interpretation. Often these descriptions come with built-in biases and perspectives, but they aren't always clearly labeled.

Of course this is a familiar problem when one selects books for class: Does the author's perspective match that of the course as a whole? But the web presents a different problem. Megabytes of data are added daily, most of it unedited and without having passed any sort of review. The nonanalytic nature of the web and its material and, at times, its abundantly clear bi-ases pointed to an opportunity for students. A goal of the course was to combine virtual visits to Jerusalem with consistent and systematic analytic perspectives found in the theoretical material from our seminar.

At the same time, my students and I have often noted that the web is entirely passive and unidirectional: Students read what others have prepared. Yet I believe that students learn best by becoming teachers; they integrate what they themselves have learned by presenting it to others. A second goal of my course was to have the students treat the web as a two-dimensional medium, in which their own insights and interpretations would be available to others.

Writing Assignments

The writing assignments for the Jerusalem seminar bear the weight of translating these goals into concrete learning for the students. In particular, I use reading responses, a scavenger hunt, collaborative teaching, and a group final project.

Reading Responses

Prepared attendance is a requirement of all my courses. In a seminar format, this is doubly important, since student-oriented discussion of assigned materials is at the core of the format. (Yet, at times, all instructors have found it difficult to induce this preparation.) In this seminar, students were given a double assignment: First, they were to prepare a one- or two-page reading response, composed of a brief selection from a primary text that illustrated the arguments of the week's reading. Second, those responses were emailed to the class mailing list three days in advance of our seminar meetings. Students were then to arrive at class ready to discuss everyone else's selections and to defend their own. The simple technology of an email list was of great advantage. Students came to class already having considered several other possible ways of reading and understanding the material. Class discussions were clearly improved by these assignments.

Web Scavenger Hunt

One of my goals in turning to the web was to allow students to see how vast and undisciplined it is. It is vital that students exercise their own judgment about the value of a given site. To get this point across, I assigned students to find at least six Jerusalem web sites, at least one of which would be focused on each of the following three issues: history, religion, and politics. Each URL was to be accompanied by a half-page explanation of the site's focus and contents. Students received two points for each URL, and four points for each URL that no one else in the course found. As an added incentive, the class agreed to make the scavenger hunt winner its guest for dinner after that week's seminar. The competitive aspect of this assignment earned the students' enthusiastic participation. They found some truly obscure web sites within the analytic categories I had assigned, some of which were downright bizarre enough to make my point about the unedited nature of the web.

Collaborative Instruction

As students presented some of their analyses on the web, a member of our information services staff became a partner in teaching the seminar. Students had two seminar meetings devoted to learning the basics of html authoring, including graphics manipulation and web site coding. Students gained a separate perspective on their work for the semester but also learned a technological skill that translated beyond the course material. In addition, they had another faculty member to draw upon for expertise and opinion.

Group Final Project

The principal work of the seminar was a research project, created as part of a publicly available web site on Jerusalem. Students worked as a single team to plan and map the web site. They then broke into small teams, each of which was assigned a portion of the methodology and theory of the seminar that was to be applied to their segment of the web site. Topics that the students proposed and executed included categories of religious experience (e.g., pilgrimage, worship), critical locations (e.g., Temple Mount, David's Tomb), and important historical moments (e.g., Solomon's rule in Jerusalem, reunification of the city in 1967). Perhaps most valuable in this project was the collaborative learning that took place in which each student became another's teacher.

LESSONS LEARNED

Innovative uses of technology force an instructor to consider a delicate balance between what is being learned and how it is learned. For example, to allow students to work on presenting their materials in a web site format, inevitably time was taken from traditional learning. We covered about one-third less material in this seminar than in a noncomputing-intensive course. This tradeoff was worthwhile in two ways: 1) Students reported uniformly that they put more effort into the presentation of their work than in the usual case, and 2) their writing was careful and clearly reflected the goal of presenting this information to a broader audience. Nonetheless, as an instructor, I have concerns about the material the students never considered. For certain subject matter, such an approach, heavy in technology skills, might well be inappropriate.

Additionally, my students and I learned a great deal about copyright rules and graphics. My students all chose to make their web sites very rich in graphics: They understood very well that pictures convey aspects of a distant locale in ways that words cannot. So they found photos on the web, scanned maps from books and articles, and, in general, cribbed, scanned, and filched images wherever they could. Unfortunately, they held the copyright on virtually none of this material. As a result, in its original incarnation, our web site was strictly an internal affair. Over the past year, I visited Jerusalem and took more than 500 photos, which have been scanned and made ready for the web site. Since this course is now being taught on a regular basis, this is work that will allow the Jerusalem web site to grow and be available to the public by the end of this year's iteration.

CONCLUSION

Innovative teaching, whether using technology or not, can be risky. My students were well aware from the first day of the seminar that they were participating in an experiment. With their good will, however, the gamble of treating traditional subject matter in a new way paid off. Their work reflected their own understanding that excellence and analysis must be the hallmarks of the material they composed for the web. Probably the greatest success of this particular experiment was the students' own adoption of this goal.

CONTACT INFORMATION

Roger Brooks, Professor
Elie Wiesel Professor of Judaic Studies
Department of Religious Studies
Campus Box 5402
Connecticut College
New London, CT 06320-4125
Email: rlbro@conncoll.edu or see
url:http://www.conncoll.edu

INDEXES

Shiavi, Richard, 40, 44
Shields, Stella F., 124
Slavit, David, 84
Soraci, Sal, 178
Spurr, Michael J., 77
Sternbach, Nancy Saporta, 253
Stewart, Concetta M., 124
Stofan, James L., 100
Sutherland, Mark, 98
Taylor, Mark C., 273
Thoennessen, Michael, 51
Treichel, Robin S., 105
Tsai, Yihjia, 51
Tschantz, Steven, 141
Urban-Lurain, Mark, 73
Vigilante, Richard, 75
Wallin, John F., 48
Walters, Richard F., 254
Waryn, Shoggy, 246
Weinshank, Donald, 73
Webster, Peter R., 215
White, Edward, 40
Willson, Robert F., 109
Wirth, James, 77
Wollaeger, Mark A., 234
Wollensak, Andrea, 200
Wolski, Stacy, 121
Wong, Yue-Ling, 26
Wright, Maurice, 217
Yeidel, Joshua, 84

COLLEGE/UNIVERSITY INDEX

American University, 87, 165, 270
Connecticut College, 95, 200, 275
Dartmouth College, 19, 267
East Carolina University, 77, 91, 198
George Mason University, 48
Harvard University, 67
Hendrix College, 98
Johns Hopkins University, 34, 100, 243
Kansas State University, 147, 195
Le Moyne College, 129, 132, 186
Massachusetts Institute of Technology, 246

Michigan State University, 51, 73, 149
Middlebury College, 81, 153, 171
Millsaps College, 22, 103, 189
New York University, 75
Northwestern University, 127, 178, 215, 220, 250
Oberlin College, 105, 183
Reed College, 24, 203, 238
Smith College, 46, 168, 253
SUNY, Potsdam, 135, 159
Temple University, 124, 217
Tufts University, 109, 173, 178, 205
University of Arizona, 56, 121, 226
University of California, Davis, 93, 111, 254
University of Missouri, Rolla, 36, 42, 229
University of Oregon, 175
University of Texas, Austin, 114, 138, 258
University of Virginia, 116, 214, 222
Vassar College, 61, 193, 232
Vanderbilt University, 40, 44, 141, 161, 234
Wake Forest University, 26, 143, 156
Washington and Lee University, 63, 224, 260
Washington State University, 84
Whitman College, 64, 118, 241
Williams College, 209, 240, 273
Worcester Polytechnic Institute, 30, 211, 263

COMPUTER TOOLS AND TECHNIQUES INDEX

Archive of Images, 203, 205, 222
Asynchronous Discussion Groups, 36, 42, 48, 51, 56, 61, 73, 77, 87, 91, 93, 95, 100, 111, 121, 124, 127, 129, 132, 147, 156, 159, 161, 165, 171, 173, 195, 200, 203, 205, 211, 215, 229, 232, 234, 243, 246, 254, 260, 273

Citations to the Web (URLs), 22, 36, 46, 48, 56, 67, 81, 87, 93, 100, 103, 105, 109, 124, 129, 132, 143, 153, 159, 189, 200, 203, 205, 209, 215, 220, 224, 226, 234, 238, 240, 243, 250, 254, 258, 260, 263
Computer Skill Exercises, 40, 73, 75, 77, 81, 91, 93, 98, 100, 132, 138, 143, 153, 156, 165, 168, 186, 189, 224, 229, 238, 240, 243, 250, 253, 254, 273, 275
Consultants and Experts in Discussion, 129, 147, 153, 156, 159, 165, 220, 229, 232, 246, 260, 263, 267
Cross-Cultural Analyses, 124, 129, 132, 205, 241, 246, 258, 270
Custom CD-ROM, 30, 42, 81, 103, 129, 135, 138, 161, 165, 183, 200, 211, 217, 250, 254, 258
Cybershows, 42, 143, 217
Electric Course Management, 36, 42, 48, 56, 64, 73, 87, 111, 124, 129, 132, 138, 143, 153, 156, 159, 183, 189, 200, 224, 258, 260
Electronic Textbook, 19, 22, 30, 36, 42, 44, 56, 75, 81, 91, 95, 149, 189, 205, 258
Email: Group and Individual, 22, 26, 40, 42, 48, 51, 56, 73, 75, 91, 93, 100, 105, 124, 129, 132, 143, 147, 159, 161, 165, 175, 183, 186, 195, 198, 200, 205, 209, 211, 229, 232, 234, 238, 246, 258, 263, 275
Hyperlinks to Related Materials, 19, 135, 200, 205, 243
Lecture Notes Online, 19, 26, 40, 42, 46, 48, 56, 67, 105, 145, 165, 189, 241, 253, 270
More Time for Class Discussion, 19, 26, 51, 64, 143, 156, 241
Multimedia Presentations, 19, 22, 24, 30, 36, 42, 56, 67, 75, 77, 81, 95, 98, 100, 103, 105, 109, 111, 114, 118, 129, 132, 135, 138, 143, 156, 178, 189, 200, 209, 211, 214, 217, 220, 222, 224, 232, 238, 240, 241, 243, 246, 253, 258, 267, 270, 273

DISCIPLINE INDEX

EDUCATIONAL BELIEFS INDEX

Interactive Learning

REFERENCES INDEX